Colt Owners Workshop Manual

Motoring Writers

and A J Jones BSc. Eng., C. Eng.

Models covered:
UK: Colt Lancer; Saloon and Estate;
1200, 1400, 1600 cc and 1600 GSR
USA: Downsized Dodge Colt; Coupe, Sedan, Hatchback
and Station Wagon; 97·5 cu in (1600 cc), 121·7 cu in (2000 cc)
155·9 cu in (2600 cc)
Including Silent Shaft and Jet Valve engined models
Does not cover Dodge Colt Challenger

ISBN 0 85696 419 0

ABCDE
FGHIJ
KLM

Printed in England *(419–2N1)*

THE
BOOK

Haynes Publishing Group
Sparkford Yeovil
Somerset B   7 LJ England

Haynes Publications Inc
861 Lawrence Drive
Newbury Park
California 91320 USA

Acknowledgements

Thanks are due to the Chrysler Corporation of the USA for the supply of technical information and certain illustrations; to Castrol Ltd for the lubrication data and the Champion Sparking Plug Company who supplied the illustrations showing the various spark plug conditions. The bodywork repair photographic sequence, used in this manual was presented by Lloyds Industries Limited who supply 'Turtle Wax', 'Dupli-color Holts', and other Holts range products.

We are also grateful for the assistance and co-operation of Four Square Garages, Bournemouth.

Last, but not least, thanks are due to all those people at Sparkford who helped in the production of this manual, to Robert Iles for editing the text and to Lee Saunders who planned the layout of each page.

About this manual

Its aims

The aim of this Manual is to help you get the best value from your car. It can do so in several ways. It can help you decide what work must be done (even should you choose to get it done by a garage), provide information on routine maintenance and servicing, and give a logical course of action and diagnosis when random faults occur. However, it is hoped that you will use the Manual by tackling the work yourself. On simpler jobs it may even be quicker than booking the car into a garage and going there twice to leave and collect it. Perhaps most important, a lot of money can be saved by avoiding the costs the garage must charge to cover its labour and overheads.

The Manual has drawings and descriptions to show the function of the various components so that their layout can be understood. Then the tasks are described and photographed in a step-by-step sequence so that even a novice can do the work.

Its arrangement

The manual is divided into twelve Chapters, each covering a logical sub-division of the vehicle. The Chapters are each divided into Sections, numbered with single figures, eg 5; and the Sections into paragraphs (or sub-sections), with decimal numbers following on from the Section they are in, eg 5.1, 5.2, 5.3 etc.

It is freely illustrated, especially in those parts where there is a detailed sequence of operations to be carried out. There are two forms of illustration: figures and photographs. The figures are numbered in sequence with decimal numbers, according to their position in the Chapter: eg Fig. 6.4 is the 4th drawing/illustration in Chapter 6. Photographs are numbered (either individually or in related groups) the same as the Section or sub-section of the text where the operation they show is described.

There is an alphabetical index at the back of the manual as well as a contents list at the front.

References to the 'left' or 'right' of the vehicle are in the sense of a person in the driver's seat facing forwards.

Whilst every care is taken to ensure that the information in this manual is correct no liability can be accepted by the authors or publishers for loss, damage or injury caused by any errors in, or omissions from, the information given.

Introduction to the Colt Lancer and Dodge Colt Lancer

The models are manufactured in Japan by the Mitsubishi Motor Corporation and are sold in North America by the Chrysler Corporation and in the UK by the Colt Car Company. In North America the models are marketed as the Dodge Colt 'Lancer', or the Dodge Colt, this model being regarded as an extension to the original Dodge Colt range.

The Lancer was introduced into the UK as a small engined saloon in 1974 and since then the range has been extended to include the Hatchback and Estate versions and a wide range of engine capacities.

The range was introduced to North America in 1977 with a minimum engine capacity of 1600cc and the option of the 'silent shaft' engine. This engine incorporates two balancing shafts which cancel the inherent vibrations of a four cylinder engine and result in uncanny smoothness.

In 1978 a further engine modification was introduced into the USA. This is the addition of a jet valve, to improve combustion and reduce exhaust emission.

Contents

Colt Lancer 1600 Sport GSR

Colt Lancer Estate

Buying spare parts and vehicle identification numbers

Buying spare parts

Spare parts are available from many sources. Colt have many dealers throughout the UK and the USA, and other dealers, accessory stores and motor factors will also stock Colt spare parts.

Our advice regarding spare part sources is as follows:

Officially appointed vehicle main dealers – This is the best source of parts which are peculiar to your vehicle and are otherwise not generally available (eg complete cylinder heads, internal transmission component badges, interior trim etc). It is also the only place at which you should buy parts if your vehicle is still under warranty. To be sure of obtaining the correct parts it will always be necessary to give the storeman your vehicle's engine and chassis number, and if possible, to take the 'old' part along for positive identification. Remember that many parts are available on a factory exchange scheme – any parts returned should always be clean! It obviously makes good sense to go straight to the specialists on your vehicle for this type of part, for they are best equipped to supply you.

Other dealers and auto accessory stores – These are often very good places to buy materials and components needed for the maintenance of your vehicle (eg oil filters, spark plugs, bulbs, fan belts,

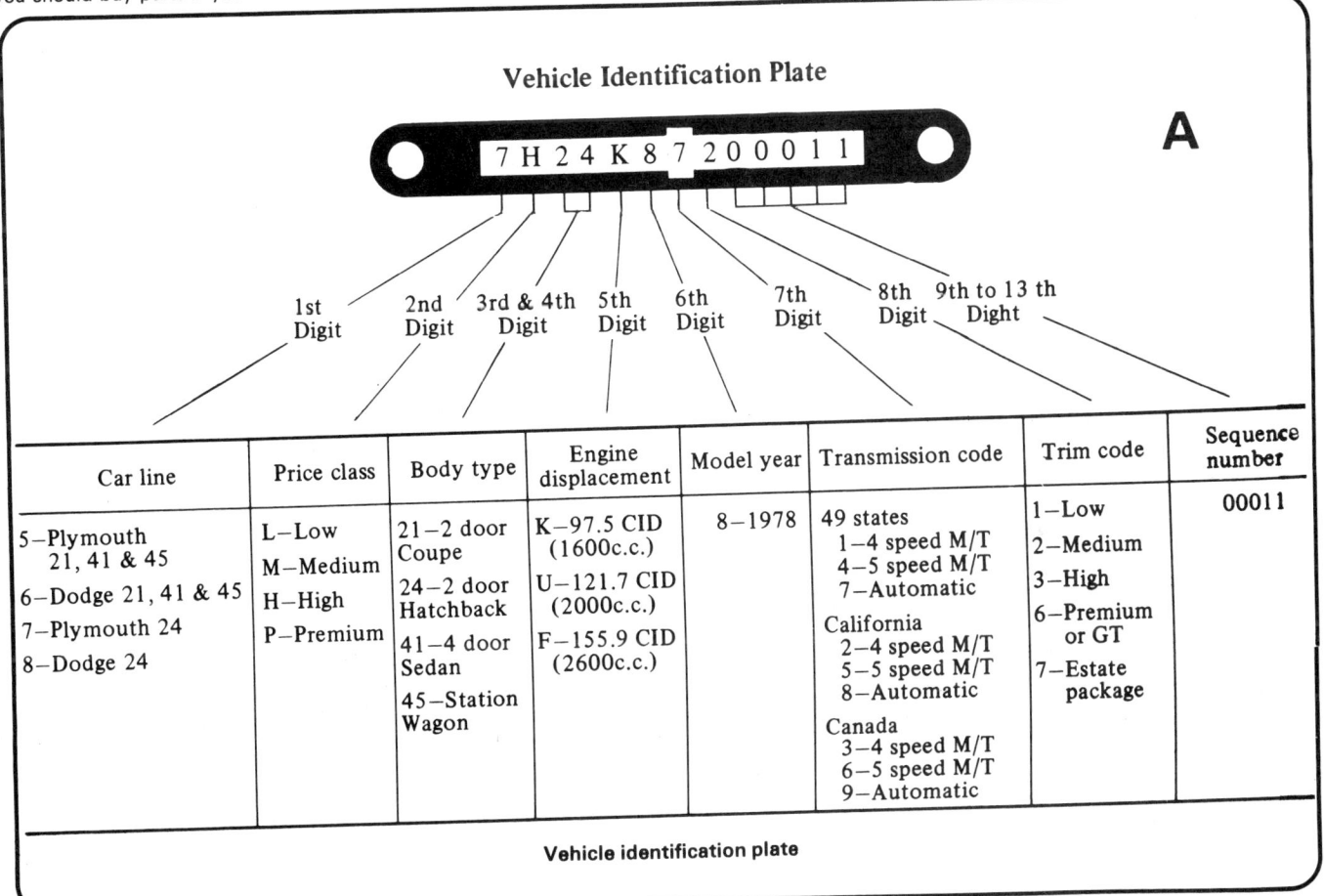

Vehicle identification plate

Car line	Price class	Body type	Engine displacement	Model year	Transmission code	Trim code	Sequence number

5–Plymouth 21, 41 & 45
 	
6–Dodge 21, 41 & 45
 	
7–Plymouth 24
 	
8–Dodge 24
	L–Low
	M–Medium
	H–High
	P–Premium
		21–2 door Coupe
		
		24–2 door Hatchback
		
		41–4 door Sedan
		
		45–Station Wagon
			K–97.5 CID (1600c.c.)
			
			U–121.7 CID (2000c.c.)
			
			F–155.9 CID (2600c.c.)
				8–1978	49 states
					  1–4 speed M/T
					  4–5 speed M/T
					  7–Automatic
					California
					  2–4 speed M/T
					  5–5 speed M/T
					  8–Automatic
					Canada
					  3–4 speed M/T
					  6–5 speed M/T
					  9–Automatic
						1–Low
						2–Medium
						3–High
						6–Premium or GT
						7–Estate package
							00011

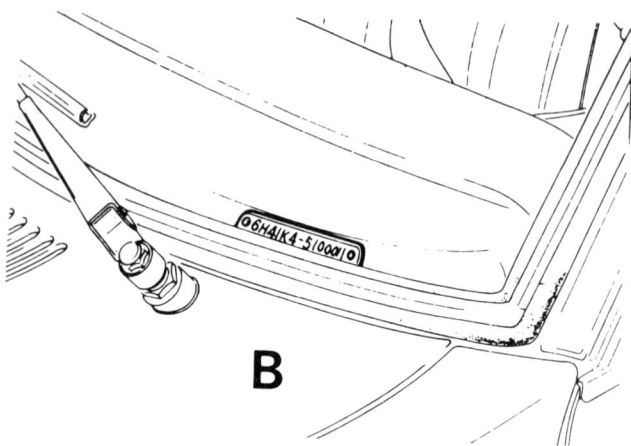

Vehicle identification number

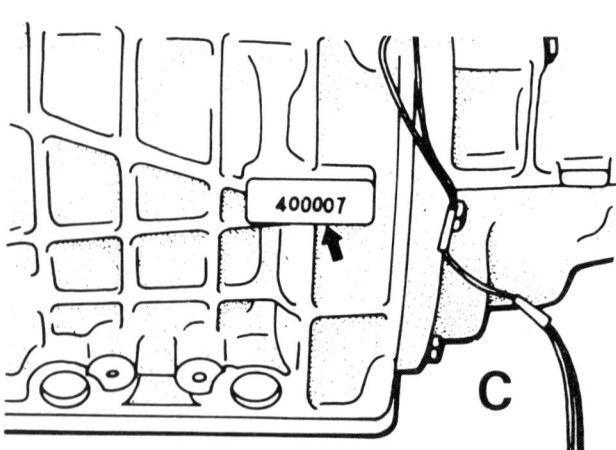

Gearbox serial number

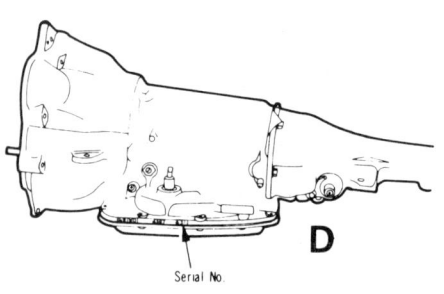

Torqueflite transmission number

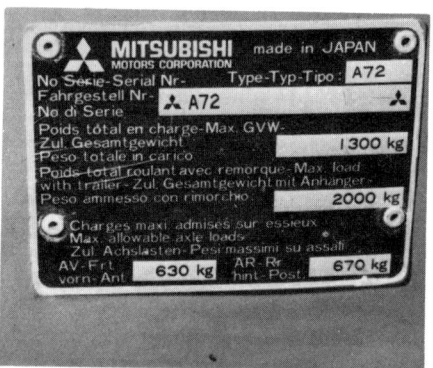

Body number

Engine number

oils and greases, touch-up paint, filler paste etc). They also sell general accessories, usually have convenient opening hours, charge lower prices and can often be found not far from home.

Motor factors – Good factors will stock of all of the more important components which wear out relatively quickly (eg clutch components, pistons, valves, exhaust systems, brake cylinders/pipes/hoses/seals/shoes and pads etc). Motor factors will often provide new or reconditioned components on a part exchange basis – this can save a considerable amount of money.

Vehicle identification numbers

All vehicle identification numbers contain 13 digits to a code shown in the illustration A. The number is located on a plate attached to the top left side of the instrument panel and visible through the windscreen (illustration B).

Body number location
The body number is stamped on the bulkhead inside the engine compartment (photo).

Engine type and number
The engine type 4G32 or 4G52 etc is cast on the left-hand side of the cylinder block, towards the bottom. The engine serial number is stamped onto the top face of the cylinder block on the right-hand side at the front (photo).

Gearbox serial number
The gearbox serial number is stamped on the left-hand side of the gearbox case (illustration C).

Automatic transmission serial number
The torqueflite serial number is stamped on to the sump mounting flange at the left-hand side (illustration D).

Use of English

As this book has been written in England, it uses the appropriate English component names, phrases, and spelling. Some of these differ from those used in America. Normally, these cause no difficulty, but to make sure, a glossary is printed below. In ordering spare parts remember the parts list will probably use these words:

English	American	English	American
Aerial	Antenna	Layshaft (of gearbox)	Countershaft
Accelerator	Gas pedal	Leading shoe (of brake)	Primary shoe
Alternator	Generator (AC)	Locks	Latches
Anti-roll bar	Stabiliser or sway bar	Motorway	Freeway, turnpike etc
Battery	Energizer	Number plate	License plate
Bodywork	Sheet metal	Paraffin	Kerosene
Bonnet (engine cover)	Hood	Petrol	Gasoline
Boot lid	Trunk lid	Petrol tank	Gas tank
Boot (luggage compartment)	Trunk	'Pinking'	'Pinging'
Bottom gear	1st gear	Propeller shaft	Driveshaft
Bulkhead	Firewall	Quarter light	Quarter window
Cam follower or tappet	Valve lifter or tappet	Retread	Recap
Carburettor	Carburetor	Reverse	Back-up
Catch	Latch	Rocker cover	Valve cover
Choke/venturi	Barrel	Roof rack	Car-top carrier
Circlip	Snap-ring	Saloon	Sedan
Clearance	Lash	Seized	Frozen
Crownwheel	Ring gear (of differential)	Side indicator lights	Side marker lights
Disc (brake)	Rotor/disk	Side light	Parking light
Drop arm	Pitman arm	Silencer	Muffler
Drop head coupe	Convertible	Spanner	Wrench
Dynamo	Generator (DC)	Sill panel (beneath doors)	Rocker panel
Earth (electrical)	Ground	Split cotter (for valve spring cap)	Lock (for valve spring retainer)
Engineer's blue	Prussian blue	Split pin	Cotter pin
Estate car	Station wagon	Steering arm	Spindle arm
Exhaust manifold	Header	Sump	Oil pan
Fast back (Coupe)	Hard top	Tab washer	Tang; lock
Fault finding/diagnosis	Trouble shooting	Tailgate	Liftgate
Float chamber	Float bowl	Tappet	Valve lifter
Free-play	Lash	Thrust bearing	Throw-out bearing
Freewheel	Coast	Top gear	High
Gudgeon pin	Piston pin or wrist pin	Trackrod (of steering)	Tie-rod (or connecting rod)
Gearchange	Shift	Trailing shoe (of brake)	Secondary shoe
Gearbox	Transmission	Transmission	Whole drive line
Halfshaft	Axleshaft	Tyre	Tire
Handbrake	Parking brake	Van	Panel wagon/van
Hood	Soft top	Vice	Vise
Hot spot	Heat riser	Wheel nut	Lug nut
Indicator	Turn signal	Windscreen	Windshield
Interior light	Dome lamp	Wing/mudguard	Fender

Miscellaneous points

An 'oil seal' is fitted to components lubricated by grease!

A 'damper' is a 'shock absorber', it damps out bouncing, and absorbs shocks of bump impact. Both names are correct, and both are used haphazardly.

Note that British drum brakes are different from the Bendix type that is common in America, so different descriptive names result. The shoe end furthest from the hydraulic wheel cylinder is on a pivot; interconnection between the shoes as on Bendix brakes is most uncommon. Therefore the phrase 'Primary' or 'Secondary' shoe does not apply. A shoe is said to be 'Leading' or 'Trailing'. A 'Leading' shoe is one on which a point on the drum, as it rotates forward, reaches the shoe at the end worked by the hydraulic cylinder before the anchor end. The opposite is a 'Trailing' shoe, and this one has no self servo from the wrapping effect of the rotating drum.

Tools and working facilities

Introduction

A selection of good tools is a fundamental requirement for anyone contemplating the maintenance and repair of a motor vehicle. For the owner who does not possess any, their purchase will prove a considerable expense, offsetting some of the savings made by doing-it-yourself. However, provided that the tools purchased are of good quality, they will last for many years and prove an extremely worthwhile investment.

To help the average owner to decide which tools are needed to carry out the various tasks detailed in this manual, we have compiled three lists of tools under the following headings: *Maintenance and minor repair, Repair and overhaul,* and *Special.* The newcomer to practical mechanics should start off with the *Maintenance and minor repair* tool kit and confine himself to the simpler jobs around the vehicle. Then, as his confidence and experience grows, he can undertake more difficult tasks, buying extra tools as, and when, they are needed. In this way, a *Maintenance and minor repair* tool kit can be built-up into a *Repair and overhaul* tool kit over a considerable period of time without any major cash outlays. The experienced do-it-yourselfer will have a tool kit good enough for most repair and overhaul procedures and will add tools from the *Special* category when he feels the expense is justified by the amount of use to which these tools will be put.

It is obviously not possible to cover the subject of tools fully here. For those who wish to learn more about tools and their use there is a book entitled *How to Choose and Use Car Tools* available from the publishers of this manual.

Maintenance and minor repair tool kit

The tools given in this list should be considered as a minimum requirement if routine maintenance, servicing and minor repair operations are to be undertaken. We recommend the purchase of combination spanners (ring one end, open-ended the other); although more expensive than open-ended ones, they do give the advantages of both types of spanner.

Combination spanners - 6, 7, 8, 9, 10, 11, & 12 mm
Adjustable spanner - 9 inch
Engine sump/gearbox/rear axle drain plug key (where applicable)
Spark plug spanner (with rubber insert)
Spark plug gap adjustment tool
Set of feeler gauges
Brake adjuster spanner (where applicable)
Brake bleed nipple spanner
Screwdriver - 4 in long x $\frac{1}{4}$ in dia (flat blade)
Screwdriver - 4 in long x $\frac{1}{4}$ in dia (cross blade)
Combination pliers - 6 inch
Hacksaw, junior
Tyre pump

Tyre pressure gauge
Grease gun (where applicable)
Oil can
Fine emery cloth (1 sheet)
Wire brush (small)
Funnel (medium size)

Repair and overhaul tool kit

These tools are virtually essential for anyone undertaking any major repairs to a motor vehicle, and are additional to those given in the *Maintenance and minor repair* list. Included in this list is a comprehensive set of sockets. Although these are expensive they will be found invaluable as they are so versatile - particularly if various drives are included in the set. We recommend the $\frac{1}{2}$ in square-drive type, as this can be used with most proprietary torque wrenches. If you cannot afford a socket set, even bought piecemeal, then inexpensive tubular box spanners are a useful alternative.

The tools in this list will occasionally need to be supplemented by tools from the *Special* list.

Sockets (or box spanners) to cover range in previous list
Reversible ratchet drive (for use with sockets)
Extension piece, 10 inch (for use with sockets)
Universal joint (for use with sockets)
Torque wrench (for use with sockets)
'Mole' wrench - 8 inch
Ball pein hammer
Soft-faced hammer, plastic or rubber
Screwdriver - 6 in long x $\frac{5}{16}$ in dia (flat blade)
Screwdriver - 2 in long x $\frac{5}{16}$ in square (flat blade)
Screwdriver - 1$\frac{1}{2}$ in long x $\frac{1}{4}$ in dia (cross blade)
Screwdriver - 3 in long x $\frac{1}{8}$ in dia (electricians)
Pliers - electricians side cutters
Pliers - needle nosed
Pliers - circlip (internal and external)
Cold chisel - $\frac{1}{2}$ inch
Scriber (this can be made by grinding the end of a broken hacksaw blade)
Scraper (this can be made by flattening and sharpening one end of a piece of copper pipe)
Centre punch
Pin punch
Hacksaw
Valve grinding tool
Steel rule/straight edge
Allen keys
Selection of files
Wire brush (large)
Axle-stands
Jack (strong scissor or hydraulic type)

Special tools

The tools in this list are those which are not used regularly, are expensive to buy, or which need to be used in accordance with their manufacturers' instructions. Unless relatively difficult mechanical jobs are undertaken frequently, it will not be economic to buy many of these tools. Where this is the case, you could consider clubbing together with friends (or a motorists' club) to make a joint purchase, or borrowing the tools against a deposit from a local garage or tool hire specialist.

The following list contains only those tools and instruments freely available to the public, and not those special tools produced by the vehicle manufacturer specifically for its dealer network. You will find occasional references to these manufacturers' special tools in the text of this manual. Generally, an alternative method of doing the job without the vehicle manufacturer's special tool is given. However, sometimes, there is no alternative to using them. Where this is the case and the relevant tool cannot be bought or borrowed you will have to entrust the work to a franchised garage.

> Valve spring compressor
> Piston ring compressor
> Balljoint separator
> Universal hub/bearing puller
> Impact screwdriver
> Micrometer and/or vernier gauge
> Carburettor flow balancing device (where applicable)
> Dial gauge
> Stroboscopic timing light
> Dwell angle meter/tachometer
> Universal electrical multi-meter
> Cylinder compression gauge
> Lifting tackle
> Trolley jack
> Light with extension lead

Buying tools

For practically all tools, a tool factor is the best source since he will have a very comprehensive range compared with the average garage or accessory shop. Having said that, accessory shops often offer excellent quality tools at discount prices, so it pays to shop around.

Remember, you don't have to buy the most expensive items on the shelf, but it is always advisable to steer clear of the very cheap tools. There are plenty of good tools around at reasonable prices, so ask the proprietor or manager of the shop for advice before making a purchase.

Care and maintenance of tools

Having purchased a reasonable tool kit, it is necessary to keep the tools in a clean serviceable condition. After use, always wipe off any dirt, grease and metal particles using a clean, dry cloth, before putting the tools away. Never leave them lying around after they have been used. A simple tool rack on the garage or workshop wall, for items such as screwdrivers and pliers is a good idea. Store all normal spanners and sockets in a metal box. Any measuring instruments, gauges, meters, etc, must be carefully stored where they cannot be damaged or become rusty.

Take a little care when tools are used. Hammer heads inevitably become marked and screwdrivers lose the keen edge on their blades fom time to time. A little timely attention with emery cloth or a file will soon restore items like this to a good serviceable finish.

Working facilities

Not to be forgotten when discussing tools, is the workshop itself. If anything more than routine maintenance is to be carried out, some form of suitable working area becomes essential.

It is appreciated that many an owner mechanic is forced by circumstances to remove an engine or similar item, without the benefit of a garage or workshop. Having done this, any repairs should always be done under the cover of a roof.

Wherever possible, any dismantling should be done on a clean flat workbench or table at a suitable working height.

Any workbench needs a vice: one with a jaw opening of 4 in (100 mm) is suitable for most jobs. As mentioned previously, some clean dry storage space is also required for tools, as well as the lubricants, cleaning fluids, touch-up paints and so on which become necessary.

Another item which may be required, and which has a much more general usage, is an electric drill with a chuck capacity of at least $\frac{5}{16}$ in (8 mm). This, together with a good range of twist drills, is virtually essential for fitting accessories such as wing mirrors and reversing lights.

Last, but not least, always keep a supply of old newspapers and clean, lint-free rags available, and try to keep any working area as clean as possible.

Spanner jaw gap comparison table

Jaw gap (in)	Spanner size
0·250	$\frac{1}{4}$ in AF
0·275	7 mm AF
0·312	$\frac{5}{16}$ in AF
0·315	8 mm AF
0·340	$\frac{11}{32}$ in AF; $\frac{1}{8}$ in Whitworth
0·354	9 mm AF
0·375	$\frac{3}{8}$ in AF
0·393	10 mm AF
0·433	11 mm AF
0·437	$\frac{7}{16}$ in AF
0·445	$\frac{3}{16}$ in Whitworth; $\frac{1}{4}$ in BSF
0·472	12 mm AF
0·500	$\frac{1}{2}$ in AF
0·512	13 mm AF
0·525	$\frac{1}{4}$ in Whitworth; $\frac{5}{16}$ in BSF
0·551	14 mm AF
0·562	$\frac{9}{16}$ in AF
0·590	15 mm AF
0·600	$\frac{5}{16}$ in Whitworth; $\frac{3}{8}$ in BSF
0·625	$\frac{5}{8}$ in AF
0·629	16 mm AF
0·669	17 mm AF
0·687	$\frac{11}{16}$ in AF
0·708	18 mm AF
0·710	$\frac{3}{8}$ in Whitworth; $\frac{7}{16}$ in BSF
0·748	19 mm AF
0·750	$\frac{3}{4}$ in AF
0·812	$\frac{13}{16}$ in AF
0·820	$\frac{7}{16}$ in Whitworth; $\frac{1}{2}$ in BSF
0·866	22 mm AF
0·875	$\frac{7}{8}$ in AF
0·920	$\frac{1}{2}$ in Whitworth; $\frac{9}{16}$ in BSF
0·937	$\frac{15}{16}$ in AF
0·944	24 mm AF
1·000	1 in AF
1·010	$\frac{9}{16}$ in Whitworth; $\frac{5}{8}$ in BSF
1·023	26 mm AF
1·062	$1\frac{1}{16}$ in AF; 27 mm AF
1·100	$\frac{5}{8}$ in Whitworth; $\frac{11}{16}$ in BSF
1·125	$1\frac{1}{8}$ in AF
1·181	30 mm AF
1·200	$\frac{11}{16}$ in Whitworth; $\frac{3}{4}$ in BSF
1·250	$1\frac{1}{4}$ in AF
1·259	32 mm AF
1·300	$\frac{3}{4}$ in Whitworth; $\frac{7}{8}$ in BSF
1·312	$1\frac{5}{16}$ in AF
1·390	$\frac{13}{16}$ in Whitworth; $\frac{15}{16}$ in BSF
1·417	36 mm AF
1·437	$1\frac{7}{16}$ in AF
1·480	$\frac{7}{8}$ in Whitworth; 1 in BSF
1·500	$1\frac{1}{2}$ in AF
1·574	40 mm AF; $\frac{15}{16}$ in Whitworth
1·614	41 mm AF
1·625	$1\frac{5}{8}$ in AF
1·670	1 in Whitworth; $1\frac{1}{8}$ in BSF
1·687	$1\frac{11}{16}$ in AF
1·811	46 mm AF
1·812	$1\frac{13}{16}$ in AF
1·860	$1\frac{1}{8}$ in Whitworth; $1\frac{1}{4}$ in BSF
1·875	$1\frac{7}{8}$ in AF
1·968	50 mm AF
2·000	2 in AF
2·050	$1\frac{1}{4}$ in Whitworth; $1\frac{3}{8}$ in BSF
2·165	55 mm AF
2·362	60 mm AF

Jacking and towing

Safety is paramount before venturing under a car to carry out any sort of maintenance or overhaul work. Placing the jack in the wrong place or using the jack on the wrong surface (too soft) or even using a worn out jack, contribute to many unnecessary accidents a year.

The jack supplied with the car is adequate for changing a wheel and that is about all. Never get under the car using just this means to support it. It is worth the effort to install stands for every task no matter how small, that demands attention underneath the car and the illustrations A and B show the points at which a trolley jack should be situated to raise the car one corner at a time and then install a stand, at the positions shown in illustrations C, D or E. However, be very careful when using this method and do it gradually, so that the car is raised evenly. Jack up one corner and install the stand with the pin in the first hole (from the top). Let the car down onto the stand and remove the jack. Move to the opposite side of the car and repeat the

operation. Then, returning to the side first raised jack up the car until the pin of the stand can be inserted into the second hole. Repeat this operation until the car is at the height required. This method may sound a little tedious and take some time but if the car was raised one corner as high as required and the stand then installed, the angle of the car to the stand may be enough to topple it once the opposite side commences to be jacked. So slowly and carefully are the key words to this operation, and do not forget to chock the wheels still left on the ground.

Towing

When towing another vehicle or when being towed always use the attachment points depicted in illustrations F and G. Attaching a tow rope to other parts of the vehicle may cause damage to that component or even an accident if it were to break off.

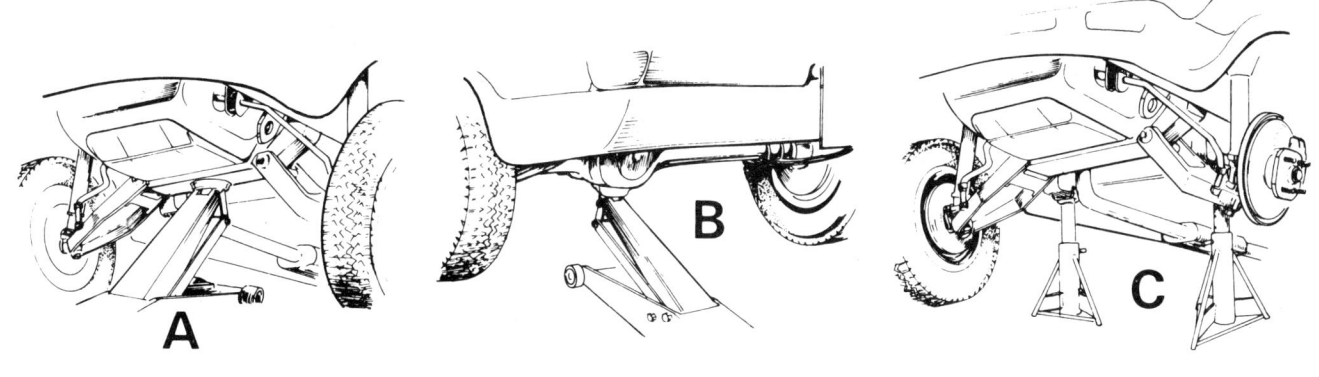

Jacking point (Front)

Jacking point (Rear)

Stand position (Front)

Stand position (Rear 1)

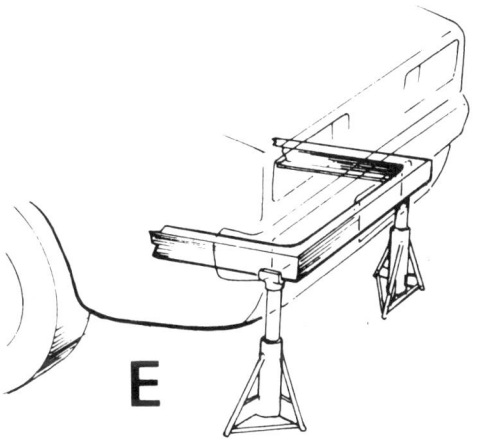

Stand position (Rear 2)

Attachment point when being towed

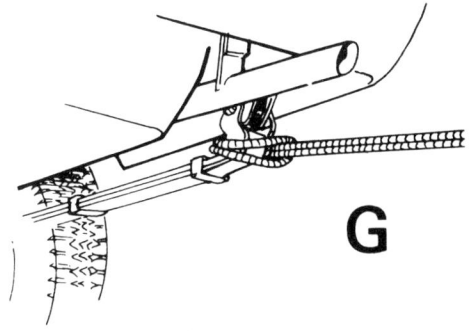

Attachment point when towing

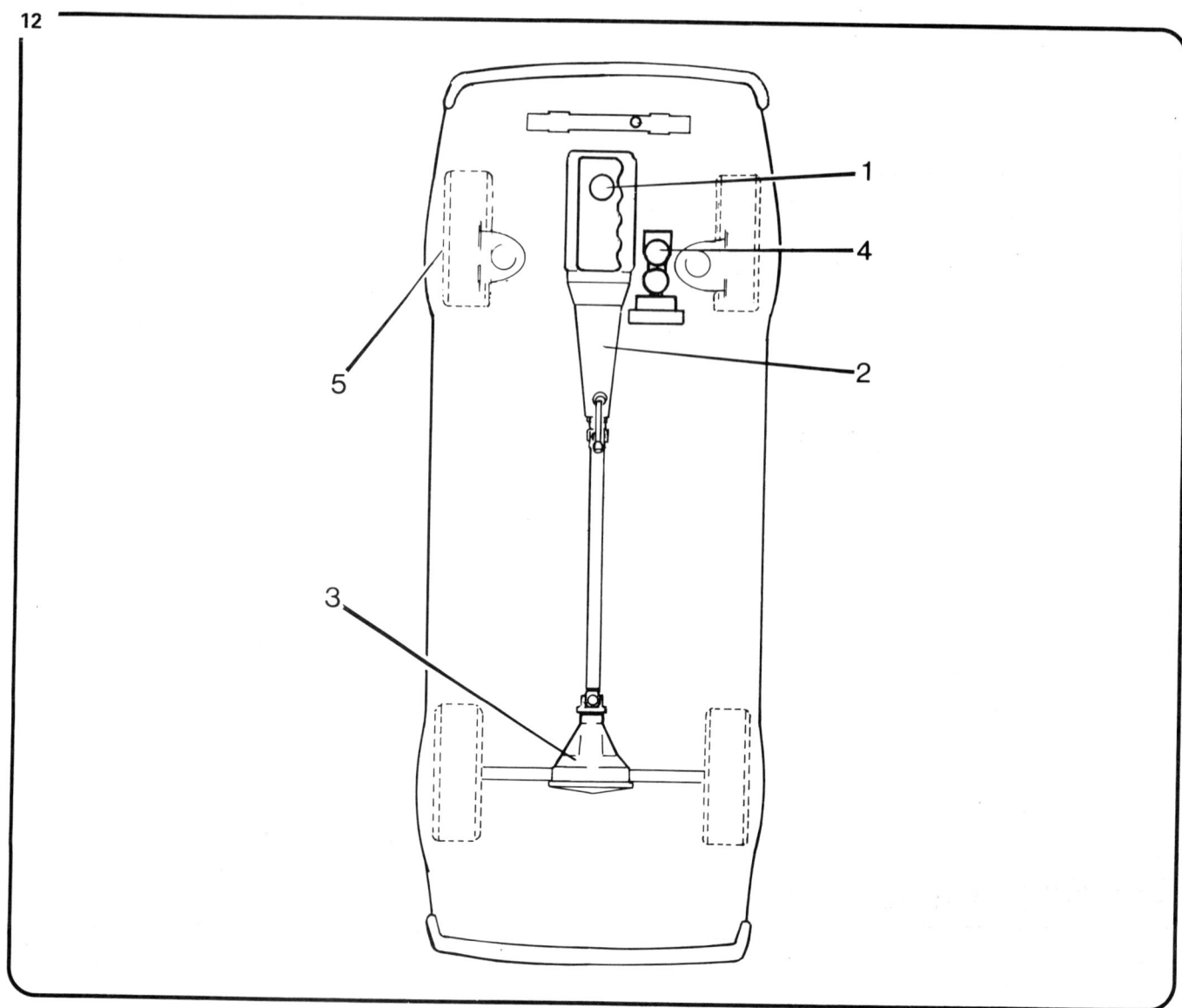

Recommended lubricants

Component	Castrol Product
Engine (1)	Castrol GTX
Transmission (2)	
Manual	Castrol Hypoy B
Automatic	Castrol TQ Dexron R
Rear axle (3)	Castrol Hypoy B
Brake system (4)	Castrol Girling Universal Brake and Clutch Fluid
Wheel bearings (5)	Castrol LM Grease
Steering gear	Castrol Hypoy B
Handbrake cable	Castrol LM Grease
Door and bonnet locks, hinges	Castrol GTX
Clutch cable and linkages	Engine oil

Note: The above are general recommendations only. Lubrication requirements vary between different operating requirements. If in doubt, consult the vehicle handbook or nearest Dealer.

Routine maintenance

Maintenance is essential for ensuring safety and reliability as well as for obtaining maximum performance and economy. Over the years the need for periodical lubrication has been reduced considerably, but for those items which are not lubricated for life it is still essential, even though the intervals may be infrequent.

Every 250 miles (400 km) or weekly

Check tyre pressure and inflate if necessary (photo)
Check engine oil level and top-up if necessary (photos)
Check battery electrolyte level and top-up if necessary (photo)
Check windscreen washer fluid level and top-up if necessary
Check coolant level and top-up if necessary (photo)
Check brake fluid level and top-up if necessary (photo)
Check operation of all lights, instruments and controls

Every 5000 miles (8000 km)

Change engine oil (photo)
Check gearbox oil or automatic transmission fluid (photo)
Check rear axle oil
Check steering gear oil
Check brake fluid
Oil locks and hinges
Check brake and coolant hoses
Inspect brake disc pads
Check fan belt tension (photo)

Every 10 000 miles (16 000 km)

Renew oil filter
Lubricate handbrake

Lubricate transmission linkage
Lubricate clutch cable
Check exhaust system for leaks
Check brake master cylinder operation
Change tyres round
Check rear brakes
Check clutch pedal movement

Every 15 000 miles (24 000 km) or annually

Lubricate distributor
Grease front wheel bearing
Check thermal reaction bolts (if fitted)
Check exhaust manifold bolts
Check and adjust carburettor linkage
Renew fuel filter
Renew air cleaner
Check heated air intake operation (if fitted)
Renew distributor points and condenser
Renew spark plugs
Check ignition wiring
Check distributor cap and rotor
Clean crankcase ventilation ports
Check evaporation control system (if fitted)
Check secondary air system (if fitted)
Check exhaust gas recirculation system (if fitted)
Check antifreeze and renew if necessary
Check all rubber and plastic components in the engine compartment

Check tyre pressures (weekly)

Check oil level (weekly)

Top up if necessary (weekly)

Check battery (weekly)

Check coolant level (weekly)

Check brake fluid (weekly)

Drain engine oil (5000 miles)

Check gearbox oil level (5000 miles)

Check fan belt tension (5000 miles)

Renew oil filter (10 000 miles)

Chapter 1 Engine

Contents

Specifications

4G3 Series

	4G32	4G32GS	4G33	4G36
Type	4 stroke, petrol	4 stroke, petrol	4 stroke, petrol	4 stroke, petrol
Number and arrangement of cylinders	4 in-line, vertical	4 in-line, vertical	4 in-line, vertical	4 in-line, vertical
Valve and camshaft arrangement	OHV OHC	OHV OHC	OHV OHC	OHV OHC
Total displacement	1597 cc (97·4 cu in)	1597 cc (97·4 cu in)	1439 cc (87·9 cu in)	1238 cc (75·5 cu in)
Bore x stroke in	3·03x3·39	3·03x3·39	2·87x3·39	2·87x2·91
mm	76·9x86	76·9x86	73x86	73x74
Compression ratio	8·5	9·5	9·0	9·0
Valve timing				
Inlet opens BTDC	20°	24°	20°	20°
Inlet closes ABDC	48°	64°	48°	48°
Exhaust opens BBDC	51°	67°	51°	51°
Exhaust closes ATDC	17°	21°	17°	17°
Firing order	1–3–4–2	1–3–4–2	1–3–4–2	1–3–4–2

Valve clearances (hot)

Inlet	0·006 in (0·15 mm)
Exhaust	0·010 in (0·25 mm)

Ignition timing at idling speed BTDC

5°±1°	13°±1°	5°±1°	5°±1°

Idling speed rpm

700±50	800±50	700±50	700±50

Crankcase ventilation system .... Closed type

Lubrication method

	Forced feed
Oil pump type	Gear type Trochoid type
Oil filter type	Full flow, cartridge
Oil capacity	3·5 qt, 4·2 US qt, 4 litres

Cooling method .... Water

Pistons and piston rings

Piston OD	3·0276 in (76·9 mm) 2·874 in (73 mm)
Piston pin hole ID	0·748 in (19 mm)
Piston oversizes	0·010 in (0·25 mm)
	0·020 in (0·50 mm)
	0·030 in (0·75 mm)
	0·040 in (1·00 mm)

Piston ring to ring groove clearance:

No 1	0·0012 to 0·0028 in (0·03 to 0·07 mm)
No 2	0·0008 to 0·0024 in (0·02 to 0·06 mm)
Oil ring	0·0010 to 0·0030 in (0·025 to 0·075 mm)
Maximum clearance (all rings)	0·006 in (0·15 mm)
Piston ring end clearance – standard	0·006 to 0·014 in (0·15 to 0·35 mm)
– maximum	0·040 in (1·0 mm)
Piston pin OD	0·7481 to 0·7483 in (19·001 to 19·007 mm)
Piston pin to piston clearance	0·0004 to 0·0005 in (0·001 to 0·0013 mm)

Connecting rod bend .... Less than 0·0012 in (0·03 mm)

Large end play – standard	0·004 to 0·01 in (0·1 to 0·25 mm)
– maximum	0·02 in (0·5 mm)

Crankshaft bearing oil clearance

	0·0006 to 0·0031 in (0·016 to 0·078 mm)
	0·006 to 0·0028 in (0·016 to 0·07 mm)
Crankshaft bearing undersizes	0·010 in (0·25 mm)
	0·020 in (0·50 mm)
	0·030 in (0·75 mm)
Crankshaft journal OD – standard	2·2441 in (57 mm)
– minimum	−0·0256 in (−0·65 mm) −0·0354 in (−0·9 mm)
Crankshaft bend	Less then 0·0012 in (0·03 mm)
Journal ovality	Less than 0·0004 in (0·01 mm)
Pin ovality	Less than 0·0004 in (0·01 mm)
End play – standard	0·002 to 0·007 in (0·05 to 0·175 mm)
– maximum	0·01 in (0·25 mm)
Undersize dimension of journals	
0·01 in (0·25 mm) undersize	2·2337 to 2·2342 in (56·735 to 56·75 mm)
0·02 in (0·50 mm) undersize	2·2238 to 2·2244 in (56·485 to 56·50 mm)
4G33 and 4G36 only:	
0·03 in (0·75 mm) undersize	2·2140 to 2·2146 in (56·235 to 56·25 mm)
Undersize dimensions of crankpin:	
0·01 in (0·25 mm) undersize	1·7612 to 1·7618 in (44·735 to 44·75 mm)
0·02 in (0·50 mm) undersize	1·7514 to 1·7520 in (44·485 to 44·50 mm)
4G33 and 4G36 only:	
0·03 in (0·75 mm) undersize	1·7415 to 1·7421 in (44·235 to 44·25 mm)

Flywheel run out – standard .... Less than 0·005 in (0·13 mm)

– maximum	0·008 in (0·2 mm)

Camshaft bend .... Less than 0·0008 in (0·02 mm)

Height of cam lobe (intake) – standard	1·4316 in (36·363 mm)
– wear limit	−0·02 in (−0·05 mm)
(exhaust) – standard	1·4336 in (36·412 mm)
– wear limit	−0·02 in (−0·05 mm)
Camshaft end play – standard	0·002 to 0·006 in (0·05 to 0·15 mm)
– maximum	0·012 in (0·3 mm)

Valves

Valve stem OD:	
Intake – standard	0·315 in (8 mm)

– wear limit	−0·004 in (−0·10 mm)
Exhaust – standard	0·315 in (8 mm)
– wear limit	−0·006 in (−0·15 mm)
Valve head thickness – standard	0·059 in (1·5 mm)
– minimum	0·039 in (1·0 mm)
Valve to guide clearance:	
Intake – standard	0·0010 to 0·0022 in (0·025 to 0·085 mm)
– wear limit	0·004 in (0·1 mm)
Exhaust – standard	0·0020 to 0·0033 in (0·05 to 0·85 mm)
– wear limit	0·006 in (0·15 mm)
Valve guide OD (intake and exhaust)	0·5118 in (13 mm)
ID Intake – standard	0·315 in (8 mm)
– wear limit	+0·004 in (+0·10 mm)
ID Exhaust – standard	0·315 in (8 mm)
– wear limit	+0·006 in (+0·15 mm)
Valve guide oversizes	0·002 in (0·05 mm)
	0·010 in (0·25 mm)
	0·020 in (0·50 mm)
Valve seat width	0·035 to 0·051 in (0·9 to 1·3 mm)
Valve seat angle	45°
Valve spring – free length	1·805 in (45·85 mmm)
– wear limit	−0·040 in (−1·0 mm)

Rocker arm

Rocker arm shaft:	
OD	0·7441 in (18·9 mm)
Bend	0·002 in (0·05 mm)
Rocker arm ID	0·7441 in (18·9 mm)
Rocker arm to shaft clearance:	
standard	0·0005 to 0·0017 in (0·012 to 0·043 mm)
wear limit	0·004 in (0·1 mm)
Chain tensioner spring free length:	
standard	2·181 in (55·4 mm)
wear limit	1·850 in (47 mm)
Spring deflection – standard	1·496 in at load of 26 lbs (38·4 mm at load of 12·6 kg)
– wear limit	1·496 in at load of 24 lbs (38·4 mm at load of 10·7 kg)

Lubrication system

Oil pressure at idling speed	11 lb/in^2 (0·8 kg/cm^2)
Oil pressure relief valve opens	56·9 to 71·1 lb/in^2 (4 to 5 kg/cm^2)
Outer rotor to inner rotor clearance:	
– standard	Less than 0·0047 in (0·12 mm)
– wear limit	0·01 in (0·25 mm)
Outer rotor to chain case clearance	
– standard	0·0039 to 0·0063 in (0·1 to 0·16 mm)
– wear limit	0·012 in (0·3 mm)
Outer rotor to cover clearance:	
– standard	0·008 to 0·0039 in (0·02 to 0·1 mm)
– wear limit	0·008 in (0·2 mm)
Relief spring free length	2·352 in (59·73 mm)

4G5 Series

	4G52	4G54
Type	4 stroke – petrol	4 stroke – petrol
Number and arrangement of cylinders	4 in-line, vertical	4 in-line, vertical
Valve and camshaft arrangement	OHV OHC	OHV OHC
Total displacement	2000 cc (121·7 cu in)	2600 cc (155·9 cu in)
Bore x stroke in	3·31 x 3·54	3·59 x 3·86
mm	84 x 90	91·1 x 98
Compression ratio	8·5	8·2
Valve timing:		
Inlet opens BTDC	25°	25°
Inlet closes ABDC	59°	59°
Exhaust opens BBDC	70°	64°
Exhaust closes ATDC	14°	20°
Jet valve opens BTDC	25°	25°
Jet valve closes ABDC	59°	59°
Firing order	1–3–4–2	1–3–4–2
Cylinder bore	3·3071 in (84 mm)	3·3071 in (84 mm)
Permissible bore wear	0·047 in (1·2 mm)	0·047 in (1·2 mm)

Pistons and piston rings

	4G52	4G54
Oversize piston sizes	3·3169 in (84·25 mm)	3·3169 in (84·25 mm)
	3·3268 in (84·50 mm)	3·3268 in (84·50 mm)
	3·3366 in (84·75 mm)	3·3366 in (84·75 mm)

	3·3465 in (85·00 mm)	3·3465 in (85·00 mm)
Piston to cylinder clearance	0·0012 to 0·0020 in (0·03 to 0·05 mm)	
Number of rings	3 (2 compression 1 oil control)	
Clearance ring and groove wall:		
No. 1	0·0024 to 0·0039 in (0·06 to 0·1 mm)	
No. 2	0·0008 to 0·0024 in (0·02 to 0·06 mm)	
Maximum clearance:		
No. 1	0·006 in (0·15 mm)	
No. 2	0·005 in (0·12 mm)	
Gap when fitted		
No. 1	0·0098 to 0·0157 in (0·25 to 0·40 mm)	
No. 2	0·0098 to 0·0177 in (0·25 to 0·45 mm)	
Oil ring	0·0079 to 0·0354 in (0·2 to 0·9 mm)	
Maximum gap, all rings	0·039 in (1·0 mm)	

Connecting rods
Permissible bend	0·0012 in (0·03 mm)
Side clearance	0·0039 to 0·0098 in (0·15 to 0·25 mm)
Maximum side clearance	0·02 in (0·5 mm)

Crankshaft
Journal diameter	2·5984 in (66 mm)
Maximum permissible wear	0·026 in (0·65 mm)
Crankpin diameter	2·0866 in (53 mm)
Maximum permissible wear	0·026 in (0·65 mm)
Minimum regrind diameter:	
Journal	2·5781 to 2·5787 in (65·485 to 65·50 mm)
Crankpin	2·0663 to 2·0669 in (52·485 to 52·50 mm)
Fillet radius, journals and crankpins	0·0020 to 0·0069 in (0·05 to 0·175 mm)
Crankshaft end play	0·010 in (0·25 mm)
Maximum end play	0·010 in (0·25 mm)

Main bearings
Diametral clearance	0·0008 to 0·0028 in (0·02 to 0·072 mm)
Maximum permissible clearance	0·005 in (0·12 mm)

Big end bearings
Diametral clearance	0·0006 to 0·0025 in (0·015 to 0·064 mm)
Maximum permissible clearance	0·004 in (0·10 mm)

Valve seats
Seat angle, inlet and exhaust	45°
Contact width, inlet and exhaust	0·035 to 0·051 in (0·9 to 1·3 mm)

Valves
Stem OD inlet and exhaust	0·315 in (8 mm)
Wear limit	
Inlet	0·004 in (0·1 mm)
Exhaust	0·006 in (0·15 mm)
Stem to guide clearance, inlet	0·001 to 0·003 in (0·025 to 0·058 mm)
Maximum permissible clearance	0·004 in (0·1 mm)
Stem to guide clearance, exhaust	0·002 to 0·0035 in (0·05 to 0·088 mm)
Maximum permissible clearance	0·006 in (0·15 mm)

Valve springs
Free length	1·891 in (48·03 mm)
Fitted length (standard)	1·5905 in (40·4 mm)
Fitted length (maximum)	1·6295 in (41·4 mm)

Timing chain tensioner
Free length	2·587 in (65·7 mm)
Minimum permissible length	2·20 in (56 mm)

Oil pump (trochoid type)
Shaft to case clearance	0·008 to 0·0022 in (0·21 to 0·57 mm)
Maximum permissible clearance	0·005 in (0·12 mm)
Inner to outer rotor clearance – less than	0·0047 in (0·119 mm)
Maximum permissible clearance	0·010 in (0·25 mm)
Rotor to cover end play	0·0008 to 0·0039 in (0·02 to 0·1 mm)
Maximum permissible end play	0·008 in (0·21 mm)

Torque wrench settings
	lbf ft	kgf m	lbf ft	kgf m
Front insulator to sub-frame	22 to 29	3·1 to 4·1	22 to 29	3·1 to 4·1
Front insulator to engine bracket	10 to 14	1·4 to 2·0	10 to 14	1·4 to 2·0
Cylinder block to engine bracket	29 to 36	4·0 to 5·0	29 to 36	4·0 to 5·0

Rear insulator to engine support bracket	10 to 12	1.4 to 1.7	10 to 14	1.4 to 2.0
Rear insulator to transmission:				
Manual	15 to 17	2.1 to 2.4	15 17	2.1 to 2.4
Automatic	9.5 to 11.5	1.3 to 1.6	9.5 to 11.5	1.3 to 1.6
Engine support bracket to body	7.2	1.0	7.2	1.0
Cylinder head attachment bolt:				
Cold engine	51 to 54	7.1 to 7.6	65 to 72	9.0 to 10.0
Hot engine	58 to 61	8.1 to 8.5	72 to 79	10.0 to 11.0
Camshaft bearing cap	13 to 14	1.8 to 2.0	13 to 14	1.8 to 2.0
Camshaft sprocket	36 to 43	5.0 to 6.0	36 to 43	5.0 to 6.0
Spark plug	15 to 21	2.1 to 3.0	18 to 21	2.5 to 2.9
Rocker cover	4 to 5	0.55 to 0.7	4 to 5	0.55 to 0.7
Heater joint	15 to 28	2.1 to 3.9		
Main bearing cap	36 to 39	5.0 to 5.5	54 to 61	7.1 to 8.5
Connecting rod cap	23 to 25	3.2 to 3.5	33 to 34	4.6 to 4.7
Flywheel or drive plate	83 to 90	11.6 to 12.6	94 to 101	13.2 to 14.2
Crank pulley	43 to 50	6.0 to 7.0	80 to 94	11.2 to 13.2
Tensioner holder	36 to 43	5.0 to 6.0		
Oil pan	4.3 to 5.8	0.6 to 0.8	4.3 to 5.8	0.6 to 0.8
Oil pan drain plug	43 to 57	6.0 to 8.0	43 to 57	6.0 to 8.0
Oil filter	8 to 9	1.1 to 1.3	8 to 9	1.1 to 1.3
Oil pump cover	11 to 14	1.5 to 2.0	11 to 14	1.5
Intake/exhaust manifold or thermal reactor	11 to 14	1.5 to 2.0	11 to 14	1.5 to 2.0
Oil temperature gauge unit	22 to 28	3.0 to 4.0	22 to 28	3.0 to 4.0
Counterbalance chamber cover			3 to 4	0.42 to 0.56
Counterbalance shaft bolts			22 to 28	3.1 to 3.9

1 General description

There are two basic models of engine, but with variations of bore, stroke and compression ratio, six different engine ratings are available. Within several of the different ratings, there is a further variation: the use of the silent shaft for engine balancing.

The engine is of the overhead camshaft type, with four vertical cylinders. The crankshaft has five main bearings of the renewable shell type and the centre bearing is flanged on both sides to accomodate camshaft thrust. The valves are operated from a five bearing overhead camshaft. Some models of engine are fitted with an additional inlet valve on each cylinder, to permit more efficient combustion and a quicker burning speed. The presence of this additional valve gives lower fuel consumption and cleaner exhaust emission. The camshaft bearings are not renewable.

The pistons have two compression rings and one oil control ring. These are graded for selective assembly to the cylinder bores. The gudgeon pins are of the semi-floating type, being a press fit in the small-end of the connecting rod. The connecting rod big-end bearings are of the renewable shell type.

The engine is liquid cooled, the coolant being circulated round the cylinder bores, combustion chambers and inlet manifold, by a centrifugal pump mounted on the timing cover and driven from the crankshaft by a belt. On some models, the cooling fan is fitted with a torque type clutch, to compensate for the increased effect of ram cooling of the radiator at higher road speeds.

Engine lubrication is by forced feed from a trochoid, or conventional gear pump, which is mounted in the bottom of the chaincase on the smaller engines and inside the sump on the larger ones. The oil is filtered continuously by a cartridge type filter mounted on the side of the engine.

2 Removal of engine and gearbox

The following sequence of operations does not necessarily need to be performed in the order given, but is a checklist of everything that needs to be disconnected or removed before the engine and gearbox can be lifted out. In a few instances items are removed to give additional clearance and so make is easier to lift out the power unit.

1 Remove the bonnet cover after disconnecting the pipe to the washer jet and put cloths, or newspapers, over the wings and grille to save them from scratches in subsequent operations.

2 Disconnect the battery leads, positive terminal first, and remove the battery.

3 Drain the coolant by removing the plug from the bottom of the radiator (photo).Using a socket spanner, remove the plug beneath the exhaust manifold.

4 Remove the front grille to avoid it being damaged. Release the two clamps on the radiator hoses and remove the hoses. Remove the four bolts securing the radiator (photo) and lift the radiator out. On automatic transmission models it will also be necessary to disconnect the pipes to 1the oil cooler.

5 Remove four bolts and take off the radiator fan and spacer (photos).

6 Remove the electrical connections from the alternator (photo). Remove the two alternator fixing bolts and lift off the alternator. Remove the fan belt and the fan pulley hub.

7 Drain the oil from the engine sump and from the gearbox. Replace and tighten the drain plugs to prevent their being lost.

8 Remove the air cleaner assembly by pulling off the breather hose, then removing the wing nut in its centre and the two nuts on its flange.

9 Remove the connections from the starter motor and its solenoid (photo), the connections to the oil pressure and coolant temperature gauge and the brake servo and distributor vacuum pipes (photo). Disconnect the distributor contact breaker lead.

10 Disconnect the earth strap on the left-hand side of the cylinder block, beneath the intake manifold (photo).

11 Unclamp the nipple on the throttle cable from the hole in the throttle lever (photo). Remove the clamp securing the choke and throttle cables to the rocker cover.

12 Disconnect the heater hoses from the engine, and the coolant pipes from the intake manifold (photo).

13 Disconnect the hose between the fuel pump and the fuel strainer.

14 Remove the brake servo pipe bracket from the rocker box cover.

15 From underneath the car, undo the exhaust pipe flange and remove the exhaust pipe support bracket.

16 Remove the split-pin from the clutch operating lever, remove two bolts from the clutch cable bracket, and disengage the clutch cable from the operating lever (photo).

17 Remove the four nuts and bolts from the propeller shaft rear axle joint flange. On models with two piece propeller shafts, remove the two nuts securing the centre bearing (photo). If the car has automatic control, it may be necessary to remove the dynamic damper (see Chapter 7).

18 Undo the bullet connectors to the reversing light (photo) and

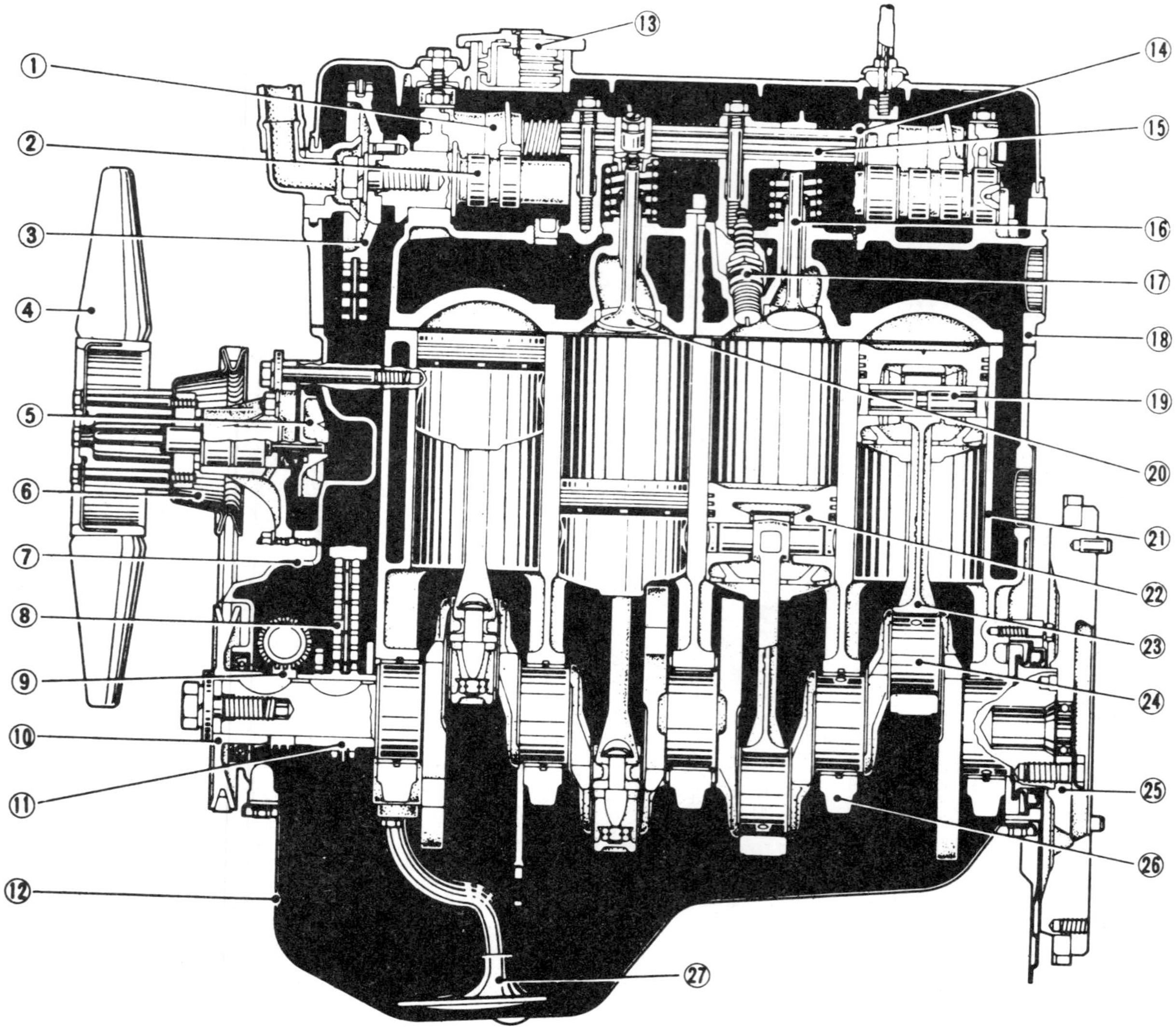

Fig. 1.1 Engine longitudinal section (4G3)

1 Rocker arm
2 Camshaft
3 Camshaft sprocket
4 Cooling fan
5 Water pump
6 Water pump pulley
7 Chain case
8 Chain
9 Crankshaft gear
10 Crankshaft pulley
11 Crankshaft sprocket
12 Sump
13 Oil filler cap
14 Rocker arm shaft spring
15 Rocker arm shaft
16 Exhaust valve
17 Spark plug
18 Cylinder head
19 Piston pin
20 Intake valve
21 Cylinder block
22 Piston
23 Connecting rod
24 Crankshaft
25 Flywheel
26 Crankshaft bearing cap
27 Oil screen

2.3 Radiator drain plug

2.4 Radiator fixing bolts

2.5a Removing the radiator fan ....

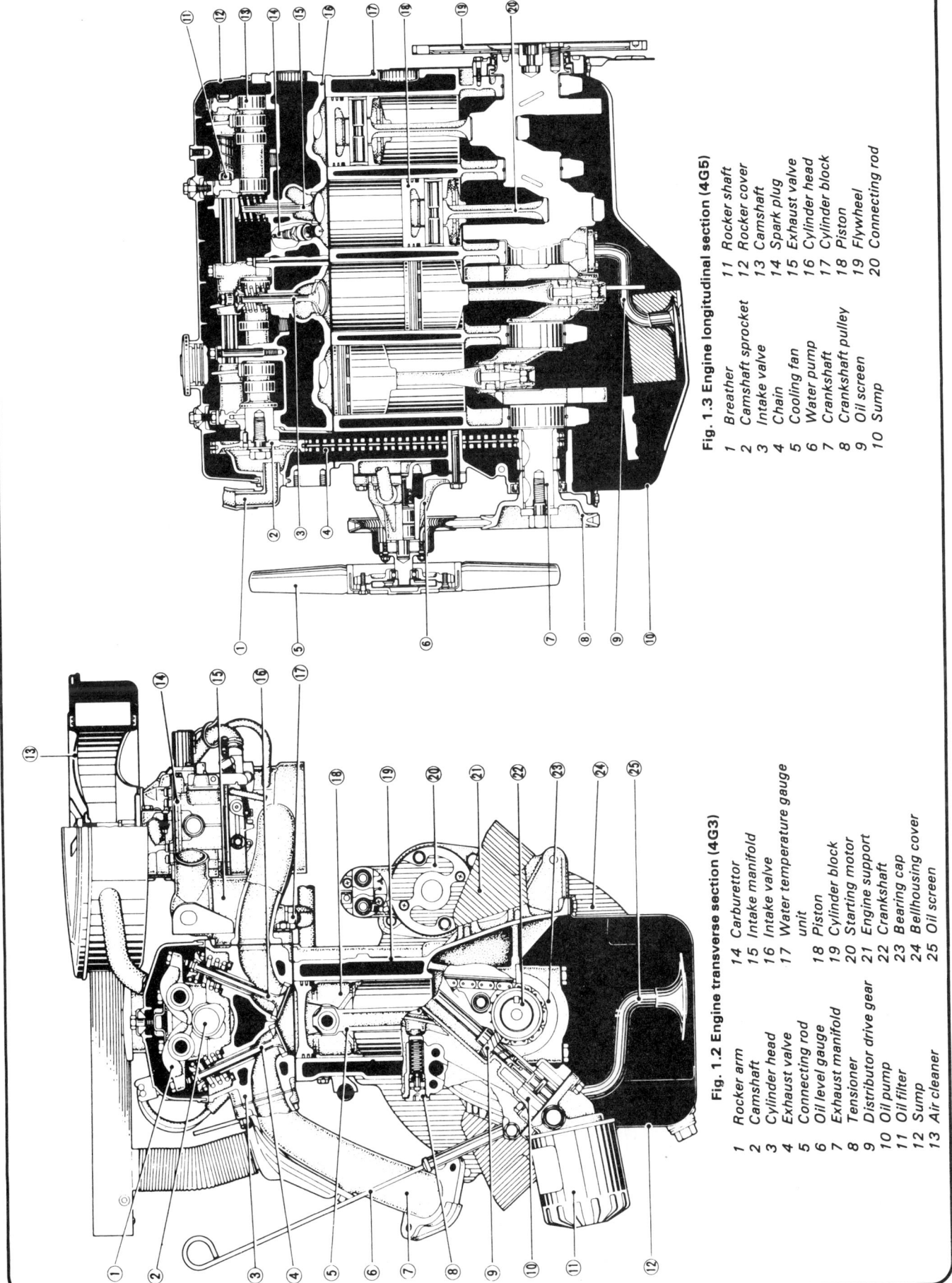

Fig. 1.3 Engine longitudinal section (4G5)

1	Breather	11	Rocker shaft
2	Camshaft sprocket	12	Rocker cover
3	Intake valve	13	Camshaft
4	Chain	14	Spark plug
5	Cooling fan	15	Exhaust valve
6	Water pump	16	Cylinder head
7	Crankshaft	17	Cylinder block
8	Crankshaft pulley	18	Piston
9	Oil screen	19	Flywheel
10	Sump	20	Connecting rod

Fig. 1.2 Engine transverse section (4G3)

1	Rocker arm	14	Carburettor
2	Camshaft	15	Intake manifold
3	Cylinder head	16	Intake valve
4	Exhaust valve	17	Water temperature gauge
5	Connecting rod		unit
6	Oil level gauge	18	Piston
7	Exhaust manifold	19	Cylinder block
8	Tensioner	20	Starting motor
9	Distributor drive gear	21	Engine support
10	Oil pump	22	Crankshaft
11	Oil filter	23	Bearing cap
12	Sump	24	Bellhousing cover
13	Air cleaner	25	Oil screen

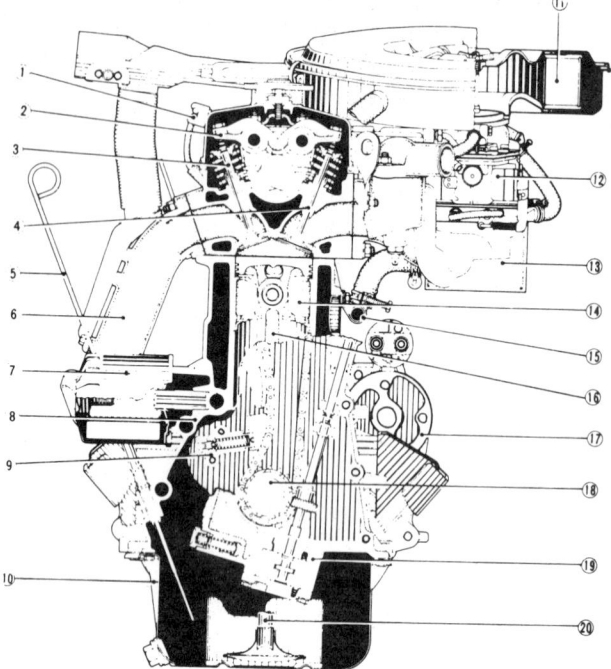

Fig. 1.4 Engine cross section (4G5)

1 Spark plug cable	8 Cylinder block	15 Heater pipe
2 Rocker arm	9 Tensioner	16 Connecting rod
3 Exhaust valve	10 Sump	17 Starting motor
4 Intake valve	11 Air cleaner	18 Crankshaft
5 Oil level gauge	12 Carburetter	19 Oil pump
6 Exhaust manifold	13 Intake manifold	20 Oil screen
7 Oil filter	14 Piston	

2.5b ... and spacer

2.6 Alternator electrical connections

2.9a Starter motor connections

2.9b Brake and distributor vacuum pipes

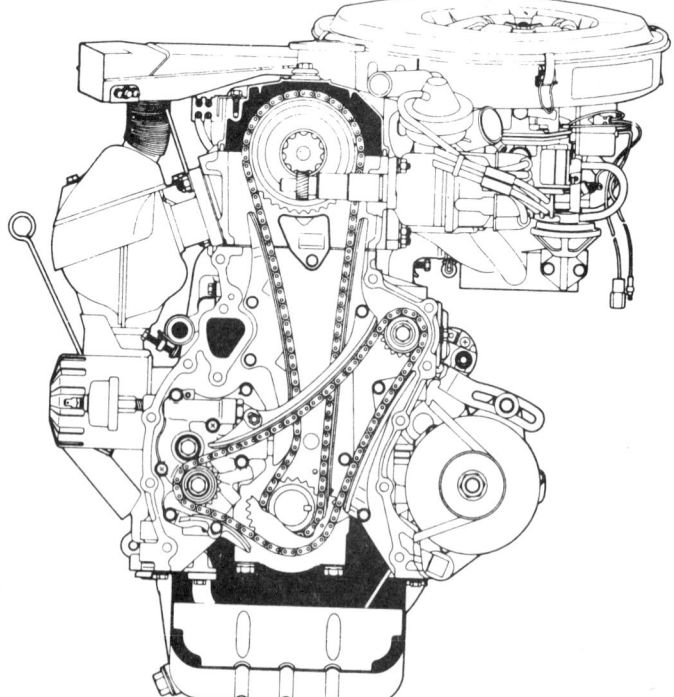

Fig. 1.5 Engine cross section (4G5 with balance shafts)

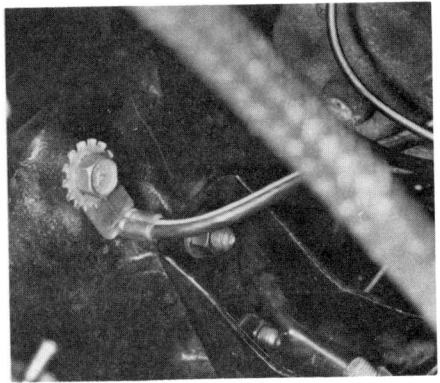

2.10 Engine earth strap

2.11 Choke and throttle connections

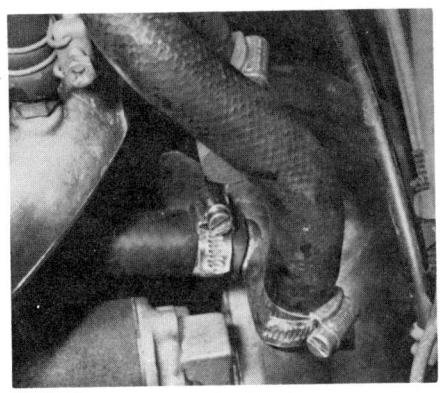

2.12 Heater and manifold coolant pipes

2.13 Clutch cable connection and bracket

2.17 Propeller shaft centre bearing bolts

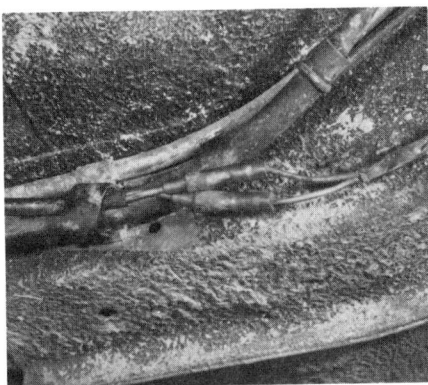

2.18 Reversing light connections

2.19 Disconnecting the speedometer drive

2.20 Gearbox and cross member fixings

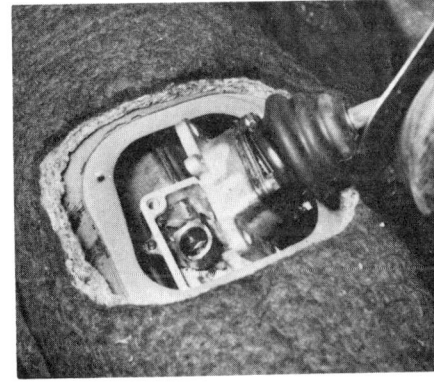

2.22 Removing the gear lever

2.23 Engine mounting nut (arrowed)

2.25 Lifting the engine out

3.2 Removing the starter motor

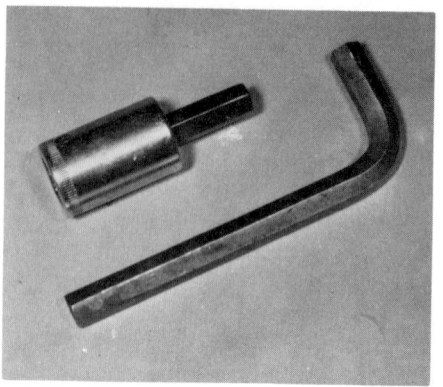

4.5 Tools for removing cylinder head bolts

5.2 Rocker cover fixing

6.2 Crankshaft pulley with key in position

6.3 Flywheel bolts and locking washer

6.4 Engine adaptor plate

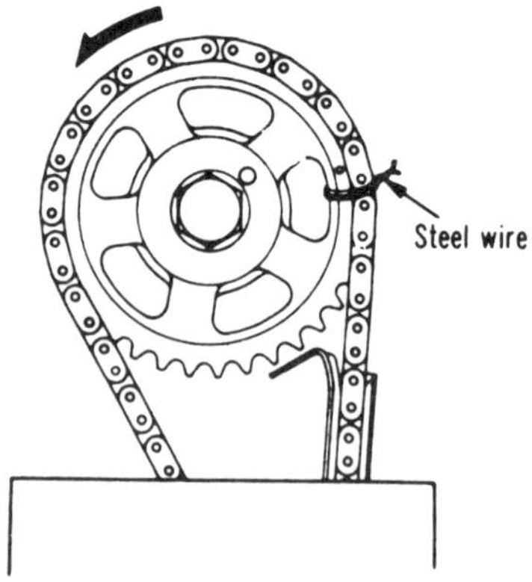

A

```
 1
    4     6    11     9     3
   O     O     O     O     O

   2     8    10     7     5
   O     O     O     O     O
 1
```
← Front

B

```
   3     5    10     8     2

   1     7     9     6     4
```

C

```
 1
    4     6    11     9     3
   O     O     O     O     O

 1
    2     8    10     7     5
   O     O     O     O     O
```

Steel wire

Fig. 1.6 Locking the timing chain

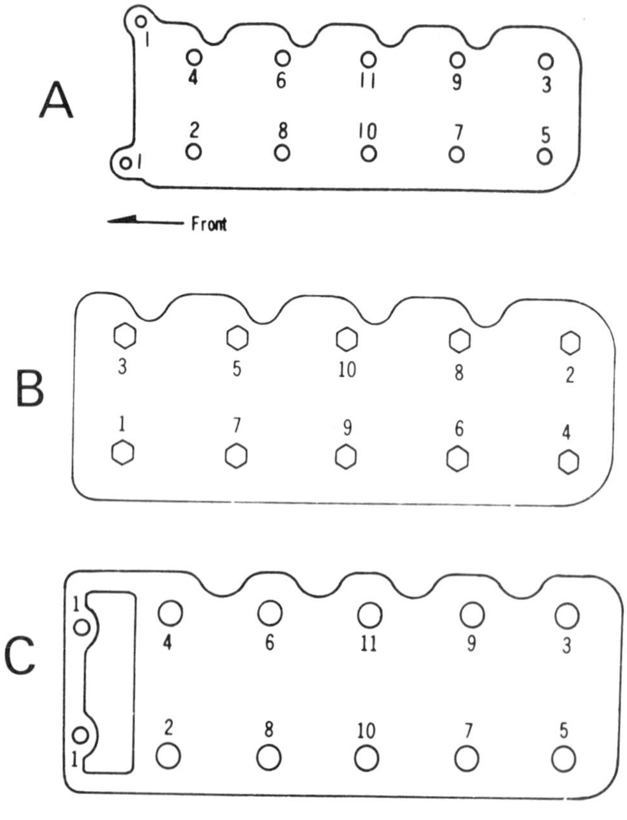

Fig. 1.7 Head bolt removal sequence

(A) 4G3 with timing chain
(B) 4G3 with timing belt
(C) 4G5

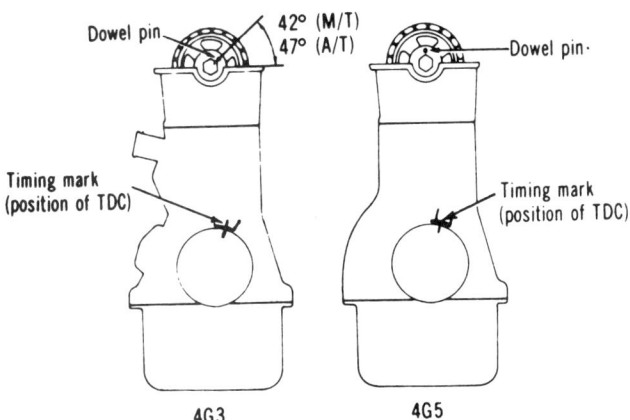

Fig. 1.8 Removing the camshaft sprocket

remove the bonding wires, cable clamps and cable stop. Secure the reversing light wires out of the way.

19 Unscrew and remove the speedometer drive from the gearbox (photo).

20 Remove the two nuts securing the gearbox to the engine rear mounting. Support the gearbox on a jack and then remove the four bolts securing the crossmember and take away the crossmember (photo).

21 Push back the carpet from around the gear lever gaiter and remove the three screws. Lift off the gaiter clamping plate.

22 Remove the bolts securing the gearbox turret and lift off the gear lever and turret assembly (photo).

23 In the engine compartment, remove the nuts securing the engine mounting bracket to the insulators (photo).

24 Sling the engine from the lifting lugs, located on each side of the rocker box, with the rear sling longer than the front one, so that the engine will lift out at an angle of about 30°. Place a rag or a plastic bag over the tail of the gearbox to catch any remaining oil which drains out when the power unit is lifted out.

25 Make a final check to see that there is nothing to prevent the engine being lifted out and then hoist slowly and carefully (photo). Watch for the bellhousing fouling the steering rod in the early stages of lifting.

26 Transfer the power unit to a suitable area and clean the outside thoroughly, using a degreasing agent which can subsequently be washed off with water.

27 If the power unit is to be dismantled, transfer it to a strong work bench.

3 Separating the engine from the gearbox

1   Support both the engine and gearbox with the engine resting on its sump.

2   Remove the starter motor (photo), which is held by two bolts.

3   Remove the remaining nuts and bolts from around the periphery of the bellhousing and ease the gearbox away from the engine. Be careful to keep the gearbox in line until it is clear of the engine, so that the input shaft is not damaged.

4 Cylinder head – removal (engine out of car)

1   Remove the two bolts securing the rocker box cover and lift it off.

2   Turn the crankshaft until No. 1 piston is at the top of its compression stroke. This is when the crankshaft pulley notch is aligned with the timing mark on the front of the timing chaincase and the dowel pin of the camshaft sprocket is in the position shown in Fig. 1.8.

3   Paint a mating mark on the timing chain in line with the mating mark on the camshaft sprocket unless the timing chain has a plated link in this position. On the 4G3 series engines the chain should be locked to the sprocket with a piece of wire as shown in Fig. 1.6.

4   Lock the flywheel pulley so that it cannot rotate. Unscrew and remove the sprocket fixing bolt and pull the sprocket off the camshaft.

5   Remove the cylinder head bolts in the sequence shown in Fig. 1.6. Each bolt should be released in about three stages, to prevent distor-

tion of the cylinder head. Later models require a $\frac{5}{16}$ hexagon wrench or socket (photo).

6   The cylinder head is located on two dowels and when all the bolts have been removed, the cylinder head should be lifted vertically, to avoid damaging the dowels.

5 Camshaft and rocker arms – removal and dismantling

1   Remove the spark plugs to avoid the risk of accidental damage to them.

2   Remove the ten camshaft bearing cap nuts and the two fixings for the rocker box cover (photo).

3   Hold the front and rear bearing caps. Apply pressure along the axis of the camshaft and remove the rocker arm assembly.

4   Separate the assembly into the caps, rocker arms, springs and wave washer, being careful to keep all the parts in the same relative positions as fitted on the shaft. Note that the bearing caps have locating dowels between them and the cylinder head. Take care not to lose any of the dowels.

6 Crankshaft pulley, clutch and flywheel – removal

1   If a major dismantling operation of the bottom end of the engine is being undertaken, it is convenient to remove the crankshaft pulley at this stage. If only the clutch and flywheel are to be removed, the pulley need not be taken off.

2   Mark the position of the distributor body on the cylinder block and the position of the rotor when No. 1 piston is at top dead centre on its firing stroke. Temporarily lock the flywheel with a suitably shaped piece of metal, and remove the crankshaft pulley bolt. Draw off the pulley, taking care not to lose the key (photo).

3   Unlock the flywheel locking tabs, mark the position of the flywheel on the crankshaft, undo the bolts from the tab washer and remove the six bolts securing the flywheel (photo).

4   Remove the bolts securing the engine adaptor plate and remove it (photo).

7 Cylinder head – dismantling

1   Remove the spark plugs and then the camshaft (Section 5).

2   Using a valve spring compressor, compress the valve springs and remove the valve collets. Carefully release the spring compressor and remove together with spring retainer, spring, spring seat and valve. The parts of each valve assembly should be kept together in the correct position for each cylinder.

3   Using a screwdriver, prise off the stem seals and discard them.

4   The valve guides are a shrink fit in the cylinder head and if they need to be removed, the cylinder head should be heated to about 480°F and the guides hammered out using a suitable drift.

8 Cylinder block – dismantling

1   Remove the oil pressure switch then turn the engine upside down and support it firmly with blocks (photo).

2   Remove the sump retaining bolts, tap the sump to break the gasket seal and remove the sump.

3   Remove the oil screen (photo).

4   Remove the timing chaincase, the chain guides and the sprocket locking bolts. If the engine is fitted with counterbalance shafts, remove the counterbalance sprockets.

5   Remove the crankshaft sprocket, camshaft sprocket and timing chain. It is necessary to depress the chain tensioner in order to remove the chain.

6   Remove the camshaft sprocket holder and the right and left-hand timing chain guides.

7   Remove the bolt locking the oil pump driven gear to the right-hand counterbalance shaft when fitted, then remove the oil pump mounting bolts and take off the oil pump (4G5).

8   Take the counterbalance shaft out of the cylinder block. If the bolt locking the oil pump gear to the counterbalance shaft is difficult to undo, remove the oil pump and counterbalance shaft as an assembly

8.1 Oil pressure switch

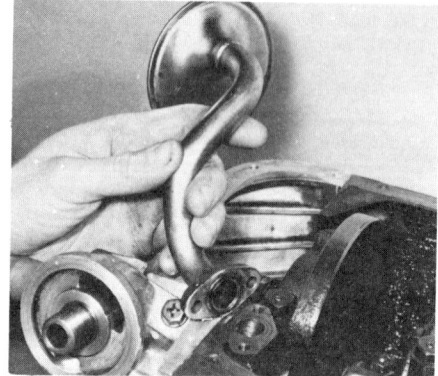

8.3 Remove the oil screen

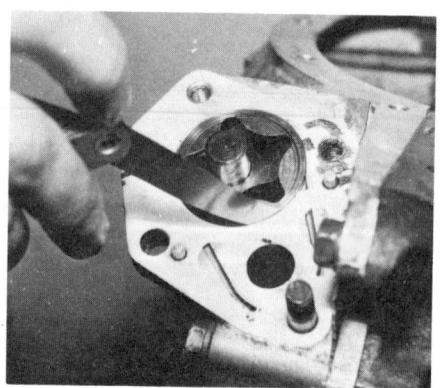

11.9a Oil pump inner rotor to body clearance

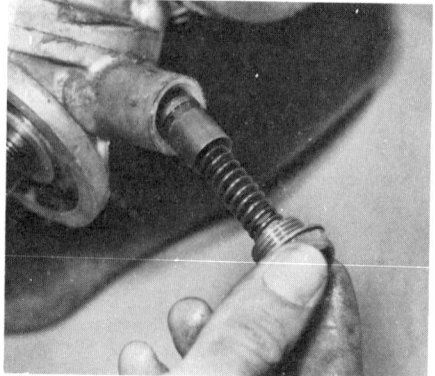

11.9b Oil relief valve plunger and spring (4G3)

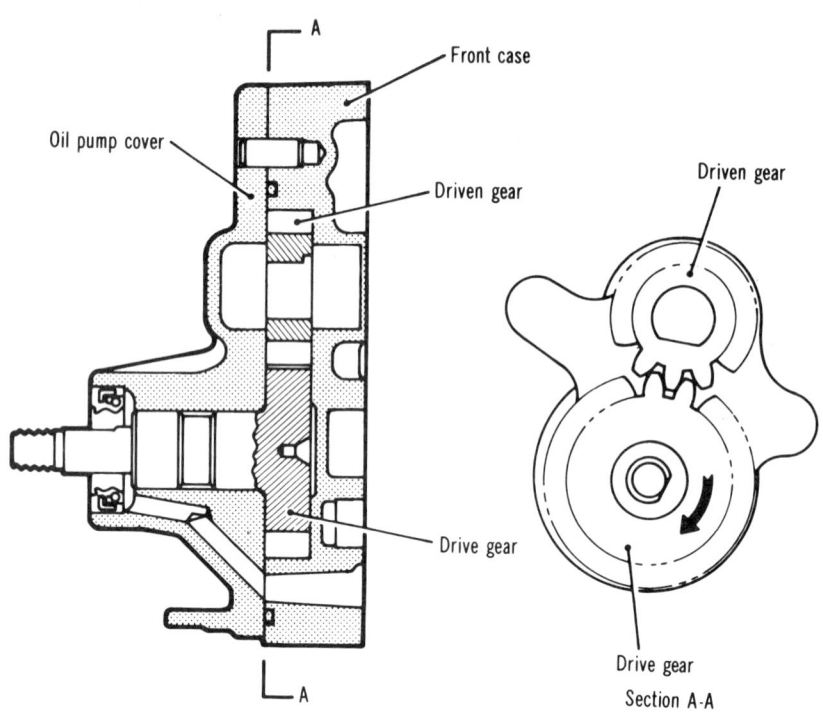

Fig. 1.9 Gear type oil pump (4G3 belt driven)

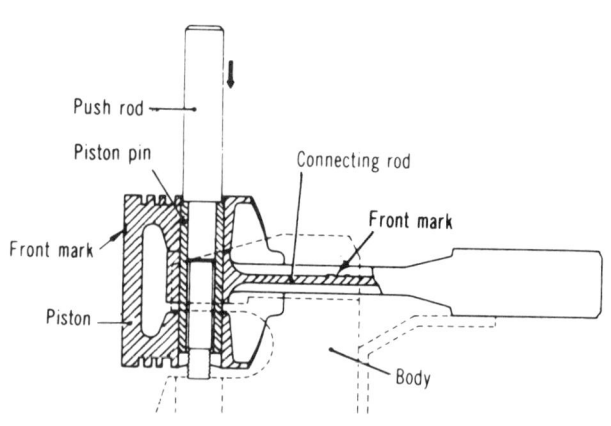

Fig. 1.10 Removing the gudgeon pin

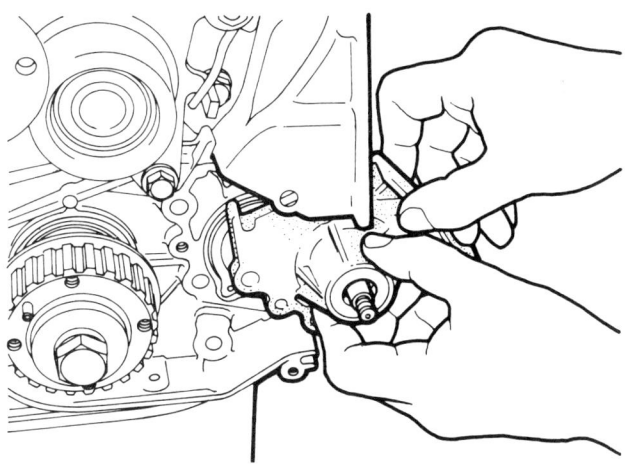

Fig. 1.11 Removing the oil pump cover (4G3 belt driven)

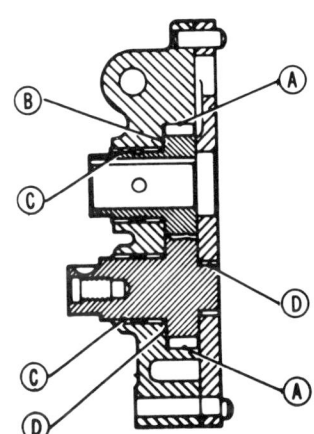

Fig. 1.12 Gear pump clearances

Clearance between gear addendum and body (A)	0.0041 to 0.0059 in
Gear end play (B)	0.0024 to 0.0047 in
Clearance between gear and bearing (C)	0.0008 to 0.0047 in
Clearance between gear and bearing (Drive gear rear end) (D)	0.0017 to 0.0026 in

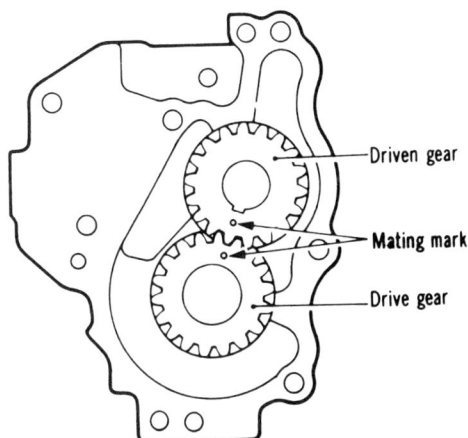

Fig. 1.13 Gear mating marks

and separate them afterwards.

9   Remove the thrust plate supporting the front of the left-hand counterbalance shaft and take the shaft out of the cylinder block. Use two bolts in the threaded holes of the flange as jacking screws to remove the thrust plate.

10   Remove the crankshaft rear oil seal housing and take out the seal and spacer.

11   Turn the cylinder block on its side, remove the connecting rod caps and push each piston out through the top of the cylinder block. Use a piece of soft wood to push them upwards, so as not to damage them. If the big-end bearings are removed and the same ones are being used again, take care to keep then in order, so that they can be refitted in exactly the same position from which they were removed.

9   Crankshaft – removal

1   Unscrew and remove the five crankshaft bearing caps.

2   Lift out the crankshaft.

3   Remove the bearings from the crankcase webs and the crankshaft bearing caps, being careful to keep them in pairs and associated with their correct journal. Also take care not to mix up the upper and lower bearings.

10   Pistons – dismantling

1   Carefully remove the piston rings to avoid damaging the piston or the piston rings, taking care to place them the same way as fitted to the piston, in order and associated with the piston from which they were removed.

2   The gudgeon pins are a press fit into the connecting rods and should not be removed unless it is absolutely necessary. To remove them without the special tool, support the piston on a piece of soft wood having a hole in it through which the gudgeon pin can pass and using a soft metal drift, drive out the gudgeon pin from the side of the connecting rod which faces the front of the engine (Fig. 1.10).

11   Oil pump – dismantling and reassembly

Gear type (Fig. 1.9)

1   Remove the two screws securing the cover and take it off.

2   Remove the plug and withdraw the relief spring and plunger.

3   Examine the pump body to see that there are no cracks, then check the gear tooth for wear. Make sure that all holes and ports in the body are clear and if necessary blow them through with compressed air. Check the cover for signs of wear from the ends of the gears and fit a new cover if the existing one is worn excessively. Check the bearings and if wear is excessive, fit a new pump body assembly.

4   Check the clearances (Fig. 1.12) after assembling the gears into the pump, then lubricate the gears.

5   Fit the relief plunger and ensure that it moves smoothly. Insert the spring, checking that it is not broken, or distorted. Oil the plunger and refit the plug.

6   Check that the gear mating marks are aligned (Fig. 1.13) then refit the cover.

Trochoid type (Fig. 1.14 and 1.15)

7   Remove the cover fixing bolts, take off the cover. Then remove and discard the gasket.

8   If it is necessary to renew the rotor assembly, or the gear, drill away the peened section of the gear fixing pin and drive out the pin (4G5).

9   Check that the rotor to cover clearance does not exceed 0.008 in (Fig. 1.16), that the outer rotor to body clearance is not more than 0.012 in (Fig. 1.17) and that the inner rotor clearance (photo) is not more than 0.010 in. Check that the relief plunger slides freely and that the oil passage and plunger bore are undamaged. Examine the spring (photo) to see that it is not broken, or distorted.

10   Reassemble the pump, using a new gasket. If the drive shaft gear has been removed, refit it with the mating marks as shown in Fig. 1.18. Fit the gear locking pin and peen it at both ends.

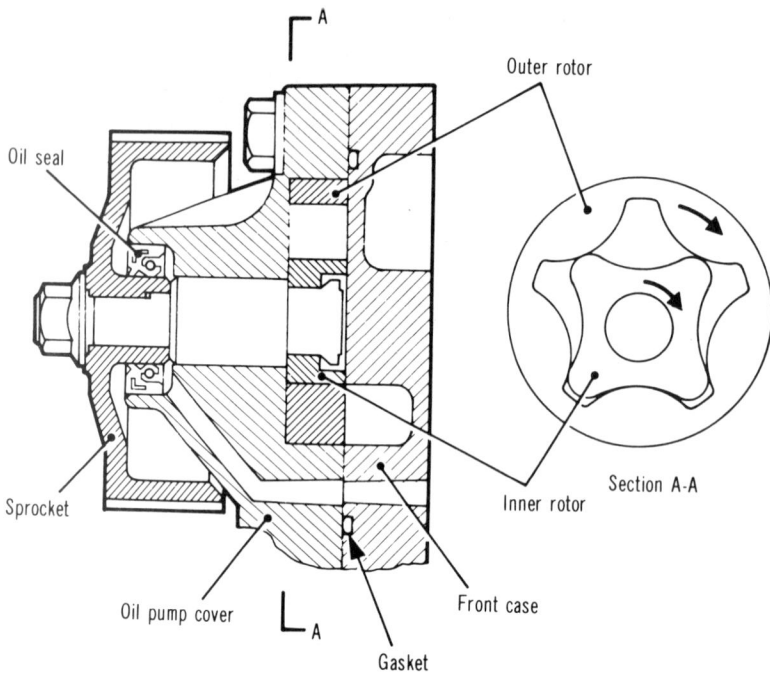

Fig. 1.14 Trochoid oil pump (4G3 belt driven)

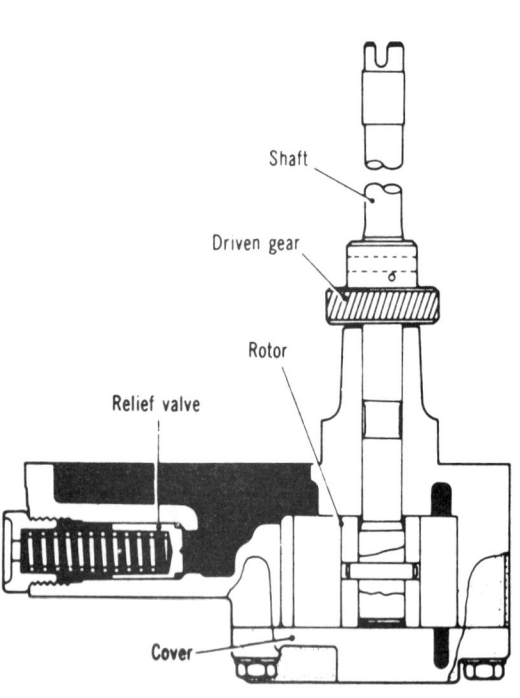

Fig. 1.15 Trochoid oil pump (shaft driven)

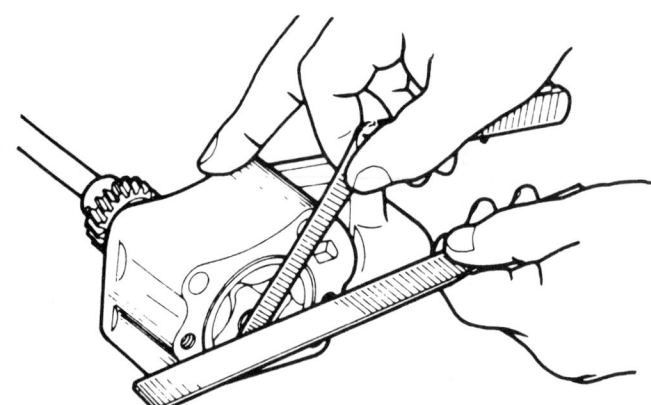

Fig. 1.16 Checking the rotor to cover clearance

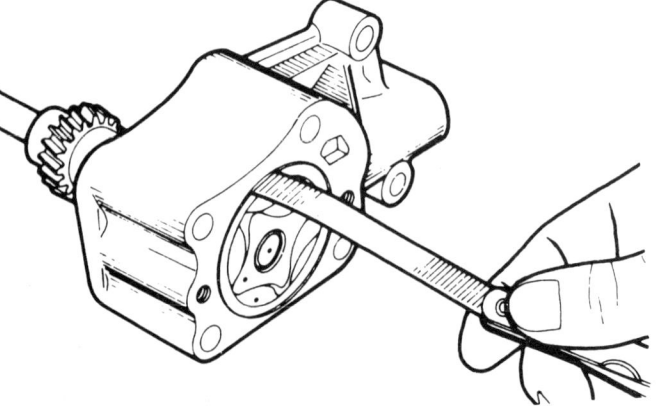

Fig. 1.17 Checking the outer rotor clearance

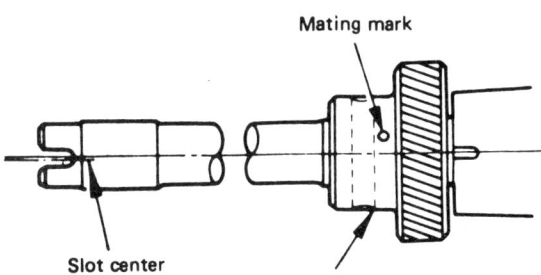

Fig. 1.18 Fitting the shaft gear on to the shaft

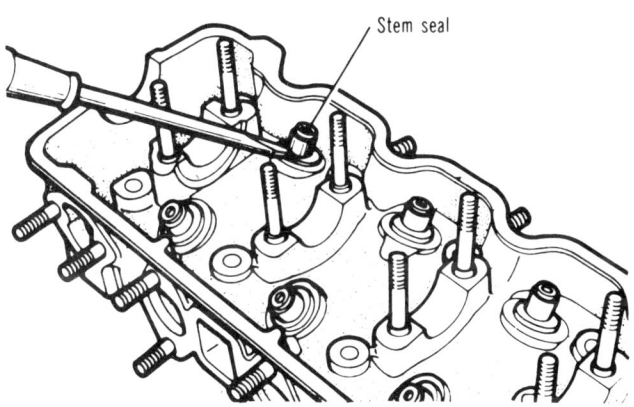

Fig. 1.19 Removing the valve stem seals

(A) using a screwdriver

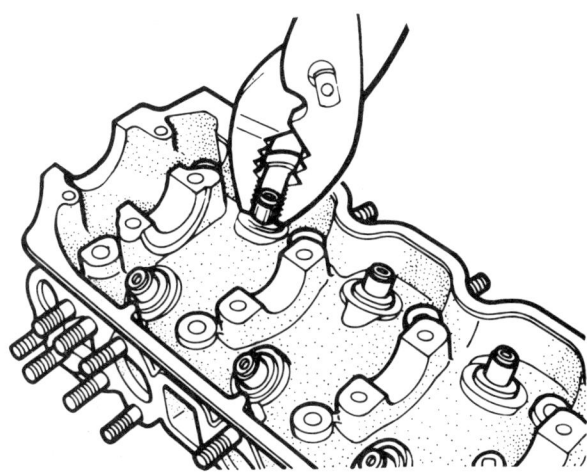

(B) using pliers

12 Valves – removal

1   Remove the spark plugs and then turn the cylinder head on to its side.
2   Carefully position a valve spring compressor over a valve and compress the spring until the collets can be removed.
3   Slowly release the spring pressure, remove the valve spring compressor and lift off the spring retainer, valve spring and spring seat.
4   Remove the valve and if the stem seals are not being removed in order to fit new ones, valve removal needs great care in order to avoid damaging the seals. If new stem seals are being fitted, prise off the old ones with a screwdriver (Fig. 1.19), or pull off with pliers.
5   Store each valve with its spring and associated parts in such a way that they can be refitted exactly as they were removed.

13 Engine components – cleaning, examination – general note

When the engine has been dismantled, thoroughly clean all components with petrol or a proprietary solvent. Remove any traces of gasket material which is still adhering, using a blunt scraper. Take care not to score any of the sealing faces.

Once the components have been cleaned, both before and after inspection, keep them wrapped or covered so that they stay clean. Renew all badly worn components.

14 Crankshaft – examination and renovation

1   Examine the crankpins and journals for signs of scoring or other damage. Using a micrometer, check the ovality of the crankpins at different points around their periphery. The crankshaft should be reground to one of the dimensions given in the Specifications if there is serious scoring, or if the ovality is greater than 0.001 in (0.025 mm). The main bearing journals should also be inspected to the same standard as the crankpins.
2   A crankshaft regrinding specialist will recondition the crankshaft and supply a set of suitable bearing shells.

15 Big-end and main bearing shells – examination

1   Big-end bearing failure produces a characteristic knocking and a drop in oil pressure. Main bearing failure is often accompanied by vibration and a pronounced drop in oil pressure.
2   Examine the bearings for signs of scoring and pitting. The bearings should be a uniform matt grey colour and with lead indium bearings the presence of a copper colour indicates that the bearing material has worn away and the underlay is exposed, necessitating new bearings.
3   If the bearings have deteriorated, but the crankshaft is serviceable, fit new bearings of standard size. If the crankshaft is reground, new bearings of the appropriate size must be fitted.

16 Cylinder bores – examination and renovation

1   Worn cylinder bores and piston rings are indicated by high oil consumption and blue smoke from the exhaust, particularly when accelerating.
2   Examine the bores for signs of scoring and for the presence of a step at the top of the bore. Bore wear may be overcome by fitting new standard size piston rings, special oil control rings, or by reboring the cylinders. The method chosen depends upon the condition of the bores and the additional mileage which is anticipated. It is best to obtain specialist advice.

17 Camshaft bearings – inspection

With the camshaft fitted and the bearing caps tightened to the correct torque wrench setting, measure the clearance between the camshaft and the bearing cap. If the clearance exceeds 0.0035 in (0.0889 mm) the bearings are worn excessively and a new cylinder head is required.

18 Valves – examination and renovation

1   Examine the heads of the valves for pitting and burning; especially the heads of the exhaust valves. The valve seating should be examined at the same time. If the pitting on the valves and seats is very light the marks can be removed by grinding the seats and the valves together with coarse and then fine, valve grinding paste. Where bad pitting has occurred to the valve seats it will be necessary to recut them to fit new valves. If the valve seats are so worn that they cannot be recut, then it will be necessary to fit new valve seat inserts. These latter two jobs should be entrusted to the local official agent or automobile engineering works. In practice it is very seldom that the seats are so badly worn that they require renewal. Normally, it is the valve that is too badly worn for refitment, and the owner can easily purchase a new set of valves and match them to the seats by valve grinding.

2   Valve grinding is carried out as follows: place the cylinder head upside down on a bench, with a block of wood at each end to give clearance for the valve stems.

3   Smear a trace of coarse carborundum paste on the seat face and apply a suction grinder tool to the valve head. With a semi-rotary action, grind the valve head to its seat, lifting the valve occasionally to redistribute the grinding paste. When a dull matt even surface finish is produced on both the valve seat and the valve, wipe off the paste and repeat the process with fine carborundum paste as before. A light spring placed under the valve head will greatly ease this operation. When a smooth unbroken ring of light grey matt finish is produced, on both valve and the valve seat faces, the grinding operation is complete.

19 Timing chain, sprockets and chain tensioner – examination and renovation

1   Examine the teeth of the sprockets and ensure that none of them are damaged or broken. If this is the case, a new sprocket must be fitted.

2   Examine the teeth for wear and if it is obvious that the teeth are no longer symmetrical because of wear on one side, the sprocket should not be refitted but renewed.

3   Because a worn timing chain causes a lot of engine noise, it is worth fitting a new timing chain when the engine is stripped down. Likewise it is worth fitting a new head to the tensioner.

20 Engine components – examination

Sump
1   Thoroughly wash out the sump to remove all sludge. Dry it with a lint-free cloth.

2   Inspect the casing for cracking or distortion. Cracks and splits may be repaired by specialist welding, but if the damage cannot be repaired satisfactorily, fit a new sump.

3   Check that the seating face is clean, has no old gasket adhering and is not distorted.

Clutch pilot bearing (spigot bush)
4   Fit the clutch shaft into the crankshaft end to see whether it is a good fit. A sloppy pilot bush will cause unnecessary wear to the gearbox front bearing, and should be renewed.

Studs, nuts and bolts
5   Examine all studs, nuts and bolts for damage and wear. For slight thread damage clean the threads up with the appropriate tap or die, otherwise fit a new fastening. Where self-locking nuts are used, any which have been removed should be renewed.

21 Decarbonising

1   Remove the cylinder head as described in Section 4 and, using a blunt screwdriver, or a rotary wire brush, remove all the carbon from the cylinder head while all the valves are still in place.

2   Remove the valves, taking the precautions given in Section 12 and remove the carbon from the valves and from the valve ports. Grind the valves in (see Section 18) and then refit them.

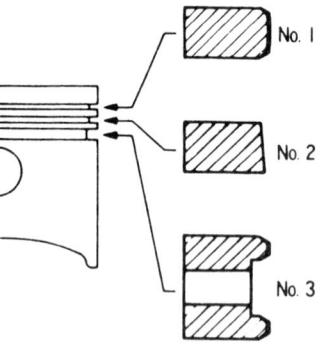

Fig. 1.20 Order of piston ring fitting (one-piece oil ring)

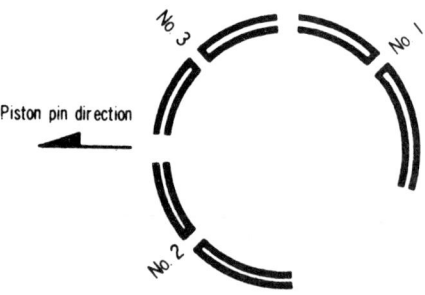

Fig. 1.21 Piston ring end position (one-piece oil ring)

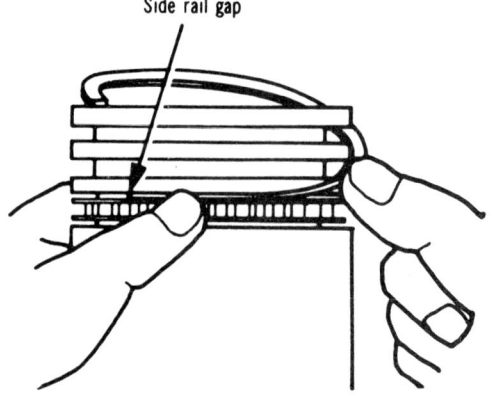

Fig. 1.22 Fitting the oil ring side rails

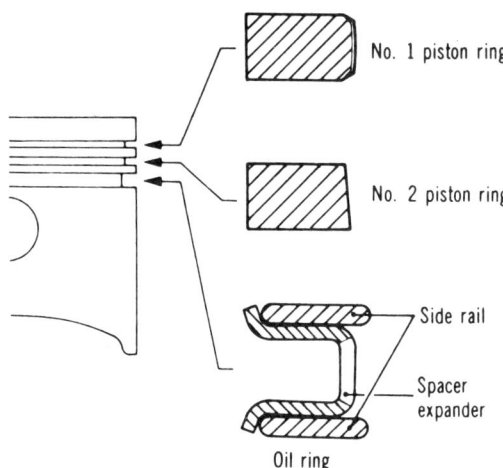

Fig. 1.23 Order of piston ring fitting (three-piece oil ring)

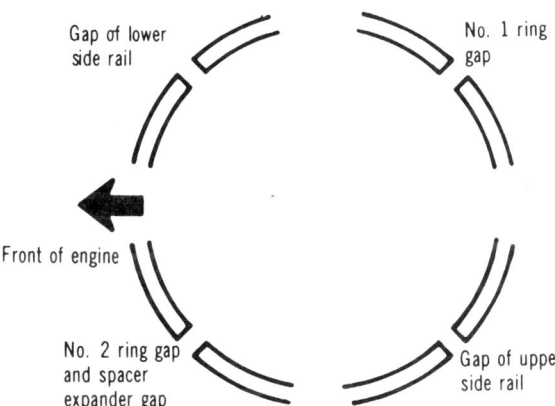

Fig. 1.24 Piston ring end positions (three-piece oil ring)

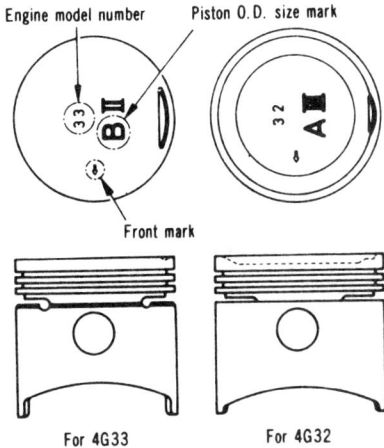

Fig. 1.25 Identifying marks on pistons

3   Turn the crankshaft so that two of the pistons are at the top of their bores. Put clean rag in the bores of the other two cylinders and cover up the waterways, then carefully scrape all the carbon from the crowns of the two exposed pistons. Use a flat, blunt scraper, taking care not to scratch the piston crowns. Ensure that no carbon gets down the side of the pistons. Carefully clean away all the loose carbon.
4   Rotate the crankshaft, so that the two clean pistons descend into their bores, insert clean rag into the bores and remove the carbon ring from the top of the cylinder. Carefully remove the rag from the bores, so that the carbon which has fallen on to it is removed with the rag.
5   Turn the crankshaft, so that the two pistons left to be decarbonised are at the top of their bores and proceed as in paragraphs 3 and 4.

22 Piston rings – refitting

1   If new pistons rings are being fitted, first insert the ring into the appropriate cylinder bore and press the ring down using the correct piston for the bore, until the ring is across an unworn part of the bore. Check that the gap between the ends of the ring is at least 0.006 in (0.15 mm), but not more than 0.40 in (1 mm). If the gap needs to be increased, remove the ring and carefully file the end of it, to achieve the required clearance.
2   Starting with the oil control ring, carefully fit the piston rings to the pistons by sliding the rings down from the piston crown. Use two feeler gauges between the ring and the piston, to slide the ring over any grooves which need to be traversed. In the case of a three piece oil control ring, first fit the spacer expander, then the upper slide rail and finally the lower slide rail. Do not attempt to open the gaps in the slide rails, but fit them as shown in Fig. 1.22, by inserting one end and holding it firmly, then gradually pressing the adjuster part into the groove until the centre ring has been fitted. Fit the side rails so that the size and maker's identification stamped on their side is uppermost Check that the upper and lower slide rails can be turned smoothly and that the gaps in the spacer expander and side rails are staggered by 45° (Fig. 1.24).
3   When fitting No. 2 piston ring, be careful to have the surface marked 'top' uppermost, because the ring section is not symmetrical. If the rings are not marked, the manufacturer's marks should be placed uppermost.
4   After fitting all the rings, check that their side clearances are as given in the Specifications and then space the ring joints so that no joint is in the direction of piston thrust, or in line with the gudgeon pin boss.

23 Engine reassembly – general note

1   To ensure maximum life and minimum trouble from a rebuilt engine, everything must be assembled correctly and must be spotlessly clean.
2   All oilways and ports must be clear. Mating surfaces must be clean and all rotating and sliding surfaces must be oiled on assembly.
3   Make sure that all nuts, bolts and washers are in good condition and are fitted exactly as they were before dismantling.
4   Check that all core plugs are in good condition and show no sign of weeping. Renew any which are suspect.
5   Have ready a supply of clean cotton rags, an oil can filled with engine oil and all the required gaskets and seals, as well as all the necessary tools.
6   Some models are fitted with socket headed cylinder head bolts. For the correct torque tightening of these, it will be necessary to have a special socket with a $\frac{5}{16}$ in (8 mm) hexagon.

24 Cylinder block assembly – engines without balance shafts

1   Ensure that the crankcase is scrupulously clean and that all oilways are clear. If possible, blow them out with compressed air. Treat the crankshaft in the same way and then inject engine oil into the crankshaft oilways.
2   Fit the upper halves of the main bearings into the webs of the crankcase, after wiping their locations clean. Note that each half bearing has a tab which locates in a groove (photo) and ensure that it is fitted correctly and that its ends are flush. The centre bearing has

24.2a Bearing locking tab and groove

24.2b Crankshaft centre bearing

24.4a Fitting the crankshaft

24.4b Fitting a crankshaft bearing cap

24.4c Tightening the main bearing cap bolts

24.5 Measuring crankshaft endfloat

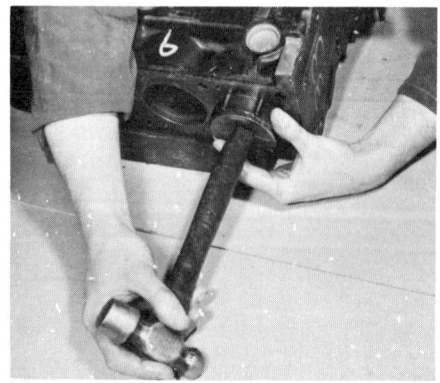
24.6a Fitting a piston

24.6b Piston 'front' mark

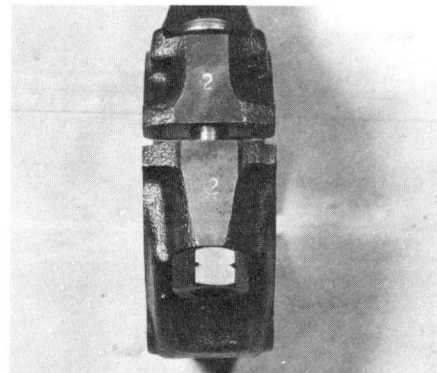
24.6c Connecting rod identification and mating marks

24.7 Fitting a big-end bearing cap

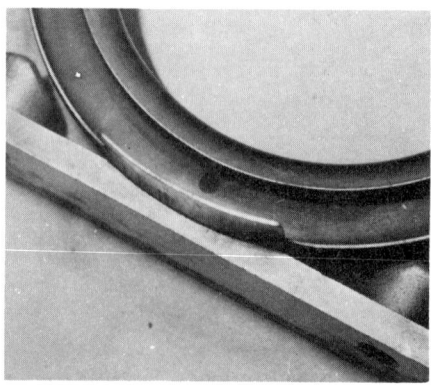
24.9a Oil hole in separator

24.9b Fitting the crankshaft rear oil seal

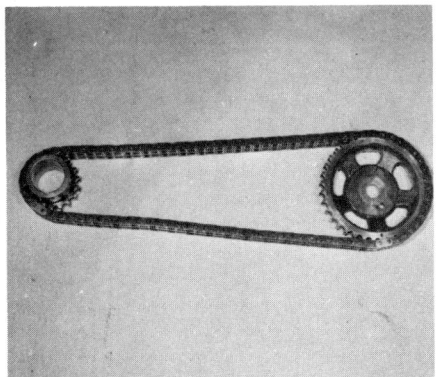

24.12a Sprocket mating marks and chain plated links

24.12b Timing chain in position (4G3)

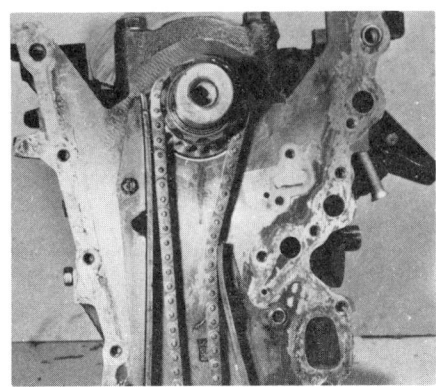

24.12c Timing chain in position (4G5)

24.12d Chain tensioner (4G5)

24.12e Crankshaft key, gear and slinger

24.13a Fitting the chaincase (4G3)

24.13b Chaincase fitted (4G5)

24.14 Fitting the chain tensioner (4G3)

24.15a Fitting the oil pump (4G5)

24.15b Oil pump mating marks (4G5)

24.16 Oil screen fitted (4G3)

thrust washers on the side (photo). If new bearings are being fitted, carefully wipe away their protective grease coating.

3   Taking the same precautions, fit the lower bearing shells to their caps.

4   Fit the crankshaft to the crankcase (photo) and fit the bearing caps (photo) noting that each one has a number to indicate its position and an arrow to show the side which must face the front of the engine. Fit the main bearing bolts and tighten them to the required torque as specified. The cap bolts should be tightened successively, in several stages (photo).

5   Ensure that the crankshaft rotates freely and has a thrust clearance at the centre bearing of between 0.002 to 0.007 in (photo).

6   Lay the cylinder block on its side, fit a piston ring compressor to a piston and insert the piston/con-rod assembly into the top of the bore (photo). Note that the piston is marked with the engine type number (Fig. 1.25) and an arrow to indicate which side of the piston should be towards the front of the engine (photo). The identification of the correct cylinder for each piston is stamped on the connecting rod (photo).

7   As each piston is inserted, fit the appropriate big-end bearing cap and fit the cap bolts or nuts finger tight (photo).

8   When all four pistons have been fitted, tighten the big-end bearing cap bolts progressively to the appropriate torque setting for the engine. Then check that the crankshaft can still be turned by hand.

9   Fit the oil seal to the crankshaft oil seal housing. Fit the separator with the oil hole at the bottom (photo) and then bolt on the oil seal assembly (photo). Smear the oil seal with engine oil when it is fitted.

10   Rotate the crankshaft so that No. 1 piston is at top dead centre.

11   With the cylinder block upside down, fit the timing chain guide, sprocket holder (4G52 only) and the tensioner. On the 4G32 engine, the chain guide must be fitted so that the jet is directed towards the chain and sprocket meshing point.

12   With the mating marks of the crankshaft sprocket and the camshaft sprocket aligned with the chrome plated links in the timing chain (photo), fit the sprocket to the crankshaft, with the chain fitted in the guide and against the tensioner (photo). Fit the key, the crankshaft gear and oil slinger, F mark (4G32), the C or A mark (4G52) towards the front of the engine and the slinger as shown (photo).

13   Fit the gasket and then bolt on the timing chaincase to the cylinder block (photo).

14   On the 4G32 engine, insert the tensioner lever plunger and spring through the hole in the right-hand side of the chaincase and tighten the holder, using a $\frac{5}{8}$ in hexagon socket wrench to the specified torque (photo).

15   On the 4G52 engine, fit the oil pump assembly beneath the timing chaincase (photo) with its mating marks lined up (photo).

16   Fit the oil screen then coat the sump joint face, the timing case to block and rear oil seal to block joints with sealer (Fig. 1.29).

17   Fit the gasket to the sump, then place the sump on the cylinder block, insert the bolts and tighten them in diagonal sequence, starting with the ones furthest from the centre. Tighten to the correct torque.

18   Fit and temporarily tighten the crankshaft pulley, taking care not to move the position of the crankshaft. Fit the oil pressure switch, then set the engine upright, again being careful not to move the crankshaft until the camshaft assembly and camshaft sprocket have been fitted.

19   Cover the top of the chaincase with rag to prevent anything from falling into it.

20   Fit the flywheel with the mating marks, made at the time of dismantling, aligned and then lock it while the mounting bolts are tightened. Fit a new tab washer and tighten the bolts to the specified torque and bend over the tabs to lock the bolts.

21   Again prevent the crankshaft from turning by locking the flywheel and finally tighten the crankshaft pulley to the appropriate torque for the engine.

22   Fit the engine support bracket.

25 Cylinder block assembly – 4G3 engine with balance shafts

1   Proceed as for the engine without balancer shafts fitted (Section 24) until the end of paragraph 9.

2   Fit the engine rear plate, then the flywheel and tighten its mounting bolts (see Section 24, paragraph 20). In the case of an engine with automatic transmission, fit the drive plate and adapter plate.

3   Fit the oil pump drive gear and driven gear into the crankcase, making sure that the timing marks on the two gears are aligned as

shown in Fig. 1.26. Apply engine oil copiously to both gears.

4   Insert the left counterbalance shaft into the driven gear and fit the retaining bolt finger tight.

5   Apply engine oil to the journals of the right counterbalance shaft and carefully fit the shaft into the cylinder block.

6   Fit a new front cover gasket and lower the front cover over the protruding shafts and fit the retaining bolts loosely.

7   Insert a screwdriver as shown in Fig. 1.28 to keep the left counterbalance shaft from rotating and tighten the bolt securing the oil pump gear to it.

8   Fit a new O-ring to the groove in the oil pump cover, fit the cover, then insert and tighten the five cover retaining bolts.

9   Fully tighten the eight retaining bolts of the front cover.

10   Fit the oil screen and tighten its fixing bolts.

11   Apply sealant to the joint faces indicated in Fig. 1.29. Fit a new sump gasket to the cylinder block, being careful to align the holes in the gasket with those in the cylinder block. Fit the sump, insert its 20 retaining bolts and tighten them in a diagonal sequence to the specified torque. Do not overtighten the sump bolts because this may cause the gasket to be squeezed out, causing leaks.

26 Cylinder block assembly – 4G5 engine with balance shafts

1   Proceed as for the engine without the balancer shafts fitted (Section 24) until the end of paragraph 9.

2   Fit the engine rear plate, then the flywheel and tighten its mounting bolts (see Section 24, paragraph 20). In the case of an engine with automatic transmission, fit the drive plate and adapter plate.

3   Fit the right-hand counterbalance shaft to the cylinder block, inserting it gently, so that it does not damage the rear bearing.

4   Fit the oil pump assembly, making sure that the keyway of the oil pump driven gear fits the Woodruff key at the end of the counterbalance shaft and that the key is not moved or displaced. After the oil pump assembly has been fitted, tighten its mounting bolts.

5   Tighten the counterbalance shaft and driven gear mounting bolt. If the fit of the Woodruff key and driven gear is too tight, first insert the counterbalance shaft into the oil pump, temporarily tighten the bolt. Insert the counterbalance shaft and oil pump as an assembly into the cylinder block.

6   Fill the oil pump with oil and tighten the counterbalance shaft to the torque figure specified.

7   Insert the left counterbalance shaft into the cylinder block, taking care not to damage the rear bearing.

8   Fit a new O-ring to the outer peripheral groove of the thrust plate (Fig. 1.34) taking care not to twist the ring. Smear the O-ring with oil and fit the thrust plate to the cylinder block. Use a bolt without a head as a guide when fitting the thrust plate, so that the plate does not have to be turned to align the holes and so possibly distort the O-ring.

9   After bolting on the thrust plate, fit the spacer.

10   Fit the sprocket holder and the right and left-hand chain guides.

11   Turn the crankshaft until the piston of No. 1 cylinder is at the top of its stroke.

12   Fit the tensioner spring and sleeve to the oil pump body.

13   Fit the camshaft sprocket, crankshaft sprocket and chain as in Section 24, paragraph 12.

14   With the parts assembled as above and being held with both hands, align the key of the crankshaft with the keyway on the crankshaft sprocket and fit the sprocket.

15   Fit crankshaft sprocket B (Fig. 1.32) (for driving the counterbalance shaft) onto the crankshaft.

16   Fit the two counterbalance drive sprockets B on to chain B (for driving the counterbalance shaft), taking care to align the mating marks (Fig. 1.31) and fit the sprockets to the shafts.

17   Tighten the locking bolts of sprockets B and temporarily install chain guides, A, B and C.

18   Adjust the tension of chain B in the following sequence.

(a)   *Firmly tighten chain guide A mounting bolt*

(b)   *Firmly tighten chain guide C mounting bolt*

(c)   *Move sprockets B to collect the slack chain at point P, then adjust the position of chain guide C so that when the chain is pulled in the direction of arrow Y with the finger tips, the clearance between chain guide B and the links of chain B will be 0.04 in to 0.14 in (1.02 to 3.56 mm), then tighten the bolts*

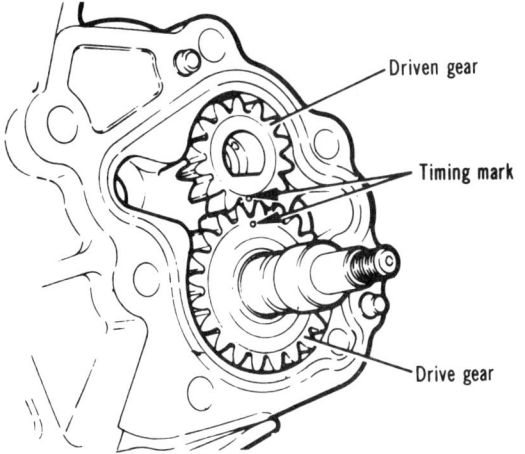

Fig. 1.26 Refitting the oil pump (4G3 with balance shafts)

Fig. 1.27 Fitting the front case

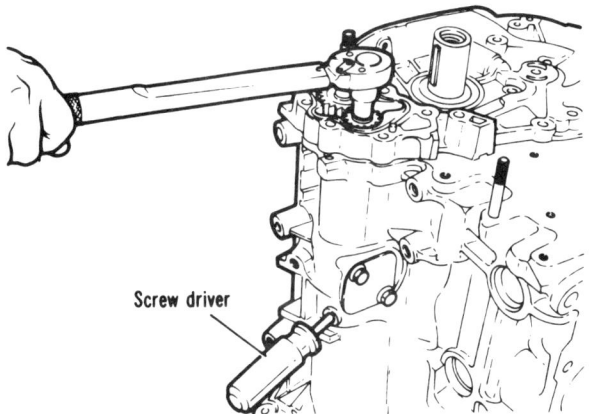

Fig. 1.28 Tightening the counterbalance shaft bolt

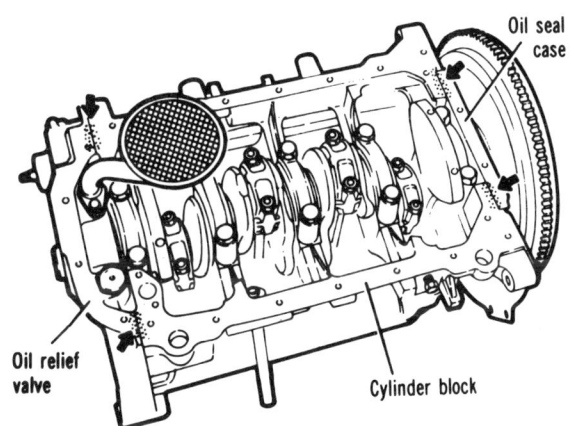

Fig. 1.29 Sealant application points (arrowed)

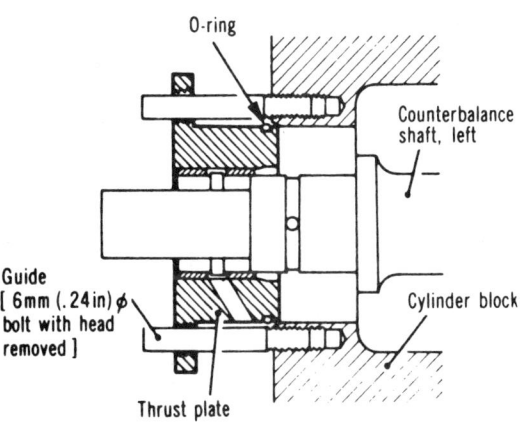

Fig. 1.30 Fitting the thrust plate

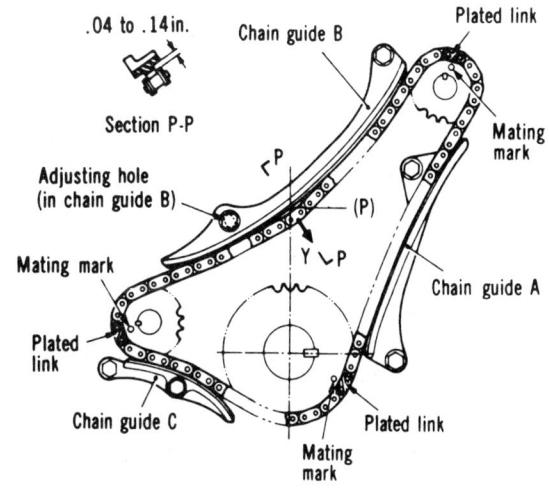

Fig. 1.31 Balancer system drive (4G5)

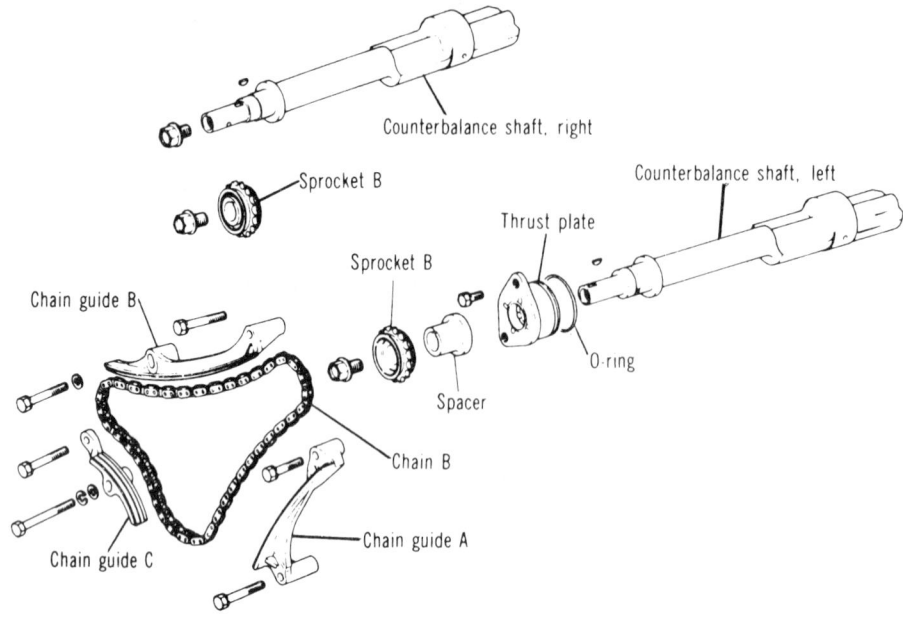

Fig. 1.32 Balance shaft assembly components (4G5)

19 Fit the timing chaincase and gasket and after refitting remove any gasket which protrudes from the top and bottom of the case.

20 Complete the assembly as in Section 24, paragraphs 16 to 22, except that the flywheel has already been fitted.

27 Cylinder head – reassembly

Valves

1 Fit the valve spring seats, then press on the valve stem oil seals (photo). Apply engine oil to each valve stem, insert the valves carefully to avoid damaging the seals (photo). Check to see that each valve moves smoothly in its guide.

2 Fit the valve springs, with the enamel identification mark on them, nearest to the rocker arm, and fit the spring retainers.

3 Compress the valve spring with a valve spring compressor, but do not compress them more than is necessary to fit the collets. If the springs are compressed too much the valve stem seal can be damaged by the lower side of the spring retainer.

4 Fit the valve collets (photo) and gradually release the pressure on the spring compressor. When the compressor has been removed, tap the top of the valve stem with a soft hammer, to make sure that the collets have seated correctly.

Jet valves

5 Jet valves should be fitted with new seals and these can only be fitted satisfactorily with a special tool (Fig. 1.38). Seals which are not fitted properly will allow oil to pass down the valve stem.

6 Apply engine oil to the jet valve stem and fit the stem into the jet body, being careful not to damage the lip of the stem seal. Check that the jet valve stem slides smoothly in the valve body.

7 Fit the jet valve spring and spring retainer. Compress the spring and fit the retainer lock. Take care not to damage the stem seal by compressing the spring until the bottom of the valve retainer presses on the seal.

8 Fit a new O-ring into the groove of the jet valve body and smear the ring with engine oil.

9 Apply engine oil to the thread of the jet valve and to its seating in the cylinder head. Then screw the valve in finger tight.

10 Tighten the jet valve with a socket spanner, taking care to keep the socket aligned with the valve stem, so that the stem is not strained.

Camshaft

11 Lubricate the camshaft lobes and the camshaft bearing journals and lay the camshaft in its location on the cylinder head (photo). Check

that its end play is within the limits 0.004 in and 0.008 in (0.1 and 0.2 mm).

12 Assemble the camshaft bearing caps, rocker arms and rocker shafts in the following way.

13 Insert the right and left-hand rocker shafts into the front bearing cap. The front bearing cap has a mating mark embossed on its front and the rocker shafts have a mark near the front end. When assembling the rocker shafts, the oil holes will be facing downwards and the mating marks on the shaft will not be visible after the shafts have been inserted correctly. The two shafts are not interchangeable. The left shaft has four oil holes at the bottom and the right-hand shaft may have either eight or twelve holes.

14 Fit the rocker arms, springs and bearing caps in the order shown in Fig. 1.35. The bearing caps are marked with their position, but although all the rocker arms are the same, they should be refitted to their original positions. Note that the springs on the right shaft are shorter than those on the left shaft. Ensure that the wave washer on the rear end of each shaft has its convex face towards the front of the engine. After fitting all the parts, insert bolts through the holes in the end caps to keep the assembly together.

15 Fit the rocker assembly to the cylinder head (photo), making sure that the dowel or keyway on the shaft is positioned correctly (see Fig. 1.37 or 1.38 as appropriate).

16 Insert the camshaft bearing bolts and screw them home finger tight. Fit the rocker box lid retainers to the front and No. 4 bearing caps (photo).

17 Sequentially tighten the bolts in stages, starting with the centre cap, then No. 2, No. 4 and the rear one in that order. On engines with timing belts, fit the distributor drive gear and camshaft spacer.

18 Fit the spark plugs and tighten them.

28 Cylinder head – refitting

Engines with timing chain

1 If there is still any covering over the top of the chaincase, remove it. Ensure that all the gasket faces of the cylinder head are clean and apply sealant to the two points indicated in Fig. 1.39.

2 Do not apply sealant to the cylinder head gasket and do not attempt to re-use an old cylinder head gasket.

3 Fit the cylinder head gasket over the dowel on the cylinder block, after ensuring that the joint between the top of the chaincase and the cylinder block is smooth.

4 Carefully lower the cylinder head onto the block after ensuring that No. 1 piston is still at the top of its cylinder. Check that the dowel hole in the camshaft sprocket is in the position shown in Fig. 1.38 or 1.46

27.1a Valve stem oil seal

27.1b Fitting a valve

27.4 Valve collets inserted

27.11 Fitting the camshaft

27.15 Fitting the rocker shaft assembly

27.16 Rocker assembly and rocker cover retainers fitted

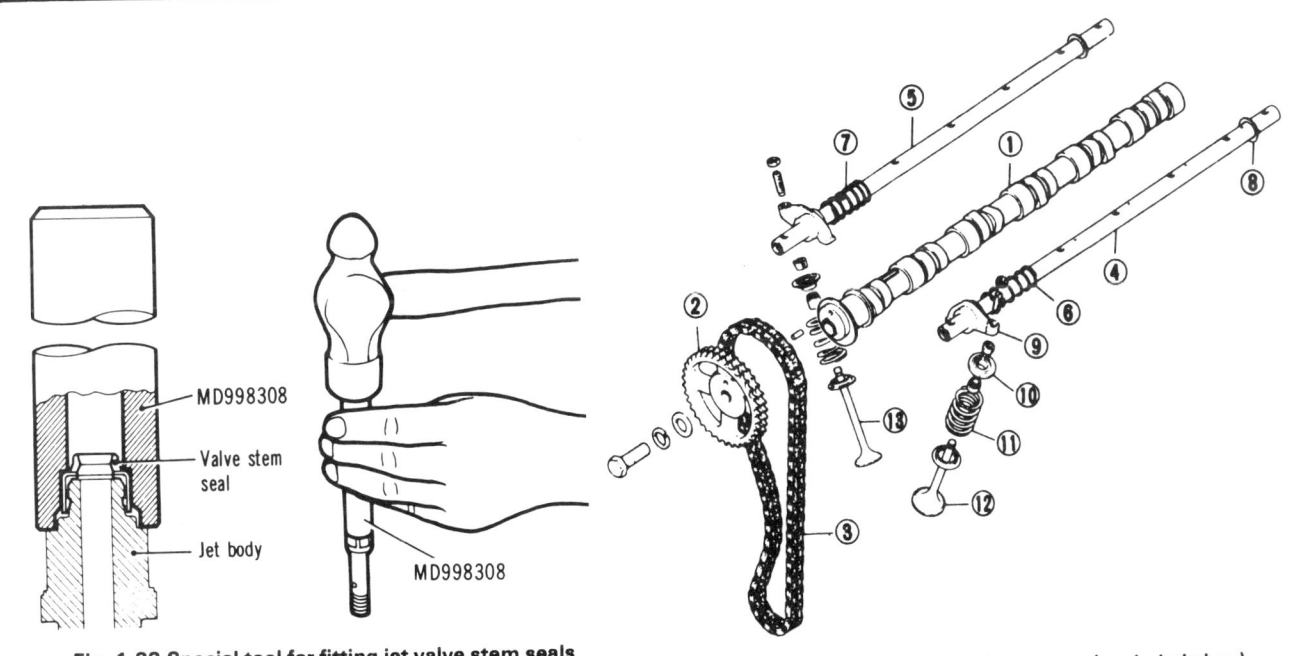

MD998308

Valve stem seal

Jet body

MD998308

Fig. 1.33 Special tool for fitting jet valve stem seals

Fig. 1.34 Chain driven timing system (exploded view)

1	Camshaft	8	Waved washer
2	Camshaft sprocket	9	Rocker arm
3	Timing chain	10	Spring retainer
4	Rocker arm shaft, left	11	Valve spring
5	Rocker arm shaft, right	12	Intake valve
6	Spring, left	13	Exhaust valve
7	Spring, right		

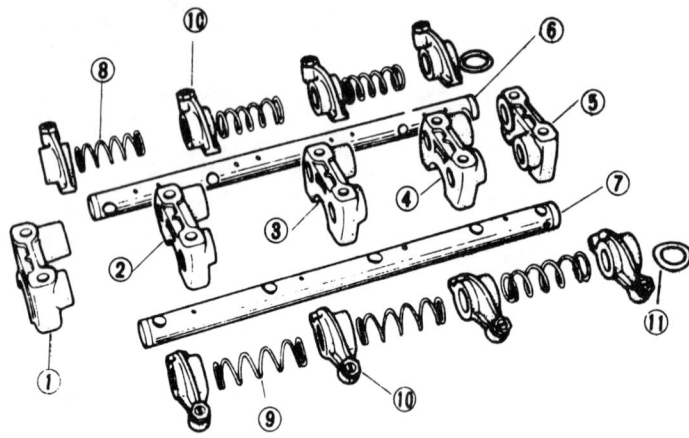

Fig. 1.35 Camshaft assembly (exploded view)

1 Camshaft bearing cap, front
2 Camshaft bearing cap, centre No 2
3 Camshaft bearing cap, centre No 3
4 Camshaft bearing cap, centre No 4
5 Camshaft bearing cap, rear
6 Rocker shaft, right (exhaust)
7 Rocker shaft, left (intake)
8 Spring, right (exhaust)
9 Spring, left (intake)
10 Rocker arm (both intake and exhaust)
11 Waved washer

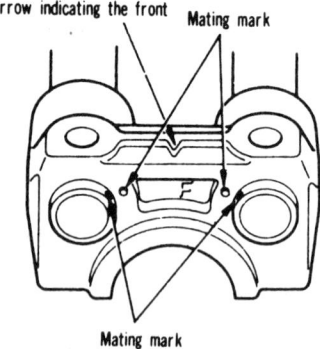

Fig. 1.36 Camshaft bearing cap identification

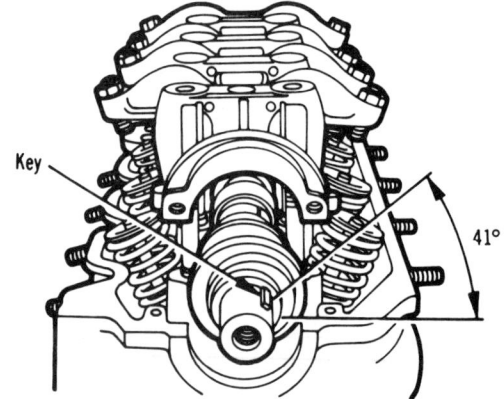

Fig. 1.37 Camshaft position (4G3)

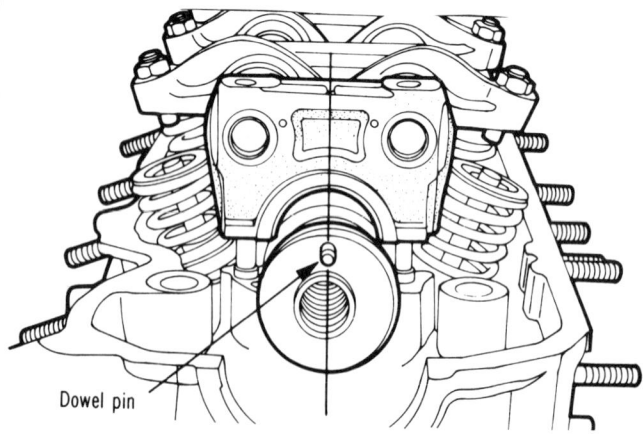

Fig. 1.38 Camshaft position (4G5)

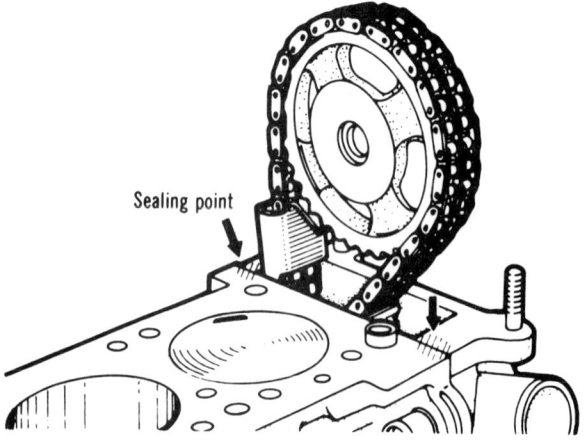

Fig. 1.39 Cylinder block sealing points

as appropriate. Because the cylinder head fits on the cylinder block dowels, it must be positioned carefully before lowering, so that it mates with the dowels.

5 Fit the cylinder head fixing bolts finger tight, then tighten them progressively in the order shown in Fig. 1.40 to a final torque wrench setting for the particular engine as given in the Specifications. After complete reassembly, and after the engine has been run for a short time, the cylinder head bolts should be retightened to the higher torque value specified.

6 Fit the camshaft sprocket over the dowel on the end of the camshaft, insert the fixing bolt and washers and tighten to the specified torque wrench setting.

Engines with timing belt

7 Ensure that all the gasket surfaces of the cylinder head and cylinder block are clean.

8 Do not apply sealant to the cylinder head gasket and do not attempt to re-use an old cylinder head gasket.

9 Fit the cylinder head gasket over the dowel on the cylinder block and then carefully lower the cylinder head on to the block, after ensuring that No. 1 piston is still at top dead centre.

10 Fit the cylinder head bolts and tighten them progressively in the order shown in Fig. 1.40, until they are all at the specified torque. This operation requires the use of a $\frac{5}{8}$ in hexagon socket.

11 Fit the timing belt upper under cover.

12 Pull the camshaft sprocket upwards and fit it to the camshaft. If the dowel pin hole in the camshaft sprocket cannot be aligned with the dowel pin at the end of the spacer, the camshaft should be turned by lightly striking the two projections provided in the rear of the exhaust cam for No. 2 cylinder. It is important that the crankshaft is not moved during any attempt to fit the camshaft.

13 Fit and tighten the sprocket attachment bolt.

29 Engine assembly – completion

Engines with timing chain

1 After applying sealant to the mating surfaces, fit the breather and

semi-circular packing at the front of the cylinder head (photo).

2 Fit the rocker cover and gasket, then tighten the fixing bolts to the torque setting given in the Specifications. Do not overtighten the fixing bolts because this can result in damage to the gasket and the leaking of oil.

3 Fit the inlet manifold (photo) and the lifting lug on its front stud. If a bonding wire was attached to the rear stud, fit this also.

4 Fit the fuel pump (photo), the water pump and the alternator (photo) if not already fitted.

5 Fit the distributor (photo) after aligning its mating marks and ensuring that the rotor is in the position for No. 1 cylinder to fire. Tighten the distributor fixing nut and reconnect the vacuum pipe.

6 Fit the exhaust manifold and the heatshield, remembering to fit the lifting lug to the rear upper stud.

7 Ensure that the cylinder block and sump drain plugs are fitted and tightened.

Engines with timing belt and balancer shafts

8 Fit the water pump assembly and tighten its four fixing bolts. Note that there are three different lengths of bolt and that the top bolt, which is the longest one, also secures the alternator brace (Fig. 1.42). The bolt immediately below the outlet pipe of the pump is of intermediate length and the two on the opposite side to the outlet are short.

9 Fit the upper under cover unless previously fitted and tighten its two bolts. Fit the lower under cover and tighten its two bolts. Because the lower of the two bolts also retains the oil pump, it should be tightened to the same torque as the oil pump cover mounting bolts.

10 Fit the spacer to the end of the right counterbalance shaft. Apply a thin coat of engine oil to the outer surface before fitting it. Fit the chamfered end first. Check to ensure that the oil seal lip has not been rolled back by the spacer.

11 Fit the counterbalance shaft sprocket with its bolt finger tight. Fit crankshaft sprocket B and align the timing marks on both sprockets with their timing marks on the front case (Fig. 1.44).

12 Fit timing belt B ensuring that there is no slack on its tension side. Then fit the tensioner, ensuring that the centre of the pulley is on the left of the mounting bolt and the pulley flange is nearest the engine.

13 Hold the tension pulley and move it in the direction of the arrow

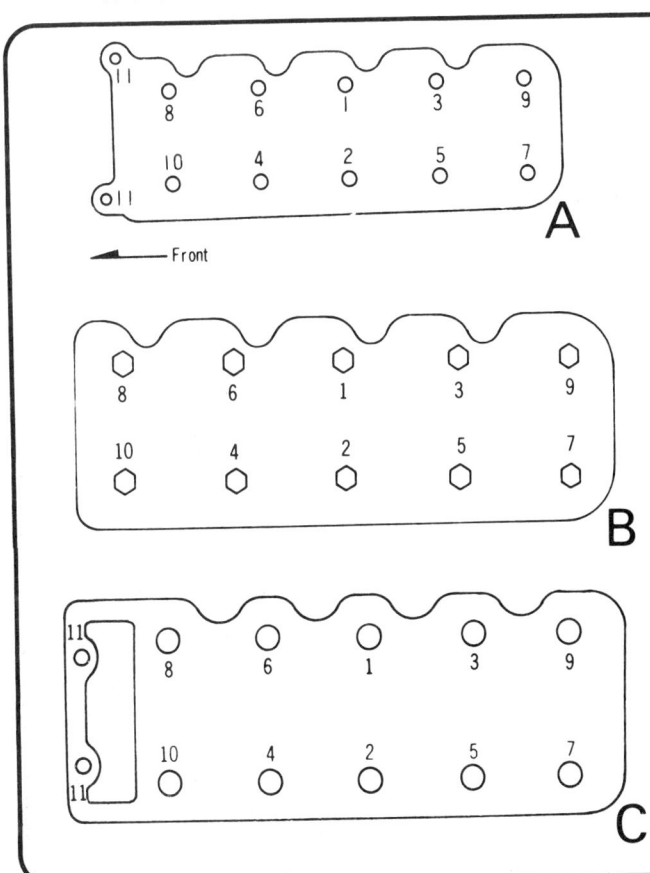

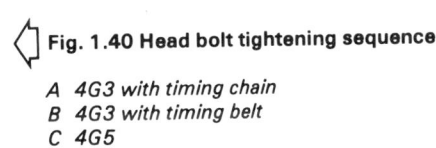

Fig. 1.40 Head bolt tightening sequence

A 4G3 with timing chain
B 4G3 with timing belt
C 4G5

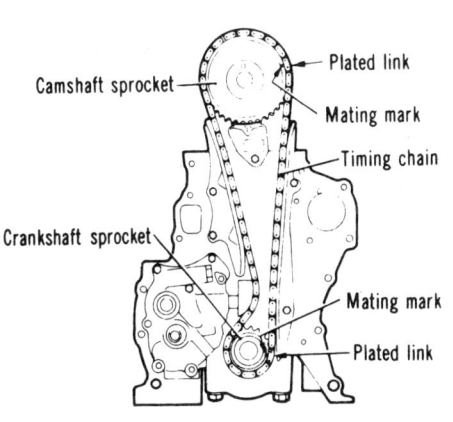

Fig. 1.41 Fitting the timing chain

29.1 Cylinder head breather

29.3a Fitting the inlet manifold

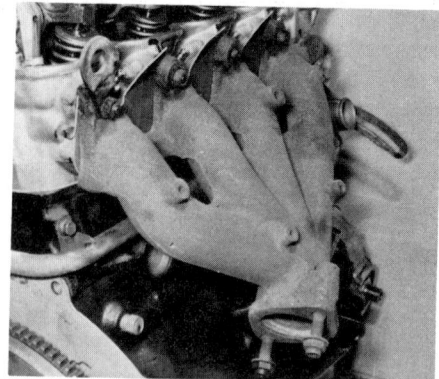
29.3b Exhaust manifold and lifting lug

29.4a Fitting the fuel pump

29.4b Alternator in position

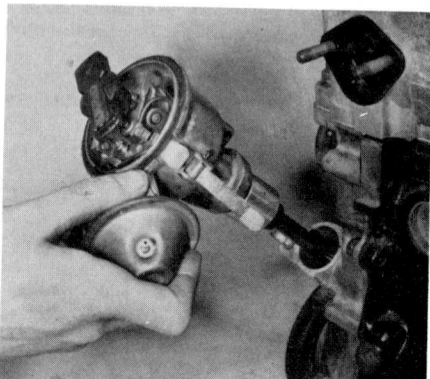
29.5 Fitting the distributor

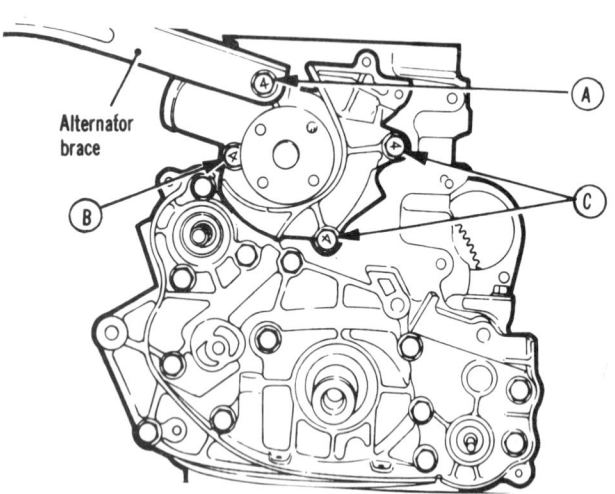

Fig. 1.42 Fitting the water pump (4G3)

A 70 mm long bolt
B 55 mm long bolt
C 28 mm long bolts

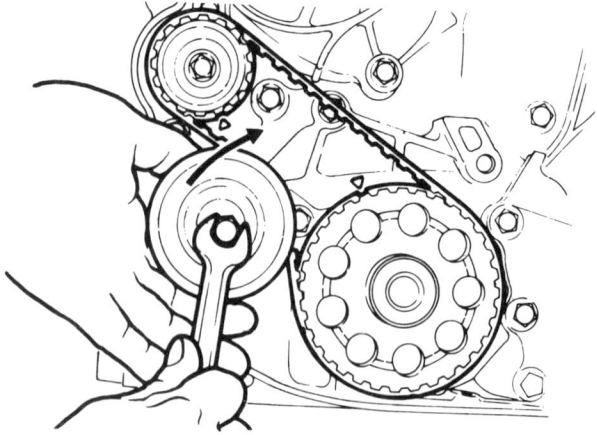

Fig. 1.43 Adjusting timing belt B tension

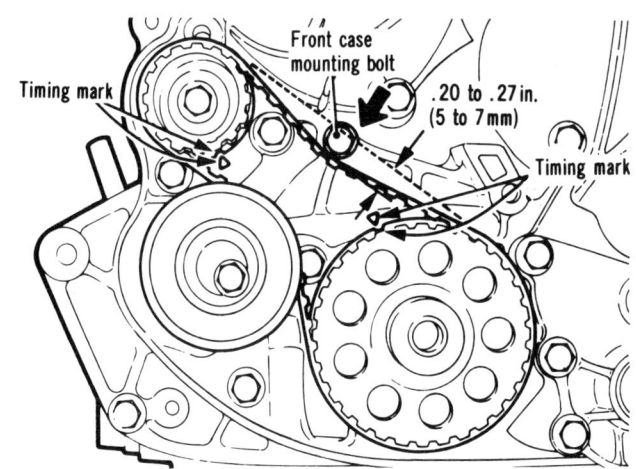

Fig. 1.44 Checking timing belt B tension

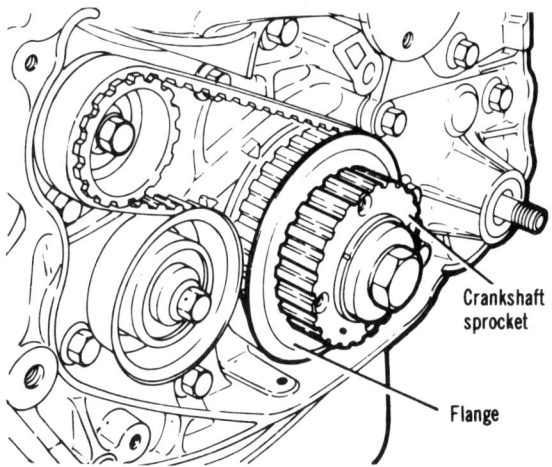

Fig. 1.45 Correct fitting of crankshaft sprocket

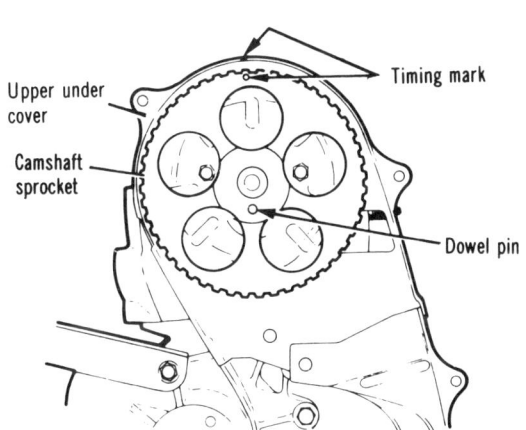

Fig. 1.46 Fitting of camshaft sprocket

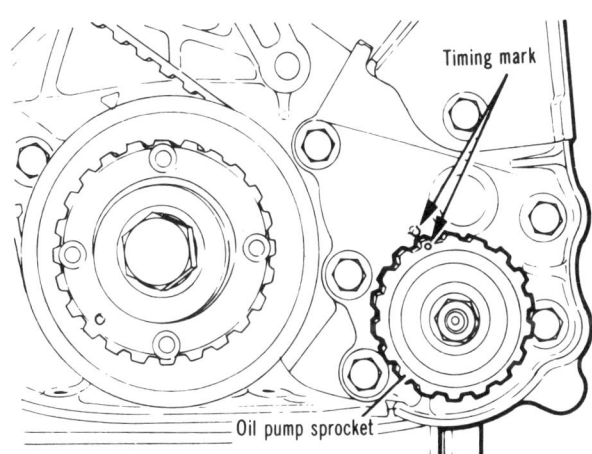

Fig. 1.47 Fitting the oil pump sprocket

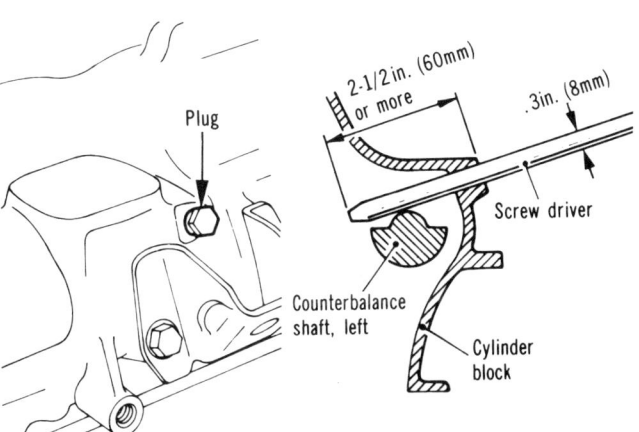

Fig. 1.48 Correct position of counterbalance shaft

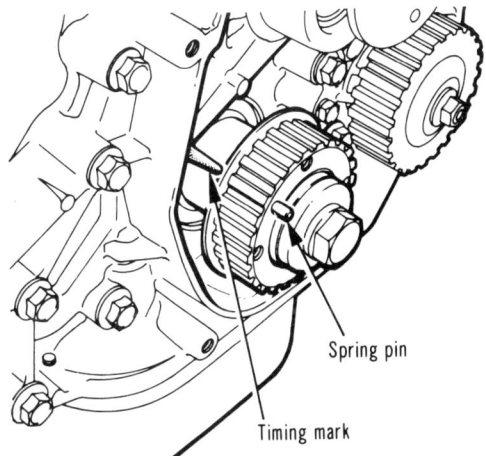

Fig. 1.49 Crankshaft pulley and timing mark (4G3 without balance shafts)

(Fig. 1.43) until the belt is tight. While tightening the tensioner, make sure that the tensioner pulley does not rotate any further, because this will result in the belt being overtightened. A belt which is too tight will cause excessive noise and one which is too loose will result in excessive belt wear, possibly resulting in the belt coming out of mesh.

14 Check that the two sprockets are still opposite their timing marks and that when the tight side of the belt is pushed with a forefinger it can just be deflected to the far side of the front case mounting bolt (Fig. 1.44). Readjust the belt tension if it is not correct.

15 Tighten the mounting bolt of the counterbalance sprocket.

16 Fit the crankshaft sprocket with its flange inwards and tighten its bolt to the specified torque.

17 Fit the camshaft spacer if not already fitted. Fit the camshaft sprocket and tighten its fixing bolt.

18 Fit the oil pump sprocket, tighten its nut to the specified torque and align the timing mark on the sprocket flange with the mark on the front cover of the pump. It is now necessary to check that the counterbalance shaft, which is meshed with the oil pump, is in the correct phase and this is done as follows.

19 Remove the plug on the left-hand side of the cylinder block and insert a screwdriver or a metal rod of 0.3 in (8 mm) diameter (Fig. 1.48). If the rod can be inserted more than about $2\frac{1}{2}$ in (60 mm), the alignment is correct. If it can only be inserted about 1 in (25 mm), rotate the oil pump pulley 360° to align with the timing mark again. Insert the rod fully and leave it in place until fitting of the timing belt has been completed.

20 Fit the tensioner spring, then the tensioner. Hold the tensioner in place by fitting its retaining nut finger tight.

21 Fit the cranked end of the tensioner spring so that it is restrained by the projection on the tensioner. Clip the straight end under the water pump body.

22 Rotate the tensioner until the hole in its lower mounting is in line with the tapped hole in the front of the engine. Insert the hinge bolt and screw it in finger tight.

23 Clamp the tensioner so that it is at the limit of its adjustment, with the tensioner pushed as far as possible towards the water pump.

24 Check that the crankshaft sprocket, oil pump sprocket and camshaft sprocket are all aligned with their timing marks. Then fit the timing belt first to the camshaft sprocket, then to the oil pump sprocket and finally to the crankshaft sprocket. When fitting the belt to each pulley, be very careful to ensure that the projections on the timing belt have engaged with the grooves in the pulley surface. If the two sets of teeth are not mated correctly, belt tension will be incorrect after the belt has slipped and engaged with the sprocket teeth.

25 Remove the screwdriver, or rod from the hole in the cylinder block. Refit the plug and tighten it.

26 Temporarily fit the crankshaft pulley so that the crankshaft sprocket cannot move out of line and misalign the timing belt.

27 Loosen the mounting bolt and nut of the tensioner. Push the tensioner outwards to make sure that the teeth of the belt and the toothed pulleys are fully engaged, then tighten the tensioner nut and bolt.

28 Turn the engine by using a spanner on the crankshaft pulley nut until it has completed one revolution in the normal direction of rotation. The tension side of the belt will then be taut, but do not touch the belt.

29 By releasing the tensioner nut and bolt, the spring will cause the tensioner pulley to apply the correct tension to the belt. Tighten the nut to the specified torque and then the bolt. If the bolt is tightened first there is a danger of the tensioner moving and making the belt too tight. At no time during belt tensioning must the belt be touched, or the crankshaft will be turned in the reverse direction.

30 On completion of tensioning, check that the timing marks are still aligned and then grip the tension side of the belt between the thumb and forefinger to check that the clearance between the outer surface of the belt and the seal line of the under cover is $\frac{1}{2}$ in (12 mm) (Fig. 1.52). Re-adjust the belt tension if necessary.

31 Remove the crankshaft pulley and fit the timing belt lower cover.

32 Fit the timing belt upper cover and then refit the crankshaft pulley, tightening its securing bolt to the specified torque.

33 Refit the distributor, fuel pump, manifolds and rocker cover as described in Sections 2 to 7.

Engines with timing belt, but without balancer shafts

34 The operations are the same as those for the engine with balancer shafts, omitting paragraphs 10 to 15 and paragraphs 19 and 25.

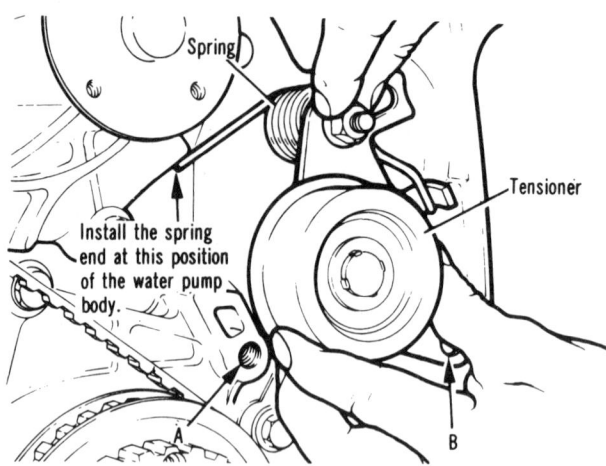

Fig. 1.50 Fitting the timing belt tensioner

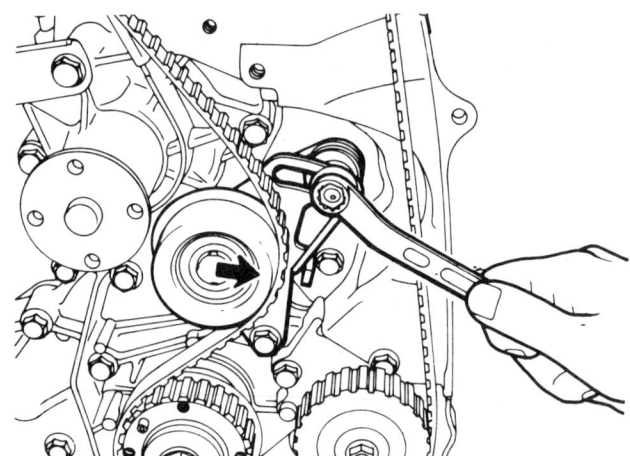

Fig. 1.51 Adjusting timing belt tension

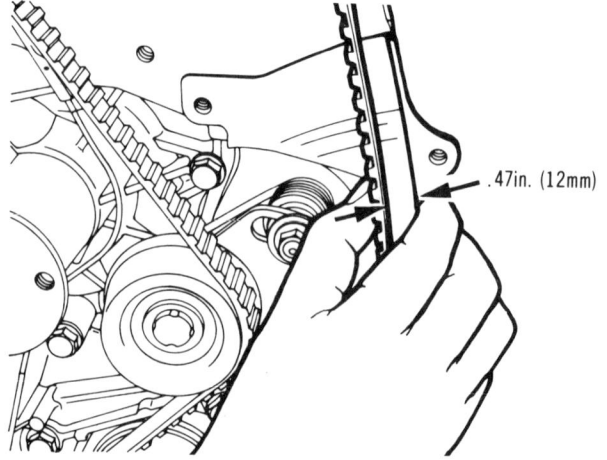

Fig. 1.52 Checking timing belt tension

30 Valves – adjustment

Inlet and exhaust

1   If the vehicle is fitted with jet valves, the jet valve clearances must be adjusted before the inlet valve clearances are adjusted.

2   If the cylinder head has been re-assembled, it will be necessary to adjust the clearances with the engine cold, proceeding as follows.

3   With each piston in turn at top dead centre, loosen the rocker arm nuts and temporarily adjust the valve clearances to 0.003 in (0.076 mm) on the intake side and 0.007 in (0.178 mm) on the exhaust side. Insert a feeler gauge to check the gap and while holding the adjusting screw so that it does not move, secure it with the locknut (photo).

4   After completion of engine assembly run the engine until the temperature of the coolant rises to between 170° and 190°F (80° to 90°C).

5   Again with each piston in turn at TDC on the compression stroke, loosen the locknut and turn the adjusting screw while measuring the clearance with a feeler gauge.

6   Adjust the clearances of the intake valves of the hot engine to 0.006 in (0.15 mm) and those of the exhaust valves to 0.010 in (0.25 mm).

7   Tighten the locknut securely, whilst holding the adjusting screw with a screwdriver to prevent it from turning.

8   After tightening the locking screw re-check the clearance and adjust again if necessary.

9   It is necessary to check the valve clearances at any time that the cylinder head bolts have been retightened.

Jet valves

10 Incorrect setting of the jet valves affects the level of exhaust emission and also has an adverse effect on engine performance.

11 To set the valves, first run the engine until the temperature of the coolant rises to between 170° and 190°F (80° to 90°C).

12 With each piston in turn at TDC on the compression stroke, carry out the following sequence of operations.

13 Release the locknut of the inlet valve and back off the adjusting screw at least two full turns.

14 Release the locknut on the adjusting screw for the jet valve.

15 Turn the adjusting screw for the jet valve anti-clockwise and insert a 0.006 in (0.15 mm) feeler gauge between the jet valve stem and the adjusting screw.

16 Tighten the adjusting screw until it just touches the feeler gauge. This operation requires great care, because the jet valve has a weak spring and it is not easy to determine if the feeler gauge is depressing the valve, particularly when the adjusting screw is stiff.

30.3 Adjusting the valve clearances

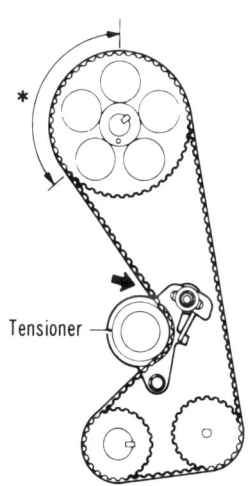

Fig. 1.53 Timing belt installed

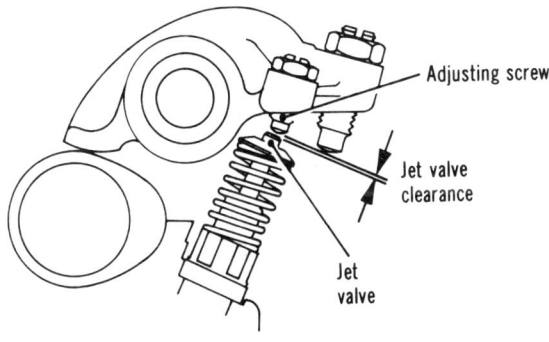

Fig. 1.54 Adjusting jet valve clearance

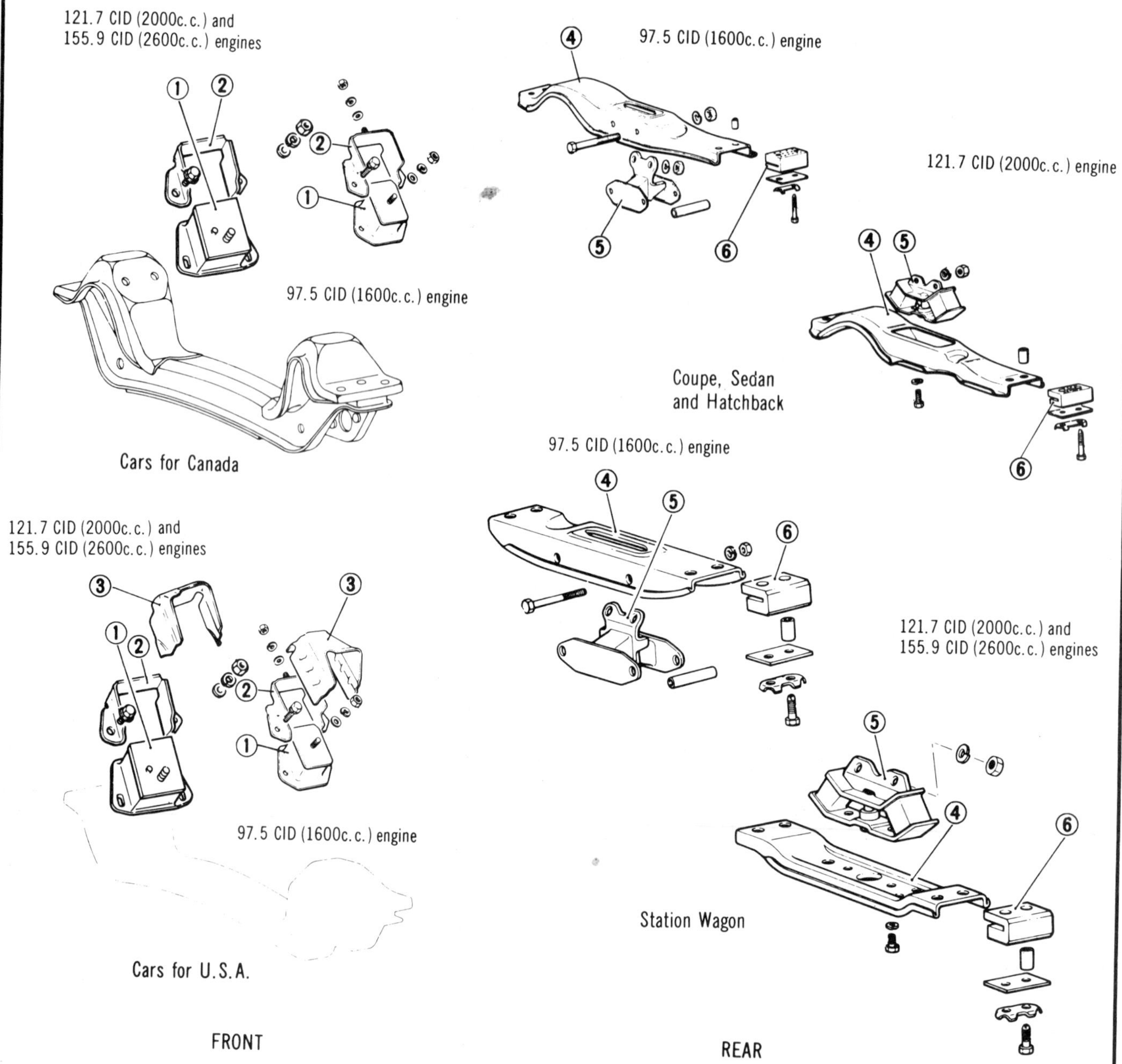

121.7 CID (2000c.c.) and
155.9 CID (2600c.c.) engines

97.5 CID (1600c.c.) engine

121.7 CID (2000c.c.) engine

97.5 CID (1600c.c.) engine

Cars for Canada

Coupe, Sedan
and Hatchback

97.5 CID (1600c.c.) engine

121.7 CID (2000c.c.) and
155.9 CID (2600c.c.) engines

97.5 CID (1600c.c.) engine

121.7 CID (2000c.c.) and
155.9 CID (2600c.c.) engines

Cars for U.S.A.

Station Wagon

FRONT

REAR

Fig. 1.55 Engine mountings (exploded view)

1   Front insulator
2   Rolling stopper
3   Heat deflector (RH side only)
4   Engine rear support bracket
5   Rear insulator
6   Pad

32.2 Engine mounting and deflector plate

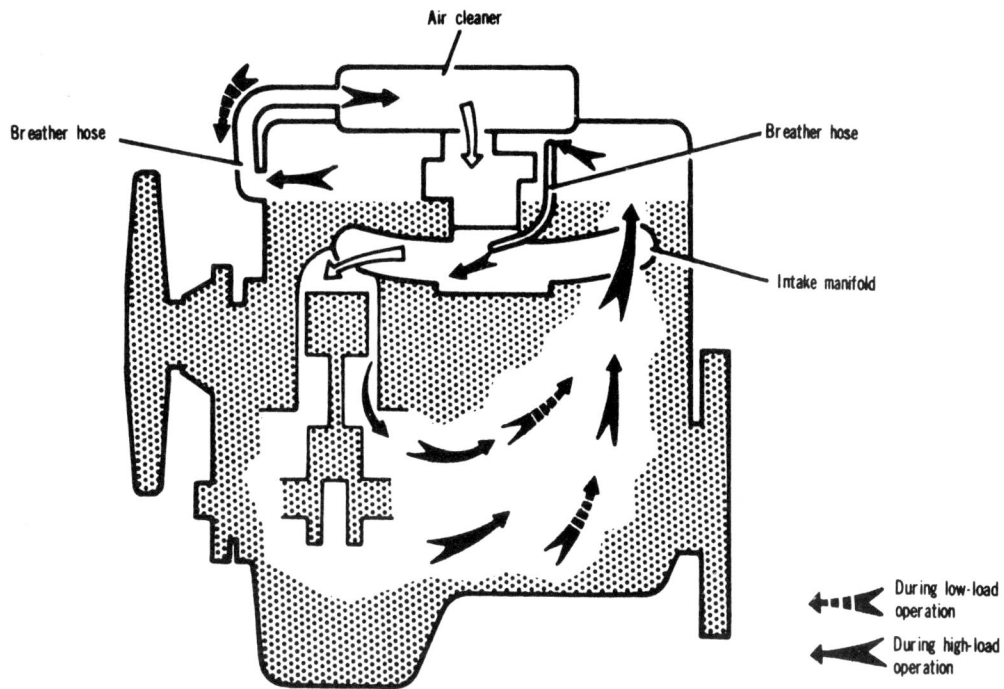

Fig. 1.56 Crankcase ventilation system

17 Whilst holding the adjusting screw with a screwdriver to prevent it from turning, tighten the locknut securely.
18 Withdraw the gauge and check that it can be re-inserted easily.
19 Adjust the inlet valve clearance as described earlier in this Section.
20 The exhaust emission should be checked after adjustment of the jet valves.

31 Engine – refitting

1 If the engine and gearbox were removed, refit them as previously described, taking care when fitting the gearbox that the input shaft is not strained.
2 Fit all the bell housing bolts and put the nuts on finger tight. Tighten them all progressively and in a diagonal sequence, except the bottom right-hand one which carries the clutch cable bracket which will be fitted later.
3 Sling the engine at an angle of about 30° (the gearbox lower than the engine) and lower it into the engine compartment until it can be fitted to its mountings. As with engine removal, it will be necessary to support the gearbox on a jack until the crossmember has been fitted.
4 The remaining operations are a reversal of those for removing the engine.

32 Engine mountings – removal and refitting

Front mountings
1 Remove the leads from the battery, then support the weight of the engine on a jack.
2 Remove the nut, spring washer and plain washer securing the rubber insulator to the engine mounting bracket. Remove the two bolts and washers securing the rubber insulator to the sub frame and remove the rubber insulator and rolling stopper, if fitted. Note that a deflector plate is fitted between the top of the rubber insulator and the engine mounting bracket on the right-hand side of the engine (photo). This protects the rubber from heat being radiated from the exhaust manifold.
3 Examine the rubbers for signs of hardening, damage or a failure of the bonding to the steel plates. Fit new ones if the old ones are suspect.
4 Refitting is the reversal of removal. The two insulators are identical.

Rear mounting
5 Support the weight of the gearbox on a jack.
6 Remove the two nuts and washers securing the rear insulator to the gearbox. Unscrew and remove the two through bolts and spacers from the crossmember and pull the rear insulator down through the slot in the crossmember.
7 To remove the crossmember pads, bend back the tabs on the locking plate, then unscrew and remove the bolts, cover plate and spacers. Pull the pad off the end of the crossmember.
8 When refitting the crossmember support bolts, first tighten them to the specified torque. If the tang of the locking tab is not parallel with one of the faces of the bolt, further tighten the bolt by the minimum amount necessary to align the bolt head with the tang. Then bend the tang to lock the bolt head.

33 Crankcase ventilation system – description

1 To reduce air pollution, the engine is fitted with a closed type of crankcase ventilation system, which prevents crankcase gas from being discharged to the atmosphere.
2 During operation of the engine under light load conditions, the crankcase gases are drawn into the intake manifold from the rocker cover bleed nipple. Fresh air is also led from the air cleaner to the front of the rocker box through the breather hose.
3 During high load operation, crankcase gases are drawn into the intake manifold from the rocker cover bleed nipple as before. These gases are also drawn from the rocker cover into the air cleaner from the breather in the front of the engine. These gases then pass into the combustion chamber.

34 Crankcase ventilation system – inspection

1 Make the following inspection and clean, or replace as appropriate any part which is dirty, or defective.
2 Check the breather hoses for cracks, damage or blocking.
3 Check that the breather hole in the rear attachment bolt of the rocker cover is clear.
4 Check that the nipple in the intake manifold is not blocked.

35 Fault diagnosis – engine

Symptom	Reason/s
Engine fails to turn over when starter switch is operated	Discharged or defective battery Dirty or loose battery leads Defective solenoid or starter switch Loose or broken starter motor leads Defective starter motor
Engine spins, but does not start	Ignition components wet or damp Spark plug insulators dirty Distributor cap 'tracking' Disconnected low tension lead Dirty contact breaker Faulty condenser Faulty coil No petrol, or petrol not reaching carburetter Faulty fuel pump Too much choke, leading to wet spark plugs Engine timing incorrect
Engine stops and will not re-start	Ignition failure Fuel pump failure No petrol in tank Water in fuel system
Engine lacks power	Burnt out exhaust valve Sticking valve Incorrect timing Blown cylinder head gasket Leaking carburetter gasket Incorrect mixture Blocked air intake, or dirty air filter Ignition automatic advance faulty
Excessive oil consumption	Defective valve stem oil seals Worn pistons and bores Blocked engine breather
Engine noisy	Incorrect valve clearances Worn timing chain Worn distributor drive Worn bearings Water pump bearing failure

Chapter 2 Cooling system

Contents

Specifications

System type	Pressurised water with thermostatic control. Pump assisted thermo-syphon with fan assisted cooling
Pump	Engine driven centrifugal

Thermostat

Type	Wax
Thermostat opening temperature:	
Europe	177 to 183°F (80·5 to 83·5°C)
USA	180°F (82°C)
Canada	190°F (88°C)
Fully open temperature:	
Europe	203°F (95°C)
USA	203°F (95°C)
Canada	212°F (100°C)
Maximum opening	More than 0·315 in (8 mm)

Pressure cap setting

High pressure side	11·4 to 14·2 lb/in^2 (0·8 to 1·0 kg/cm^2)
Vacuum side	−0·7 to −1·4 lb/in^2 (−0·05 to −0·10 kg/cm^2)
Antifreeze type	Ethylene glycol with inhibitors for mixed metal engines (Specifications SAE J1034, BS3151, or BS3152)

Cooling system capacity

1600 cc engine	6·4 qts, 7·7 US qts, 7·3 litres
2000 cc engine	7·9 qts, 9·5 US qts, 9·0 litres
2600 cc engine	8·1 qts, 9·7 US qts, 9·2 litres

Fan type

	4G3 Direct drive	4G5 & 4G32 GS Torque clutch
Blade diameter		
1200 cc, 1400 cc & 1600 cc Europe	12·6 in (320 mm)	12·6 in (320 mm)
1600 cc USA	13·39 in (340 mm)	13·39 in (340 mm)
1600 cc GS	13·39 in (340 mm)	13·39 in (340 mm)

	lbf ft	kgf m
1600 cc Canada	12·6 in (320 mm)	12·6 in (320 mm)
2000 cc & 2600 cc	15 in (380 mm)	15 in (380 mm)

Number of blades

1200 cc Europe	4	4
1200 cc (except Europe)	5	5
1400 cc and 1600 cc Europe	5	5
1600 cc GS	7	7
1600 cc USA and Canada	5	5
2000 cc and 2600 cc	6	6

Torque wrench settings

	lbf ft	kgf m
Fan blades	10	1·4
Water pump bolts	15	2·1
Thermostat housing bolts	20	2·8
Alternator mounting and adjusting bolts	20	2·8
Heater joints	15	2·1
Water temperature sensor	25	3·5

1 General description

The engine coolant is circulated by a pump assisted thermo-system and the whole system is pressurised so that the boiling point of the coolant is raised considerably. The pressure is controlled by the radiator filler cap which vents the system to the overflow pipe when the correct pressure is exceeded. It is therefore important to ensure that the cap is fitted properly and that the sealing washer and its spring are in good condition.

The cooling system consists of a radiator, water pump on which the radiator cooling fan is mounted, thermostat and interconnecting hoses. Some of the heat from the system is used for interior heating and for heating the inlet manifold and automatic choke.

The system functions by the pump drawing water from the bottom of the radiator and circulating it around the passages in the cylinder block to take away the heat of combustion and keep the cylinder bores and pistons cool. The water then passes to the cylinder head and circulates around the combustion areas and valve seats to the thermostat. When the engine has reached its correct operating temperature, the thermostat opens and coolant flows into the radiator header tank. Coolant from the header tank passes through the radiator core where it is cooled rapidly by the airflow resulting from the fan and

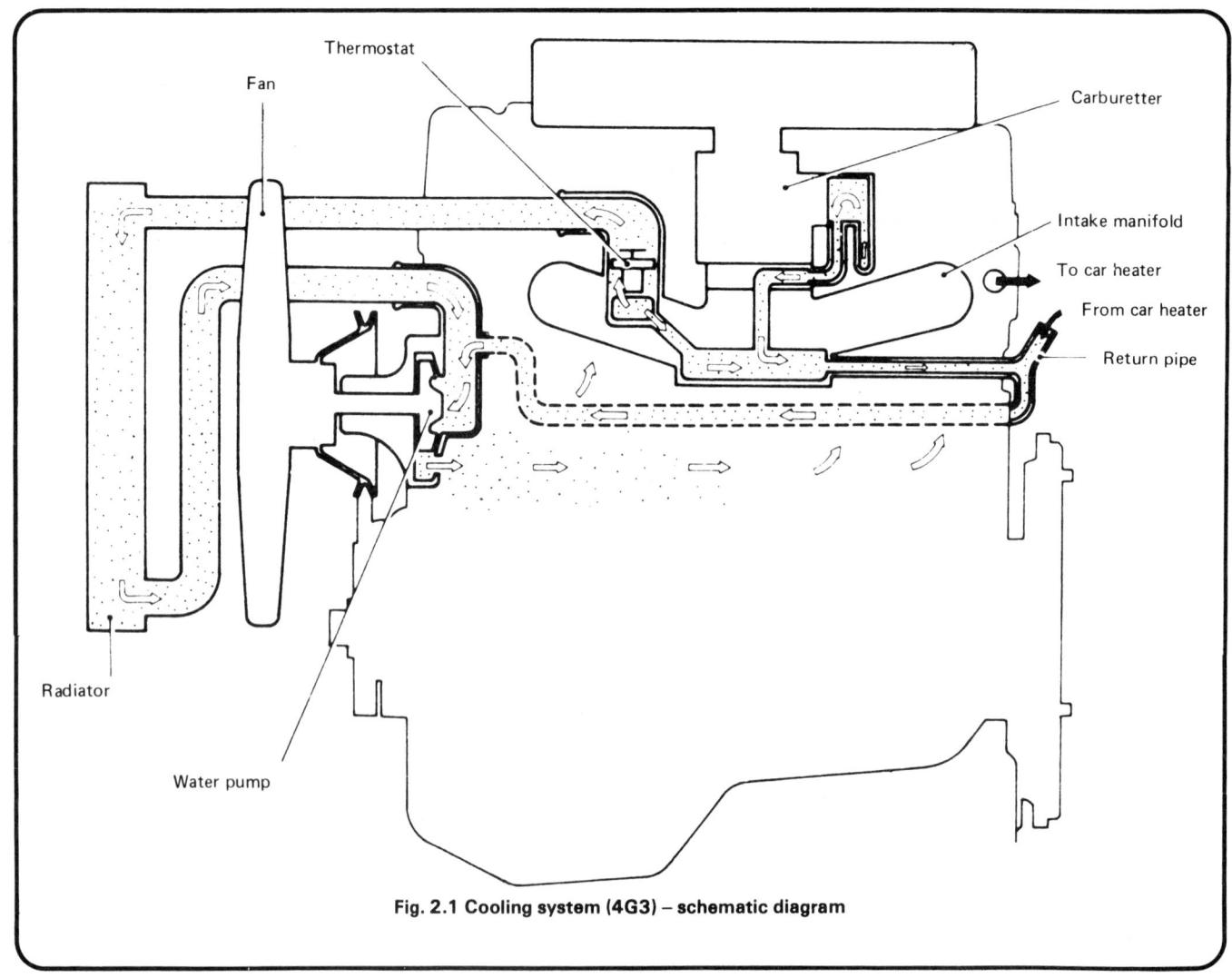

Fig. 2.1 Cooling system (4G3) – schematic diagram

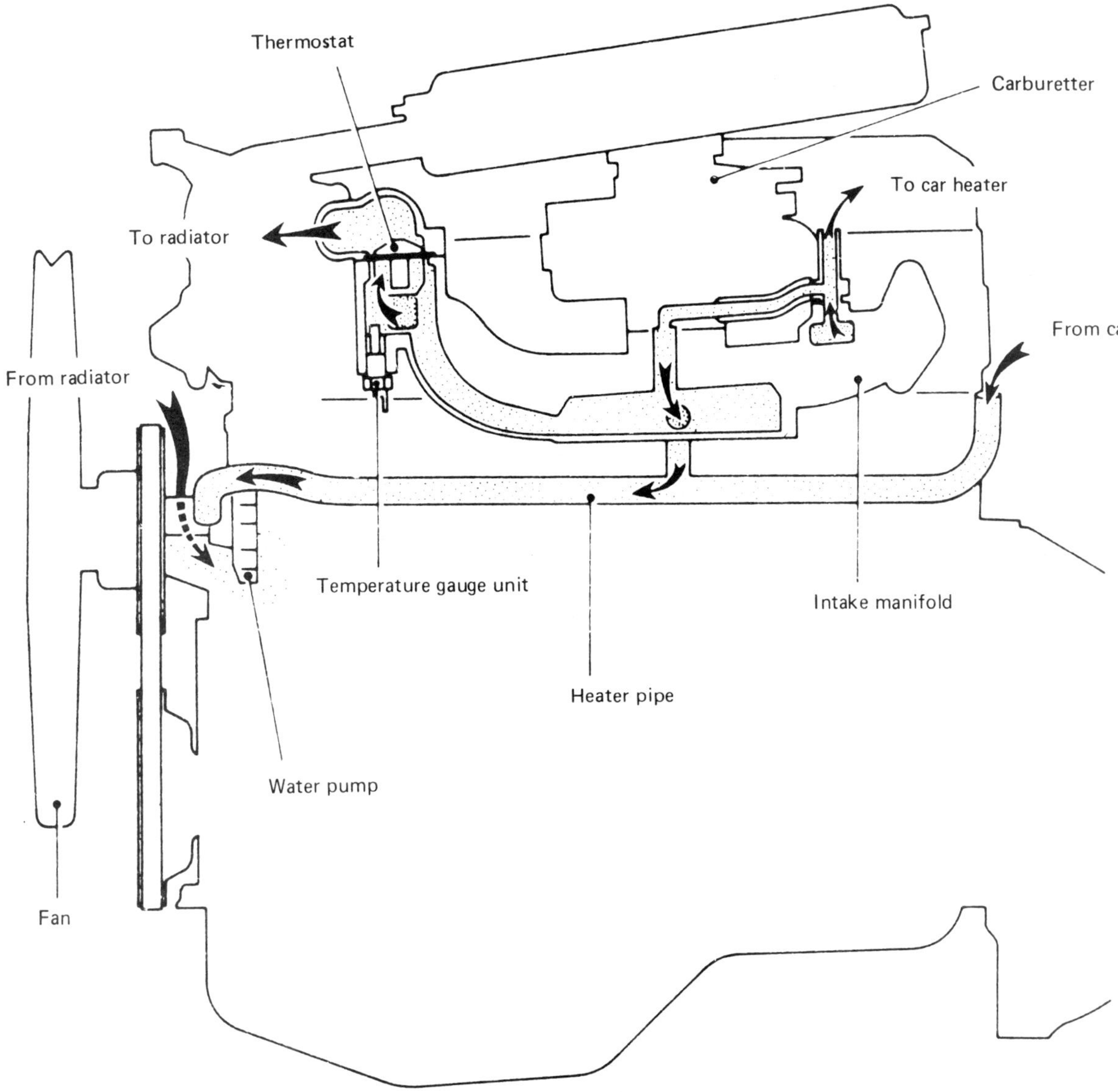

Thermostat

Carburetter

To car heater

To radiator

From car heater

From radiator

Temperature gauge unit

Intake manifold

Heater pipe

Water pump

Fan

Fig. 2.2 Cooling system (4G5) – schematic diagram

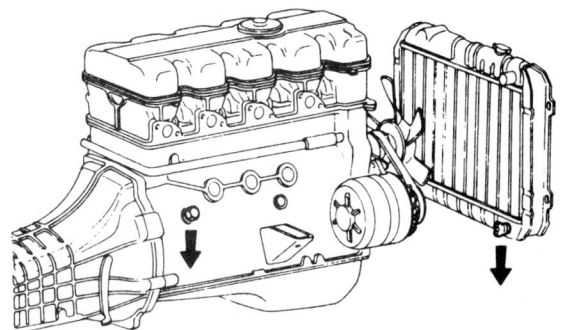

Fig. 2.3 Cooling system drain points (arrowed)

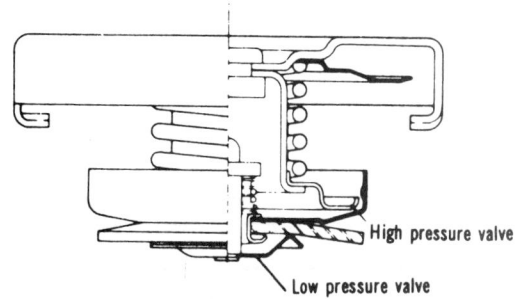

High pressure valve

Low pressure valve

Fig. 2.4 Radiator cap

the forward motion of the vehicle. On reaching the bottom of the radiator, the cooled liquid is recirculated. When the engine is cold, the thermostat is closed and maintains the recirculation of the same coolant in the engine. Only when the correct minimum operating temperature has been reached, as shown in the Specifications, does the thermostat begin to open and allow coolant to return to the radiator.

There are some variations in the system and the position of components on different models. Some have a fan fitted with a torque type clutch, which governs the fan speed when pulley speed increases beyond a certain value. This speed reduction is independent of ambient temperature and is to reduce loss of engine power in the fan drive at high speeds.

On models fitted with automatic transmission, the base of the radiator is fitted with a cooler, through which the automatic transmission oil is recirculated.

2   Cooling system – draining

1   Unscrew and remove the radiator cap (Fig. 2.4). If the engine is hot, this operation should be done slowly and carefully because the cooling system will be under pressure.
2   If the engine contains antifreeze which is less than two years old and is therefore reusable, place a clean container below the radiator drain plug. Otherwise allow the coolant to run to waste. Remove the radiator drain plug.
3   Place a container below the cylinder block drain plug and remove the plug.

3   Cooling system – flushing

1   With the passing of time, the cooling system will gradually lose its efficiency as the radiator becomes choked with rust, scale deposits from water and other sediment. To clear the system out, initially drain the system as described previously, then allow water from a hose to run through from the top hose connection and out of the bottom hose connection for several minutes. Fit the cylinder block drain plug while this is being done.
2   Refit the hoses and fill the system with fresh, 'soft' water (use rain water if possible) and a proprietary flushing compound, following the manufacturer's instructions carefully. (Refer to the next Section).
3   If the cooling system is very dirty, reverse flush it, by forcing water from a hose up through the bottom hose connection for about five to ten minutes, then complete the operation as described in paragraph 2, of this Section.

4   Cooling system – filling

1   Ensure that the radiator drain plug and cylinder block drain plugs are screwed in fully and that all the hoses have been fitted with their clips tightened.
2   Remove the radiator cap and pour in a mixture of water and antifreeze through the radiator filler until the system is full. If the radiator starts to overflow before the volume of coolant given in the Specifications has been poured in, there is an air lock in the system. To remove this, undo and remove a heater hose and pour coolant into the radiator until a stream of coolant comes out of the heater, then refit and clamp the heater hose.
3   After filling the system, fit the radiator cap and run the engine for about three minutes. Carefully remove the filler cap after stopping the engine and top-up the cooling system if necessary.

5   Antifreeze solution

1   As modern antifreeze compounds contain corrosion inhibitors, it is advantageous to have antifreeze in the engine throughout the year. Unless the antifreeze is known to be of the long life type which may be left in the system for two years, the system should be drained and refilled every year.
2   Any antifreeze which conforms with specification 'SAE J1034', 'BS 3151' or 'BS 3152' can be used. Never use an antifreeze with an

alcohol base.
3   Antifreeze can be left in the cooling system for up to two years, but after six months it is advisable to have the specific gravity of the coolant checked at your local garage, and thereafter, every three months.
4   Listed below are the amounts of antifreeze which should be added to ensure adequate protection down to the temperature given:

Percentage of antifreeze by volume	Protection provided down to:
25%	–13°C (+9°F)
33%	–19°C (–2°F)
50%	–36°C (–33°F)
55%	–45°C (–49°F)

6   Fan – removal and refitting

Fixed hub fan

1   Unscrew and remove the four bolts securing the fan blades, distance piece and pulley hub to the water pump flange. Then lift off the blades.
2   Remove the distance piece from the pulley hub.
3   Loosen the alternator fixing bolts, swing the alternator towards the engine to slacken the fan belt, then remove the pulley hub from the water pump flange.
4   Refit the pulley hub, distance piece and fan blades in that order. Insert the four bolts and tighten to the torque given in the Specifications.
5   Adjust the tension of the fan belt as described in the following Section.

Torque hub fan

6   Remove the six bolts securing the fan to the torque hub and lift the fan off.
7   Undo the four nuts securing the torque hub to the studs of the water pump flange and remove the torque hub (photo).
8   Loosen the alternator fixing bolts, swing the alternator towards the engine to slacken the fan belt, then remove the pulley hub from the flange.
9   Refit the pulley hub, torque hub and fan blades in that order. Tighten the fixing nuts and bolts.
10   Adjust the tension of the fan belt as described in the following Section.

7   Fan belt – removal and adjustment

1   Loosen the alternator fixing bolts and lift the alternator in towards the engine to release the tension on the fan belt.
2   Remove the fan belt from the alternator pulley and then lift it clear of the crankshaft and fan pulleys. If the belt shows any sign of cracking, damage or excessive wear, fit a new belt.
3   After fitting the belt over the fan and crankshaft pulleys and then over the alternator pulley, tension the belt by lowering the alternator. Correct belt tensioning is when a load of 22 lbs (9.98 kg) applied at right angles to the mid point of the span between the fan pulley and alternator pulley, will deflect the belt between 0.28 and 0.35 in (7.1 and 8.89 mm) (Figs. 2.6 and 2.7).
4   Having checked that the belt tension is correct, fully tighten the alternator fixing bolts.

8 Radiator – removal and refitting

1   If a special shield is fitted beneath the engine remove its fixing bolts and lift it off.
2   Remove the radiator filler cap and radiator drain plug. Drain the radiator, saving the coolant if antifreeze is being used and is under two years old.
3   Unclamp and remove the hoses from the top and bottom of the radiator. On models fitted with automatic transmission, remove the oil feed and return lines from the bottom of the radiator after placing a

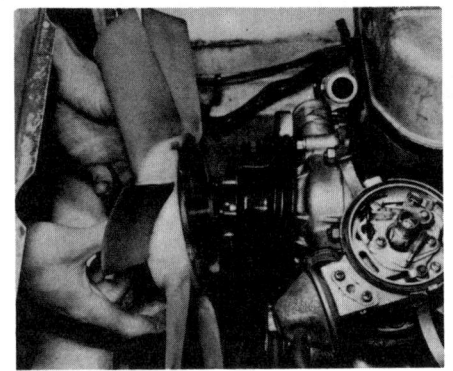

6.7 Removing the fan and torque hub (4G5)

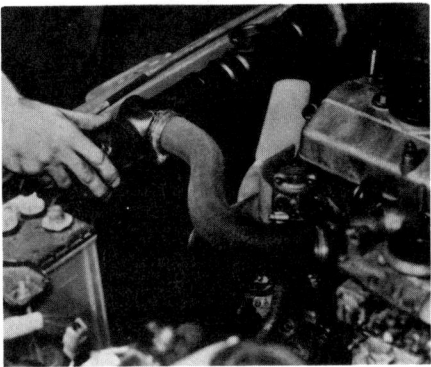

8.6 Refitting the radiator (4G3)

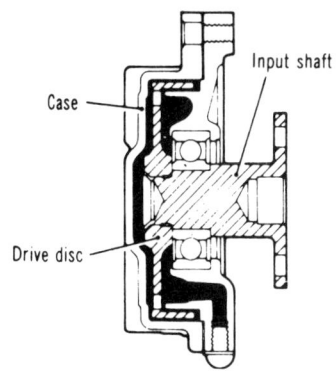

Fig. 2.5 Torque hub – sectional view

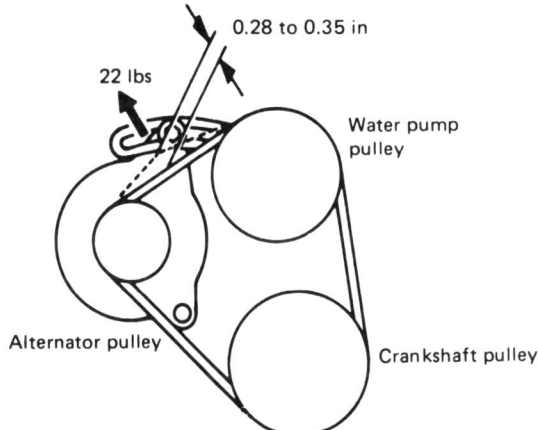

Fig. 2.6 Fan belt adjustment (4G3)

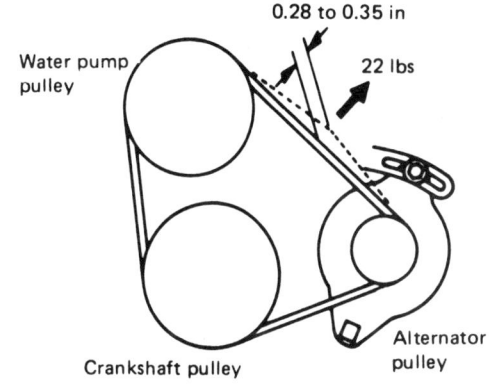

Fig. 2.7 Fan belt adjustment (4G5)

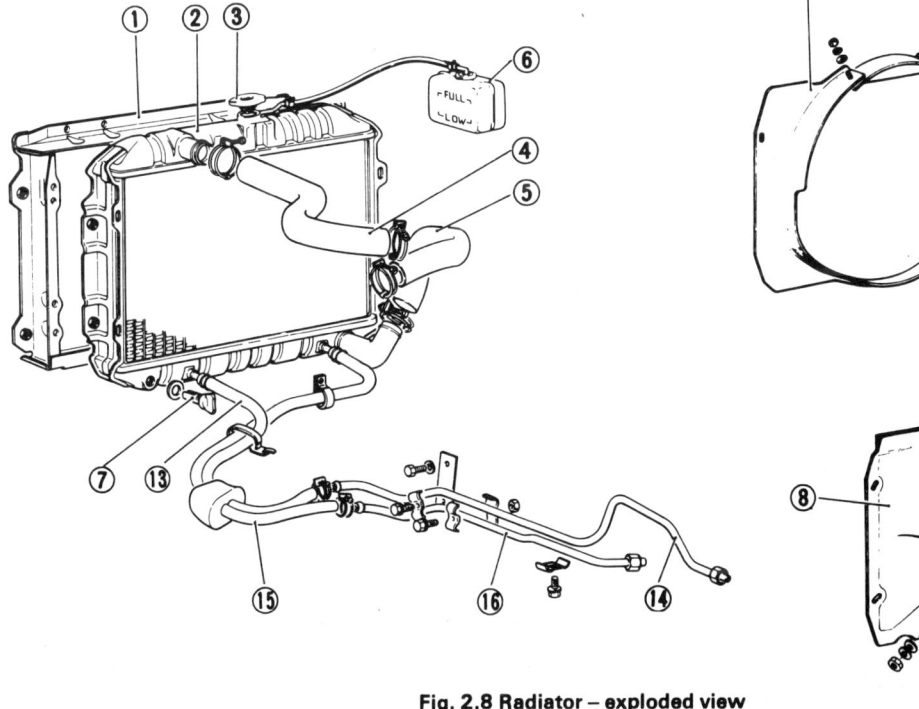

Fig. 2.8 Radiator – exploded view

1 Radiator cowl (4G3)	5 Radiator hose (bottom)	9 Left shroud (4G3)	13 Oil feed hose (AT)
2 Radiator	6 Reservoir tank	10 Lower shroud (4G3)	14 Oil feed tube (AT)
3 Radiator cap	7 Drain plug	11 Upper shroud (4G5)	15 Oil return hose (AT)
4 Radiator hose (top)	8 Upper shroud (4G3)	12 Right shroud (4G5)	16 Oil return tube (AT)

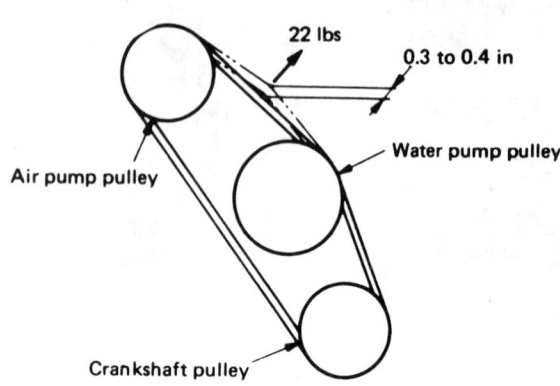

Fig. 2.9 Fan belt adjustment for vehicles with air pumps

22 lbs

0.3 to 0.4 in

Air pump pulley

Water pump pulley

Crankshaft pulley

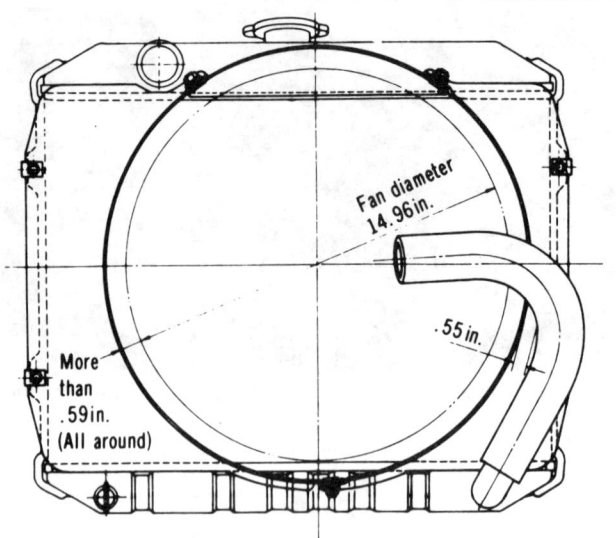

Fan diameter 14.96 in.

More than .59 in. (All around)

.55 in.

Fig. 2.10 Shroud to fan clearance (4G5)

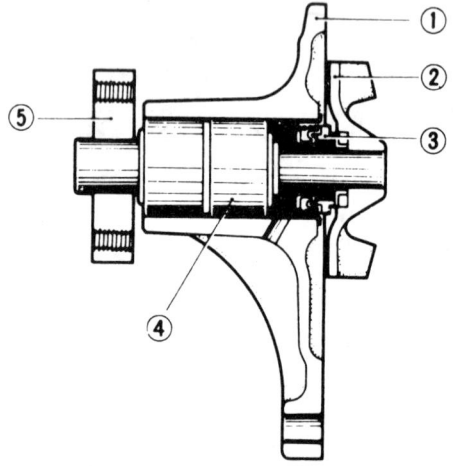

Fig. 2.11 Water pump construction (4G3)

1   Pump body   4   Shaft assembly
2   Impeller   5   Pump flange
3   Seal assembly

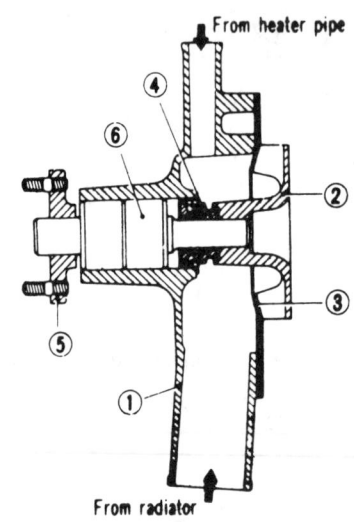

From heater pipe

From radiator

Fig. 2.12 Water pump construction (4G5)

1   Pump body   4   Seal assembly
2   Impeller   5   Pump flange
3   Water pump plate   6   Shaft assembly

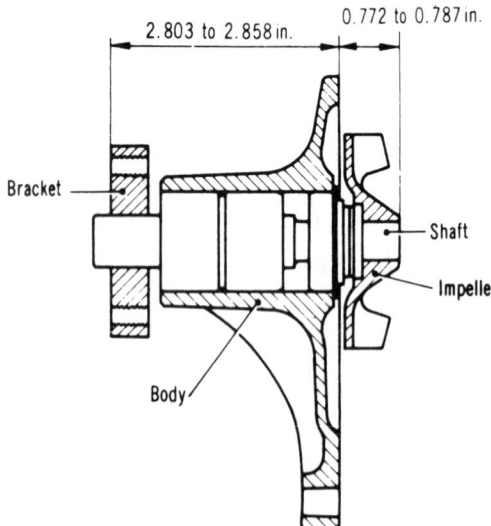

2.803 to 2.858 in.

0.772 to 0.787 in.

Bracket

Shaft

Impeller

Body

Fig. 2.13 Flange and impeller settings (4G3)

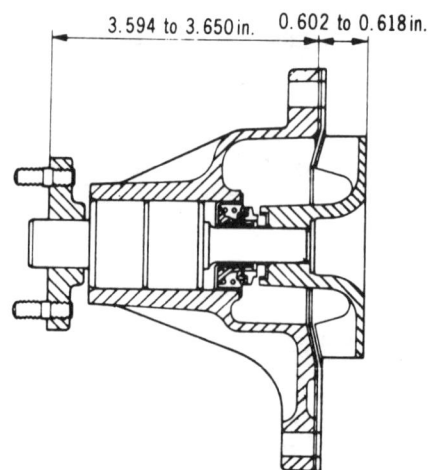

3.594 to 3.650 in.

0.602 to 0.618 in.

Fig. 2.14 Flange and impeller settings (4G5)

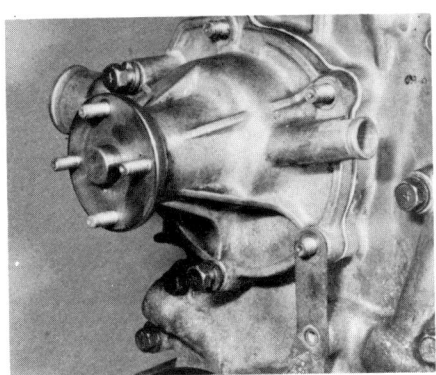

9.3 Thermostat and housing (4G3)   10.9a Fitting the water pump (4G3)   10.9b Fitting the water pump (4G5)

drip tray beneath the unions to catch any oil that runs out. Plug the oil pipe ends and cooler connections to prevent unnecessary loss of oil and the entry of dirt.

4   On vehicles fitted with a radiator shroud, remove the nuts and washers which attach the upper part of the shroud to the lower part. Remove the bolts securing the upper part of the shroud to the radiator and remove the upper shroud. Remove the lower shroud.

5   Remove the four bolts securing the radiator to the front panel and lift the radiator out, taking care not to damage the fan or the radiator matrix.

6   Having removed the radiator, examine it for leaks and damage. Flush the radiator thoroughly while it is off the vehicle and brush away any accumulated dirt and debris from the radiator core. If the radiator hoses are cracked, damaged or no longer supple, discard them and fit new ones.

7   Refit the radiator and shroud, if appropriate. Check that the drain plug and all hose connections are fitted and fully tightened. Then refill the cooling system (photo).

8   Examine the radiator cap for deterioration of the washer and spring. Fit a new cap if either the spring or the sealing washer are damaged.

9   Thermostat – removal, testing and refitting

A wax type thermostat is fitted and when this type fails, they do so in the closed position, which will lead to the system boiling and losing coolant.

The removal procedure is as follows:-

1   Drain the coolant until it is below the level of the thermostat.

2   Unclamp the hose at the thermostat housing and pull off the hose.

3   Remove the nuts and washers from the thermostat housing and pull off the housing. If necessary, tap the housing gently with a soft hammer to release it.

4   Note which way round and which way up the thermostat is fitted and carefully pull it out (photo).

5   Examine the thermostat for damage. If the valve is not closed tightly at room temperature, the thermostat is defective and a new one must be fitted.

6   To test the thermostat, place it in a pan of water, with a thermometer capable of indicating at least 212°F (100°C). Raise the temperature of the water and note the temperature at which the thermostat starts to open and is fully open. Fit a new thermostat if either valve is significantly outside the specified limits.

7   Refit the thermostat, taking care that it is properly sealed. Refit the

thermostat housing using a new gasket. Apply sealant to both sides of the gasket. All traces of the old gasket and sealant must be removed from the thermostat housing and its mating face before the new gasket is fitted.

10   Water pump – removal and refitting

To dismantle the pump requires a special puller and also a press. If these are not available it is preferable to fit a new or factory reconditioned pump.

1   Drain the cooling system, unclamp and remove the pump hose. On the 4G5 engine the heater hose must also be disconnected from the pump.

2   Remove the fixing nuts and washers and carefully prise off the pump. On the 4G5 engine, where the water pump is integral with the timing chain cover, there is a water pump plate between the pump body and the timing chain cover (Fig. 2.12). Care must be taken to remove the pump so that this plate is not damaged and its gasket remains intact. If this gasket is damaged, it can only be renewed if the pump impeller is removed.

3   To dismantle the pump, pull off the impeller, using a suitable puller.

4   Remove the seal assembly by prising it out with a screwdriver.

5   Heat the pump body in boiling water and push out the shaft assembly, using a press. If the pump is cold, a force of at least a ton is required to press out the shaft assembly.

6   Check the parts for damage, or excessive wear and renew where necessary. The bearings are grease packed and sealed for life, so do not require any other lubrication. If the bearings are worn, or the pump shaft does not rotate freely and smoothly, renew the shaft assembly.

7   To reassemble the pump, heat the pump body in boiling water and press the pump shaft assembly in until the end face of the bearing is flush with the pump body (Fig. 2.11 and 2.12).

8   Fit new seals to the body and the impeller end. Then press the impeller on until the end of the shaft is flush with the end of the impeller bore. Check the distance between the body end face and the shaft end face to ensure that it is as shown in Fig. 2.13 and 2.14 as appropriate. On the 4G5 engine, the water pump plate and gasket must be fitted before the impeller is pressed on.

9   Refit the pump, using new gaskets coated on both sides with a jointing compound. Fit the securing bolts or nuts and tighten them to the specified torque (photo).

10   Reconnect the hose, or hoses to the pump, refill the cooling system and adjust the fan belt tension.

Fault diagnosis overleaf

11 Fault diagnosis – cooling system

Symptom	Reason/s
Coolant loss	Faulty, or incorrect radiator pressure cap Split hose, or leaking hose joint Leaking water pump to engine joint Leaking water pump shaft seal Leaking core plug Blown cylinder head gasket
Overheating	Low coolant level Faulty radiator pressure cap Thermostat failed and stuck shut Drive belt broken, or loose and slipping Ignition timing incorrect Carburetter mixture incorrect Blocked radiator Corroded cooling system
Cool running	Defective or incorrect thermostat Outside temperature excessively low

Chapter 3 Carburation, fuel, exhaust and emission control systems

Contents

Specifications

Air filter .... Renewable element type

Carburetter
Type .... Downdraught, twin-barrel

4G3 series

	4G32, 4G33, 4G3 (except Europe and Cal)	4G32, 4G33, 4G36 for Europe	4G32 for California	4G32 GS
Throttle bore – primary	1·102 in (28 mm)	1·102 in (28 mm)	1·102 in (28 mm)	1·102 in (28 mm)
– secondary	1·256 in (32 mm)	1·256 in (32 mm)	1·256 in (32 mm)	1·256 in (32 mm)
Main jet – primary	92·5	92·5	101·3	95
– secondary	190	190	185	165
Pilot jet – primary	55	55	60	55
– secondary	70	70	70	60
Enrichment jet	60	60	40 (2 off)	40
Fast idle opening	0·0413 in (1·05 mm)	0·056 in 1·42 mm)	0·047 in (1·2 mm)	0·028 in (0·7 mm)

	4G32 except Cal, 4G2, 4G435	4G32 GS	4G32 for California
Idling speed	700 ± 50 rpm	800 ± 50 rpm	850 ± 50 rpm

4G5 series
Throttle bore – primary	1·181 in (30 mm)
– secondary	1·260 in (32 mm)

4G52 (2000 cc)

	California	49 states	Canada
Main jet – primary	103·8	105	106·3

– secondary	190	190	190
Pilot jet – primary	57·5	57·5	55
– secondary	60	60	60
Enrichment jet	50	50	40 (2 off)
Auto choke set temperature	71·2°F (21·5°C)	73·8°F (23·5°C)	73·8°F (23·5°C)

4G54 (2600 cc)

Main jet – primary	106·3	107·5	107·5
– secondary	185	185	185
Pilot jet – primary	60	60	55
– secondary	60	60	60
Enrichment jet	45	45	40
Auto choke set temperature	71·2°F (21·5°C)	73·8°F (23·5°C)	73·8°F (23·5°C)

Fuel pump

Type .... Mechanical, diaphragm

	4G3	4G5
Discharge rate at engine speed 5000 rpm	0·36 gal/min 0·43 US gal/min 1·6 litres/min	0·44 gal/min 0·53 US gal/min 2 litres/min
Discharge pressure	3·7 to 5·1 lb/in²	4·6 to 6 lb/in²

Fuel tank capacity:

4G3 – except 1400 cc estate car .... 11 gall, 13 US gall, 50 litres

     – 1400 cc estate car .... 8·8 gall, 10·4 US gall, 40 litres

4G5 – 2000 cc and 2600 cc .... 13·2 gall, 15·8 US gall, 60 litres

Torque wrench settings

	lbf ft	kgf m
Fuel pump cap screw	0·5 to 1·6	0·07 to 0·22
Fuel pump body screw	1·4 to 3·6	0·2 to 0·5
Fuel tank band nuts	12·3 to 16·6	1·7 to 2·3
Accelerator rod to yoke locking nut	11 to 14	1·5 to 1·9
Exhaust manifold	10 to 14	1·4 to 1·9
Exhaust pipe to bellhousing	26 to 32	3·6 to 4·5
Front pipe to main silencer	15 to 21	2·1 to 2·9
Front pipe to centre pipe (estate car)	15 to 21	2·1 to 2·9
Centre pipe to main exhaust (estate car)	15 to 21	2·1 to 2·9
Main exhaust to tail pipe	7 to 11	1·0 to 1·5
Vapour check valve	25 to 28	3·5 to 3·9

1 General description

The fuel system consists of a rear mounted fuel tank, a mechanical fuel pump which is driven from the engine camshaft, a carburetter and all the necessary fuel lines, filters and a fuel gauge. Refinements to the system provide facilities for preventing vapour locking. On the 4G3 series engine this is achieved by fitting a thermostatically controlled non-return valve in the fuel return hose from the carburetter to the fuel tank. On the 4G5 series engines a vapour separator is fitted to achieve the same result.

Cars operating in North America are equipped with a variety of emission control systems. The type of system depends upon operating territory and the production date of the vehicle. The various systems are described later in the Chapter.

2 Air cleaner – dismantling, cleaning and reassembly

The air cleaner uses a filter cloth element having a high filtration efficiency and low suction resistance. To the air cleaner body is connected a breather hose, through which blow-back from the engine is sent with the intake air into the combustion chambers. The air cleaner has an adjustable spout, so that during cold weather it can be turned to take in warm air from the exhaust manifold.

1   To remove the filter, undo the clips securing the lid of the cleaner and take the lid off (photo).

2   Remove the element, clean the inside of the casing and at the same time check the casing and sealing washers for signs of damage.

3   If the existing element is reusable, clean it by tapping the element lightly on a flat surface and then blowing compressed air from the inside.

4   Fit the element into the cleaner body, making sure that it is properly seated and sealed. If you are reusing an element, ensure that the oil stained part is placed by the engine breather inlet, so that the oil stained area will not spread.

5   Refit the cover, lining up the mating marks on it and refasten the clips.

6   Check that the position of the air intake pipe is drawing in hot air or cold air as appropriate to the time of year (photo).

3 Fuel strainer – cleaning and refitting

The cartridge type fuel strainer is held by a spring clip (photo) on the side of the engine compartment.

1   Check the fuel strainer for damage and an excessive accumulation of dirt and water. Renew it if it is defective.

2   When there is only a small quantity of water inside, remove the strainer from its clip and with the outlet direction downwards blow compressed air through the fuel inlet pipe (Fig. 3.2).

3   Refit the filter in its clip, or if it has been in service for 12 000 miles fit a new one, then refit the inlet and outlet hoses and tighten their clips.

4 Fuel pump – description

1   The fuel pump is mounted on the left-hand side of the engine and is driven by a separate lobe, mounted on the camshaft (photo).

2   A rocker arm, which is spring loaded, moves a diaphragm up and down as the cam rotates.

3   When the diaphragm rises, fuel is sucked into the pump and as the diaphragm is depressed, the fuel is ejected into the outlet pipe. Non-return valves within the pump prevent fuel being sucked from the carburetter or being pumped back into the inlet pipe.

5 Fuel pump – removal and refitting

1   Loosen the hose clamps and remove the fuel pump inlet and outlet

Fig. 3.1 Fuel system components

1 Fuel hose (separator to pump)
2 Fuel hose (separator to carburetter)
3 Fuel hose (pump to tank return)
4 Fuel hose (carburetter to tank return)
5 Fuel hose (filter to pump)
6 Fuel hose (carburetter to return valve)
7 Vapour separator
8 Fuel filter
9 Fuel return valve
10 Fuel return pipe
11 Main fuel pipe
12 Fuel tank

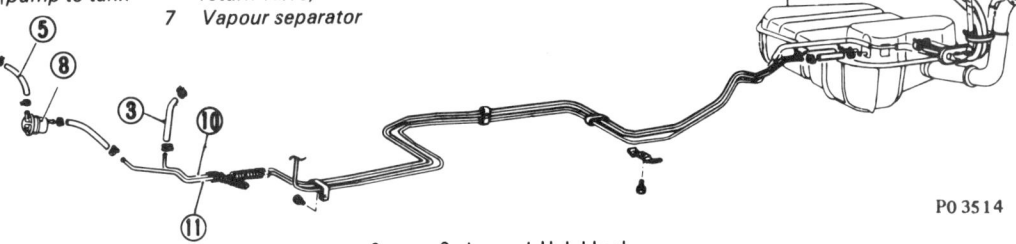

PO 3514

Coupe, Sedan and Hatchback

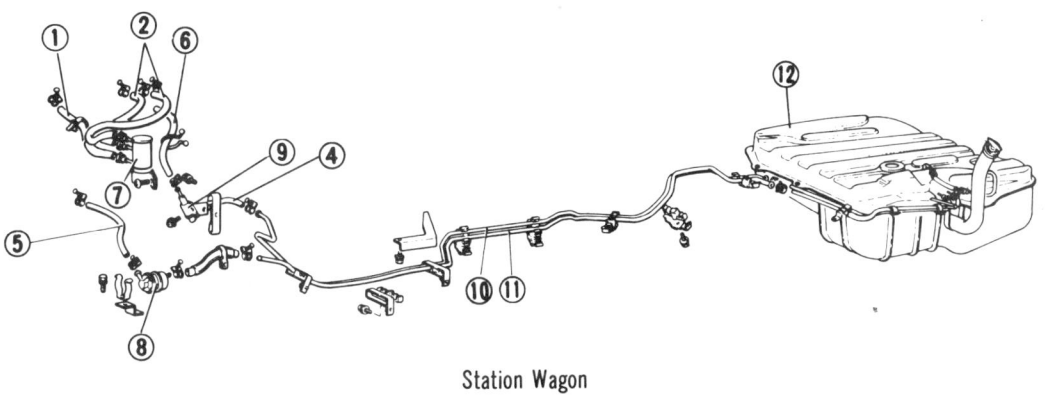

Station Wagon

2.1 Removing the air cleaner

2.6 Air intake summer and winter positions

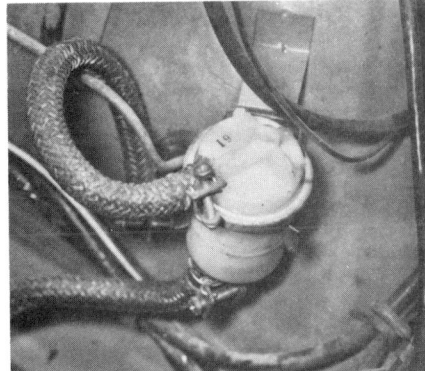

3.1 Fuel strainer

4.1a Fuel pump 4G3

4.1b Fuel pump 4G5

pipes.

2   Remove the two fixing bolts, then lift the pump upwards to disengage the rocker arm from the camshaft lobe and so allow the pump to be withdrawn.

3   Remove the insulator and the two gaskets from the cylinder head.

4   When refitting the pump, fit a new gasket to both sides of the insulator and apply jointing compound to both sides of each gasket.

5   On the 4G3 series, fit the rocker arm lever beneath the camshaft (Fig. 3.3). On the 4G5 engine fit the lever above the camshaft (Fig. 3.4), then position the pump so that the bolts can be inserted.

6   Fit the bolts and tighten them to the torque given in the Specifications.

7   Fit the fuel hoses to the appropriate nipple, pushing the hoses on as far as possible, then clamp them firmly with hose clips.

8   Start the engine and check for fuel leaks.

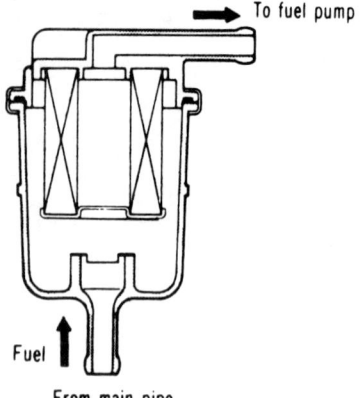

Fig. 3.2 Fuel strainer

6   Fuel pump – dismantling and reassembly

The fuel pump on the 4G3 series of engine cannot be dismantled. To dismantle the pump on the 4G5, proceed as follows:-

1   Remove the cap and the diaphragm from the upper body and then separate the upper body from the lower body. The two valves are sealed into the body and no attempt should be made to remove them.

2   Pull out the rocker arm pivot pin and dismantle the pump into the component parts, the diaphragm assembly, seal, rocker arm, diaphragm spring and rocker arm spring.

3   Examine the diaphragm carefully and look for cracks, tears or porosity. Check the valves for full movement and correct seating. Examine the end of the rocker arm which bears against the camshaft lobe and check that it is not damaged, or worn excessively. Check the pivot pin hole and pivot pin for wear. Look for signs of cracking in the pump body.

4   Reassemble the pump in the reverse order, pushing the centre of the diaphragm down when inserting it and making sure that it is not creased or folded.

5   After refitting the cap, screw on the cap nut to the specified torque. It is important that the cap is not overtightened.

6   After reassembly, move the rocker arm up and down to ensure that it moves freely and smoothly with a full range of movement.

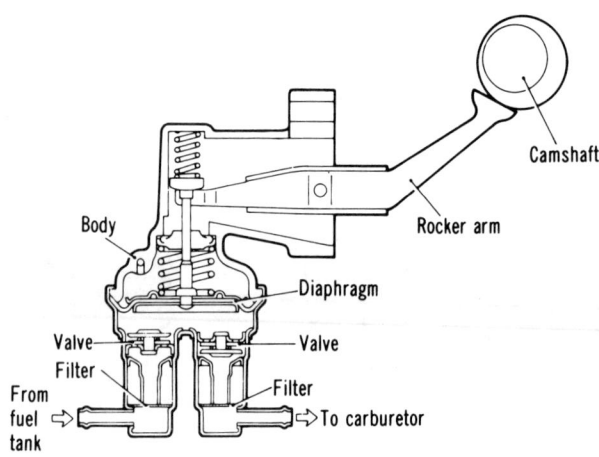

Fig. 3.3 Fuel pump (4G3) – sectional view

7   Fuel pump – testing

1   Remove the outlet hose from the pump and connect the pump outlet to a pressure gauge having a range of 0 to 10 lb/in². Spin the engine with the starter motor and check pump pressure which should be between 3.7 and 5.1 lb/in² for 4G3 engines and 4.6 and 6 lb/in² for 4G5 engines.

2   After checking the pressure, carefully inspect the pump to make sure that there are no fuel leaks.

8   Vapour separator – fitting and inspection

The vapour separator (Fig. 3.5) is only fitted on 4G5 engined cars for the USA market. Fuel from the fuel pump passes into the vapour separator through a nipple roughly in the middle of it and flows out to the carburettor through a nipple at the bottom. Vapour separated from the fuel passes to the upper part of the separator and out through the top nipple. After being passed to the accelerator pump to cool it, the vapour is returned to the fuel tank.

1   Always fit the vapour separator with the red mark uppermost (Fig. 3.5).

2   To eliminate the possibility of error, the nipples are colour coded and the two different systems of marking used are down in Fig. 3.8. The correct connections are as follows:

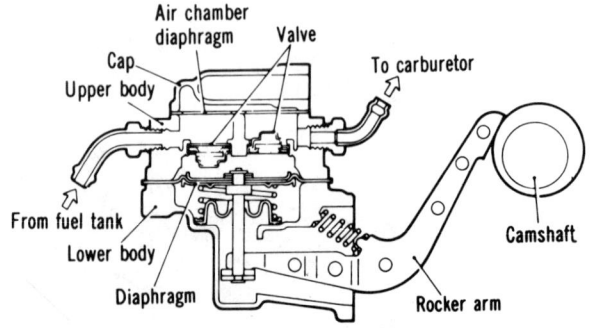

Fig. 3.4 Fuel pump (4G5) – sectional view

Top (Red) nipple on separator to	*nipple at the bottom of the accelerator pump on carburetter (with red mark)*
Middle (Green) nipple on separator to	*nipple at outlet of fuel pump (with green mark)*
Bottom (Yellow) nipple on separator to	*nipple at inlet of carburetter (with yellow or no colour mark)*

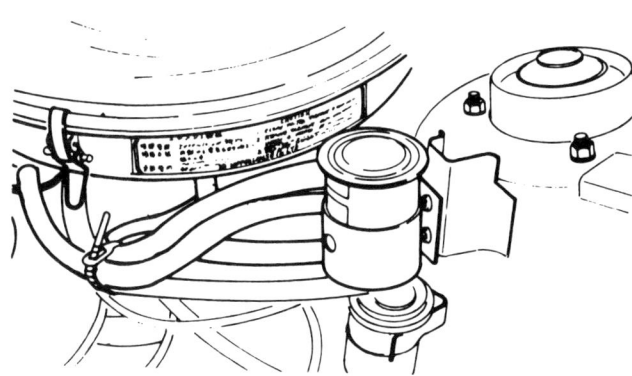

Fig. 3.5 Vapour separator position

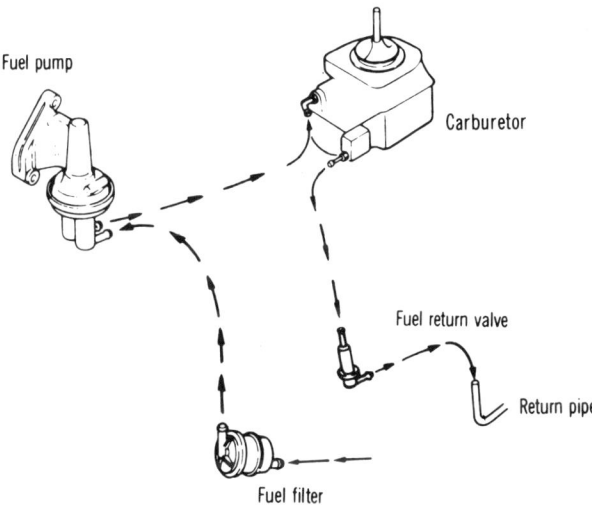

Fig. 3.6 Fuel control system (4G3)

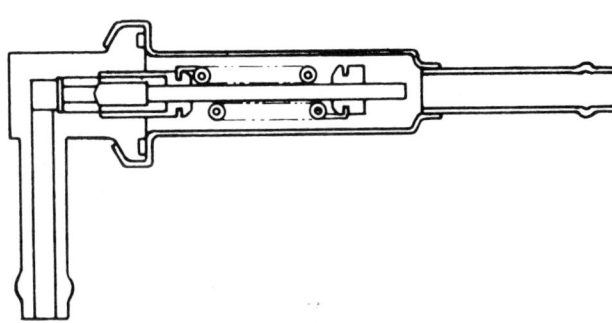

Fig. 3.7 Fuel return valve

3   Push the hoses as far as possible on to the nipples and then clamp firmly with a hose clip. Check each hose for signs of cracking and damage. Renew if necessary.
4   Start the engine and make a careful check that there is no leakage from any joint.

9   Fuel return valve – description and inspection

1   The fuel return valve is only fitted to cars with 4G3 series engines for the US market. It is fitted in the return hose between the carburetter and the return pipe of the fuel tank and it contains a spring loaded valve which is controlled by a bimetallic strip.
2   When the valve is closed, a normal amount of fuel can pass to the carburetter. When the temperature of the fuel rises to 108 to 127°F (42 to 53°C) the valve opens, allowing more fuel to flow from the pump, through the carburetter and back to the tank, to minimise the risk of vapour locking.
3   Inspect the valve for signs of obvious damage and blow through it to ascertain that it is not blocked. If the valve is blocked, it must be discarded and a new one fitted.
4   Check that the hose connectors to the valve are not leaking and that the hoses are in good condition.

10   Carburetter – general description

The carburetter is of the dual barrel downdraught type and has four basic fuel metering systems. The slow running system provides a mixture for idling and low speed operation; the main system gives optimum mixture for economical cruising conditions; the accelerator pump provides additional fuel during acceleration and the enrichment system provides a richer mixture when high power output is required.

In addition to these four basic systems, there is a fuel inlet system which provides a constant supply of fuel to the metering systems and a choke to enrich the mixture to make starting and cold running easier. The choke may be manual or automatic, depending upon the model of the vehicle. Engines with manual transmission are equipped with a dashpot to retard the return of the throttle to the idling position.

11   Carburetter – inlet system adjustment

There is a sight glass (Fig. 3.9) in the float chamber and the level of fuel should be within the limits of the level mark. If it is necessary to adjust the level:
1   Remove the air cleaner.
2   Disconnect the fuel inlet pipe and remove the screws securing the float chamber cover. Remove the float chamber cover and gasket.
3   Pull out the float pivot pin and remove the float and jet needle.
4   Unscrew and remove the needle valve and adjust the number of packing washers to achieve the correct level. A sheet of needle valve packing washers are 0.039 in (0.99 mm) thick. Inserting or removing a sheet of packing washers will change the float level by 0.118 in (2.997 mm).
5   Even if the fuel mark is about 0.16 in (4 mm) above, or below the mark, it will not affect the performance of the carburetter, or engine. The fuel level need not be adjusted while it stays within this range.

12   Idle mixture adjustment

Cars for Europe
1   Check that the ignition timing is correct and adjust it if necessary.
2   On vehicles with automatic transmission set the control lever to the N (neutral) position and if an air conditioning system is fitted, turn it off.
3   Run the engine at idling speed until the coolant temperature reaches 170 to 190° (80 to 90°C).
4   Set the engine speed in accordance with the following table, by turning the idle speed adjusting screw (Fig. 3.10).

4G32 (except GS), 4G33 and 4G36	700 ± 50 rpm
4G32 GS	800 ± 50 rpm
4G52 and 4G54	850 ± 50 rpm

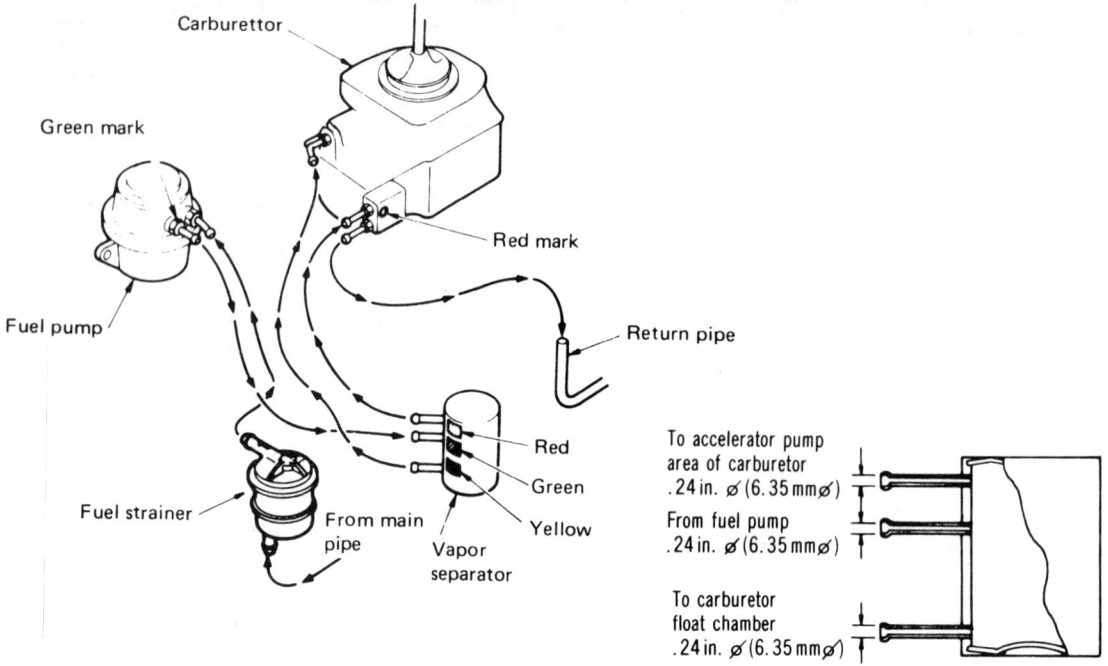

Carburettor

Green mark

Red mark

Fuel pump

Return pipe

Fuel strainer

From main pipe

Red

Green

Yellow

Vapor separator

To accelerator pump area of carburetor .24 in. ⌀ (6.35 mm⌀)

From fuel pump .24 in. ⌀ (6.35 mm⌀)

To carburetor float chamber .24 in. ⌀ (6.35 mm⌀)

Fig. 3.8 Vapour control system

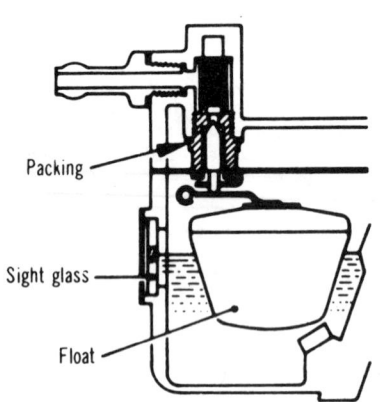

Packing

Sight glass

Float

Fig. 3.9 Float level adjustment

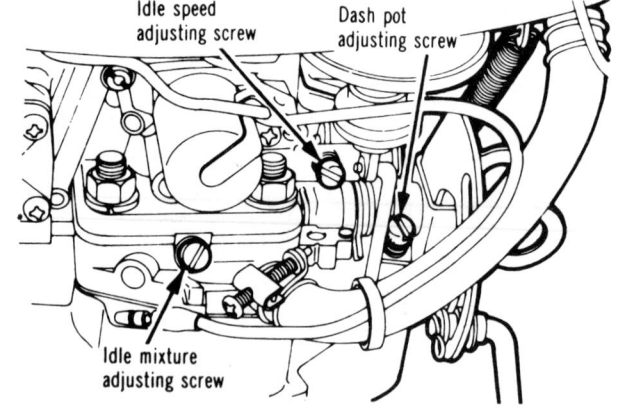

Idle speed adjusting screw

Dash pot adjusting screw

Idle mixture adjusting screw

Fig. 3.10 Carburetter adjusting screws

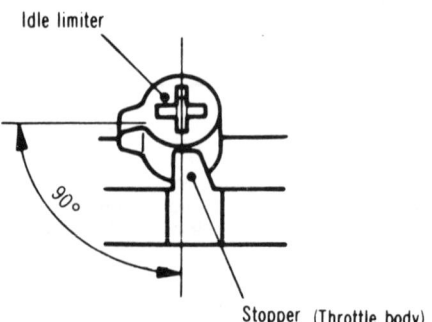

Idle limiter

90°

Stopper (Throttle body)

Fig. 3.11 Idle limiter

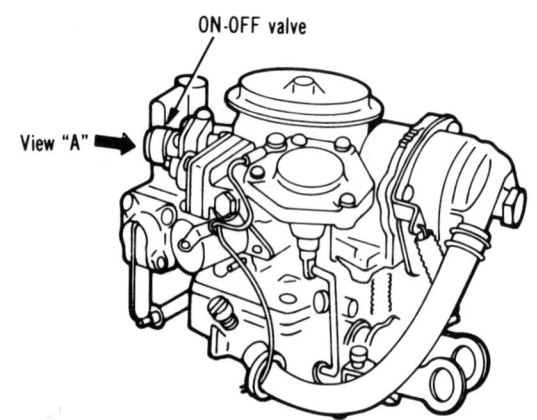

ON-OFF valve

View "A"

Fig. 3.12 Altitude compensator valve

High altitude set   Above 4,000 ft.
(1,219 m)

View "A"

Low altitude set   Below 4,000 ft.
(1,219 m)

View "A"

Fig. 3.13 Altitude compensator valve settings

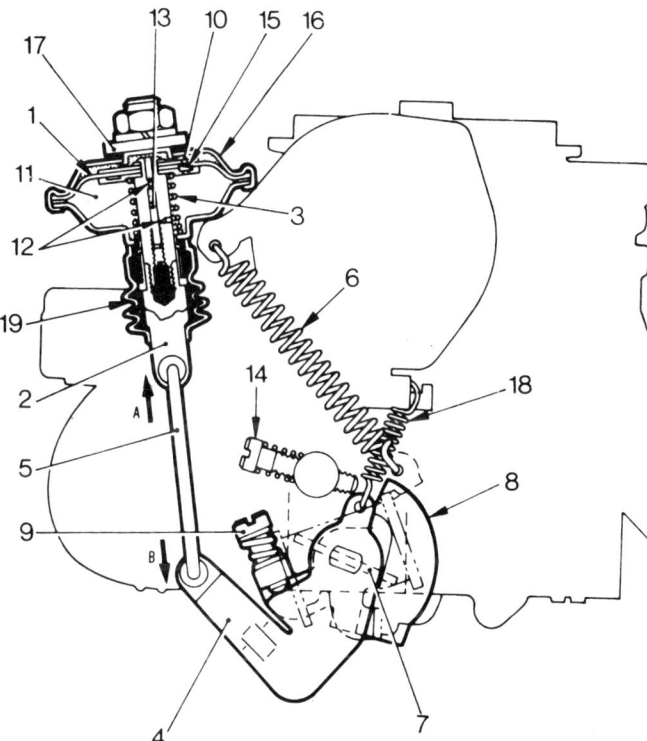

Fig. 3.14 Dashpot construction

1   Diaphragm
2   Rod
3   Diaphragm spring
4   Lever
5   Link
6   Throttle return spring
7   Throttle valve
8   Abatement plate
9   Adjusting screw
10 Diaphragm chamber
11 Diaphragm chamber
12 Jet
13 Needle screw
14 Speed adjusting screw
15 Check valve
16 Dashpot body
17 Bracket
18 Lever spring
19 Cover

5   Turn the idle mixture screw by increments of $\frac{1}{8}$ turn at a time to give the leanest mixture which is possible without misfiring.
6   Increase engine speed to 2500 rpm by opening the throttle. Check that when the throttle is released, the engine returns to its correct idling speed. Repeat the test two or three times.
7   When the adjustment has been completed, fit the idle limiter to the idle mixture adjustment screw (Fig. 3.10)
8   The foregoing adjustment is a basic one and final adjustment can only be made with an exhaust gas analyser. This checks that the carbon monoxide content is 2.5 $\pm$ 1.0%, at such lower limit as may be specified to meet legal requirements where these apply.

Cars for USA
9   After carrying out the steps detailed in paragraphs 1 to 3, check that where an altitude compensator knob is fitted (Fig. 3.12), this is set correctly as shown in Fig. 3.13.
10 Set the engine speed and idle CO concentration in accordance with the following table by making the appropriate adjustments to the idle speed screw and idle mixture screw.

Engine	Transmission	Curb idle speed rpm	Curb idle CO %	Enriched idle speed rpm	Enriched idle CO %
1600 cc	Manual	650±50	Below 0·1	730	1·0
1600 cc	Automatic	700±50	Below 0·1	780	1·0
2000 cc	Manual	650±50	Below 0·1	730	1·0
2000 cc	Automatic	700±50	Below 0·1	780	1·0
2600 cc (California)	Manual	700±50	Below 0·1	780	1·0
2600 cc (California)	Automatic	750±50	Below 0·1	830	1·0
2600 cc (49 states)	Manual	850±50	Below 0·1	930	1·0
2600 cc (49 states)	Automatic	850±50	Below 0·1	930	1·0

11 Reset the engine speed to the normal curb idle speed shown above by adjusting mixture adjusting screw.
12 Check that the idle speed and idle CO are within the specification and readjust if necessary by turning the idle mixture screw so as not to cause any misfiring.
13 After adjustment, fit the idle limiter to the idle mixture adjustment screw.

Cars for Canada
14 After carrying out the steps detailed in paragraphs 1 to 3, set the engine speed and idle CO to the following valves:

Engine	Idle speed rpm	Idle CO %
1600 cc and 2000 cc	850 ± 50	0.5 to 2.0
2600 cc	850 ± 50	1.0 to 2.5

15 Make adjustments to the idle speed adjusting screw and idle mixture adjusting screw until CO is the lowest value within the specified range which can be achieved without misfiring.
16 After adjustment, fit the idle limiter to the idle mixture adjustment screw.

13 Carburetter – dashpot adjustment

1   This adjustment is only applicable to cars with manual transmissions which are fitted with exhaust emission control.
2   After completing the idling adjustments, push up the lower end of the dashpot rod until it comes up against its stop and then check the engine speed to see that it is between 2000 and 2100 rpm.
3   Release the pushrod quickly and check the time that elapses before the engine speed drops to 900 rpm. This should be between 3 and 6 seconds.
4   If necessary, adjust the dashpot adjusting screw to achieve the correct timing (Fig. 3.14).

14 Carburetter – fast idle adjustment

Automatic choke
1   With the fast idle cam set on the 4th step, adjust the connecting

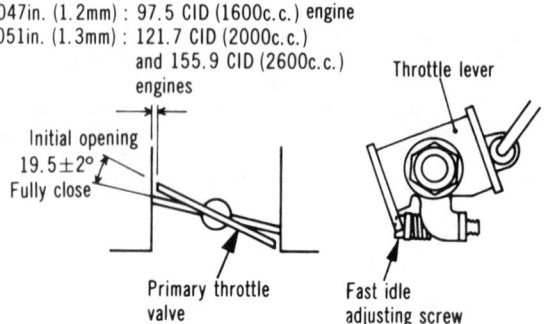

.047in. (1.2mm) : 97.5 CID (1600c.c.) engine
.051in. (1.3mm) : 121.7 CID (2000c.c.)
and 155.9 CID (2600c.c.)
engines

Initial opening
19.5±2°
Fully close

Throttle lever

Primary throttle valve

Fast idle adjusting screw

Fig. 3.15 Fast idle adjustment (automatic choke)

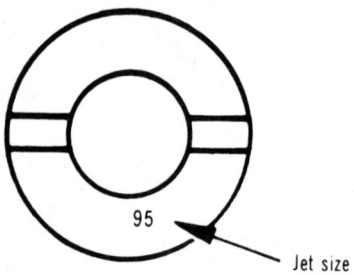

95

Jet size

Fig. 3.16 Jet identification marking

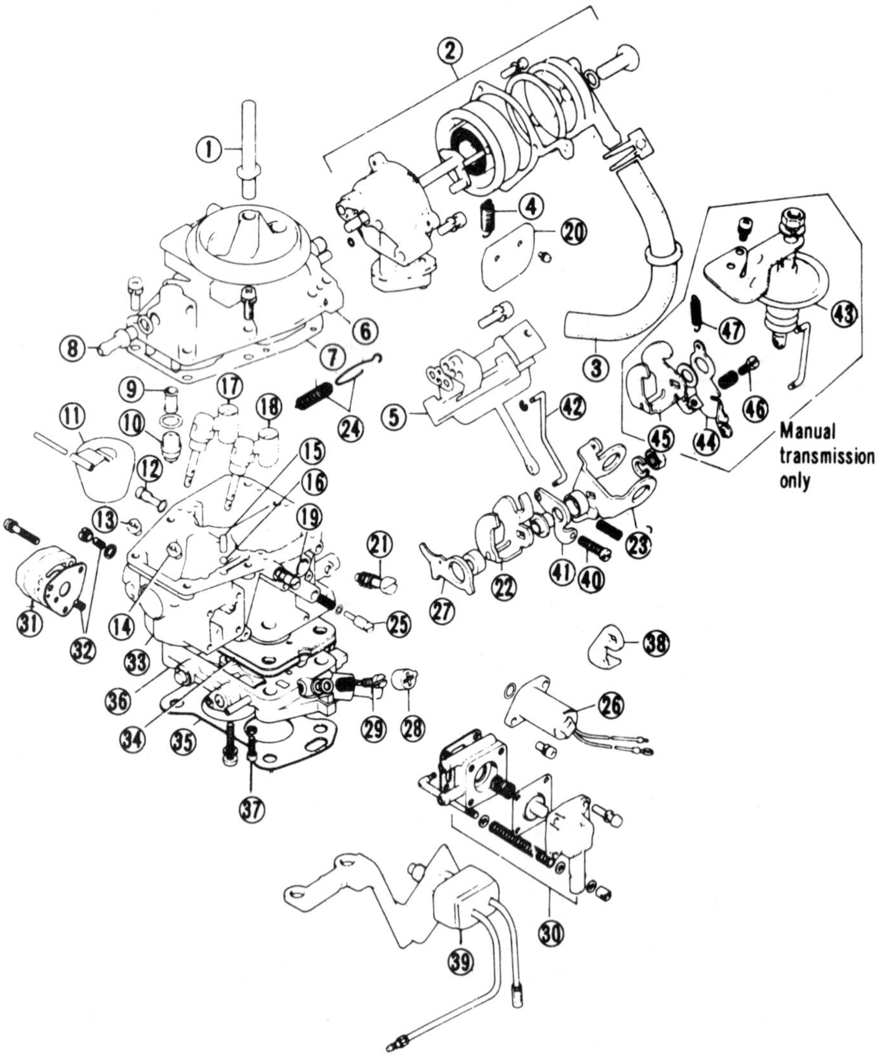

Fig. 3.17 Carburetter – exploded view

1   Stud
2   Auto-choke
3   Water hose
4   Return spring
5   Depression chamber
6   Float chamber cover
7   Float chamber packing
8   Fuel inlet nipple
9   Filter
10 Needle valve
11 Float
12 Secondary pilot jet
13 Secondary main jet
14 Primary main jet
15 Valve weight
16 Check valve
17 Inner secondary venturi
18 Inner primary venturi
19 Primary pilot jet
20 Choke valve
21 Throttle stop screw
22 Abatement plate
23 Throttle lever
24 Throttle return spring
25 Bypass screw
26 Fuel cut solenoid
27 Intermediate lever
28 Idle limiter
29 Pilot screw
30 Accelerator pump
31 Enrichment body assy
32 Enrichment jet
33 Main body
34 Insulator
35 Carburetter gasket
36 Throttle body
37 Throttle stop screw
38 Lever (AT)
39 Kickdown switch (AT)
40 Screw
41 Lever
42 Choke rod
43 Dashpot
44 Lever
45 Abatement plate
46 Adjusting screw
47 Lever spring

Manual transmission only

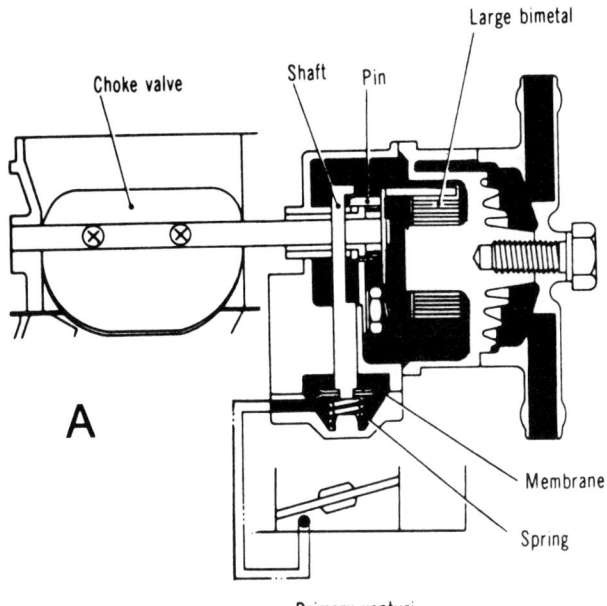

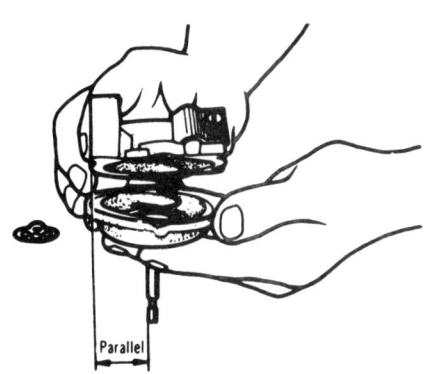

Fig. 3.19 Reassembling the depression chamber

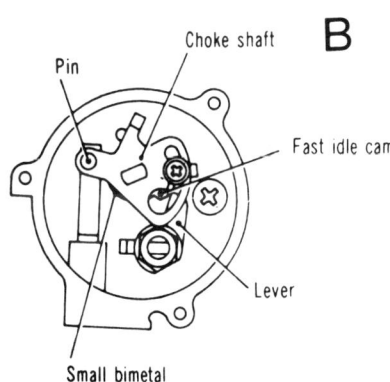

Fig. 3.18 Automatic choke

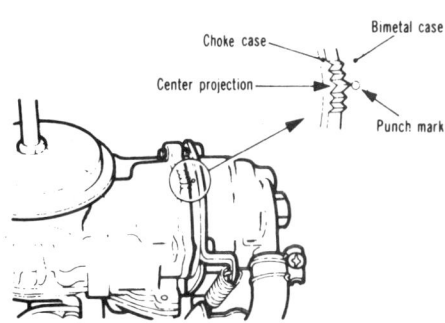

Fig. 3.20 Mating mark of automatic choke

rod with the fast idle adjusting screw so that the throttle will open to the clearance given in Fig. 3.15. The clearance is that between the edge of the valve plate and the throttle bore.

2 Check the engine speed and if it is in excess of 2000 rpm, turn the adjusting screw until the speed of the engine falls to 2000 rpm.

Manual choke

3 Set the bent end of the throttle rod so that when the choke valve is fully closed, the throttle valve will be open by the amount shown in Fig. 3.15. The clearance is that between the edge of the valve plate and the throttle bore.

15 Carburetter – removal and refitting

1 Remove the air cleaner breather hose and undo the clips, or ring nuts, of the air cleaner cover. Remove the cover and the element. Remove the fixing bolts of the air cleaner case and remove the case.

2 Disconnect the accelerator cable, the choke cable (manual choke models) at the carburetter, then remove the vacuum and fuel pipes.

3 Place a clean container underneath the cylinder block drain plug (Chapter 2, Section 2) remove the plug and drain the coolant. Remove the hose between the carburetter and the cylinder head.

4 Remove the bolts from the carburetter mounting flange and remove the carburetter.

5 Refit the carburetter in the reverse order, using a new gasket between the carburetter flange and the intake manifold. Apply jointing compound to both faces of the gasket before fitting it.

16 Carburetter – dismantling, cleaning and reassembly

The dismantling and reassembly of a carburetter requires clean conditions and systematic methods of working. Make sure that all spanners and screwdrivers are a good fit, so that they do not damage the components and use only lint-free cleaning cloths. As each unit of the carburetter is dismantled, keep all its parts together, preferably in an individual container and lay all the parts out in the exact position and order in which they were removed. The following procedure relates specifically to a carburetter with automatic choke, but the method for a manual choke carburetter does not differ significantly.

1 Wash the outside of the carburetter with petrol and dry it with a clean lint-free cloth.

2 Remove the throttle return spring and the intermediate return spring, disconnect the choke rod and the depression chamber rod end and disconnect the coolant hose.

3 Remove the float chamber cover and gasket, then the accelerator pump valve ball and weight. Extract the float pin and remove the float, clip and needle valve. Remove the valve seat, packing washers and

filter.

4   Remove the depression chamber and dismantle it into the body cover, diaphragm and spring.

5   Remove the idling cam assembly of the automatic choke (Fig. 3.16) then the water case and gasket, the bimetal case and plate, then remove the choke valve and shaft, the membrane cover, spring and membrane. Remove the recessed screws and withdraw the automatic choke body. It is not necessary to dismantle the automatic choke assembly.

6   Disconnect the accelerator pump lever rod at the throttle shaft, remove the screws from the throttle body and separate the main body from the throttle body. Remove the gasket and spacer. The pump lever rod nut is factory adjusted and should not be removed.

7   Remove the accelerator pump cover (photo). Remove the spring and the membrane.

8   Remove the enrichment cover, the spring and the valve body. It is not necessary to dismantle the valve body.

9   Remove the main and pilot jets, but do not attempt to remove the inner venturi and do not remove the bypass screw, which is sealed with white paint.

10 Remove the throttle lever nut, throttle lever, collar abutment plate and intermediate lever. When fitted, remove the dashpot fixing screws and dashpot assembly. Do not attempt to dismantle the throttle shaft and valve.

11 Clean all components in clean petrol and blow them dry.

12 Check the carburetter body and the water passages for cracks, sealing or blockage. Check the needle valve seat for wear, the filter for damage and blockage, and the jets for damage and blockage. Do not attempt to clean out any jet or air passage with wire. If the dirt cannot be dislodged by blowing, use a nylon bristle or a piece of nylon line.

13 Check each membrane for damage, examine the pilot screw seat for wear of the contact surface, the throttle valve shaft for wear and distortion and the linkage for smoothness of operation.

14 Check the float for damage and leaks, the lip for damage, the float lever pin locations for wear and the float lever bracket for deformation.

15 Using new packings and gaskets and making sure that they are fitted properly, reassemble, by first fitting the intermediate lever of the throttle body then fitting the thin collar, abutment plate, thick collar and throttle lever on to the primary throttle shaft. Secure them with a nut and spring washer. When a dashpot assembly is fitted it should be refitted at this stage. (Fig. 3.14)

16 Adjust the secondary throttle valve stop screw with the throttle in the fully closed position, rotate it a quarter of a turn and secure it with the locknut.

17 Fit the main jets and pilot jets, noting that each jet has an identification mark on its end (Fig. 3.16). The correct jet sizes are given in the Specifications.

18 Fit the enrichment valve, checking that the free length of the spring is nominally 1 in (25 mm) and then fit the accelerator pump and pump cover. The length of the accelerator pump spring is nominally 0.5 in (13 mm).

19 Fit the throttle body and the main body, connect the pump rod end to the throttle shaft, then fit the idle compensator within the float chamber cover. Fit the case of the automatic choke, then the membrane and spring. The free length of the spring should be 1.3 in (33 mm). Fit the choke shaft and valve, taking care to ensure that the valve is the right way round.

20 Ensure that the diaphragm ring fits snugly in the groove in the body then assemble the depression chamber. (Fig. 3.19) so that the float chamber joint face and the shaft on to which the nylon bearing is fitted, are parallel and the small diameter end of the bushing is facing outward.

21 Fit the depression chamber to the float chamber cover, then fit the filter and valve seat. Do not overtighten the valve seat because this can cause damage to the filter.

22 Fit the needle valve and retaining clip, then fit the float and its support pin. Fit the accelerator pump ball and weight, then fit the float chamber cover.

23 Connect the bent section of the choke connecting rod and with the fast idle cam engaged in the third stage turn the fast idle adjusting screw so that the clearance between the throttle valve and bore is 0.063 to 0.071 in (1.6 to 1.8 mm).

24 Insert the choke ring in the bimetal and tighten with the red line on the case aligned with the highest part of the automatic choke case (Fig. 3.20). Set the choke valve to a fully closed position at an ambient temperature of about 73°F.

17 Emission control systems – description

All vehicles are fitted with a positive crankcase ventilation system (Chapter 1, Section 33) and a variety of other systems may be fitted to vehicles which operate in countries where anti-pollution laws require them. These systems are:-

(a) Evaporation control, in which a canister of activated charcoal is fitted between the fuel tank and the air cleaner (Fig. 3.22). Petrol vapours are directed to the canister (Fig.3.23) for temporary storage and while the engine is running, air is drawn through the canister to purge it and the air vapour mixture is then routed to the combustion chambers through the air cleaner. In cars for the USA, a fuel check valve is fitted, which is closed when the engine is idling, to prevent vapourised fuel entering the air cleaner and giving excessive carbon monoxide emission during idling. The purge control valve is closed when the engine is idling so that vapourised fuel cannot enter the air cleaner and increase carbon monoxide emission. This is particularly important when engines are idling at high ambient temperature.

(b) Temperature controlled ignition, (Figs. 3.25 and 3.26) is fitted to offset the low exhaust gas temperature and consequent incomplete combustion which occurs when the engine is idling, operating at low speeds, is lightly loaded or decelerating. Under these conditions, ignition timing is retarded. To prevent the engine coolant from overheating after prolonged periods of idling with retarded ignition and also from periods of overload, or high ambient temperatures, a thermo-valve is fitted. The thermo-valve removes the vacuum from the retard side of the distributor diaphragm, so that spring B (Fig. 3.25) causes the ignition to advance with a consequent increase in engine speed and fan speed until the coolant temperature drops, the thermo-valve restores the vacuum on the retard side of the diaphragm and the ignition is retarded again. On cars fitted with automatic transmission the increase in idling speed produced by temperature controlled ignition is prevented by an idle speed control system (Fig. 3.26). This is done to prevent creep during idling and to reduce shift shock. A vacuum motor is fitted to the throttle lever and is controlled by the pressure output of the thermo-valve. When the thermo-valve is in the normal position, ie closed, manifold vacuum is applied to the vacuum motor, and the vacuum motor pulls the throttle in opposition to the throttle spring against the stop screw C. When the thermo-valve opens and vents to the atmosphere, the vacuum motor spring pushes the rod downwards. This and the throttle spring allow the throttle to close slightly until limited by the stop screw B.

(c) Heated air intake, is fitted (Fig. 3.28) to prevent the lean mixture and lower engine output which results from the incomplete vaporisation of fuel and cold air. A cowl is fitted over the thermal reactor and is joined by a duct to the air intake. A flap valve, controlled by a bimetallic element, ensures that all intake air is sucked over the thermal reactor, if the under bonnet temperature is less than 41°F. When the underbonnet air temperature exceeds 100°F, the valve prevents any further air from being drawn over the thermal reactor and air flows directly to the air cleaner.

(d) Jet air system, (Figs. 3.29 and 3.30) has an additional inlet valve which provides for air, or a super lean mixture to be drawn from the air intake into the cylinder head. The jet valve is operated by the same cam as the inlet valve. There is a common rocker arm, so that the jet valve and the inlet valve open and close simultaneously.

On the suction stroke, fuel/air mixture flows through the intake port into the combustion chamber. At the same time, jet air is forced into the combustion chamber because of the pressure difference between the jet intake in the throttle bore and the jet valve in the cylinder as the piston moves down. At small throttle openings there is a large pressure difference, giving the jet air a high velocity. This scavenges the residual gases around the spark plug and creates good ignition conditions. It also produces a strong swirl in the combustion chamber which lasts throughout the compression stroke and improves flame propogation after ignition, assuring high combustion efficency. As the throttle opening is increased, less jet air is forced in and jet swirl diminishes, but the increased flow through the intake valve ensures satisfactory combustion.

(e) Exhaust gas recirculation, dilutes the air fuel mixture in the engine cylinders in order to reduce the oxides of nitrogen in the exhaust gases. The quantity of exhaust gas being used is controlled by a valve which operates according to engine temperature. When the engine is cold, the level of oxides of nitrogen in the exhaust is low and there is no recirculation. When engine temperature rises above 131°F, the

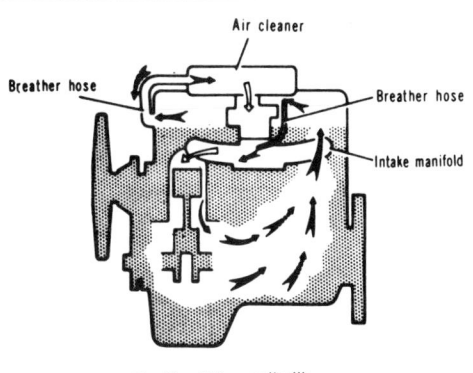

Fig. 3.21 Crankcase ventilation system

←•◄ At partially-open throttle
←◄ At wide-open throttle

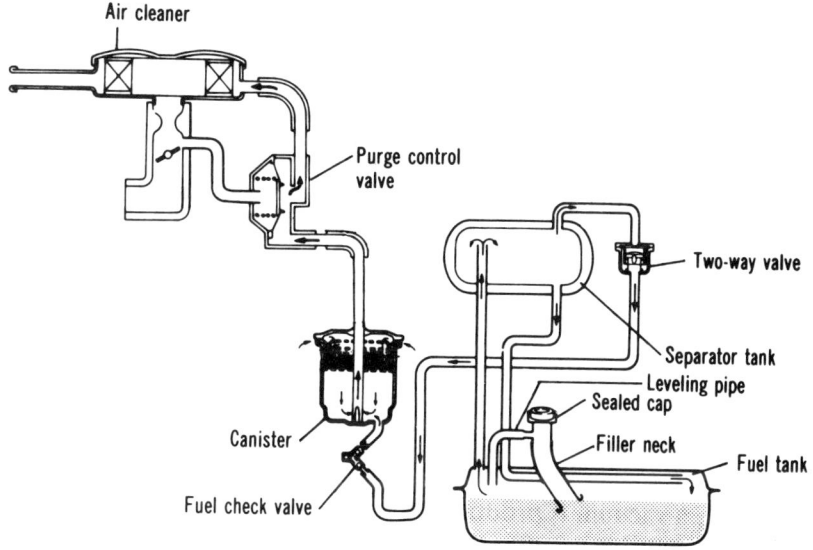

Coupe, Sedan and Hatchback

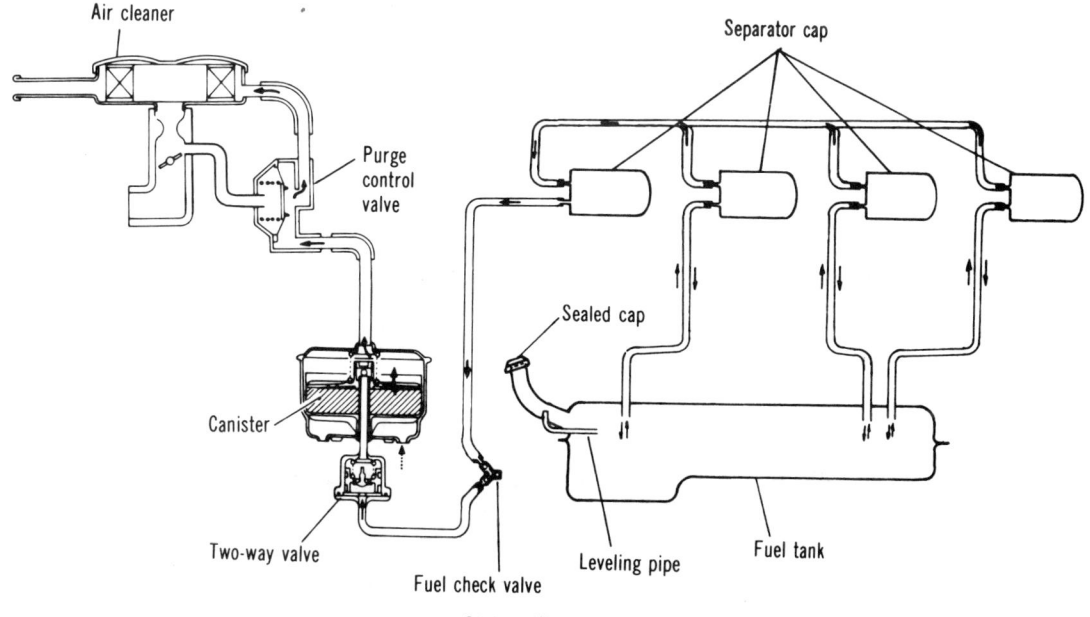

Station Wagon

Fig. 3.22 Evaporation control schematic

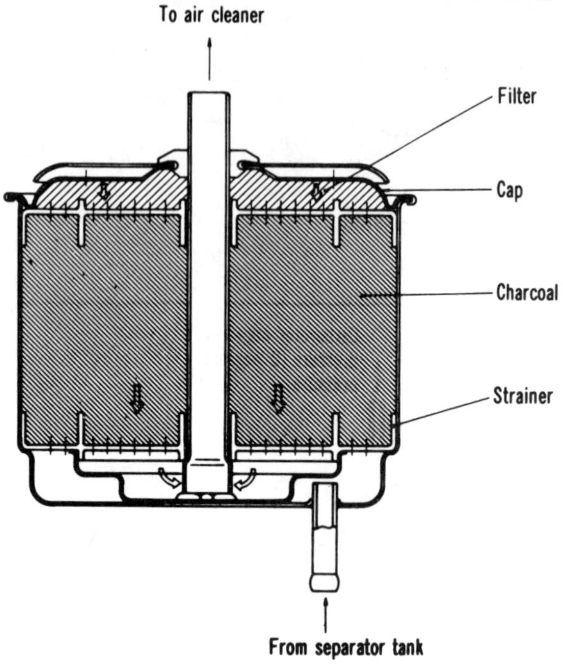

To air cleaner

Filter

Cap

Charcoal

Strainer

From separator tank

Fig. 3.23 Filter canister

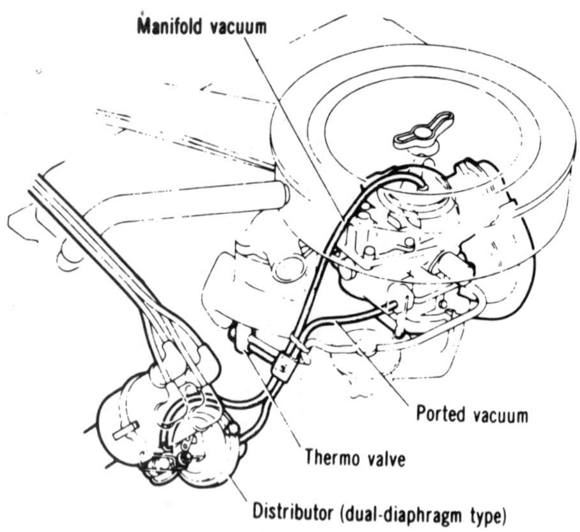

Manifold vacuum

Ported vacuum

Thermo valve

Distributor (dual-diaphragm type)

Fig. 3.24 Ignition timing control system

Orifice

Manifold

Thermo valve

Retard

Spring (A)

Spring (B)

Diaphragm on retard side

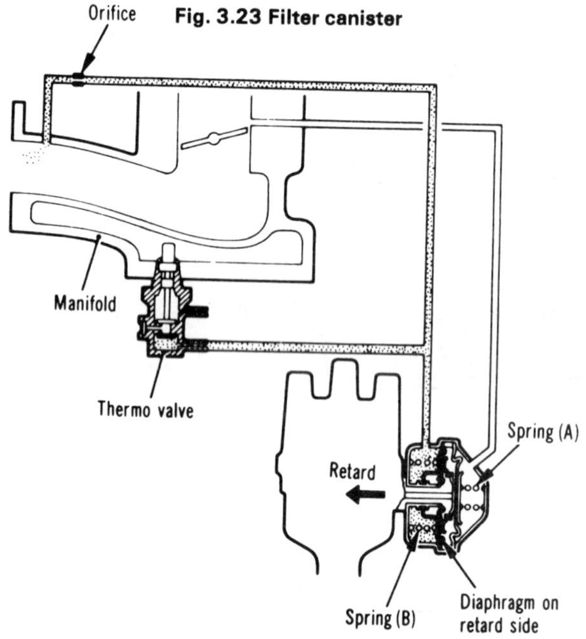

Fig. 3.25 Operation of ignition timing control system (normal idling)

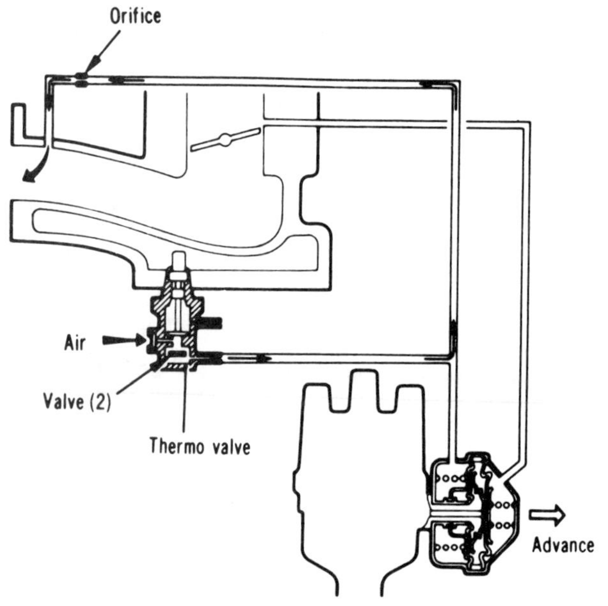

Orifice

Air

Valve (2)

Thermo valve

Advance

Fig. 3.26 Operation of ignition timing control system (at high temperature)

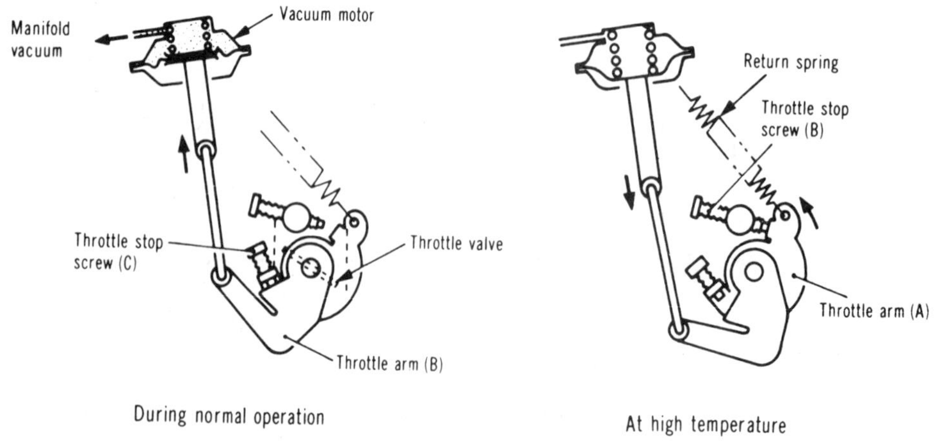

Manifold vacuum

Vacuum motor

Throttle stop screw (C)

Throttle valve

Throttle arm (B)

During normal operation

Return spring

Throttle stop screw (B)

Throttle arm (A)

At high temperature

Fig. 3.27 Operation of throttle adjuster

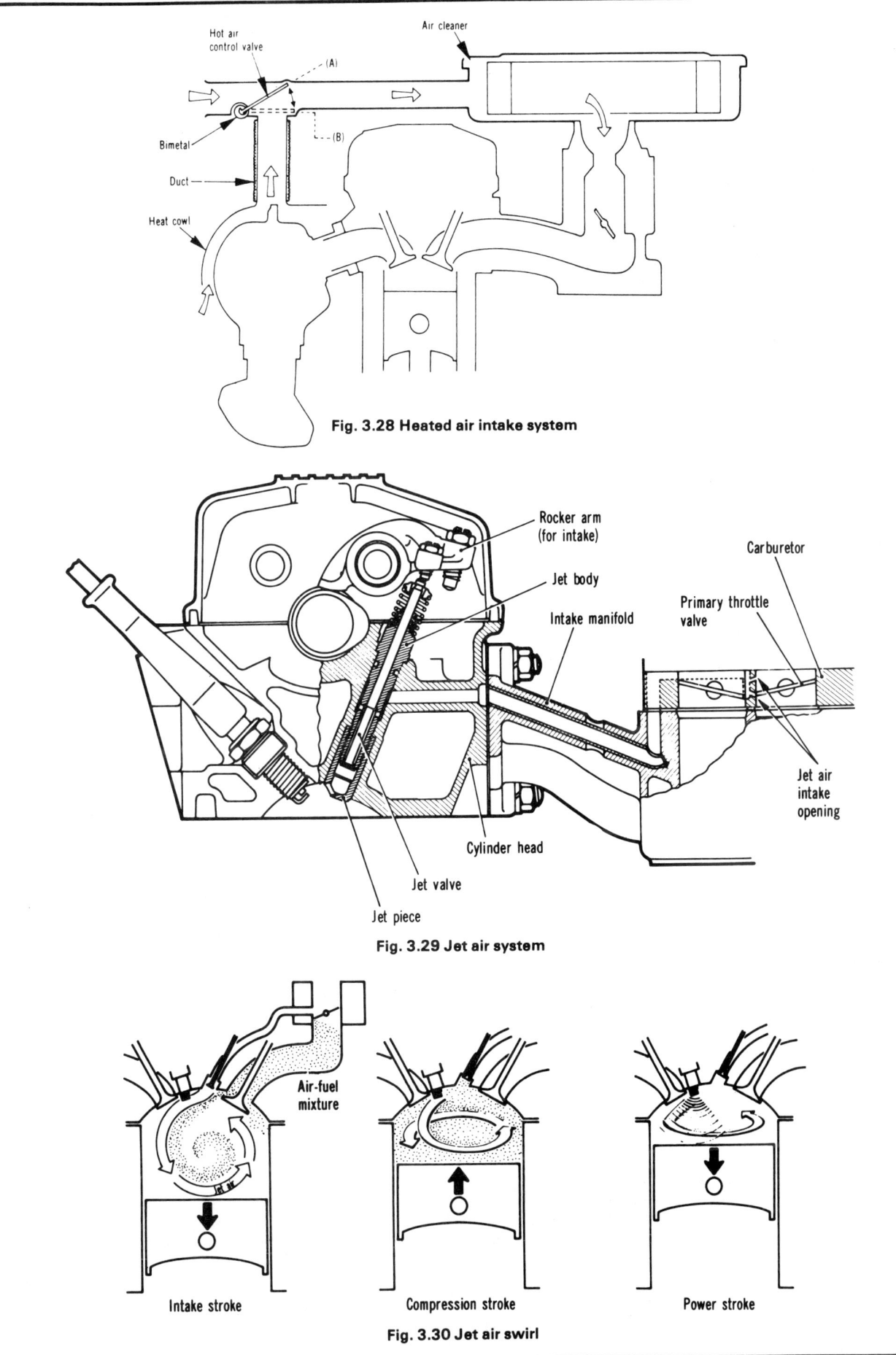

Fig. 3.28 Heated air intake system

Fig. 3.29 Jet air system

Fig. 3.30 Jet air swirl

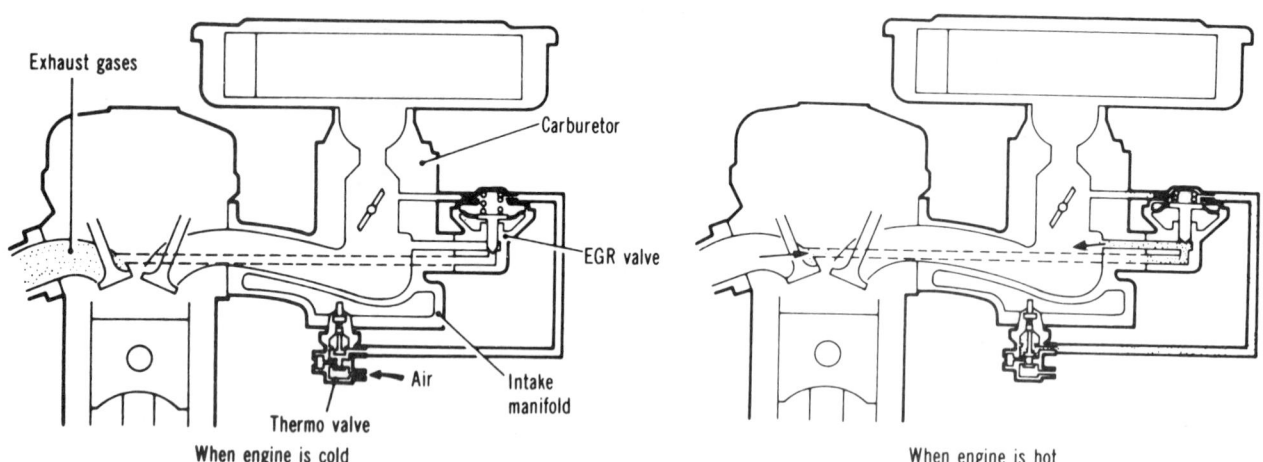

Fig. 3.31 Exhaust gas recirculation system

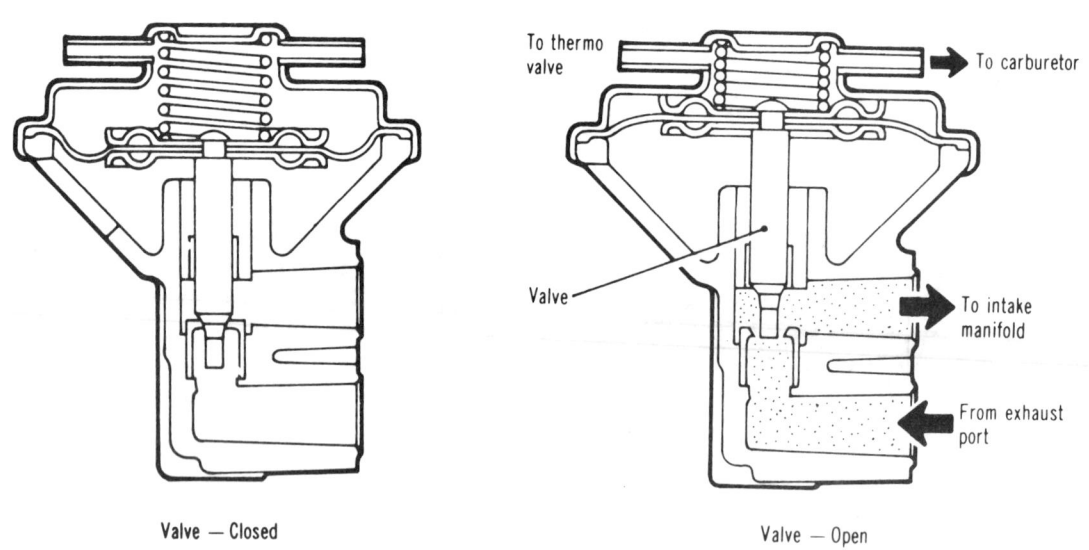

Fig. 3.32 EGR valve

thermo-valve connects manifold suction to the EGR (Fig. 3.32) valve which opens and allows recirculation. During engine idling, manifold vacuum is too low to keep the EGR valve open, even though the thermo-valve is above its operating temperature.

(f) Catalytic converter fitted in the exhaust manifold. This consists of a stainless steel core which is fitted with an oxidizing catalyst to oxidize any residual hydrobcarbons and carbon monoxide in the exhaust gases.

(g) Deceleration device to decrease hydrocarbon emissions during deceleration. This may be a servo operated mixture control valve built into the carburetter, or a dash pot mounted externally.

The mixture control valve, which is operated by the inlet manifold vacuum supplies additional air to the inlet manifold during deceleration, to reduce hydrocarbon emission. At constant vehicle speed, an orifice maintains a balanced vacuum in the spring chamber and reservoir so that the valve is closed by its spring. When the throttle is closed suddenly, a high vacuum from the inlet manifold in the spring chamber forces the diaphragm to move and open the valve, so admitting air to the intake manifold.

The dashpot, which is controlled by a servo valve, delays the closure of the throttle valve to its normal idling position. The servo valve detects inlet manifold vacuum and closes if the vacuum is above

a pre-set value. When the servo is closed, the air in the diaphragm chamber of the dashpot cannot leak out and the throttle opening position is maintained.

(h) High altitude system to compensate for the reduction in the density of the air at high altitudes. It consists of a manually operated ON-OFF valve on the carburetter which controls additional air passages to the primary main well and slow fuel passage. There is also a connection from the altitude valve to the EGR system, so that at high altitude the EGR flow through the secondary valve is decreased.

18 Emission control systems – maintenance and testing

Positive crankcase ventilation

1   Check the crankcase ventilation breather hoses and jet to make sure that they are not blocked. Clean them if necessary. An indication of poor crankcase breathing is a build up of deposits inside the rocker box cover.

Evaporation control

2   Every 15 000 miles (24 000 km) disconnect both ends of the vapour vent line and blow through it to ensure that it is clear.

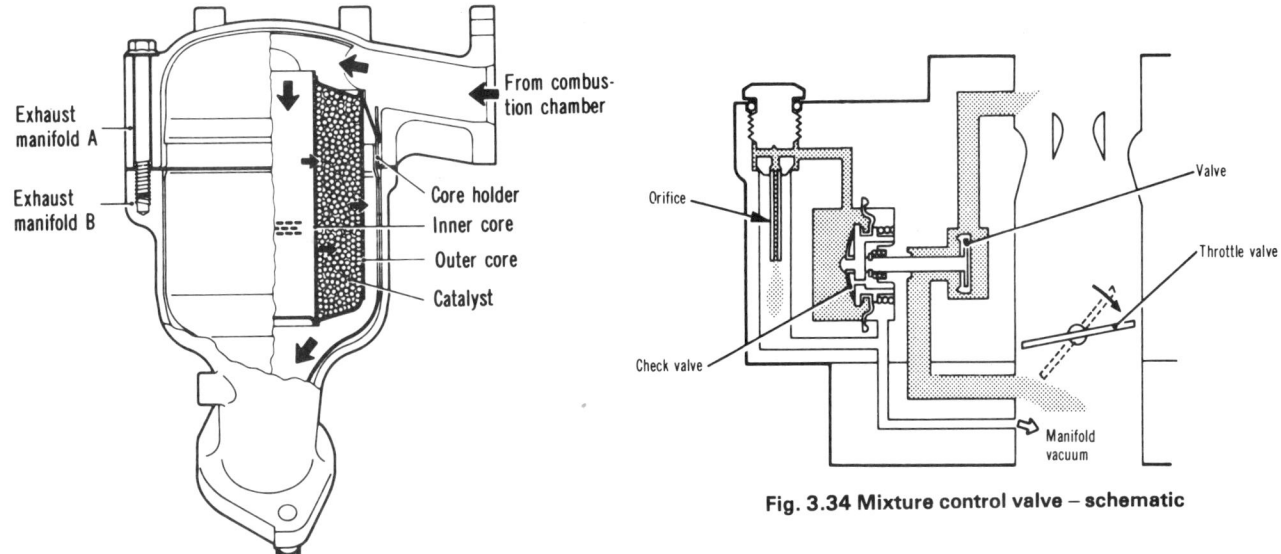

Exhaust manifold A

Exhaust manifold B

From combustion chamber

Core holder
Inner core
Outer core
Catalyst

Fig. 3.33 Catalytic converter – part sectional view

Orifice

Valve

Throttle valve

Check valve

Manifold vacuum

Fig. 3.34 Mixture control valve – schematic

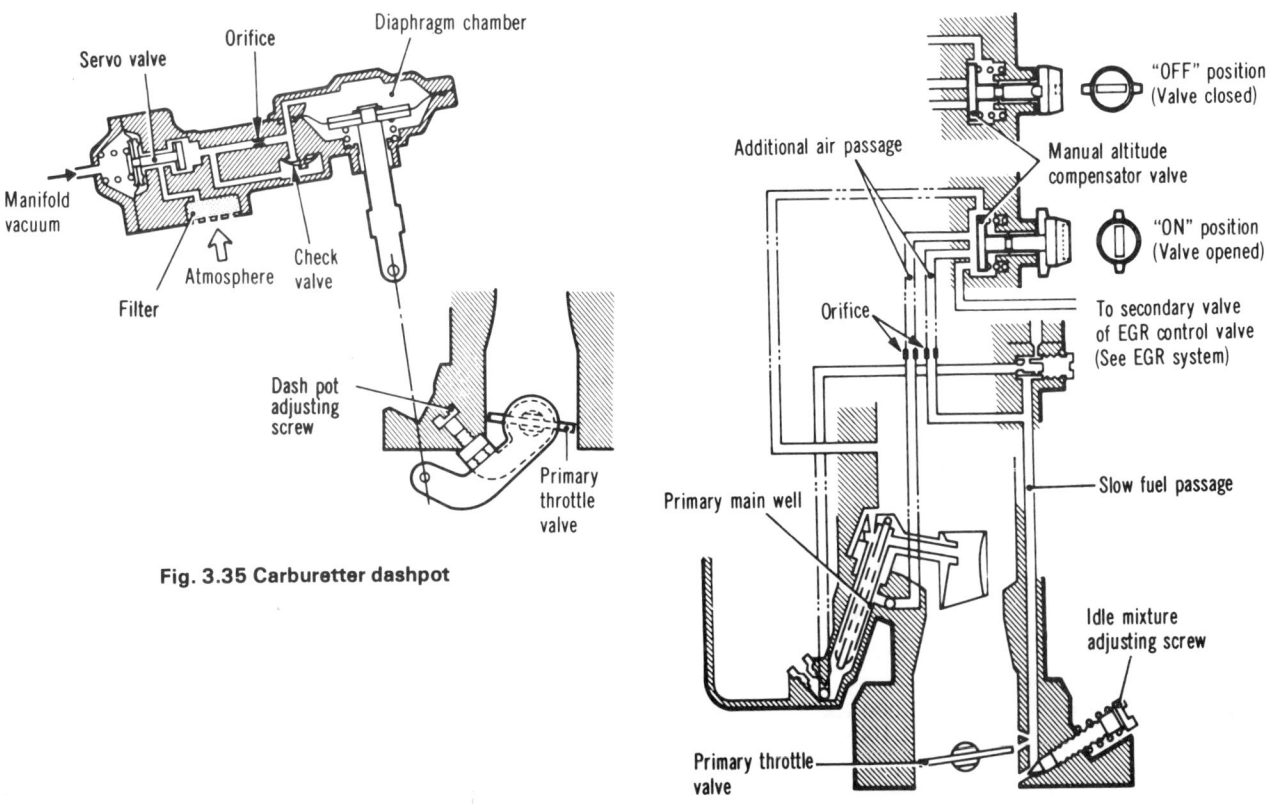

Servo valve
Orifice
Diaphragm chamber

Manifold vacuum

Atmosphere
Filter
Check valve

Dash pot adjusting screw

Primary throttle valve

Fig. 3.35 Carburetter dashpot

"OFF" position (Valve closed)

Additional air passage

Manual altitude compensator valve

"ON" position (Valve opened)

Orifice

To secondary valve of EGR control valve (See EGR system)

Slow fuel passage

Primary main well

Idle mixture adjusting screw

Primary throttle valve

Fig. 3.36 High altitude compensation system

3   Dust tends to accumulate round the suction port of the canister. This reduces its efficiency. The port should be cleaned every 15 000 miles (24 000 km) and a new canister should be fitted every 30 000 miles (48 000 km). When the canister is replaced, inspect the rubber and vinyl hoses and fit new ones if the existing ones have deteriorated.
4   Inspect the vapour check valve for clogging every 15 000 miles (24 000 km). If necessary wash the valve in petrol so that the check ball moves freely.

Temperature controlled ignition

5   The construction, operation and checking of the distributor are given in Chapter 4.
6   To check the thermo valve, first inspect the vacuum hose to ensure that it is not kinked, or damaged.
8   Connect a tachometer and a timing light to the engine and run the engine until it achieves normal operating temperature.
9   Remove the rubber cap from the retard side of the distributor and check that the timing advances, and then retards again when the plug is refitted.
10   Cover the radiator so that the coolant temperature rises, but take care not to let the coolant boil.
11   If ignition timing has not advanced to basic ignition timing by the time the coolant temperature has reached 203°F (95°C), the thermo-valve is not functioning properly and a new one should be fitted.

Heated air intake

12   When the engine is cool, check that the hot air control valve has closed the cold air intake. Run the engine until the under bonnet temperature exceeds 108°F and check that the heated air intake is fully closed. Check the air cleaner cover and case for damage and distortion. Renew if necessary.
13   The air control valve is integral with the air cleaner case and the case must be renewed if the valve is faulty. Check that the air cleaner element is not excessively dirty and that the gaskets and sealing washers are in good condition.

Jet air system

14   Check the jet valve clearances as detailed in Chapter 1.
15   Check that the valve moves freely without sticking.

Exhaust gas recirculation

16   To check the EGR valve, warm the engine up until the coolant

temperature is 176°F, then set the engine speed to 3000 to 3200 rpm. Disconnect the vacuum hose to the valve and check that the diaphragm lowers and closes the valve. Reconnect the vacuum hose and check that the diaphragm rises and allows exhaust gas to recirculate. If these conditions are confirmed, the valve is satisfactory. After completing the checks, re-set the EGR warning lamp (Chapter 10).

Catalytic converter

17   Check that the case and core of the converter are not damaged and that the flange connections are gas tight. The converter can only be tested by checking the idle CO and hydrocarbon contents of the exhaust gas after first ensuring that the ignition timing and idle mixture are adjusted correctly.

---

19 Accelerator pedal – removal and refitting

1   Loosen the clamp bolt on the yoke and pull the accelerator rod out of the yoke.
2   Remove the two fixing bolts of the accelerator arm support and withdraw the assembly.
3   Remove the split cotter from the accelerator arm and withdraw the arm.
4   When refitting the pedal support to the body, apply a sealant to the threaded holes.
5   Apply multi-purpose grease to the points indicated by arrows in Fig. 3.38.

---

20 Accelerator pedal – adjustment

1   Release the locknut of the pedal stop adjusting bolt and turn the bolt until its projection is within the limits shown in Fig. 3.39. Hold the bolt in this position and tighten the locknut.
2   To fit the accelerator pedal in its correct position, thread the gaiter on to the accelerator rod until the lip of the gaiter fits into the groove in the accelerator rod.
3   Holding the pedal lightly against its stop and with the engine running at idling speed, offer the assembly up and thread the accelerator rod through the yoke.
4   Clamp the rod by tightening the yoke clamp bolt to the specified torque.

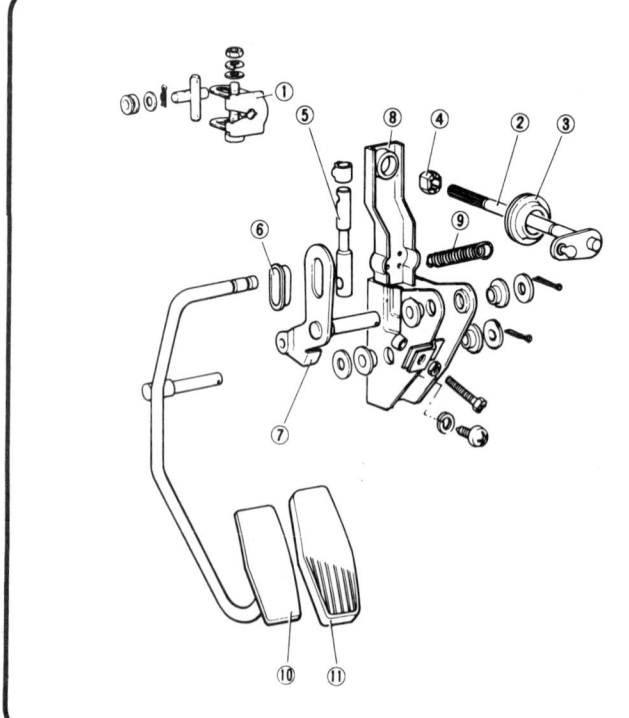

Fig. 3.37 Accelerator pedal assembly – exploded view

1   Yoke
2   Accelerator rod
3   Gaiter
4   Bearing
5   Connecting rod
6   Bushing
7   Lever
8   Accelerator arm support
9   Return spring
10 Accelerator pedal
11 Pedal rubber

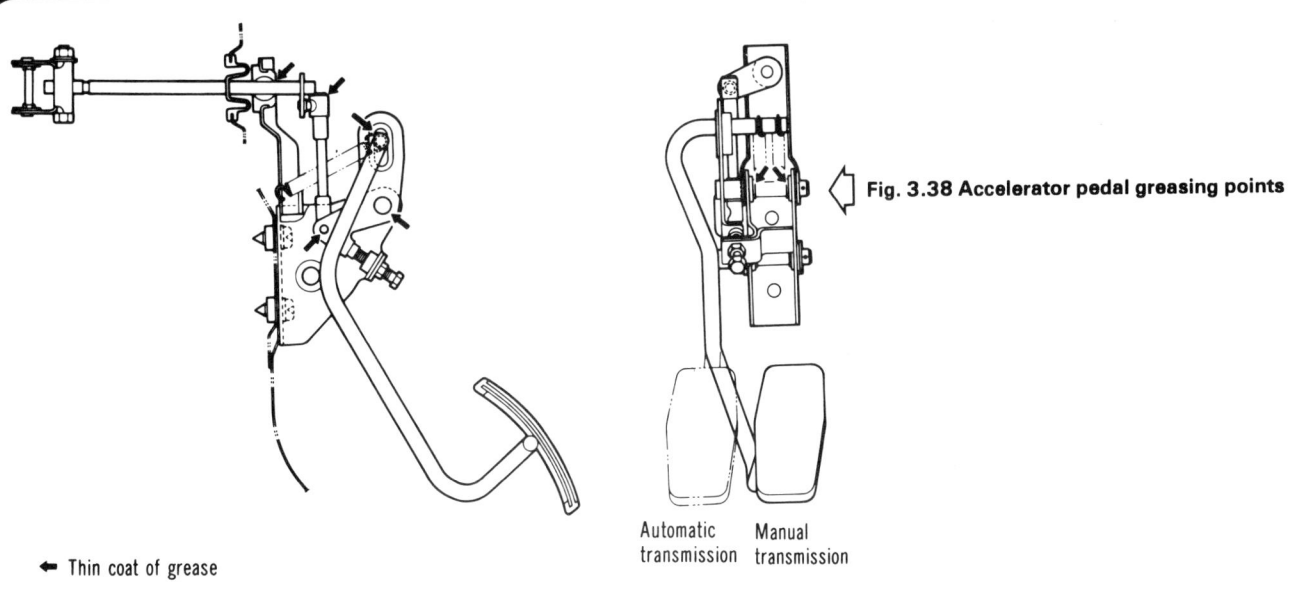

Fig. 3.38 Accelerator pedal greasing points

Automatic transmission   Manual transmission

← Thin coat of grease

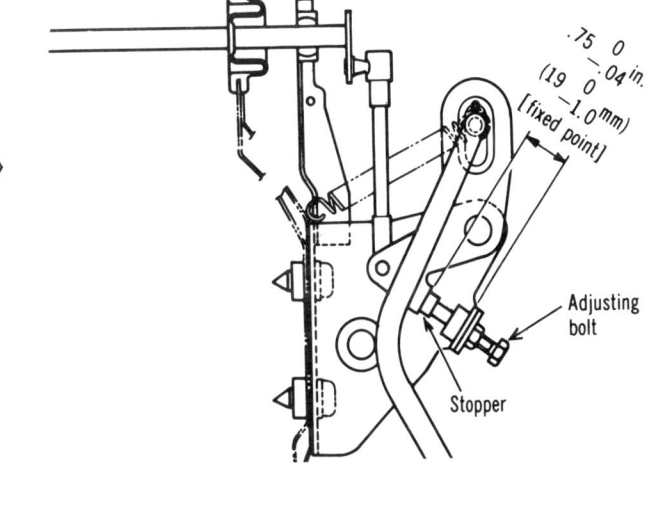

Fig. 3.39 Accelerator pedal adjustment

$.75 \quad 0 \quad .04$ in.
$(19 \quad 0 \quad 1.0$ mm$)$
[fixed point]

Adjusting bolt

Stopper

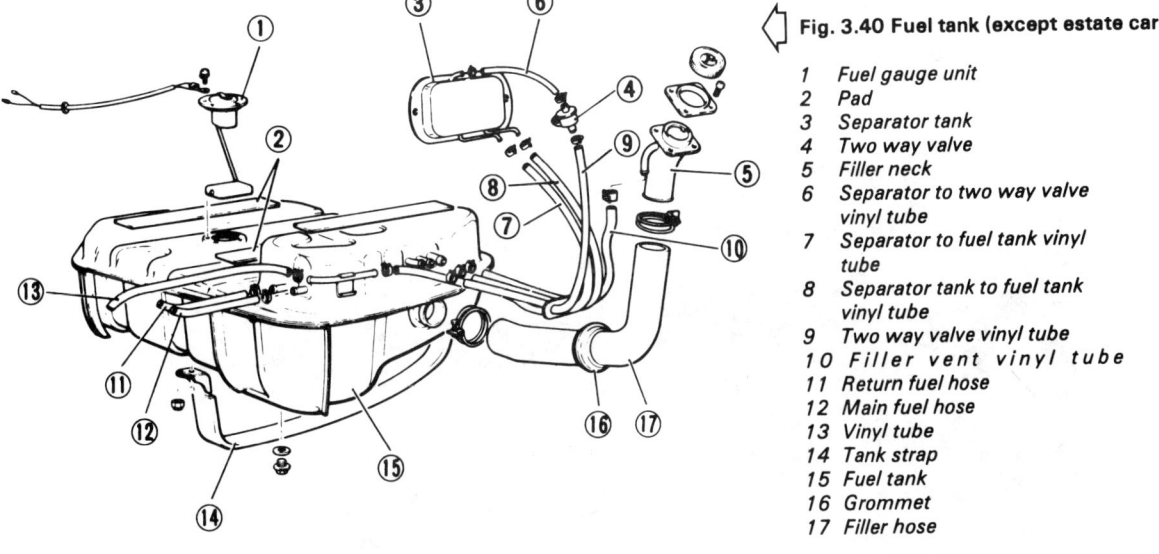

Fig. 3.40 Fuel tank (except estate car)

1   Fuel gauge unit
2   Pad
3   Separator tank
4   Two way valve
5   Filler neck
6   Separator to two way valve vinyl tube
7   Separator to fuel tank vinyl tube
8   Separator tank to fuel tank vinyl tube
9   Two way valve vinyl tube
10 Filler vent vinyl tube
11 Return fuel hose
12 Main fuel hose
13 Vinyl tube
14 Tank strap
15 Fuel tank
16 Grommet
17 Filler hose

Fig. 3.41 Fuel tank (estate car)

1 Fuel gauge unit
2 Fuel tank
3 Fuel tank cap
4 Separator tank
5 Return fuel hose
6 Main fuel hose
7 Vinyl hose
8 Vinyl hose
9 Vapour hose
10 Vapour hose
11 Vapour hose
12 Vapour hose
13 Vapour hose
14 Vinyl tube
15 Vinyl hose
16 Vapour hose
17 Vapour hose
18 Vapour hose
19 Breather hose

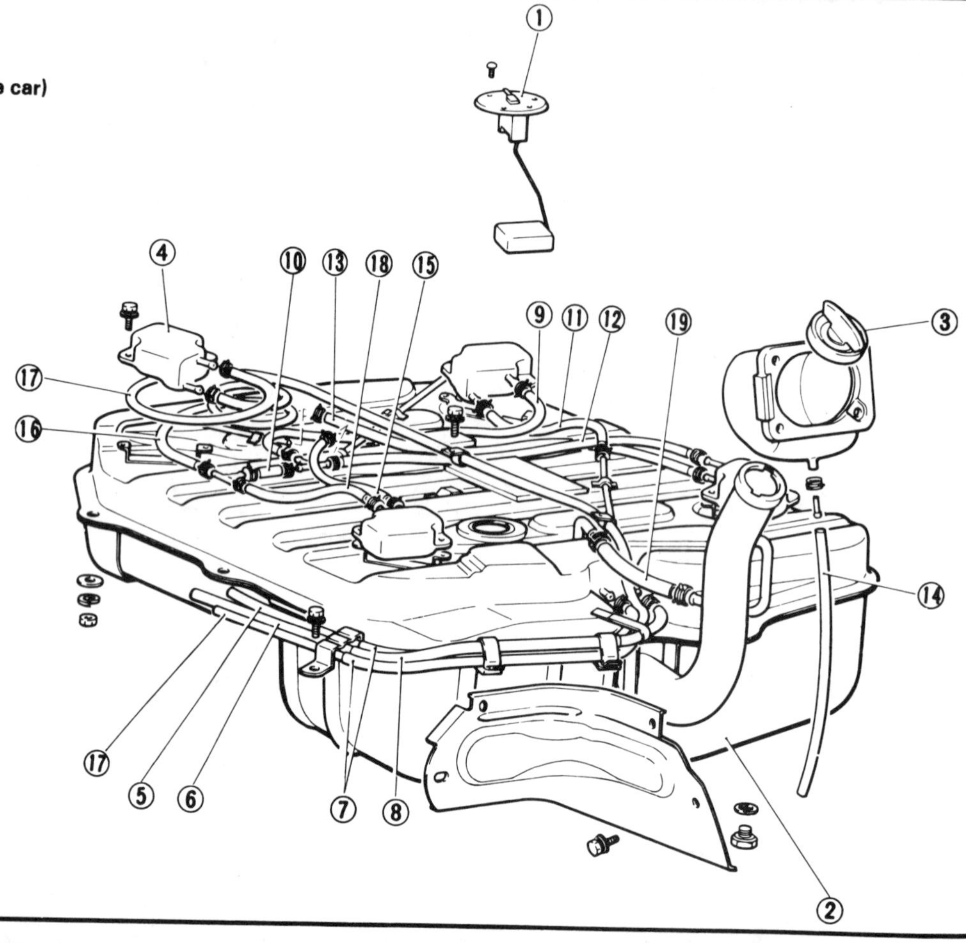

22.5 Tail pipe joint and heat deflector bolts

22.6 Tail pipe hanger (early type)

22.7 Front pipe to manifold joint

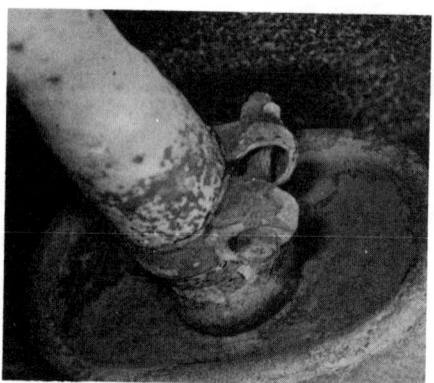

22.8 Front pipe to main exhaust joint

22.10 Main silencer support (early type)

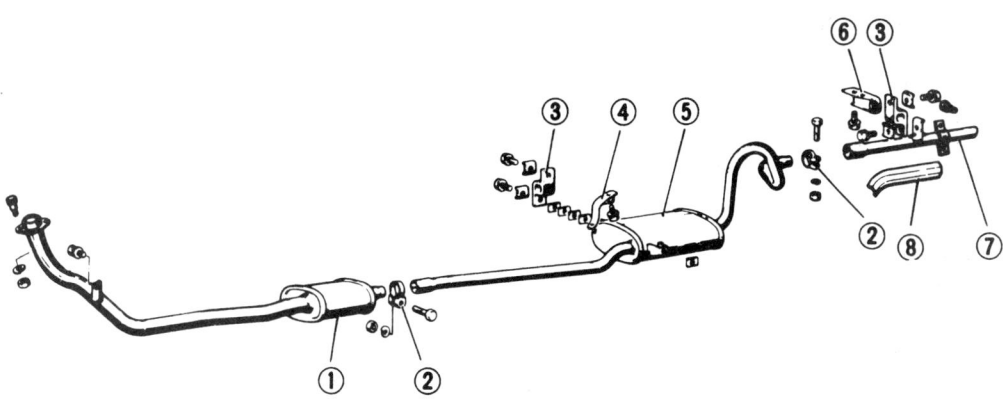

Fig. 3.42 Exhaust system components (early models)

1	Exhaust pipe assembly	5	Main silencer assembly
2	Exhaust clamp	6	Tail pipe bracket
3	Silencer hanger	7	Tail pipe
4	Silencer bracket	8	Heat shield

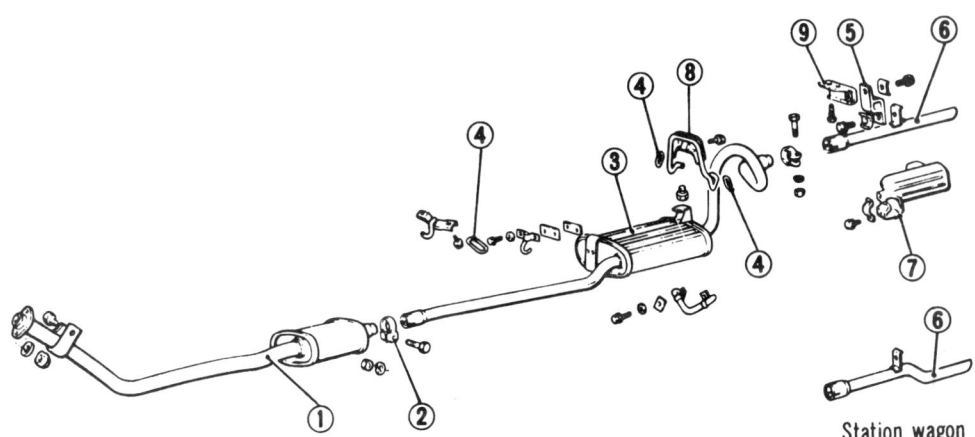

Station wagon

Fig. 3.43 Exhaust system components (later models)

1	Front exhaust pipe	6	Tail pipe
2	Clamp	7	Heat shield (Cars for Europe
3	Main silencer assembly		except estate car)
4	O ring	8	Bracket
5	Tail pipe hanger	9	Tail pipe bracket

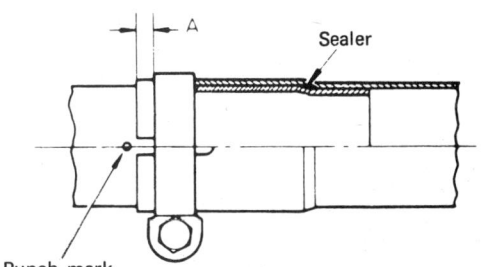

Sealer

Punch mark

▷ **Fig. 3.44 Pipe clamping position**

Pipe to clamp end clearance A $\frac{1}{4}$ in (6 mm)

21 Fuel tank – removing and refitting

Before removing the fuel tank, reduce the quantity of fuel in it as much as possible by normal usage.

1   With the vehicle in a well ventilated place, free from naked lights, or sources of sparking, remove the battery leads, then remove the drain plug from the tank and run the fuel into a metal container with a vapour tight lid. Label the container and store it safely. On the estate car, remove the spare tyre and its hanger.

2   Loosen the clamps of the main and return fuel hoses and then disconnect the hoses from the fuel tank.

3   Loosen the clamps at the side of the separator tank and remove the vent lines.

4   Loosen the hose clamp on the side of the tank and pull off the filler hose.

5   Remove the rear floor covering and disconnect the fuel tank gauge from the wiring harness.

6   Remove the fuel tank mounting bolts, lower the tank sufficiently to unclamp and remove the vent lines and then remove the tank.

Caution: *Never bring any naked light near a fuel tank, nor attempt to solder, or weld it unless it has been steamed out for at least two hours.*

7   When fitting the tank, check that fuel pipes are free from cracks, damage and corrosion.

8   Ensure that the main and return hoses, and vent lines are connected to their outlets and that they will not be kinked, trapped or strained. Make sure that all hose clamps are fitted and tightened adequately.

9   When pipes pass through places in the body, ensure that there is a grommet correctly and securely fitted to the hole and that the grommet and pipe are sealed.

10   If the gauge unit is removed from the tank, refit it using a new gasket and coat both sides of the gasket with sealant.

22 Exhaust system – removal and refitting

1   A two silencer exhaust system is fitted to all vehicles except the 2600 cc for Canada, which has an additional silencer on the centre pipe. The heat shield is only fitted on vehicles for the USA.

2   The exhaust system should not be removed unless it requires repair, the renewal of part of the system, or the sealing of gas leaks. It is usually easier to remove the entire system, rather than try to take out only part of it. When renewal is required, it is often cheaper to have the job done by an exhaust fitting specialist.

3   With the car over a pit, or with the rear axle supported as high as possible on firmly based axle stands, proceed as follows.

4   Because exhaust system fixings are usually corroded severely, saturate them all with an anti-corrosion fluid or penetrating oil before making any attempt to undo them.

5   Remove the tail pipe heat deflector plate, if fitted, then undo the clamp bolt of the main muffler to tail-pipe joint (photo).

6   Remove the bolt from the tail-pipe hanger and pull the tail-pipe off (photo).

7   Disconnect the exhaust pipe from the manifold by removing the flange fixings (photo).

8   Release the front pipe clamp and remove the connecting bolts from the joint between the front pipe and the main silencer assembly (photo).

9   On vehicles fitted with a front pipe heatshield, remove the heatshield.

10   Remove the main silencer supports, which may be either flexible supports secured by bolts, or hooks and O-rings. In the case of O-ring supports, pull the silencer to one side and lever the O-ring off the hook, taking care not to damage the O-ring.

11   Remove the front pipe and main silencer as an assembly and then separate them.

12   When fitting the system, temporarily connect the front pipe, tail pipe and main silencer in that order and leave all the bolts and fixings loose. Use an exhaust system sealing compound on the joints between the front pipe and the main silencer, and the main silencer and the tail pipe.

13   When connecting the different parts of the system, insert them as far as they will go, which for sleeve joints should be about 3 in (75 mm).

14   Ensure that there is a clearance of 1 in (25 mm) between every part of the exhaust system and the nearest point of the body.

15   Tighten the fixings to the specified torque, starting at the exhaust manifold and working towards the tail-pipe.

23 Fault diagnosis – fuel system

Unsatisfactory engine performance and excessive fuel consumption are not necessarily the fault of the fuel system or carburetter. In fact they more commonly occur as a result of ignition faults. Before acting on the fuel system it is necessary to check the ignition system first. Even though a fault may lie in the fuel system it will be difficult to trace unless the ignition is correct.
The table below therefore, assumes that the ignition system is in order.

Symptom	Reason/s
Smell of petrol when engine is stopped	Leaking fuel lines or unions Leaking fuel tank
Smell of petrol when engine is idling	Leaking fuel line unions between pump and carburetter Overflow of fuel from float chamber due to wrong level setting Ineffective needle valve or punctured float
Excessive fuel consumption for reasons not covered by leaks or float chamber faults	Worn needle Sticking needle
Difficult starting, uneven running, lack of power, cutting out	Incorrectly adjusted carburetter Float chamber fuel level too low or needle sticking Fuel pump not delivering sufficient fuel Intake manifold gaskets leaking, or manifold fractured

24 Fault diagnosis – emission control system

Symptom	Reason/s
Low CO content of exhaust gases (weak or lean mixture)	Fuel level incorrect in carburetter Incorrectly adjusted carburetter
High CO content of exhaust gases (rich mixture)	Incorrectly adjusted carburetter Choke sticking

Chapter 4 Ignition system

Contents

Specifications

Distributor

	4G3	4G5
Model	T3T 03872	LB–615, LB–63 (Canada)
Rotation	Clockwise	
Contact breaker gap	0·018 to 0·022 in (0·45 to 0·55 mm)	
Dwell angle	49 to 55°	
Condenser capacity	0·15 μF	

Centrifugal advance:
Initial	0° at 500 rpm	
Final	10° at 2,200 rpm	

Vacuum advance:
Initial	0° at 2·36 in Hg (60 mm Hg)	
Intermediate	4·5° at 5·91 in Hg (150 mm Hg)	
Final	10° at 14·17 in Hg (360 mm Hg)	

Ignition timing

Static . . . . 3° BTDC
Basic (engine idling) . . . . 5° BTDC at 700 rpm

Ignition coil

Type LB63
Primary coil resistance . . . . 1·4 ohms
Secondary coil resistance . . . . 10·2 K ohms
External resistor resistance . . . . 1·35 ohms
Insulation resistance at 500V . . . . Over 60 megohms

Spark plug type . . . . NGK BPR 5E3, Champion N12Y
Spark plug gap (except USA) . . . . 0·028 to 0·032 in (0·7 to 0·8 mm)
           (USA) . . . . 0·039 to 0·043 in (1·0 to 1·1 mm)

Firing order 1–3–4–2

Torque wrench setting

	lbf ft	kgf m
Spark plug	14 to 21	1·9 to 3·0

1 General description

In order that the engine may run correctly, the fuel/air charge in the cylinder needs to be ignited at exactly the right moment and the optimum time depends upon engine load and speed.

The ignition system ignites the charge by producing a high voltage electrical discharge between the electrodes of the spark plug. The moment of discharge is automatically varied to suit the engine load and speed.

The system has two main components, the ignition coil (photo), which consists of a low voltage and a high voltage winding which are coupled electromagentically, and the distributor, which is a mechanically operated switch, which helps to produce a spark at the required moment and routes it to the appropriate cylinder. During engine starting, the high current required by the starter motor produces a drop in the output voltage of the battery, and the ignition coil is designed to give its optimum output at this voltage and so ensure easy starting. When the engine is running and the battery output voltage rises, a resistor is switched into the ignition coil circuit so that the coil will be not overloaded.

Ignition timing is controlled automatically by a mechanical governor which produces the timing variations required at different engine speeds. A vacuum control (Fig. 4.2), which is operated by the suction of the induction manifold, varies the ignition timing according to engine load. On some engines there is a dual diaphragm vacuum control to provide the additional facility of retarding the ignition during idling to comply with anti-pollution legislation (Chapter 3, Section 17b).

2 Distributor – removal

1 Using a spanner on the crankshaft pulley nut, rotate the pulley until the notch in its rim is in line with the T mark on the indicator plate (photo).

2 Disconnect the battery leads, pull the ignition leads off the spark plugs and the high tension leads from the coil. Remove the low tension lead from the contact breaker, then unclip and remove the distributor cap.

3 Disconnect the vacuum hose(s) from the vacuum unit(s) taking care to label them if there is more than one.

4 Mark the position of the distributor mounting flange in relation to the cylinder block and note the position of the rotor arm.

5 Remove the distributor fixing screw and pull out the distributor.

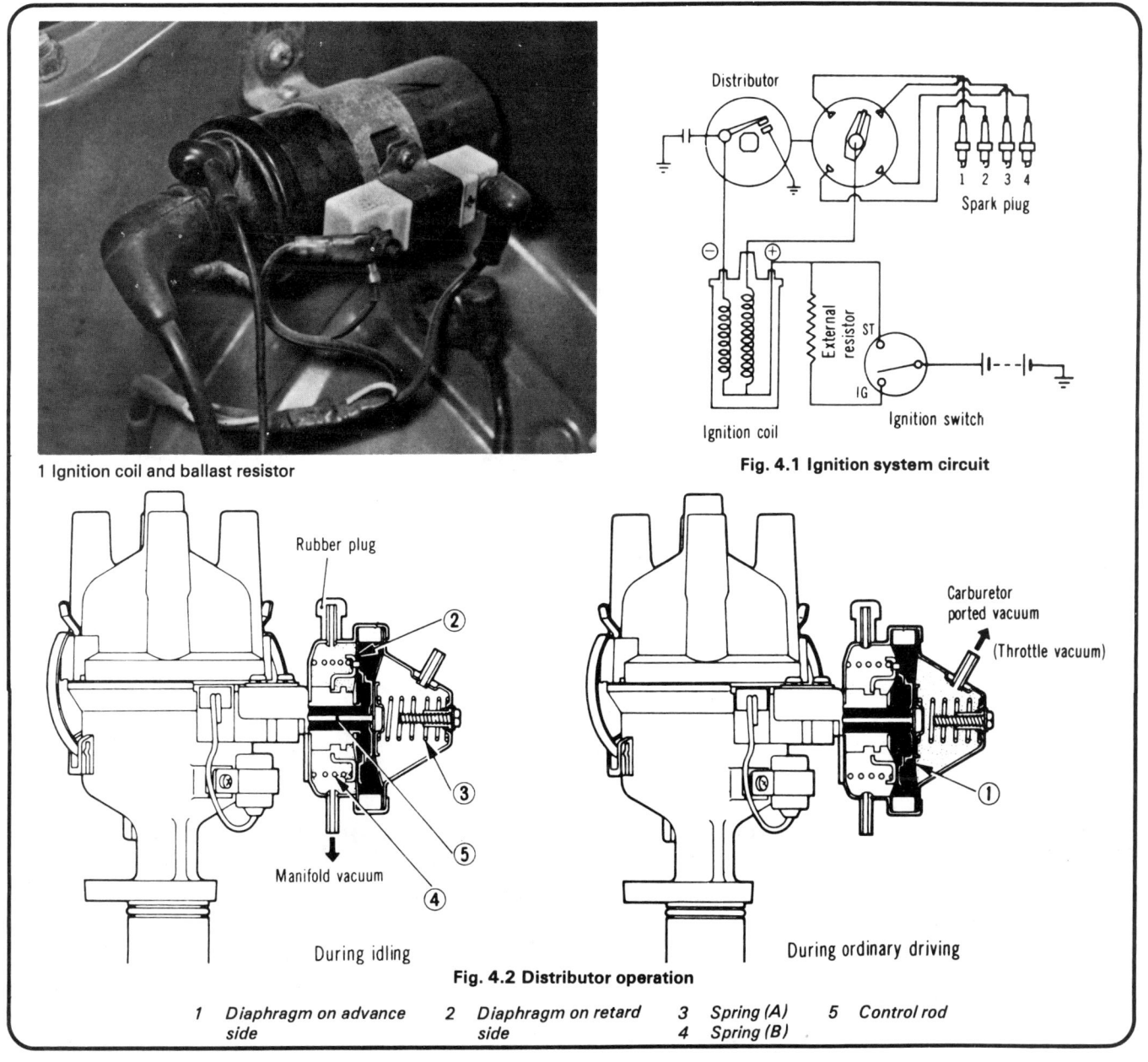

1 Ignition coil and ballast resistor

Fig. 4.1 Ignition system circuit

Fig. 4.2 Distributor operation

| 1 | Diaphragm on advance side | 2 | Diaphragm on retard side | 3 | Spring (A) | 5 | Control rod |
| | | | | 4 | Spring (B) | | |

3 Distributor – refitting

1   Turn the crankshaft until number 1 piston is at top dead centre on its compression stroke and the notch in the rim of the crankshaft pulley is opposite the T mark on the timing plate.

2   Turn the oil pump driveshaft until the slot in its end is at right angles to the centre line of the crankshaft, as shown in Fig. 4.3. The oil pump shaft can be turned easily with a long screwdriver.

3   Turn the distributor rotor until it is in position A of Fig. 4.5 and insert the distributor until it fits snugly into the oil pump groove. If the distributor shaft and the oil pump spindle do not engage with each other, turn the distributor spindle slightly until they are felt to engage. As the distributor drive gear engages with the gear on the camshaft, the rotor arm will turn slightly. When the distributor has been fitted, the rotor position should be as B in Fig. 4.6

4   Fit the distributor clamping nut and washer, and tighten the nut.

5   Adjust the contact breaker gap (see Section 6).

6   Fit the distributor cap. Reconnect the low tension lead, the spark plug leads and the high tension lead to the ignition coil.

7   Connect the vacuum hose, making sure that the hose is pushed firmly on to the distributor vacuum unit nipple.

8   Check the ignition timing as described in Section 7.

2.1 Crankshaft pulley notch and timing marks

4 Distributor – dismantling and reassembly

1   Remove the distributor from the car as described previously and then remove the rotor arm.

2   Remove the circlip from the vacuum control post on the contact breaker baseplate and lift the vacuum control rod off the post (photo).

3   Remove its two fixing screws then take off the vacuum control unit.

4   Remove the low tension lead to the contact breaker and remove the contact breaker assembly.

5   Remove the contact breaker baseplate assembly (photos).

6   Put mating marks on the gear and shaft, then, using a pin punch, drive out the pin, and remove the gear, collar and washer.

7   From the top of the distributor, pull out the governor and shaft assembly.

8   With the exception of the contact breaker assembly, wash all the parts in petrol and allow to dry.

9   Examine the gear for signs of wear and fit a new gear if the wear is excessive.

10 Check the shaft for excessive play, in its bearing, and endfloat. Renew if necessary.

11 Examine the contact breaker for signs of roughness and damage of the contact points. Unless the contacts are almost free from any signs of wear, fit a new contact breaker assembly.

12 Reassemble the distributor after lightly lubricating the spindle, pivots of the centrifugal weights and the bore of the cam. Smear a small quantity of multipurpose grease on to the cam surface.

13 Before refitting the distributor cap, suck the vacuum connection and check that the diaphragm is not punctured and that the rod moves and turns the contact breaker plate.

4.2 Vacuum control post and circlip (arrowed)

5 Distributor lubrication

1   It is important that the distributor is lubricated every six months or 6000 miles whichever comes sooner.

2   Remove the distributor cap and rotor arm. Apply a single drop of engine oil to the contact breaker pivot and the vacuum rod eye.

3   Smear oil onto the surface of the cam and apply as many drops of oil, as it will absorb, to the cam felt.

4   Apply two drops of oil to the recess in the top of the cam spindle and refit the rotor arm and distributor cap (Fig. 4.9).

6 Contact breaker – adjustment

1   Turn the engine over until the contact breaker points are as wide apart as possible. Check the gap. If it is incorrect proceed as follows:

2   Loosen the two contact breaker assembly clamping screws (Fig. 4.10) and insert a screwdriver into hole A. Fit the screwdriver to the edge of the visible part of the contact breaker base, so that as the

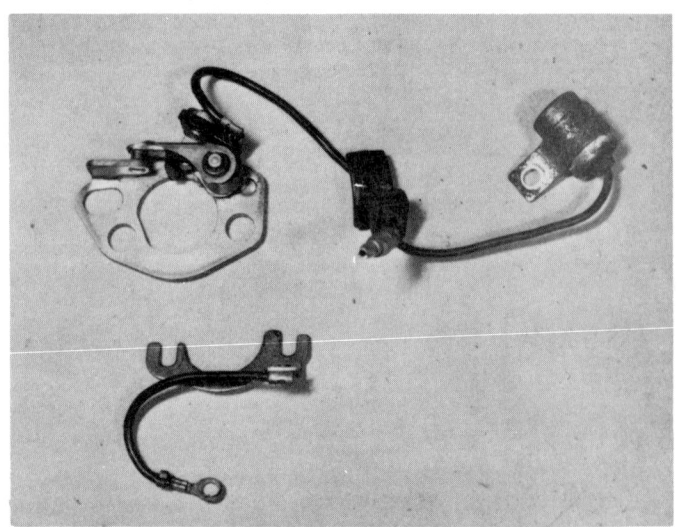

4.5a Contact breaker assembly (early version)

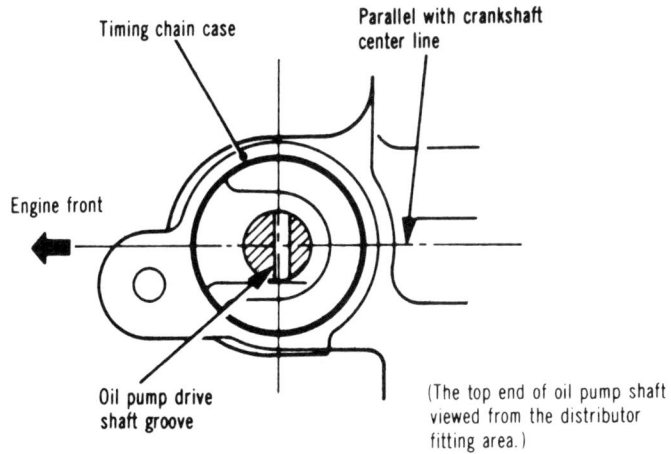

Fig. 4.3 Oil pump shaft position

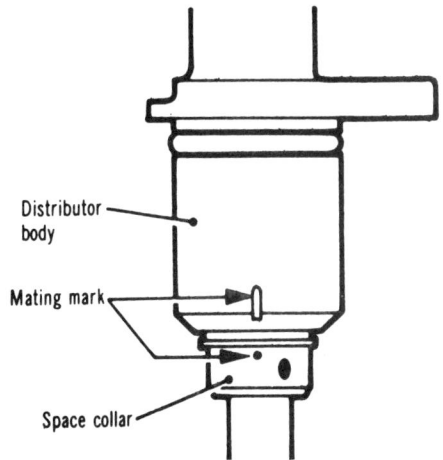

Fig. 4.4 Distributor mating mark 4G3

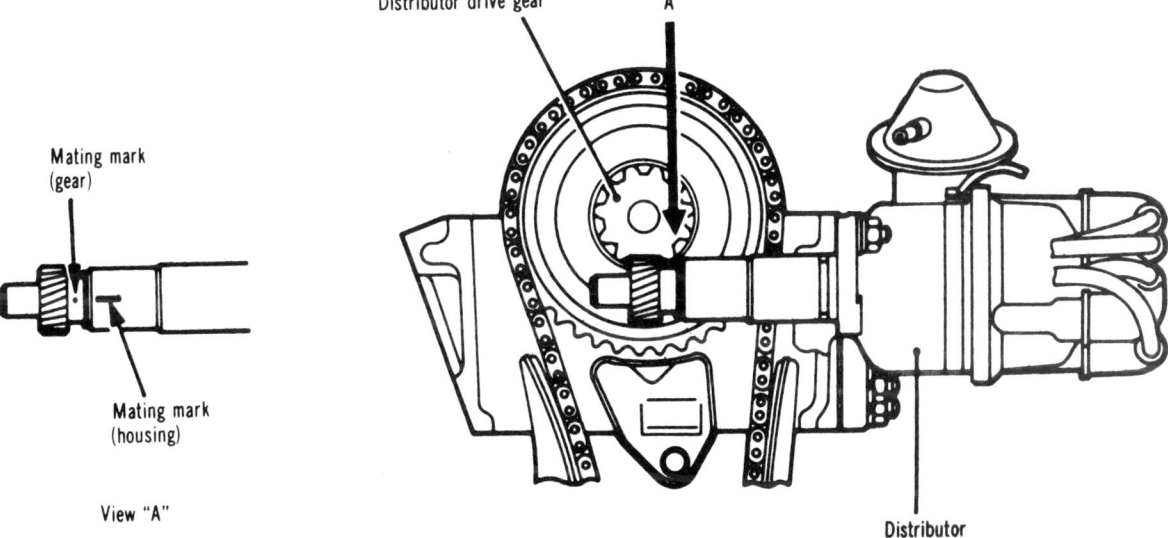

View "A"

Fig. 4.5 Engaging the distributor drive 4G5

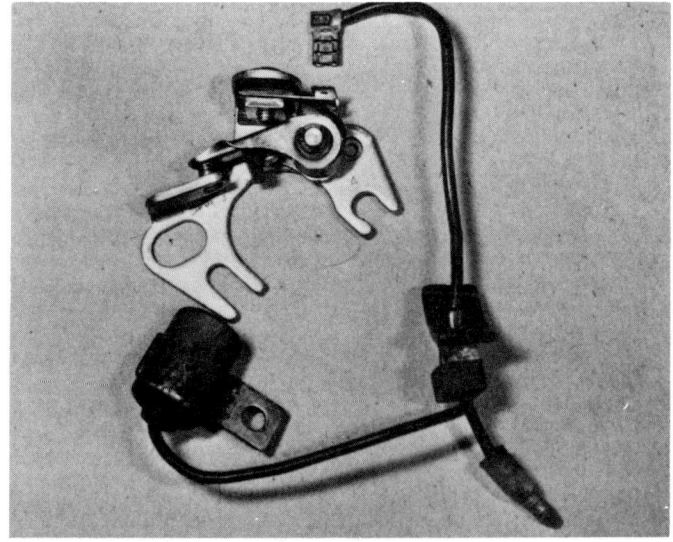

4.5b Contact breaker assembly (later version)

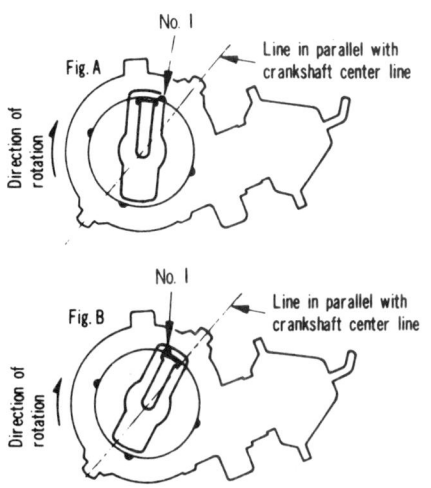

Fig. 4.6 Fitting the distributor

screwdriver is turned, the top plate moves and alters the separation of the contacts.

3   Adjust the gap between the contact to 0·018 to 0·021 in (0·457 to 0·533 mm) and tighten the clamping screws. When checking the gap, take care to wipe the feeler gauge to free it of any oil or dirt before inserting it between the contacts.

7   Ignition timing – setting and adjustment

Procedures are given for static setting and for dynamic setting. Although the static setting is generally satisfactory, dynamic setting is preferable because it is easier to compensate for backlash and wear in the distributor drive.

Static setting

1   Check the contact breaker gap as described in Section 6.
2   Take a 12V bulb of low wattage, such as a panel lamp or sidelamp and if no lamp holder is available, solder a wire to each of its contacts.
3   Turn the engine until the contact on the rotor arm points in the direction of where the number 1 cylinder plug lead segment in the distributor cap should be, and the notch in the crankshaft pulley rim is opposite the T mark on the timing plate. Then turn the crankshaft pulley until the notch is opposite the basic ignition timing position given in the Specifications.
4   Loosen the distributor fixings so that the distributor can be rotated between its end stops. Unlock the adjustment plate and set the ignition adjuster to its middle position (Fig. 4.11 and 4.12).
5   Disconnect the low tension lead to the contact breaker. Connect the contact breaker terminal to one of the test lamp wires. Connect the other test lamp wire to the positive terminal of the battery.
6   Switch on the ignition and if the contact breaker points are closed the test lamp will light and if they are open the lamp will not be lit. Turn the distributor head until a position is found where the lamp just goes from *on* to *off* ie the contacts start to separate.
7   Tighten the distributor fixings, taking care not to move the distributor from this position.

8   Rotate the crankshaft until the crankshaft pulley notch again approaches the basic timing mark, then, turning the crankshaft as slowly as possible, check that the lamp goes out as the motor passes the basic timing mark.
9   Switch off the ignition, remove the test lamp, reconnect the lead to the distributor contact breaker and refit the distributor cap.

Dynamic setting

10   Connect a timing light in accordance with its manufacturer's instructions.
111   Start the engine and, if possible, using an external tachometer, set it to the timing speed given in the Specifications and check whether the timing is correct.
12   To alter the timing, switch the engine off, undo the two locking screws of the ignition timing adjuster (Fig. 4.11 and 4.12), insert a Phillips type screwdriver and turn the adjuster in the required direction. Turning the adjuster alters the timing about 4° of crank angle for every division on the scale.
13   Start the engine again and recheck that the adjustment is correct. If so, stop the engine, lock the distributor adjuster and remove the timing light.

8   Distributor – advance and retard check

1   Connect a timing light in accordance with its manufacturer's instructions.
2   With the engine idling, check the timing as in the previous Section.
3   Disconnect the pipe from the intake manifold to the vacuum unit or remove the rubber plug, if fitted (Fig. 4.13). Increase engine speed to about 2000 rpm. Check that the ignition advances by about 10° as engine speed is increased, and retards when the speed falls to idling. If the timing does not change in this way, the centrifugal advance mechanism is not functioning.
4   Reconnect the vacuum pipe or refit the rubber plug and repeat the test. If the vacuum unit is satisfactory the ignition advance will be about 10° greater than in the previous test. If there is no difference, fit a new vacuum unit.

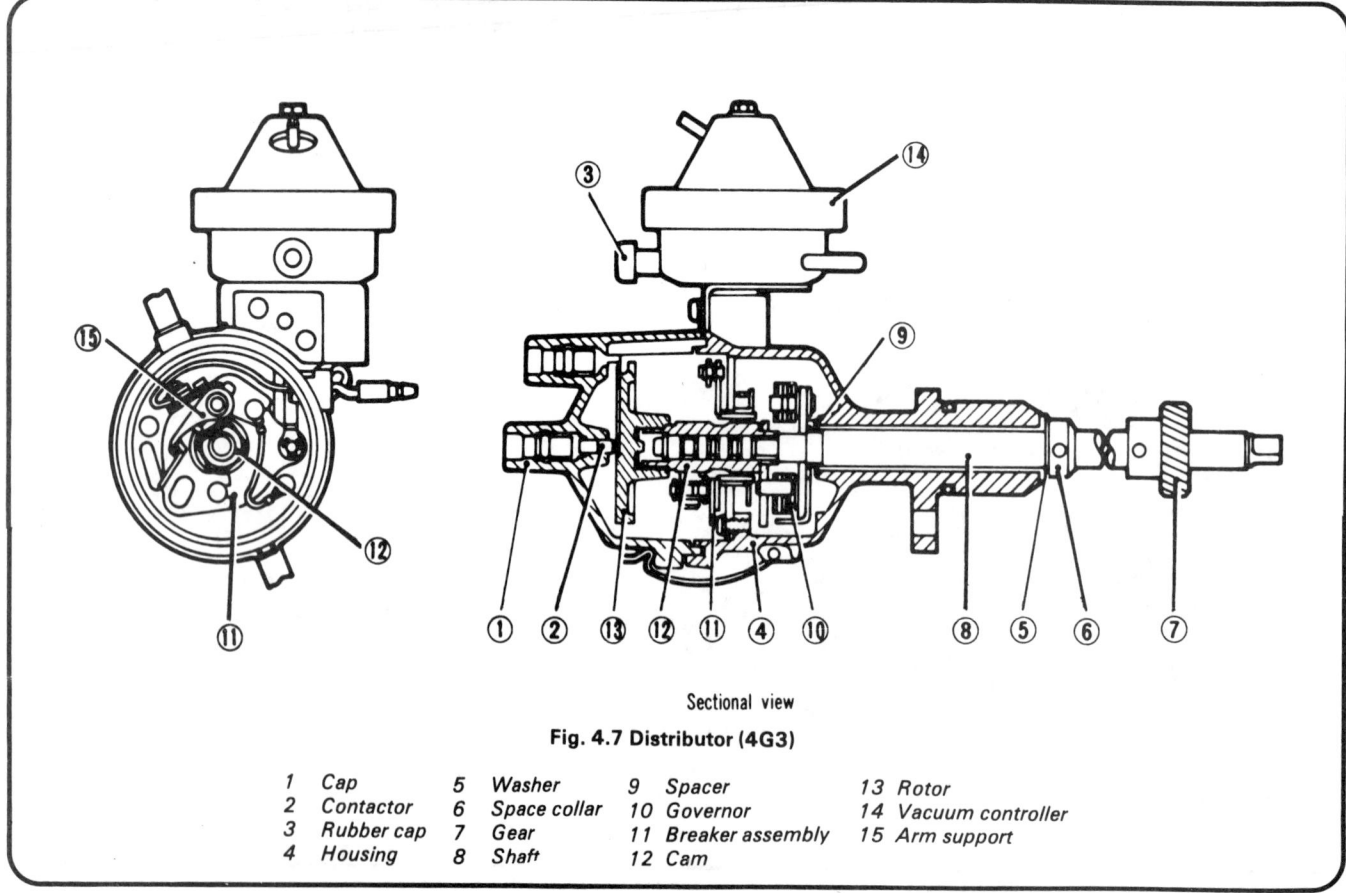

Sectional view

Fig. 4.7 Distributor (4G3)

1	Cap	5	Washer	9	Spacer	13	Rotor
2	Contactor	6	Space collar	10	Governor	14	Vacuum controller
3	Rubber cap	7	Gear	11	Breaker assembly	15	Arm support
4	Housing	8	Shaft	12	Cam		

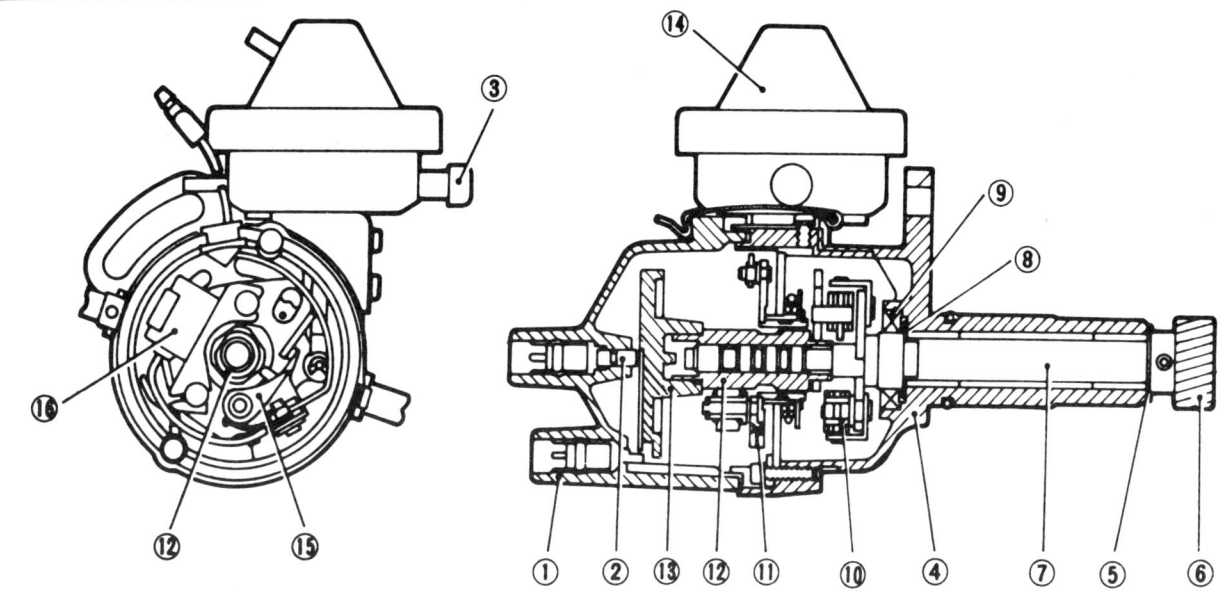

Sectional view

Fig. 4.8 Distributor (4G5)

1	Cap	9	Oil seal
2	Contactor	10	Governor
3	Rubber cap	11	Breaker assembly
4	Housing	12	Cam
5	Washer	13	Rotor
6	Gear	14	Vacuum controller
7	Shaft	15	Arm support
8	Washer	16	Condensor

7.2 Position of rotor for No 1 cylinder

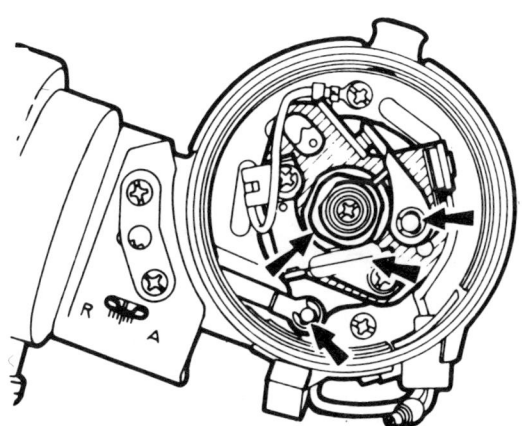

Fig. 4.9 Distributor lubrication points

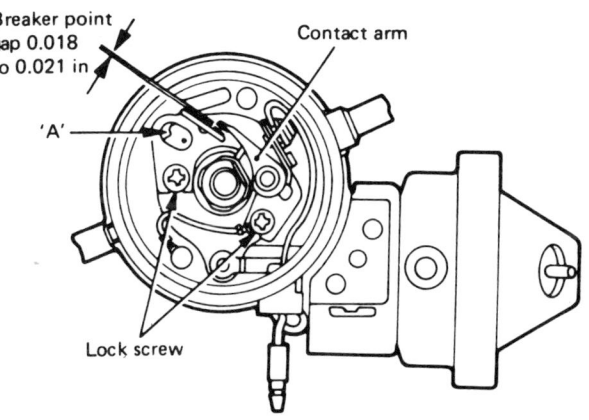

Fig. 4.10 Contact breaker adjustment

9 Distributor – capacitor check

A faulty capacitor will give bad starting and cause excessive burning of the contact breaker points.

1   Connect a 500V Megger between the positive capacitor terminal and the case. The capacitor is satisfactory if a reading of 5 Megohms or more is obtained.

2   While the Megger is still turning, disconnect it from the capacitor and immediately bring the capacitor positive wire close to the case. If the capacitor is satisfactory, a spark will jump from the wire to the case.

3   If no capacitor testing equipment is available, the unit can be checked by separating the points by hand with the ignition switched on. If this is accompanied by a flash it is indicative that the capacitor has failed. If the capacitor is suspect the quickest method of testing is to renew the unit and to note if there is any improvement.

10 Spark plugs and HT leads

See illustrations on page 83.

1   The correct functioning of the spark plugs is vital for the smooth running and efficiency of the engine.

2   At intervals of 5000 miles (8000 km), the plugs should be removed, examined, and cleaned. The condition of the spark plugs will also tell much about the overall condition of the engine. The plugs should be renewed at intervals of 15 000 miles (24 000 km).

3   If the insulator nose of the spark plug is clean and white, with no deposits, this is indicative of a weak mixture, or too hot a plug (a hot plug transfers heat away from the electrode slowly – a cold plug transfers it away quickly).

4   The plugs fitted as standard are as listed in Specifications at the head of this Chapter. If the tip and insulator nose are covered with hard black looking deposits, then this is indicative that the mixture is too rich. Should the plug be black and oily, then it is likely that the engine is fairly worn, as well as the mixture being too rich.

5   If the insulator nose is covered with light tan or greyish brown deposits, then the mixture is correct and it is likely that the engine is in good condition.

6   If there are any traces of long brown tapering stains on the outside of the white portion of the plug it will have to be renewed. This shows that there is a faulty joint between the plug body and the insulator, and compression is being allowed to leak away.

7   Plugs should be cleaned by a sand blasting machine which will free them from carbon more thoroughly than cleaning by hand. The machine will also test the condition of the plugs under compression. Any plug that fails to spark at the recommended pressure should be renewed.

8   The spark plug gap is of considerable importance, as, if it is too large or too small, the size of the spark will be incorrect and its efficiency will be seriously impaired. The spark plug should be set to the figure given in Specifications at the beginning of this Chapter.

9   To set it, measure the gap with a feeler gauge, and then bend open or close, the outer plug electrode until the correct gap is achieved. The centre electrode should never be bent as this may crack the insulation and cause plug failure if nothing worse.

10   When refitting the plugs, remember to use new plug washers. Refit the leads from the distributor in the correct firing order, which is 1, 3, 4, 2, No. 1 cylinder being the one nearest the radiator.

11   The plug leads require no routine attention other than being kept clean and wiped over regularly.

12   At intervals of 5000 miles (8000 km) or 3 months, however, pull the leads off the plugs and distributor one at a time and make sure no water has found its way on to the connections. Remove any corrosion from the brass ends, wipe the collars on top of the distributor, and refit the leads.

11 Ignition system – fault diagnosis

There are two main symptoms indicating faults. Either the engine will not start or fire, or the engine is difficult to start and misfires. If it is a regular misfire, ie the engine is only running on two or three cylinders, the fault is almost sure to be in the secondary, or high tension circuit. If the misfiring is intermittent, the fault could be in

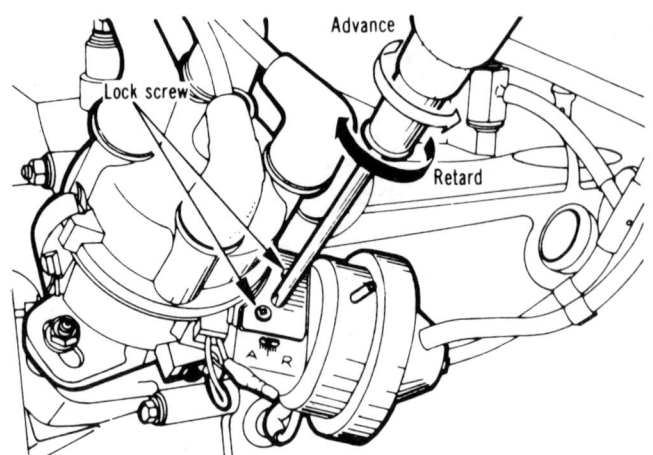

Fig. 4.11 Ignition adjustment (4G3)

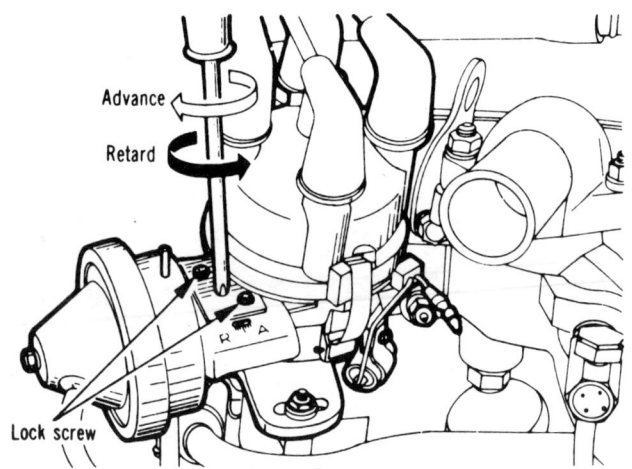

Fig. 4.12 Ignition adjustment (4G11)

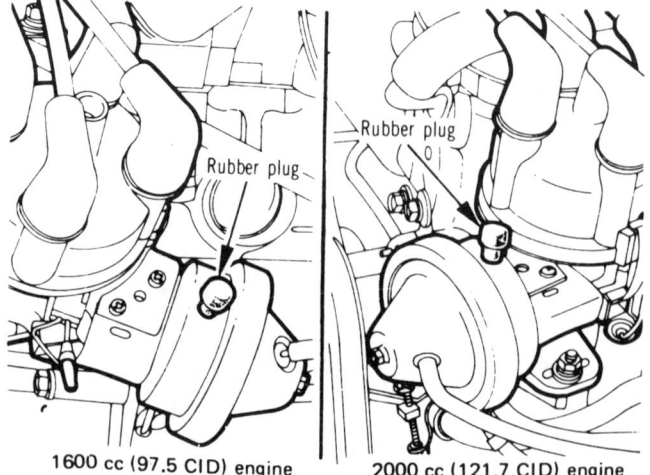

1600 cc (97.5 CID) engine   2000 cc (121.7 CID) engine

Fig. 4.13 Distributor rubber plug

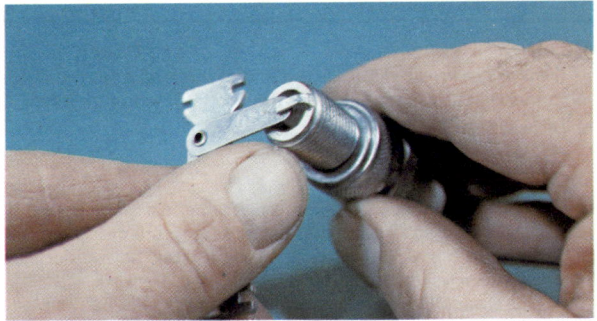

Measuring plug gap. A feeler gauge of the correct size (see ignition system specifications) should have a slight 'drag' when slid between the electrodes. Adjust gap if necessary

Adjusting plug gap. The plug gap is adjusted by bending the earth electrode inwards, or outwards, as necessary until the correct clearance is obtained. Note the use of the correct tool

Normal. Grey-brown deposits, lightly coated core nose. Gap increasing by around 0.001 in (0.025 mm) per 1000 miles (1600 km). Plugs ideally suited to engine, and engine in good condition

Carbon fouling. Dry, black, sooty deposits. Will cause weak spark and eventually misfire. Fault: over-rich fuel mixture. Check: carburettor mixture settings, float level and jet sizes; choke operation and cleanliness of air filter. Plugs can be re-used after cleaning

Oil fouling. Wet, oily deposits. Will cause weak spark and eventually misfire. Fault: worn bores/piston rings or valve guides; sometimes occurs (temporarily) during running-in period. Plugs can be re-used after thorough cleaning

Overheating. Electrodes have glazed appearance, core nose very white – few deposits. Fault: plug overheating. Check: plug value, ignition timing, fuel octane rating (too low) and fuel mixture (too weak). Discard plugs and cure fault immediately

Electrode damage. Electrodes burned away; core nose has burned, glazed appearance. Fault: pre-ignition. Check: as for 'Overheating' but may be more severe. Discard plugs and remedy fault before piston or valve damage occurs

Split core nose (may appear initially as a crack). Damage is self-evident, but cracks will only show after cleaning. Fault: pre-ignition or wrong gap-setting technique. Check: ignition timing, cooling system, fuel octane rating (too low) and fuel mixture (too weak). Discard plugs, rectify fault immediately

either the high or low tension circuits. If the car stops suddenly or will not start at all, it is likely that the fault is in the low tension circuit. Loss of power and overheating (apart from carburation or emission control system faults – see Chapter 3), are normally due to faults in the distributor or incorrect ignition timing.

Engine fails to start

1   If the engine fails to start and the car was running normally when it was last used, first check there is fuel in the petrol tank. If it turns over normally on the starter motor and the battery is evidently well charged, then the fault may be in either the high or low tension circuits. First check the HT circuit. **Note:** *If the battery is known to be fully charged, the ignition light comes on, and the starter motor fails to turn the engine check the tightness of the leads on the battery terminals and the secureness of the earth lead at its connection to the body.* It is quite common for the leads to have worked loose, even if they look and feel secure. If one of the battery terminal posts gets very hot when trying to work the starter motor, this is a sure indication of a faulty connection to that terminal.

2   One of the commonest reasons for bad starting is wet or damp spark plug leads and distributor. Remove the distributor cap. If condensation is visible internally dry the cap with a rag and also wipe over the leads. Refit the cap.

3   If the engine still fails to start, check that current is reaching the plugs, by disconnecting each plug lead in turn at the spark plug end, and holding the end of the cable about $\frac{3}{16}$ in (5 mm) away from the cylinder block. Spin the engine on the starter motor.

4   Sparking between the end of the cable and the block should be fairly strong with a strong regular blue spark. (Hold the lead with rubber to avoid electric shock). If current is reaching the plugs, then remove them and clean and regap them to 0·030 in (0·76 mm).

5   If there is no spark at the plug leads take off the HT lead from the centre of the distributor cap and hold it to the block as before. Spin the engine on the starter once more. A rapid succession of blue sparks between the end of the lead and the block indicate that the coil is in order and that the distributor cap is cracked, the rotor arm faulty, or the carbon brush in the top of the distributor cap is not making good contact with the spring on the rotor arm. Possibly, the points are in bad

condition.

6   If there are no sparks from the end of the lead from the coil, check the connections at the coil end of the lead. If it is in order start checking the low tension circuit.

Engine misfires

7   If the engine misfires regularly run it at a fast idling speed. Pull off each of the plug caps in turn and listen to the note of the engine. Hold the plug cap in a dry cloth or with a rubber glove as additional protection against a shock from the HT supply.

8   No difference in engine running will be noticed when the lead from the defective circuit is removed. Removing the lead from one of the good cylinders will accentuate the misfire.

9   Remove the plug lead from the end of the defective plug and hold it about $\frac{3}{16}$ in (5 mm) away from the block. Re-start the engine. If the sparking its fairly strong and regular the fault must lie in the spark plug.

10   The plug may be loose, the insulation may be cracked, or the points may have burnt away giving too wide a gap for the spark to jump. Worse still, one of the points may have broken off. Either renew the plug, or clean it. Reset the gap, and then test it.

11   If there is no spark at the end of the plug lead, or if it is weak and intermittent, check the ignition lead from the distributor to the plug. If the insulation is cracked or perished, renew the lead. Check the connections at the distributor cap.

12   If there is still no spark, examine the distributor cap carefully for tracking. This can be recognised by a very thin black line running between an electrode and some other part of the distributor. These lines are paths which now conduct electricity across the cap thus letting it run to earth. The only answer is a new distributor cap.

13   Apart from the ignition being incorrect, other causes of misfiring have already been dealt with under the Section dealing with the failure of the engine to start. These are:

   (a) *The coil may be faulty giving an intermittent misfire*
   (b) *There may be a damaged lead or loose connection in the low tension circuit*
   (c) *The condenser may be short circuiting*
   (d) *There may be a mechanical fault in the distributor*

Chapter 5 Clutch

Contents

Specifications

	4G32	4G33	4G52	4G54
Type	Single dry disc	Single dry disc	Single dry disc	Single dry disc
Clutch control	Cable operated	Cable operated	Cable operated	Cable operated
Clutch dimensions (OD x ID x thickness)	7·874 x 5·512 x 0·138 in (200 x 140 x 3·5 mm)	7·252 x 5·000 x 0·126 in (184·2 x 127 x 3·2 mm)	8·465 x 5·906 x 0·126 in (215 x 150 x 3·2 mm)	8·86 x 5·91 x 0·307 in (225 x 150 x 7·8 mm)
Facing area	24·8 in² (160 cm²)	21·7 in² (140 cm²)	28·8 in² (190 cm²)	34·2 in² (220 cm²)
Facing material		Semimold		Special woven
Pressure plate type	Diaphragm spring	Diaphragm spring	Diaphragm spring	Diaphragm spring
Setting load	793·7 lbs (360 kg)	727·5 lbs (330 kg)	882 lbs (400 kg)	904 lbs (410 kg)

	4G3	4G52	4G54
Distance between clutch pedal and toe-board	6·8 in (175 mm)	6·8 in (175 mm)	7·2 in (185 mm)
Clutch pedal stroke	5·5 in (140 mm)	5·5 in (140 mm)	5·9 in (150 mm)

Adjusting nut to cable holder clearance
1600 cc models . . . . 0·2 to 0·24 in (5 to 6 mm)
2000 cc estate car . . . . 0·14 to 0·18 in (3·5 to 4·5 mm)
One turn of the nut alters the clearance 0·06 in (1·5 mm)

Adjusting nut to insulator clearance
2600 cc estate car . . . . 0·12 to 0·16 in (3 to 4 mm)

Clutch pedal free play
Except estate car . . . . 0·8 to 1·2 in (20 to 30 mm)
Estate car . . . . 0·4 to 0·6 in (10 to 15 mm)

Clearance between toe board and clutch pedal when pedal is depressed fully
Except estate car . . . .   0·59 in (15 mm) minimum
Estate car . . . .   1 in (25 mm) minimum

Torque wrench settings

	lbf ft	kgf m
Pressure plate mounting bolts	11 to 15	1·5 to 2·2

1   General description

The clutch enables the engine torque to be applied progressively to the gearbox for starting from rest smoothly and isolates engine torque whilst changing gear. The pressure plate is of the single dry plate type, with a diaphragm spring. A cable transfers the force applied to the pedal and operates the clutch lever and shaft assembly.

The clutch plate is riveted together and should not be dismantled. No adjustment is required during the life of the clutch facing and when necessary, the complete plate assembly is renewed.

2   Clutch – removal, inspection and refitting

1   Remove the gearbox from the engine as described in Chapter 6.
2   Mark the clutch cover and flywheel so that the clutch may be refitted in its original position, unless it is to be renewed. The clutch cover, pressure plate and diaphragm spring assembly must be renewed as a unit if it is found to be faulty. Only the clutch plate is able to be renewed as a separate component.
3   Insert a clutch centralising tool, or a suitable piece of round material into the clutch plate, so that it does not fall out when the pressure plate is removed. Progressively slacken the six pressure plate to flywheel bolts, a turn at a time, so releasing them evenly. As they are being released, check that the pressure plate flange is not binding on the dowels, otherwise it could fly off.
4   Lift away the six bolts and spring washers, followed by the pressure plate assembly and clutch plate. *Note which way round the clutch plate is fitted.* The longer boss is facing towards the gearbox.

5   Using a stiff brush or clean rags, clean the face of the flywheel, the pressure plate assembly and the clutch plate. Note that the dust is harmful to the lungs as it contains asbestos, so do not inhale it.
6   It is important that neither oil or grease comes into contact with the clutch facings, and that absolute cleanliness is observed at all times.
7   Inspect the friction surfaces of the clutch plate and, if worn, a complete new assembly must be fitted. The linings are completely worn out when the faces of the rivets are flush with the lining face. There should be at least 0.012 in (0.3 mm) of lining material left clear of the rivet faces, or the clutch plate is not worth refitting. Check that the friction linings show no signs of heavy glazing or oil impregnation. If evident, a new assembly must be fitted. If a small quantity of lubricant has found its way on to the facing, it will be burnt off. This will be indicated by darkening of the facings. This is not too serious provided that the grain of the facing material can be clearly identified. Fit a new assembly if there is any doubt at all. It is important that if oil impregnation is present, the cause of the oil leak is found and rectified to prevent recurrence.
8   Carefully inspect the pressure plate and flywheel contact faces for signs of overheating, distortion, cracking and scoring; if any serious evidence of scoring exists, then it will probably be necessary to have the flywheel skimmed; if you simply renew the clutch plate, you could very soon be faced with the same faulty condition. Renew the pressure plate assembly if necessary.
9   Mount the clutch plate onto the input shaft and check for looseness or wear on the hub splines. Also check the clutch plate damper springs for damage or looseness.
10 Remove the spring clip retaining the bearing carrier (photo), then

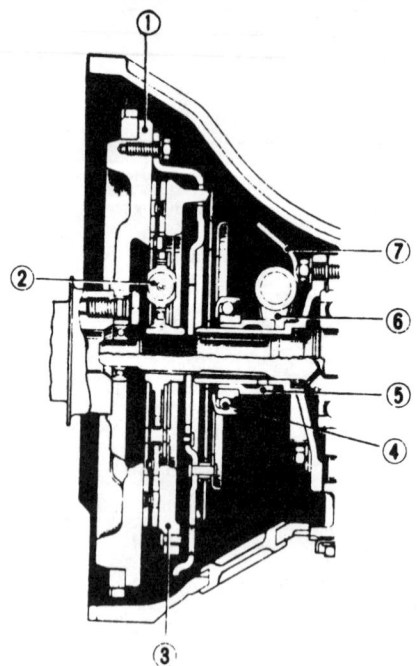

Fig. 5.1 Clutch – sectional view

1 Flywheel	5 Bearing carrier
2 Friction plate	6 Shift fork
3 Pressure plate	7 Return spring
4 Release bearing	

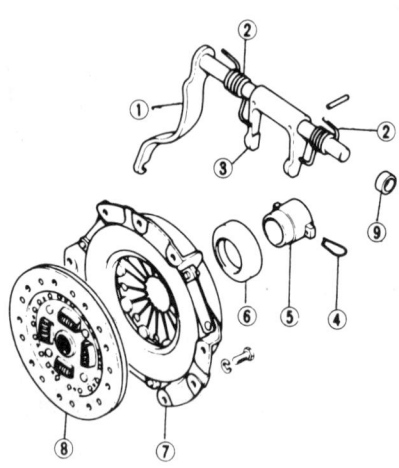

Fig. 5.2 Clutch components

1 Clutch shaft	6 Release bearing
2 Return spring	7 Pressure plate assembly
3 Shift fork	8 Friction plate
4 Clip	9 Felt
5 Bearing carrier	

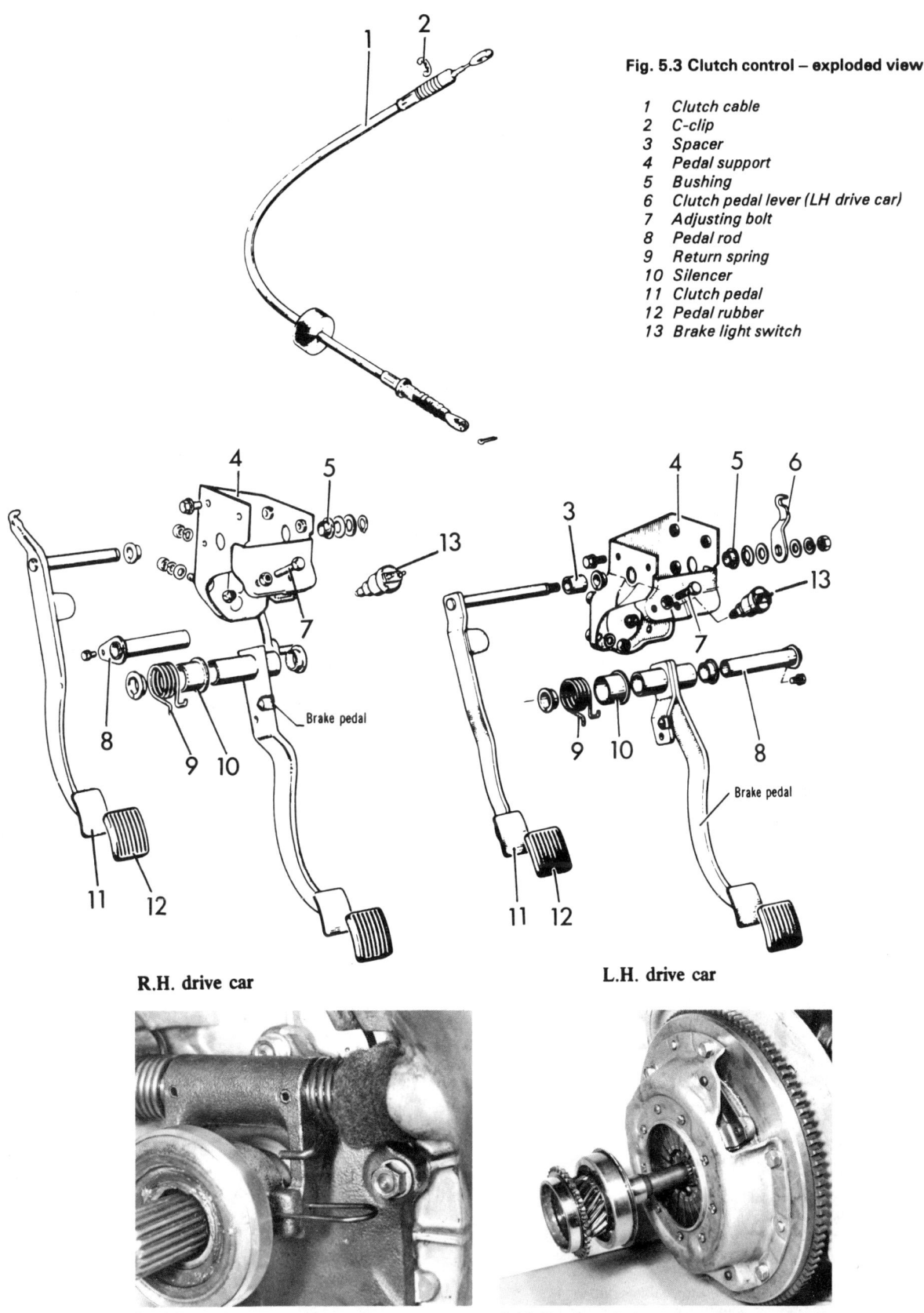

Fig. 5.3 Clutch control – exploded view

1   Clutch cable
2   C-clip
3   Spacer
4   Pedal support
5   Bushing
6   Clutch pedal lever (LH drive car)
7   Adjusting bolt
8   Pedal rod
9   Return spring
10 Silencer
11 Clutch pedal
12 Pedal rubber
13 Brake light switch

Brake pedal

Brake pedal

R.H. drive car

L.H. drive car

2.10 Clutch bearing and retainer

2.14 Gearbox shaft used as clutch centralising tool

remove the bearing carrier and bearing.

11 Drive out the two lock pins from the shift arm and remove the shift arm, springs and felts.

12 Clean the clutch bearings, but do not use any solvent because the bearing is grease packed. If the bearing shows any signs of burning, roughness, sloppiness or abnormal wear of the contact face against the diaphragm claws, fit a new bearing. Also clean the components of the release mechanism, examine them for wear and renew as required.

13 Check the condition of the clutch pilot bearing (spigot bush). Further reference to this is made in Chapter 1, Section 20.

14 Using a clutch centralising tool, or a makeshift means of keeping the clutch plate concentric with the spigot bush (photo) fit the clutch plate. If the clutch plate is not centralised accurately, it will be very difficult to insert the gearbox first motion shaft into the clutch when refitting the gearbox. Ensure that the clutch plate is fitted so that the larger boss is towards the gearbox.

15 Offer up the pressure plate assembly, align the scribed marks if refitting the original assembly, refit the fixing bolts and washers then tighten the bolts progressively a turn at a time until the recommended torque wrench setting is achieved. It will be necessary to prevent the flywheel from rotating while tightening the pressure plate bolts. This can be done by engaging a suitable piece of metal in the flywheel teeth (photo), or by jamming a spanner on the crankshaft pulley.

16 Smear a little thin grease or engine oil on to the splines of the gearbox shaft and refit the gearbox.

3 Clutch bearing – removal, inspection and refitting

When it is required to remove the bearing, without dismantling the clutch assembly, it is only necessary to carry out the operations described in paragraphs 1, 10, 11, 12 and 16 of the previous Section.

4 Clutch cable – removal and refitting

1 Loosen the cable adjusting wheel inside the engine compartment, or pull off the cable adjuster snap-ring (photo) in the engine compartment, depending on which method of adjustment is used.

2 Loosen the lock nut on the clutch pedal adjuster bolt and back off the bolt as far as possible.

3 Remove the cotter pin from the clutch shift lever on the bellhousing.

4 Unhook the cable eye from the lever on the clutch pedal and withdraw the cable assembly from inside the engine compartment.

5 Inspect the cable for breakage and damage, renewing it if necessary.

6 Lubricate the cable with engine oil, refit it reversing the removal procedure and adjust it as described in Section 6.

7 After fitting the cable, use pads at the following points to prevent the cable from chafing:

RH drive cars – side of alternator (photo) and at the inner side of the engine front mounting
LH drive cars – intake manifold side of engine and rear of engine front mounting

5 Clutch pedal – removal and refitting

1 Remove the clutch cable from the clutch pedal as described in the previous Section.

2 Withdraw the split cotter and pull out the clevis pin connecting the pedal to the push rod yoke of the brake servo.

3 Remove the nuts securing the brake servo to the front bulkhead and withdraw the servo. On the estate car it is only necessary to remove the nuts.

4 On RH drive cars, slacken the accelerator cable adjuster fully, to provide maximum travel for the accelerator pedal, then remove the split cotter and washer from the pedal pivot. Remove the pedal.

5 Remove the pedal support bolts and nuts (bolts only on estate car) and remove the clutch pedal, brake pedal and pedal support as an assembly.

6 Pull the snap-ring off the RH end of the clutch pedal shaft and

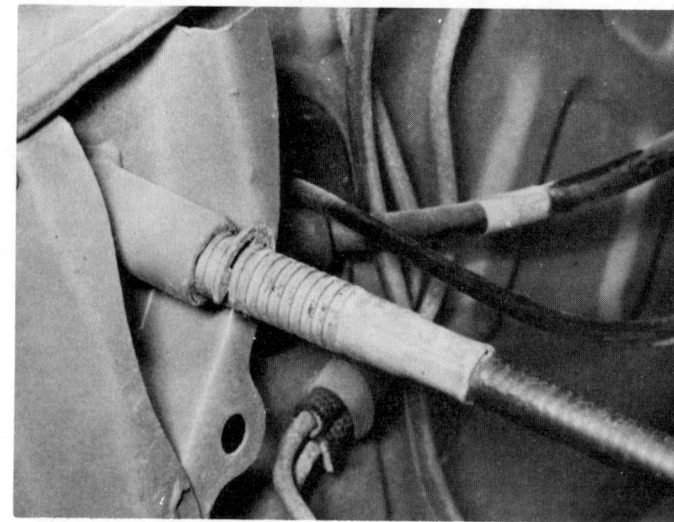
4.1 Snap-ring cable adjuster

4.7 Clutch cable buffer

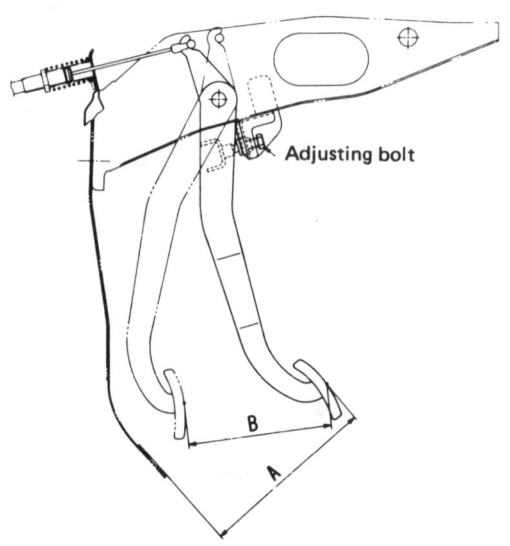
Adjusting bolt

Fig. 5.4 Clutch pedal adjustment

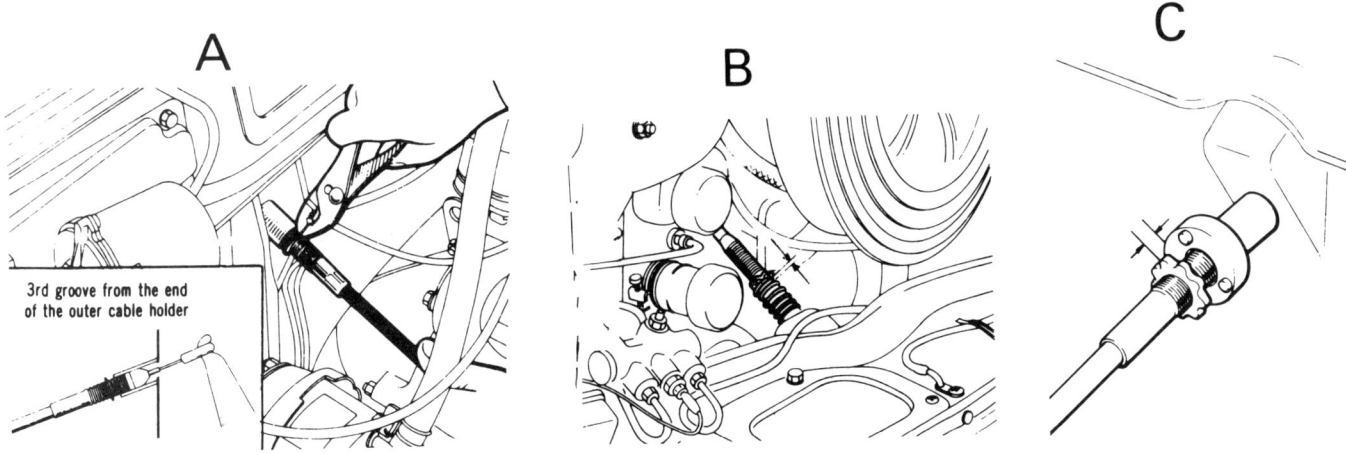

Fig. 5.5 Clutch cable adjustment   *A C-clip adjustment*   *B Wheel adjustment (except estate car)*   *C Wheel adjustment (estate car)*

withdraw the pedal (RHD), or remove the nut from the end of the clutch pedal shaft (LHD).
7   Check the pedal shaft bushes for wear and fit new ones if necessary.
8   Refit the pedal as the reverse of removal. Apply grease to the pedal shaft, to the connections of the cable to the pedal and to the clutch operating lever.
9   Check the adjustment of the clutch pedal stroke (Section 6) and adjust the clutch cable.
10   Refit the accelerator pedal and adjust its cable (RHD).

6   Clutch pedal and clutch cable – adjustment

1   Slacken the locknut of the clutch pedal adjuster bolt and turn the

bolt until the pedal height from the floor is as given in the Specifications.
2   On models which are fitted with a C-clip adjuster, remove the C-clip from the outer cable in the engine compartment. Pull the outer cable until all the slack has been taken up and resistance is being felt. Then fit the C-clip in the third groove from the end of the cable holder (Fig. 5.5).
3   On models with screw adjusters, pull the cable gently from the cable holder on the toe board and turn the adjuster until the free play is as given in the Specifications.
4   Check that the pedal stroke is as specified. Insufficient pedal stroke results in insufficient clutch movement for complete disengagement. If necessary re-adjust the clutch pedal stop to give the correct pedal travel and then tighten the pedal stop locknut.

7   Fault diagnosis – clutch

Symptom	Reason/s
Judder when taking up drive	Loose engine mountings Worn, or oil contaminated clutch plate friction linings Worn splines on clutch plate hub, or gearbox input shaft Worn crankshaft spigot bush (pilot bearing)
Clutch slip	Damaged or distorted pressure plate assembly Clutch plate linings worn, or oil contaminated
Noise on depressing clutch pedal	Dry, worn, or damaged clutch release bearing Excessive play in input shaft splines
Noise as clutch pedal is released	Distorted clutch plate Broken, or weak, clutch plate hub cushion coil springs Distorted, or worn, input shaft Release bearing loose
Difficulty in disengaging clutch for gearchange	Clutch operation cable incorrectly adjusted, or damaged Gearbox drive shaft splines worn, or damaged Gearbox drive shaft splines need lubricating

Chapter 6 Manual gearbox and automatic transmission

Contents

Part A – Manual gearbox

Part B – Automatic transmission

Specifications

Four-speed gearbox

Number of gears	4 forward, 1 reverse
Synchromesh	All forward gears
Ratios	
First	3·525 : 1
Second	2·193 : 1
Third	1·442 : 1
Fourth	1·000 : 1
Reverse	3·867 : 1
Control system	Floor shift
Oil capacity	3·0 pints (1·8 US qts, 1·7 litres)

Five-speed gearbox

Number of gears	5 forward, 1 reverse
Synchromesh	All forward gears
Ratios	
First	3·369
Second	2·035
Third	1·360
Fourth	1·000

Fifth	0·856
Reverse	3·635

Control system .... Floor shift

Oil capacity .... 4·0 pints (2·4 US qts, 2·3 litres)

Torqueflite automatic transmission

Stalling torque ratio .... 2·5 : 1

Torque converter
Nominal diameter .... $9\frac{1}{2}$ in

Ratios

First	2·45 : 1
Second	1·45 : 1
Third	1·00 : 1
Reverse	2·2 : 1

Fluid .... Dexron type

Refill capacity .... 1·4 gal (1·7 US gal, 6·4 litres)

Torque wrench settings	lbf ft	kgf m
Manual gearbox		
Transmission mounting bolts	22 to 30	3 to 4·2
Starter mounting bolts	15 to 21	2 to 3
Mainshaft locknut	36 to 72	5 to 10
Front bearing retainer	7 to 9	1 to 1·3
Extension housing bolts	11 to 16	1·5 to 2·2
Bottom cover bolts	5·8 to 7·2	0·8 to 1
Automatic transmission		
Converter drive plate to crankshaft	83 to 90	11·5 to 12·4
Converter housing	22 to 30	3 to 4·1
Kickdown band adjusting screw	6	0·8
Kickdown band locknut	35	4·8
Low and reverse band adjuster	3·4	0·47
Low and reverse band locknut	30	4·1
Oil pan	12·5	1·75
Cooler line nuts	7	0·98
Transmission mounting bolts	21 to 25	2·9 to 3·5
Bottom cover attachment bolts	6 to 7	0·8 to 1·0

Part A Manual gearbox

1 General description

The manual transmission fitted to models covered by this manual will be one of two types, depending upon the engine capacity, model type and intended market. The number of forward gears may be four, or five, all of them being synchromesh. A reverse gear of the sliding spur type is fitted to both gearboxes and the operation of all the gears is by a floor mounted gear shift lever.

A Torquelite automatic transmission is available on some models and information on this is given in Part B of this Chapter.

2 Manual gearbox – removal and refitting

1 Remove the air cleaner and battery leads.
2 Remove the starter motor.
3 Remove the two bolts from the top of the gearbox.
4 From inside the car remove the console base. For cars not fitted with the console base, remove the transmission tunnel carpet.
5 Remove the dust cover retaining plate by removing the lock screws.
6 Remove the four attaching bolts at the lower part of the extension housing. For the four or five speed gearbox, remove the gear shift lever assembly. **Note**: *On cars fitted with the 4-speed gearbox, remove the gearshift lever while it is in the second gear position. On cars fitted with the 5-speed gearbox, remove the gear shift lever while it is in the first speed position.*
7 With the car supported on stands, drain the transmission fluid.

8 Remove the speedometer cable and the reversing light switch wiring from the gearbox.
9 Remove the bolts from the propeller shaft and draw the propeller shaft out of the gearbox.
10 Disconnect the exhaust pipe from its bracket.
11 Disconnect the clutch cables.
12 With the gearbox supported on a trolley jack, remove the insulator from the members by removing the attaching bolts.
13 Detach each member from the frame and pull them off sideways.
14 Remove the bellhousing cover.
15 Remove the remaining bolts from the gearbox and carefully draw it rearwards from the engine.
16 Refitting is a reversal of the removal procedure but note the following:

   (a) Check that the bellhousing cover is not bent
   (b) When refitting the gear shift assembly, place the shift lever in the second gear position for the 4-speed gearbox and in the first speed position for the 5-speed gearbox. Carefully refit the linkage on the 3-speed gearbox
   (c) Adjust the clutch if it is out of adjustment
   (d) Refill the gearbox with the correct grade of oil
   (e) Tighten all bolts to the correct torque wrench settings

3 Five-speed gearbox – dismantling

1 Before starting to dismantle the gearbox, clean the exterior with a water-soluble degreasing agent. This will make the gearbox easier to handle and will lessen the chance of the interior being contaminated with dirt.

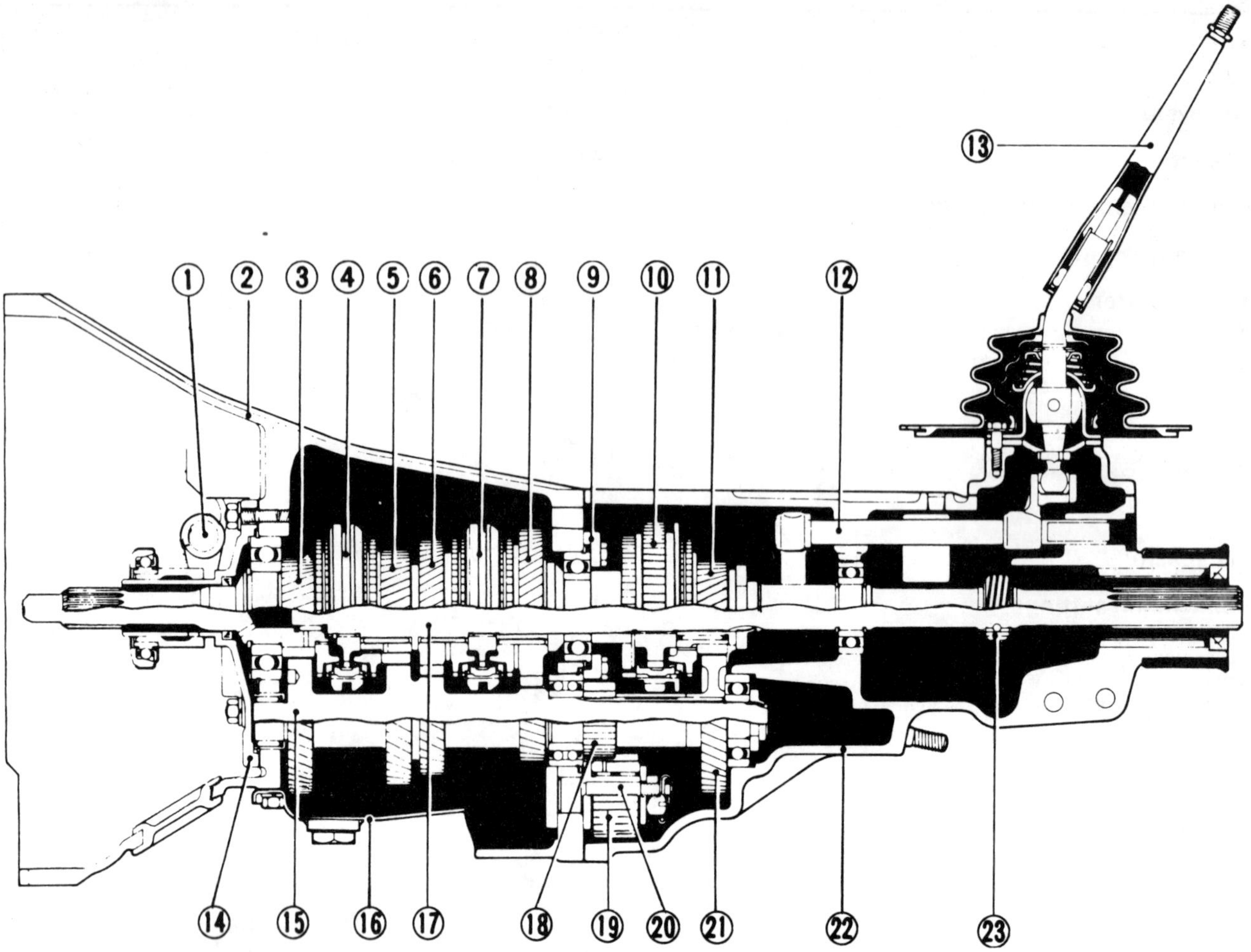

Fig. 6.1 Five speed gearbox – sectional view

1 Clutch control shaft	7 Synchronizer (1-2 speed)	12 Control shaft	18 Counter reverse gear
2 Transmission case	8 1st speed gear	13 Control lever	19 Reverse idle gear
3 Main drive gear	9 Rear bearing retainer	14 Front bearing retainer	20 Reverse idle gear shaft
4 Synchronizer (3-4 speed)	10 Synchronizer (reverse and overdrive)	15 Countershaft gear	21 Counter overtop gear
5 3rd speed gear		16 Under cover	22 Extension housing
6 2nd speed gear	11 Overdrive gear	17 Mainshaft	23 Speedometer drive gear

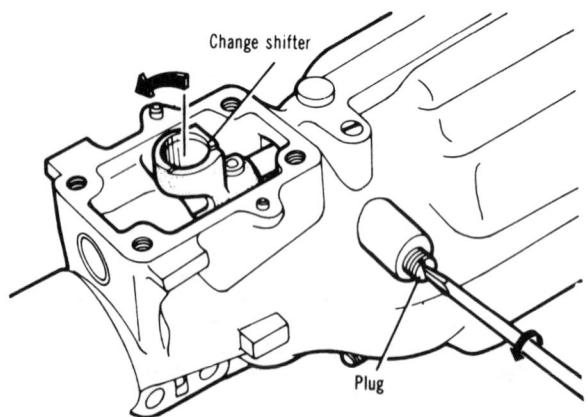

Fig. 6.2 Removing the extension housing

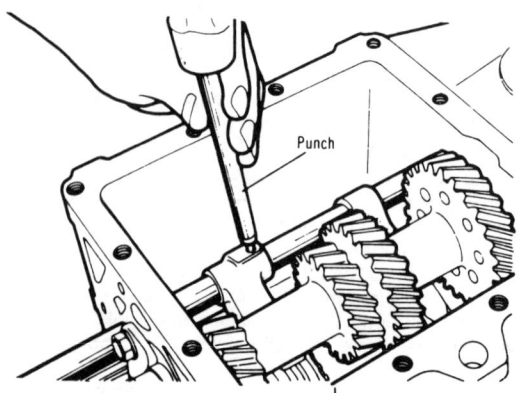

Fig. 6.3 Removing the shift fork pin

3.3 Front bearing retainer and spacer

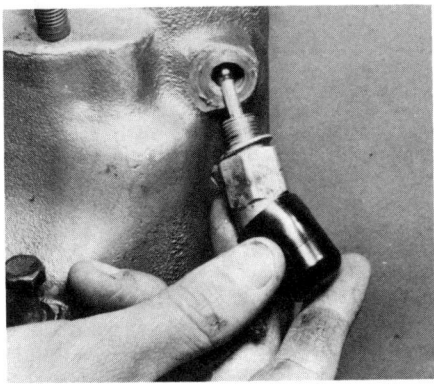
3.4 Reversing light switch and ball

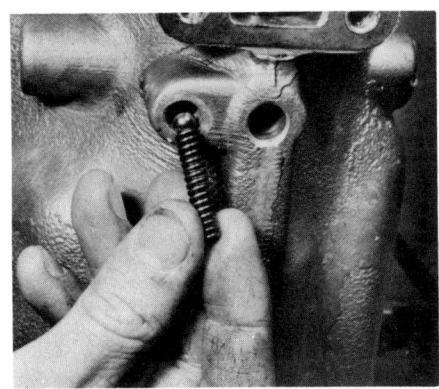
3.6 Removing a poppet spring and ball

3.9 Countershaft gear and bearing

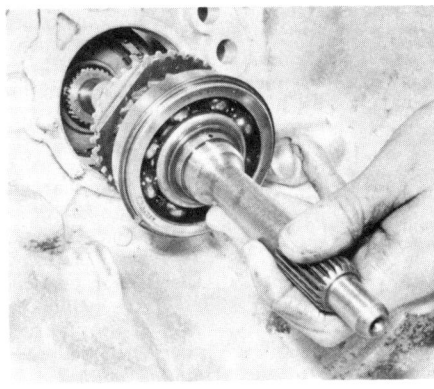
3.16 Removing the main drive pinion

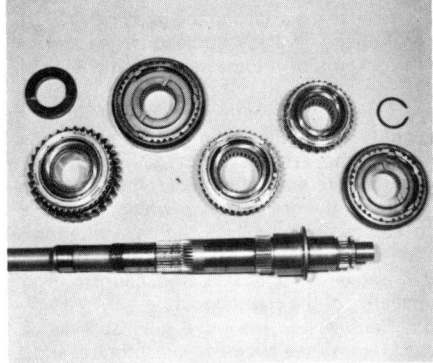
3.17 Mainshaft assembly dismantled

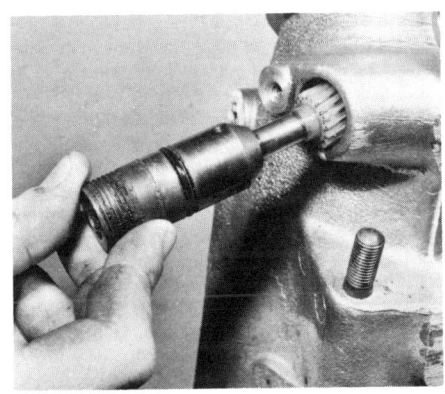

◁ 3.18 Removing the speedometer drive

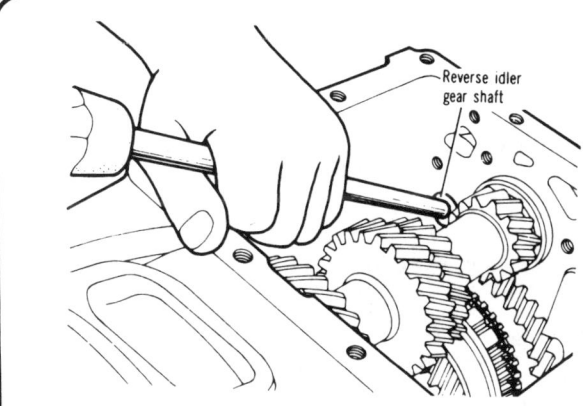
Fig. 6.4 Removing the reverse idler gear shaft

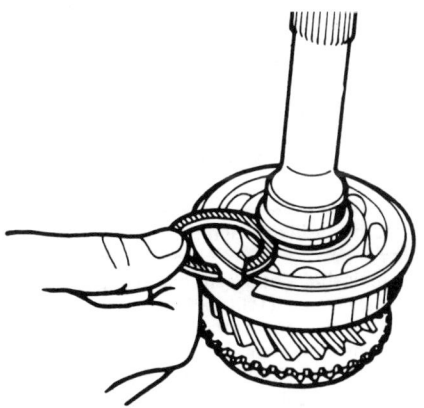
Fig. 6.5 Main drive pinion assembly

2   Ensure that the gearbox oil has been drained out and that the plug is refitted securely.

3   Remove the clutch release bearing and operating levers as described in Chapter 5, then remove the front bearing retainer and its spacer (photo).

4   Remove the bolts attaching the extension housing, then remove the reversing light switch, taking care not to lose the ball (photo). Unscrew the plug of the neutral return plunger on the right of the turret mounting until about one complete thread is still screwed in and then turn the gear shifter anticlockwise (Fig. 6.2). With the gear shifter held as far as it will go in this direction, pull back the extension housing until it is free.

5   Remove the circlip, the speedometer drive gear, the ball from the end of the mainshaft and then the second circlip.

6   Unscrew and remove the three poppet spring plugs, then remove the three poppet springs and three balls (photo).

7   Drive out the spring pins from the 3rd/4th and 1st/2nd speed shift forks inside the gearbox (Fig. 6.3) and the pin from the overdrive and the reverse gear outside the gearbox.

8   Engage reverse and second gears to lock the gear train, unpeen the locknuts of the mainshaft and countershaft, unscrew and remove the two nuts.

9   Using a claw extractor, pull off the countershaft gear and bearing (photo) which will then make it possible to withdraw the 1st/2nd gear selector rod. Withdraw the 3rd/4th gear and overdrive reverse selector rods, then remove the selector forks from the synchronizers. Shake out the two interlock plungers which engage in the shift rods and place these, the poppet valves and balls with the selector fork spring pins in a suitable container.

10   Remove the spacer, the counter reverse gear and the second spacer from the countershaft.

11   Remove the overdrive gear and sleeve from the mainshaft and then remove the overdrive synchronizer and spacer.

12   Pull out the split-pin, loosen the nut and then remove the reverse idler gear.

13   Remove the three bolts and lift off the retainer of the mainshaft rear bearing. Then remove the four bolts from the reverse idler gear shaft mounting. The shaft is spigot mounted into the end of the gearbox and should be driven out from inside the gearbox (Fig. 6.4).

14   Press the countershaft gear to the rear and remove the circlip from the rear bearing. Using a drift from inside the gearbox, drive out the countershaft rear bearing.

15   Remove the circlip from the countershaft front bearing. Insert a nut between the largest gear and the front bearing and tap the gear assembly forward so that the bearing is pushed out of the front of the box. Remove the bearing with a puller and then lift the countershaft from inside the box.

16   Pull the main drive pinion assembly from the front of the box (photo). Push the mainshaft assembly as far as possible to the rear, remove the bearing circlip and carefully tap the bearing off the mainshaft. Lift the mainshaft assembly from inside the gearbox.

17   Dismantle the mainshaft in the following order and place all the components on the bench in the same relative position as when they were assembled.

   (a)   Pull off the 1st speed gear, the 1st/2nd speed synchronizer and the 2nd speed gear

   (b)   Remove the circlip from the forward end of the mainshaft, then remove the 3rd/4th speed synchronizer and the 3rd speed gear (photo)

18   Dismantle the extension housing by removing the locking plate and pulling out the speedometer drive (photo). Remove the three plugs and remove three springs, two neutral return plungers and one ball.

4   Five-speed gearbox – inspection

1   Support the mainshaft between centres and check that the maximum bend in it is less than 0.0008 in (0.02 mm).

2   Check the synchronizer taper surfaces for wear and damage.

3   Check all gear teeth for wear and damage. The faces of the teeth should be highly polished and free from defects.

4   Check the clutch disc splines for wear and damage, ensure that the disc slides freely and smoothly along it without excessive play.

5   Examine all bearings for damage and wear. Because dismantling the gearbox is a major operation and undertaken infrequently, it is worth fitting new bearings unless the existing ones have only had a little service.

6   With each synchronizer hub and sleeve assembled, check for excessive clearance and see that they slide smoothly. Check the hubs and sleeves for wear, ensure that the springs are not distorted or broken. Examine the fork grooves for wear and damage.

7   Examine the shift rods for signs of damage and excessive wear.

5   Five-speed gearbox – reassembly

Renew all gaskets and oil seals. Apply jointing compound to all gaskets before fitting them. Ensure that all parts are clean before reassembly and apply oil to all sliding and rotating parts as they are assembled. Do not re-use any spring pins which are removed and only re-use circlips if they are not bent. Apply grease to the lips of all oil seals after they have been inserted.

1   Fit the bearing to the main drive pinion with the groove in the outer track away from the pinion and secure it with a circlip. Check the clearance between the circlip and the bearing, which should not exceed 0.0024 in (0.06 mm) (Fig. 6.7). Different thickness circlips are available to give the correct clearance. Fit a circlip in the outer track groove.

2   Assemble the mainshaft in the following order: First fit the needle cage, then the 3rd speed gear, the 3rd/4th synchronizer and the front circlip. Note that the large chamfer on the synchronizer is towards the rear of the gearbox. Check that the end play between the circlip and synchronizer does not exceed 0.0031 in (0.08 mm) and if necessary fit a selective circlip to achieve this clearance. Fit the 2nd speed gear bearing, followed by the 2nd speed gear (photo) the 1st/2nd synchronizer and 1st speed gear. Fit the bearing spacer and with the spacer pushed forward check that the 1st and 2nd speed gears end play does not exceed 0.0016 to 0.0079 in (0.04 to 0.2 mm). Identification of the 1st/2nd speed and 3rd/4th speed synchronizers and the correct fitting of the synchronizer spring is shown in Fig. 6.7.

3   Insert the assembled mainshaft into the case (photo) and drive in the rear bearing with its outer circlip fitted whilst holding the end of the mainshaft at the front of the case.

4   Fit the needle bearing and the synchronizer ring to the main drive pinion assembly and insert the assembly through the front of the case, tapping it until the bearing circlip is against the casing. Using a brush, rub clutch grease MC2 on to the splines on which the clutch plate slides.

5   Fit the countershaft gear into the casing (photo) and after fitting the circlip to the countershaft front needle bearing (photo) drive the bearing into the case by tapping the outer race with a soft faced mallet. Fit the circlip to the countershaft rear bearing and tap it fully home.

6   Fit a new oil seal to the front bearing retainer, fit the front bearing spacer, smear the oil seal lip with gear oil. Apply jointing compound to both faces of the gasket, then fit the gasket and bearing retainer. Tighten the retaining nuts (photo).

7   Fit the rear bearing retainer.

8   Fit the reverse idler gear shaft, line up the bolt holes by inserting one bolt (photo) and then insert the remaining bolts and tighten progressively.

9   Fit the needle bearing, the reverse idler gear (photo) and thrust washer, the ground face of the washer being towards the gear. Screw on and fully tighten the nut, then fit a split-pin to prevent it from unscrewing (photo).

10   Assemble the overdrive synchronizer hub and sleeve as shown in Fig. 6.8. Fit the spacer and stop plate to the mainshaft (photo) and then fit the synchronizer assembly (photo) followed by the overdrive gear bearing sleeve, needle bearing and synchronizer ring. Fit the overdrive gear (photo) followed by the locknut which should be screwed on lightly.

11   The overdrive countergear has to be fitted at the same time as the 3rd/4th gear shift rod. Fit the spacer, reverse countergear (photo) and second spacer (photo) to the countershaft end, then insert the two interlock plungers between the shift rods, the three shift forks and the 1st/2nd gear and overdrive/reverse shift rods. Fit the 3rd/4th gear shift rod and whilst holding the overdrive countergear against the flat on the rod (photo) fit the gear to the countershaft (photo). Fit the ball bearing on top of the gear and then the countershaft nut (photo).

12   Engage reverse and 2nd gears to lock the shafts then fully tighten the nuts on the mainshaft and countershaft. When tight, peen the nuts

5.2a Fitting second speed bearing and gear

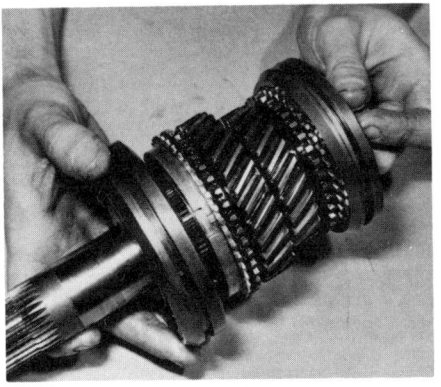
5.2b ... the 1–2 synchronizer ...

5.2c ... and the first speed gear

5.2d Mainshaft bearing spacer

5.3 Inserting the mainshaft

5.5a Inserting the countershaft

5.5b Inserted main drive pinion assembly and countershaft front bearing

5.5c Countershaft rear bearing and circlip

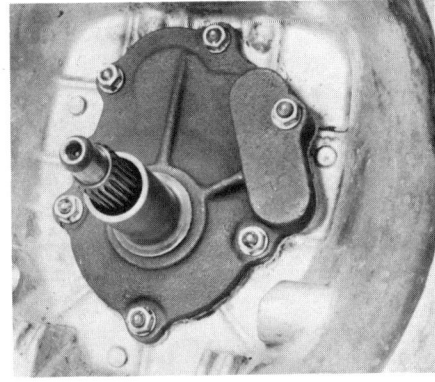
5.6 Front bearing retainer installed

5.7 Fit the rear bearing retainer

5.8 Lining up the reverse idler shaft

5.9a Reverse idler gear and bearing

5.9b Washer and nut installed on gear

5.10a Mainshaft spacer and stop ring

5.10b Fitting the overdrive synchronizer

5.10c Fitting the overdrive gear and bearing

5.11a Spacer, reverse counter gear ...

5.11b ... and second spacer

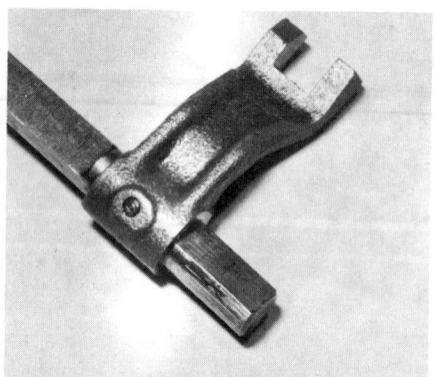

5.11c Flat on the 3rd–4th gear rod

5.11d Fitting the shift rod and overdrive counter gear

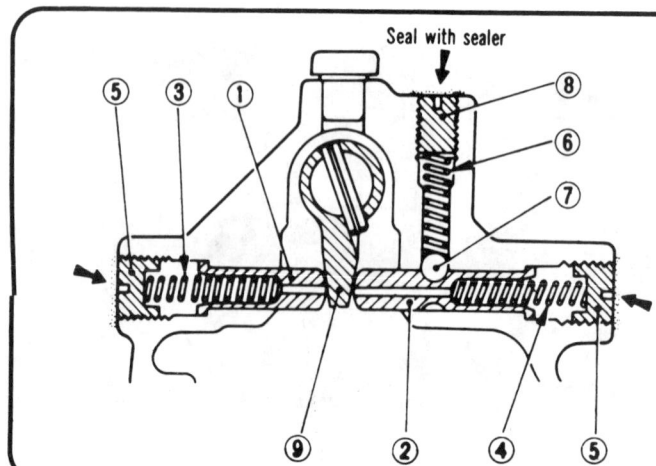

Fig. 6.6 Installing the neutral return plungers

1 Neutral return plunger A
2 Neutral return plunger B
3 Spring A
4 Spring B
5 Plug

6 Resistance spring
7 Ball
8 Plug
9 Neutral return finger

5.11e Countershaft ball bearing and nut

5.13 Inserting spring pins in shift forks

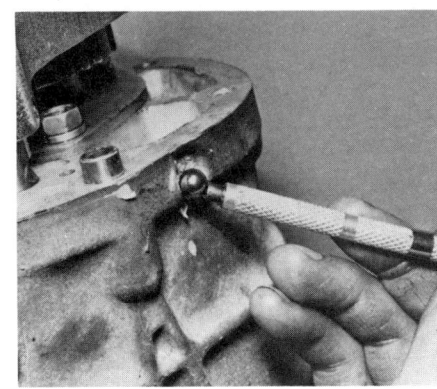

5.14a Poppet ball

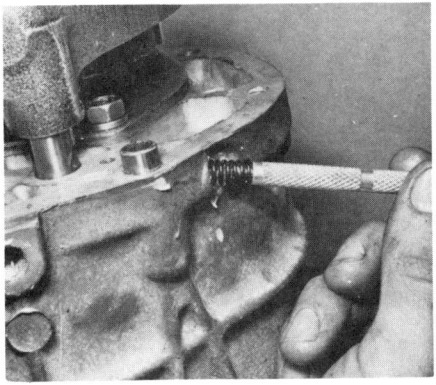

5.14b ... poppet spring

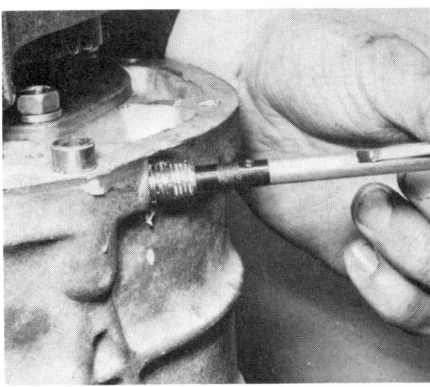

5.14c ... and plug

5.15 Ballrace at end of mainshaft

5.16 Circlip, speedometer gear and ball

5.19 Speedometer drive locking plate

5.20 Fitting the reversing light cable

5.22a Fitting spring pin to installed clutch arm

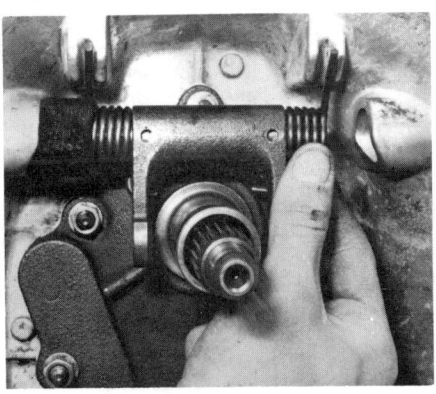

5.22b Locating upper end of clutch rod springs

5.22c Inserting a clutch bearing retainer

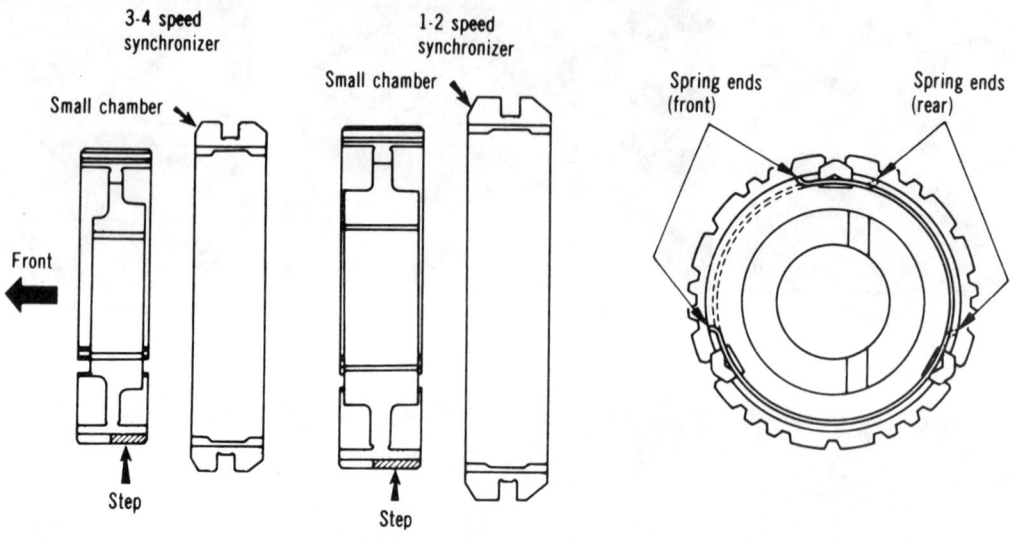

Fig. 6.7 Synchronizer identification and spring installation

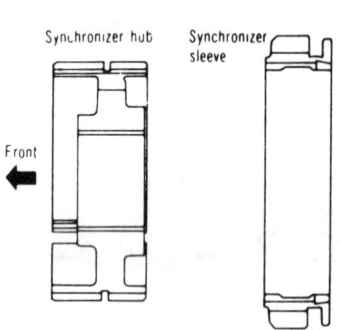

Fig. 6.8 Overdrive synchronizer identification

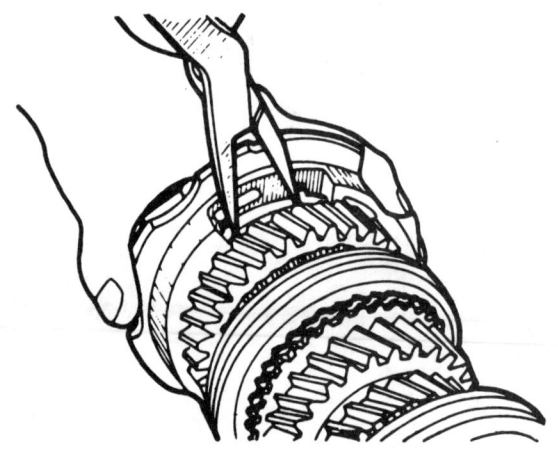

Fig. 6.9 Removing the rear bearing retainer

into the slots in their shafts.

13 Line up the holes in the shift forks and those in the selector rods, fit the new spring pins (photo) with their slots in line with the axis of the shift rod and drive the pins in fully.

14 Fit a ball (photo) and poppet spring (photo) into each shift rail, the smaller diameter end of the spring being against the ball. Screw in the plugs (photo) until their top faces are about 0.23 in (6 mm) below the surface. Seal the plug heads with sealer KE41, or a similar non-hardening sealer.

15 Fit the ballrace to the rear end of the mainshaft (photo).

16 Fit the front circlip of the speedometer drive, insert the ball into the shaft, slide the gear over it (photo) and then fit the rear circlip.

17 Apply jointing compound to both sides of the gearbox extension gasket and to the threads of the attachment bolts. Line up the slots in the lugs of the three shift levers, then, while holding the gear shifter of the extension housing as far over to the left as it will go. Fit the extension housing to the gearbox casing. Make sure that the forward end of the control finger is fitted snugly into the slots of the shift lugs. Fit the fixing bolts, except the two bottom ones, and tighten, ensuring that the washers have their convex side towards the bolt head.

18 Fit the neutral return plungers and springs (Fig. 6.6) then the ball and spring. The spring for the ball is shorter than the return plunger springs. Insert and tighten the screw plugs until their heads are flush with the casting boss and seal with KE41 or a similar non-hardening sealer.

19 Apply jointing compound to the outside surface of the sleeve of the speedometer drive and fit it into its pocket in the extension housing. Check that the gear is properly meshed then insert the locking

plate (photo) into the locking plate groove and insert and tighten the bolt.

20 Apply sealer to the threads of the reversing light switch, drop the ball into the reversing light pocket in the extension housing, then insert the switch and tighten it. Fit the two remaining housing extension bolts after threading them through the reversing light cable clips and tighten the bolts (photo).

21 Fit the gearbox cover and gasket, then insert and tighten the retaining bolts to a torque wrench setting as specified. Do not over-tighten the bolts, because this will cause the gasket to be squeezed out and may result in oil leakage.

22 Grease the shaft of the clutch arm. Enter the clutch arm into the bellhousing and thread on to it a felt packing, spring, clutch shift arm, spring and felt packing in that order. Insert the two spring pins with their slots in line with the axis in the shaft and drive them in fully (photo). Locate the upper ends of the springs in the grooves in the housing casting (photo) and the lower ends against the front faces of the clutch shift arms. Fit the clutch thrust bearing and its two retaining spring clips (photo).

23 After completing the assembly, check the correct operation of the clutch arm. Check the correct operation of the shift rods and the selection of all six gears and make sure that the drive pinion can be rotated freely in every gear. If it is felt that the gear lever does not go fully forward when engaging first gear, remove the extension housing and check for dirt or any burrs in the hole for it in the housing. This shaft fits into a blind hole and the condition of its bore is very important for correct engagement of 1st gear.

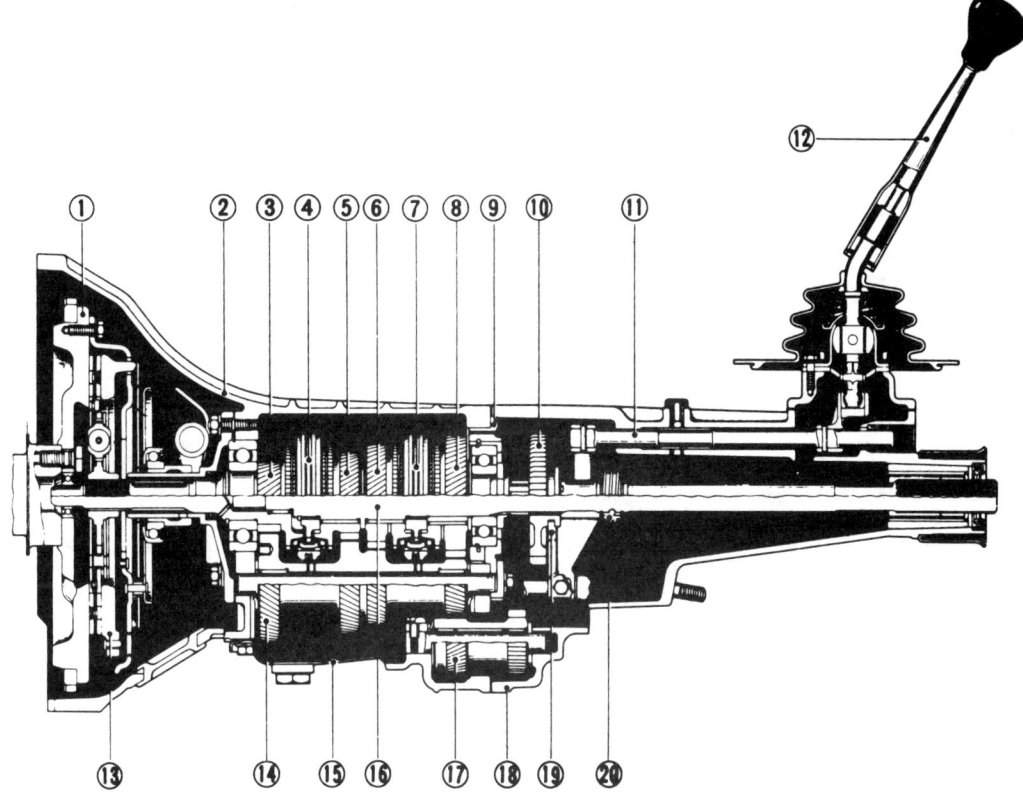

Fig. 6.10 Four speed gearbox – sectional view

1 Flywheel	6 Second-speed gear	11 Control shaft	16 Mainshaft
2 Transmission case	7 Synchronizer sleeve (for	12 Gearshift lever assembly	17 Reverse idler gear
3 Main drive gear	first-second speeds)	13 Pressure plate assembly	18 Extension housing
4 Synchronizer sleeve (for	8 First-speed gear	14 Counter gear	19 Shift fork (reverse)
third-fourth speeds)	9 Rear bearing retainer	15 Under cover	20 Speedometer drive gear
5 Third-speed gear	10 Reverse gear		

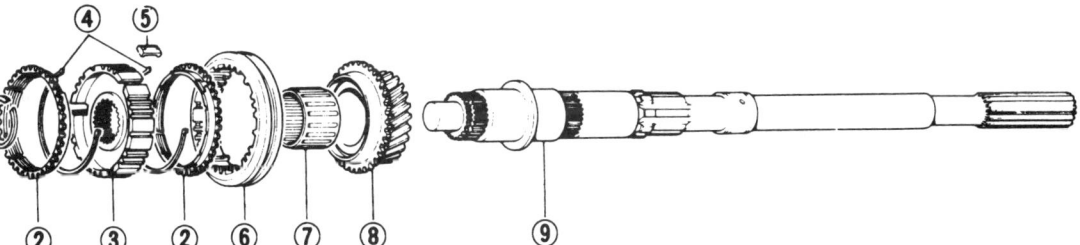

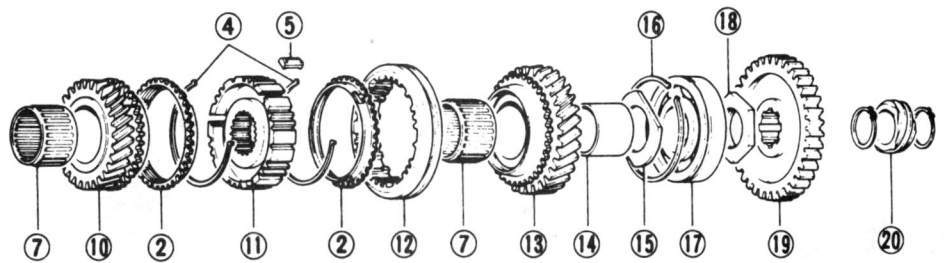

Fig. 6.11 Mainshaft components

1 Snap-ring	6 Synchronizer sleeve (3rd-	11 Synchronizer hub (1st-2nd	15 Spacer
2 Synchronizer ring	4th speeds)	speeds)	16 Snap-ring
3 Synchronizer hub (3rd-	7 Needle bearing	12 Synchronizer sleeve (1st-	17 Ball bearing
4th speeds)	8 3rd-speed gear	2nd speeds)	18 Lock nut
4 Synchronizer spring	9 Mainshaft	13 1st speed gear	19 Reverse gear
5 Synchronizer piece	10 2nd-speed gear	14 Spacer bushing	20 Speedometer drive gear

6   Four-speed gearbox – dismantling

1   Remove the clutch operating lever, extension housing and speedometer gear as described in detail in Section 3, paragraphs 1 to 5.

2   Remove the bearing retainer of the main drive gear (Fig. 6.10). If it is stuck hard, tap it lightly with a soft hammer.

3   Remove the countershaft retaining plate and pull the countershaft towards the rear of the case. Remove the countergear, a total of 42 needle rollers from the front and rear ends and also a spacer together with a thrust washer from both the front and the rear end.

4   Remove the rear thrust washer, rear idler gear, needle bearing and spacer from the reverse idler gear shaft.

5   Remove the gear shaft locking bolt and pull the shaft out towards the rear of the case. Remove the other needle bearing, front thrust washer and front idler.

6   Remove the three plugs from the right-hand side of the case and extract the three poppet springs and three balls.

7   Unscrew the locking bolt on the reverse gear shift fork and remove the shift fork and distance piece.

8   Drive out the spring pins from the two remaining shift forks and pull out the shift rods with their selectors. Do not remove the selectors from the shift rods. Remove the two shift forks from the box then shake out the two interlock plungers which are fitted between the shift rods.

9   Remove the reverse gear and then pull the mainshaft assembly to the rear until the bearing retainer is free. The assembly can then be removed. Take the assembly out and also remove the synchronizer ring from the main drive gear.

10   Dismantle the mainshaft assembly by expanding the circlip with a pair of pliers and pulling the rear bearing retainer off the bearing. Remove the locking nut, lever and tap off the bearing if a special bearing puller is not available and then proceed as follows:

  (a)   *Remove the spacer, first gear, needle bearing, spacer bushing, synchronizer ring. 1st/2nd speed synchronizer assembly, synchronizer ring, second speed gear and needle bearing. Lay all the parts out in the exact order and facing in the same relative directions as when fitted (Fig. 6.11).*

  (b)   *Remove the circlip from the front end of the mainshaft and pull off the 3rd/4th speed synchronizer assembly, synchronizer ring, third speed gear and needle bearing.*

  (c)   *Dismantle each synchronizer assembly into the synchronizer sleeve, synchronizer hub, two springs and three fingers. All parts other than the hubs are identical on the three synchronizers, but it is good practice to refit all parts in the same position as that from which they were removed.*

11   Remove the main drive gear assembly from the front of the box. Remove the circlips from the shaft and from the outer track of the bearing and pull the bearing off.

7   Four-speed gearbox – inspection

The points to be checked are essentially the same as those detailed in the inspection of the five-speed gearbox in Section 4. However, the maximum bend in the mainshaft is different and should not exceed 0.001 in (0.03 mm).

8   Four-speed gearbox – reassembly

Renew all gaskets and oil seals, and apply jointing compound to all the gaskets before fitting them. Ensure that all parts are clean before reassembly. Apply oil to all sliding and rotating parts as they are assembled. Do not re-use any spring pins which are removed and only re-use circlips if they are not bent. Apply grease to the lips of all oil seals after they have been inserted.

1   Fit the bearing to the main drive pinion with the groove in its outer track away from the pinion. Secure it with a circlip. Check the clearance between the circlip and the bearing. This should not exceed 0.0024 in (0.061 mm). Different thickness circlips are available to give the correct clearance. Fit a circlip in the outer track groove.

2   Assemble the synchronizers with the sleeve and hub in the correct directions and the spring fitted as shown in Fig. 6.13.

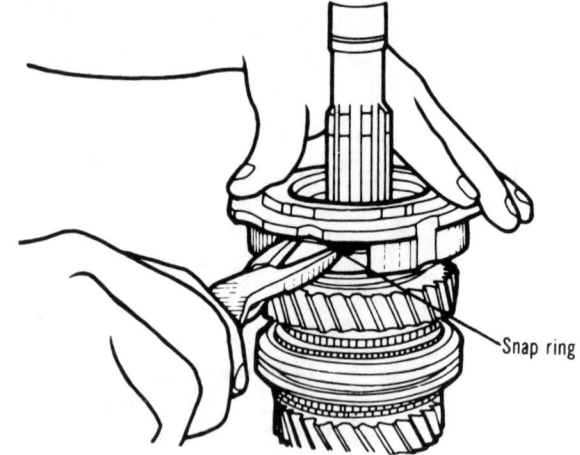

Fig. 6.12 Fitting the rear bearing retainer

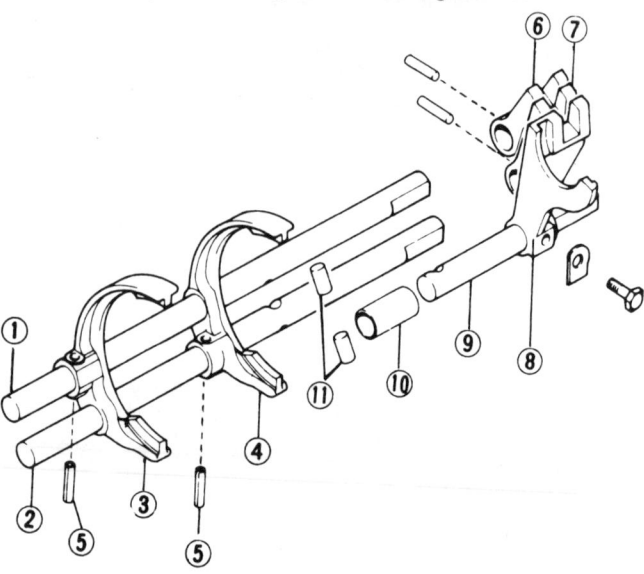

Fig. 6.13 Shift rod assembly components

1 *Shift rail (3rd-4th speed)*	7 *Selector (1st-2nd speed)*
2 *Shift rail (1st-2nd speed)*	8 *Shift fork (reverse)*
3 *Shift fork (3rd-4th speed)*	9 *Shift rail (reverse)*
4 *Shift fork (1st-2nd speed)*	10 *Distance piece*
5 *Spring pin*	11 *Interlock plunger*
6 *Selector (3rd-4th speed)*	

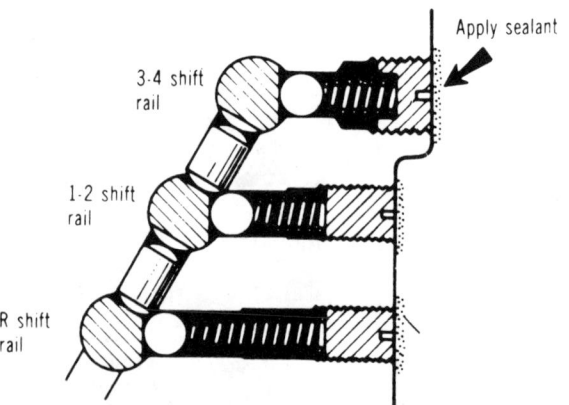

Fig. 6.14 Fitting the poppet balls, springs and plugs

Plugs should be screwed in flush

8.3a Mainshaft with 2nd speed gear and synchronizer ring

8.3b ... the 1st/2nd gear synchronizer

8.3c ... first gear sleeve ...

8.3d ... and first gear

8.3e Spacer and bearing

8.3f Bearing nut tightened and peened

8.4 Bearing retainer circlip jammed open with block of metal

8.5a Needle bearing and 3rd speed gear

8.5b ... the 3rd/4th speed synchronizer

8.5c ... and then a circlip

8.6 Inserting the mainshaft assembly

8.7a Main drive gear assembly needle bearing

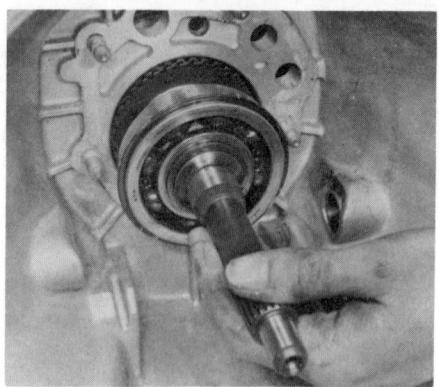

8.7b Inserting the main drive gear assembly

8.8 Fitting reverse gear

8.10a Inserting 1st/2nd gear shift rod

8.10b Fitting the interlock plunger

8.10c Spring pin slot in line with axis of shift rod

8.11a Entering the reverse gear shift rod

8.11b Interlock plunger for 3rd/4th speed shift rod

8.11c Inserting the second interlock plunger

8.12a 3rd/4th gear shift rod poppet ball ...

8.12b ... spring and plug

8.12c Reverse gear shift rod poppet ball ...

8.12d ... spring and plug

8.13a Reverse idler gear assembly fitted

8.13b Shaft securing bolt fitted and locked

8.14a Inserting the countershaft

8.14b Correct position of countershaft end

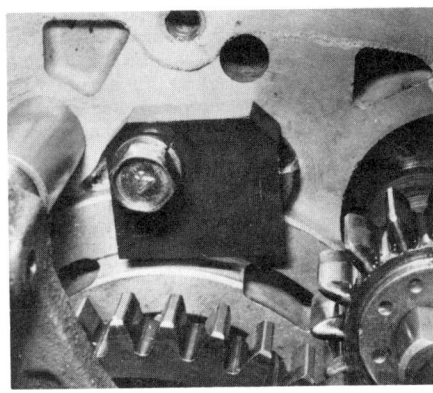

8.14c Countershaft stop plate

8.15 Fitting the speedometer gear

8.16a Front bearing cover and spacer

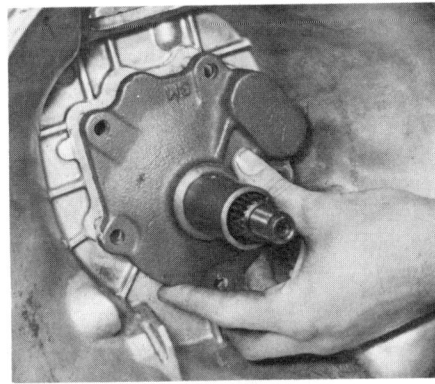

8.16b Fitting the bearing cover

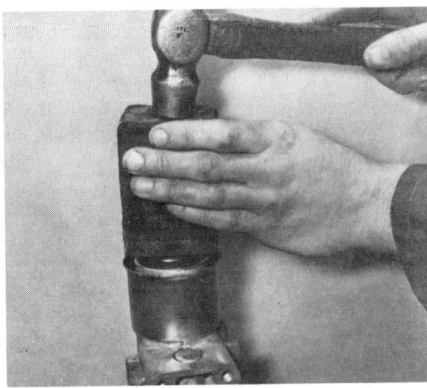

8.17a Fitting the gearbox extension housing oil seal

8.17b Position of gear shifter lever for fitting the extension housing

8.17c Fitting the gearbox extension housing

8.18 Speedometer drive locking plate and bolt

3   Fit the needle bearing and the 2nd speed gear to the rear of the mainshaft, followed by a synchronizer ring (photo), the 1st/2nd gear synchronizer (photo), 1st gear sleeve (photo) and first gear (photo). The spacer must be fitted so that the identification mark 'I' is towards the rear. Press or tap the bearing on, with the groove in the outer bearing track towards the gear (photo). Screw on the locking nut and tighten it fully before peening the collar of the nut into the keyway of the mainshaft (photo).

4   Fit the circlip into the rear bearing retainer and keep it in place by spreading its ends and jamming a piece of metal between them (photo). Fit the retainer over the bearing and then remove the metal block so that the circlip locates in the groove in the outer track of the bearing.

5   Fit the needle bearing and 3rd gear to the front of the mainshaft (photo), followed by the synchronizer ring, the 3rd/4th gear synchronizer (photo) and then a circlip (photo). The width of the circlip should be selected to give a third speed gear end play of 0.001 to 0.007 in (0.03 to 0.19 mm) and a synchronizer hub end play of 0 to 0.003 in (0 to 0.08 mm).

6   Insert the mainshaft assembly through the rear end of the gear case (photo).

7   Fit the needle bearing into the bore of the main drive gear assembly (photo) and insert the assembly into the front of the gearbox (photo) to mesh with the mainshaft.

8   Fit the reverse gear to the mainshaft (photo) and then by reference to Fig. 6.15, insert the shift forks into the grooves in the appropriate synchronizer sleeves.

9   The fitting of the shift rods varies, according to whether the reverse shift fork is bolted to its rod, as in Fig. 6.15, or is permanently pinned to the rod as on the model used for this manual.

10   For a bolted-on reverse gear shift fork proceed as follows. Holding the selector forks, with one hand inside the case, insert the 3rd/4th speed shift assembly into the case through each fork. Fit an interlock plunger and push it down until it engages the 3rd/4th speed shift rod. Fit the 1st/2nd speed shift rod into the case through the middle hole and push it through the shift forks (photo). Set the rods in their correct position relative to the case. Align the holes in the shift forks with those in the shift rods. Insert spring pins, with the slot in the pin, in line with the axis of the shift rods (photo). Tap the pins in fully. Fit the other interlock plunger to engage the 1st/2nd speed shift rod. Fit the reverse gear shift fork into the groove of reverse gear and push the reverse gear shift rod through the hole in the fork. Fit the distance piece over the end of the rod, then push the rod through its hole in the end of the case. When the rod is in its correct position with the hole in the rod and the hole in the fork aligned, fit and tighten the fork locking bolt.

11   For a pinned reverse gear fork proceed as follows. Fit the sleeve to the reverse gear shift lever. With the fork fitted into the groove in the reverse gear, enter the end of the shift rod into its lobe in the gear case (photo). Fit the 3rd/4th speed shift rod assembly through the lowest

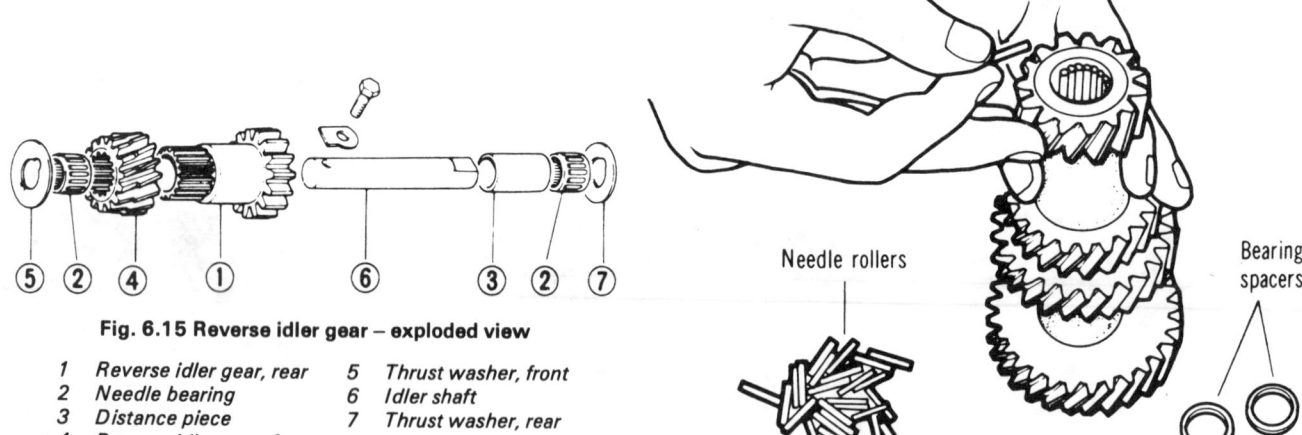

Fig. 6.15 Reverse idler gear – exploded view

1   Reverse idler gear, rear   5   Thrust washer, front
2   Needle bearing   6   Idler shaft
3   Distance piece   7   Thrust washer, rear
4   Reverse idler gear, front

Fig. 6.16 Fitting the needle rollers

8.19 Reversing light switch and ball

8.21 Reassembling the clutch operating mechanism

hole of the case and push its end through each fork. Fit an interlock plunger and push it down until it engages the 3rd/4th speed shift rod (photos). Insert the 1st/2nd gear shift rod into the centre hole. With the reverse gear shift rod pulled back, so that it is clear of the plunger bore, insert an interlock plunger and push it down on to the 1st/2nd gear shift rod. Align the shift forks and push them all forward together. Insert the spring pins through the shift forks as in paragraph 10.

12 Fit the three poppet balls and then insert the springs with the smaller diameter end against the ball (photos). Note that the reverse shift fork spring is longer than the other two (photo). Screw in the plugs until their tops are flush with the surface of the case. Move the shift rods to ensure that the gears engage easily, but positively. If necessary adjust the plugs a quarter of a turn at a time until satisfactory operation is achieved and then seal the plugs with a non-hardening sealer.

13 Assemble the components of the reverse idler gear assembly by fitting the front gear to the rear gear and inserting the spacer and two needle bearings into the bore (Fig. 6.15). Fit the larger thrust washer so that its tongue engages in the slot in the idler shaft mounting and insert the gear assembly through the rear of the gear case. Insert the shaft with its circular end first. When the hole in the shaft and the hole in the mounting are aligned (photo) insert and tighten the bolt and bend up the tab washer to lock it (photo). Fit the smaller thrust washer over the exposed end of the shaft.

14 Fit 21 needle rollers and a spacer into each end of the bore of the countergear (Fig. 6.16), packing the needles in grease, so that they do not drop out. The spacer is fitted outside the needle rollers. Grease the larger of the two thrust washers (35 mm dia) and attach it to the front of the countergear. Grease the smaller one (30 mm dia) and attach it to the rear end. Hold the assembly in its place and insert the shaft (photo), making sure that the tang of the thrust washer fits properly into the slot in the case. Secure the rear end of the countershaft (photo) by fitting the stop plate.

15 Fit the front circlip of the speedometer drive gear, the ball, speedometer gear (photo) and the rear circlip.

16 Fit a new oil seal to the front bearing retainer. Insert the spacer (photo) and fit the assembly (photo) using a new gasket, coated with jointing compound on both sides.

17 Fit a new oil seal to the gearbox extension housing (photo). Apply jointing compound to both sides of the gearbox extension gasket and to the threads of the attachment bolts. Line up the slots in the lugs of the three shift levers. Whilst holding the gear shifter of the extension housing as far over as it will go (photo), fit the extension housing to the gearbox casing (photo). Make sure that the forward end of the control finger is fitted snugly into the slots of the shift lugs. Fit the fixing bolts, except the two bottom ones which secure the reversing switch cable, and tighten, ensuring that the washers have their convex sides towards the bolt head.

18 Apply jointing compound to the outside surface of the sleeve of the speedometer drive shaft and fit it into its pocket in the extension housing. Check that the gear is properly meshed, then insert the locking plate into the locking plate groove. Then insert and tighten the bolt (photo).

19 Apply sealer to the threads of the reversing light switch. Drop the ball into the reversing light pocket in the extension housing, then insert the switch and tighten it (photo). Fit the two remaining housing extension bolts after threading them through the reversing light clips. Tighten the bolts.

20 Fit the gearbox cover and gasket, then insert and tighten the retaining bolts to the torque wrench setting specified. Do not over-tighten the bolts, because this will cause the gasket to be squeezed and may result in oil leakage.

21 Grease the shaft of the clutch arm. Enter the clutch arm into the bellhousing and thread on to it a felt packing, spring, clutch shift arm, spring and felt packing, in that order (photo). Insert the two spring pins, with their slots in line with the axis of the shaft and drive them in fully. Locate the upper ends of the springs in the grooves in the housing casting. Locate the lower ends against the front faces of the clutch shift arms. Fit the clutch thrust bearing and its two retaining clips.

22 After completing the assembly, check the correct operation of the clutch arm. Check the correct operation of the shift rods and the selection of all five gears, making further adjustment to the poppet spring plugs if necessary. If it is felt that the gear lever does not go fully forward when engaging first gear, remove the extension housing and check for dirt or any burrs in its location hole in the housing. This shaft fits into a blind hole and the condition of its bore is very important for correct engagement of 1st gear.

9 Fault diagnosis – manual gearbox

Symptom	Reason/s
Weak or ineffective synchromesh	Malfunction of gear shift lever or control shaft Synchronising cones worn, split or damaged Synchronising spring weak or damaged Synchronising dogs worn or damaged
Jumps out of gear	Shift fork worn or poppet spring broken Gearbox coupling dogs worn Selector fork groove worn excessively Gear or bushing worn
Excessive noise	Incorrect grade, or insufficient oil in gearbox Bearings worn excessively, or damaged Gear teeth worn excessively or damaged
Gears difficult to engage	Selector rods not moving freely, or having restricted travel
Difficult to engage reverse gear	Ball of reversing light switch not free in its bore

Part B Automatic transmission

10 General description

The Torqueflite automatic transmission combines a torque converter with a fully automatic three speed gear system. The torque converter is a sealed unit and cannot be dismantled. The hydraulic control system and the clutch systems are complex and it is not recommended that stripping the unit is attempted. Certain auxiliary parts of the system can be changed and the procedures for doing these are given.

When the unit is faulty and the fault cannot be rectified, repair should be entrusted to a specialist.

11 General precautions

Parking

When parking, the selector lever must not be moved to the

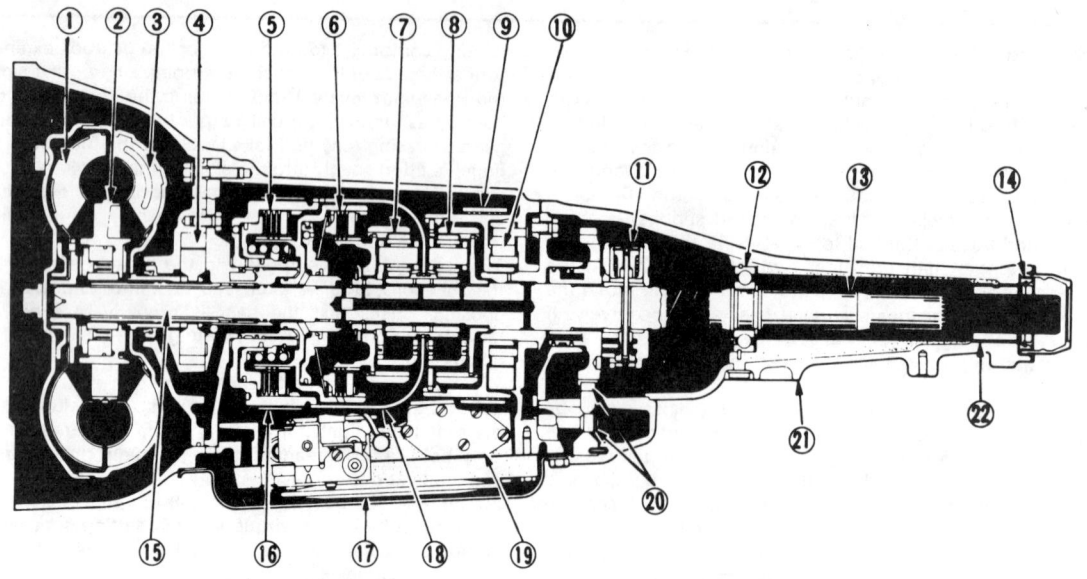

Fig. 6.17 Torqueflite automatic transmission – sectional view

1 Turbine	7 Front planetary gear set	13 Output shaft	18 Sun gear driving shell
2 Stator	8 Rear planetary gear set	14 Seal	19 Valve body
3 Impeller	9 Low and reverse band	15 Input shaft	20 Parking lock assembly
4 Oil pump	10 Over-running clutch	16 Kickdown band	21 Extension housing
5 Front clutch	11 Governor	17 Oil filter	22 Bushing
6 Rear clutch	12 Bearing		

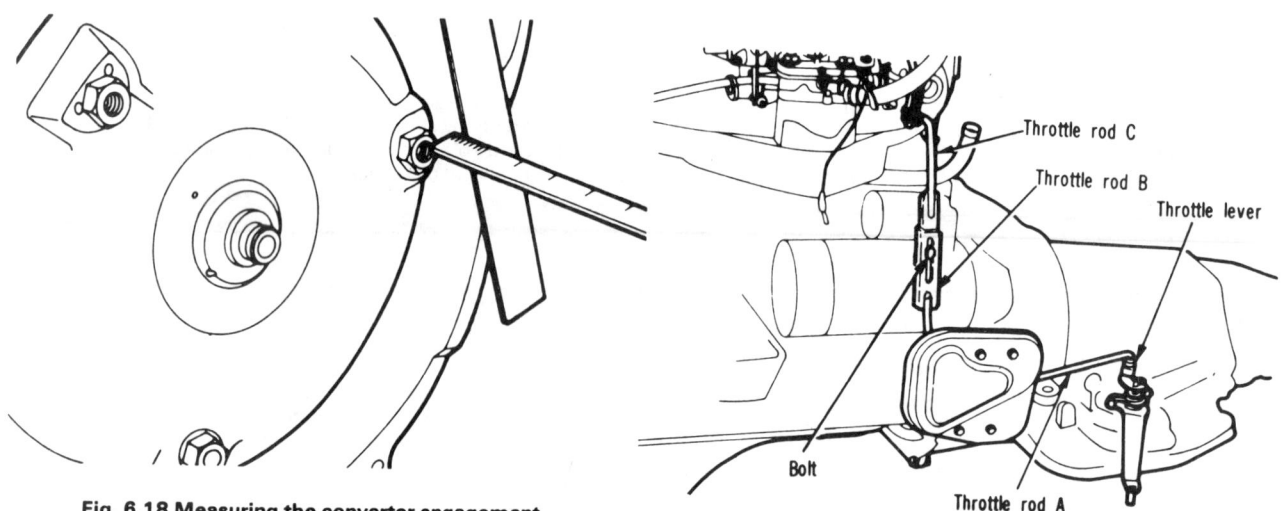

Fig. 6.18 Measuring the converter engagement

Fig. 6.19 Throttle rod adjustment

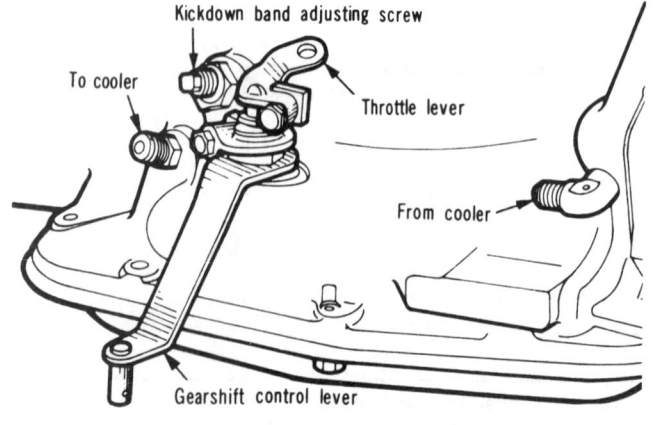

Fig. 6.20 Kickdown band adjustment

Chapter 6 Manual gearbox and automatic transmission

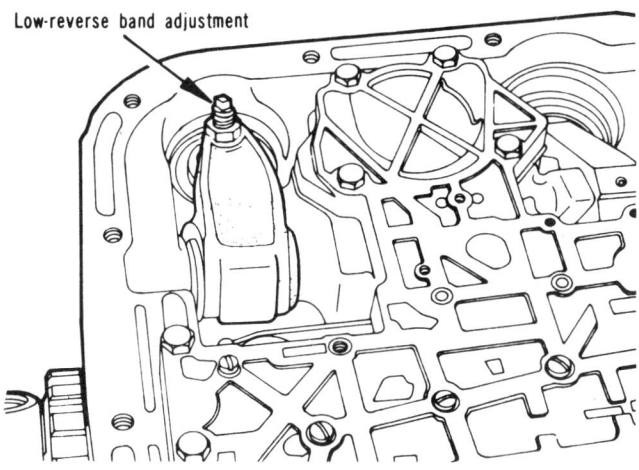

Fig. 6.21 Low and reverse band adjustment

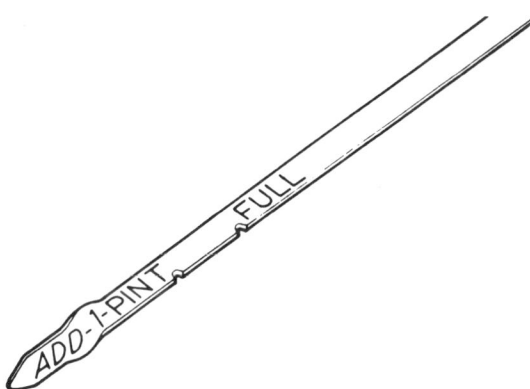

Fig. 6.22 Dipstick markings

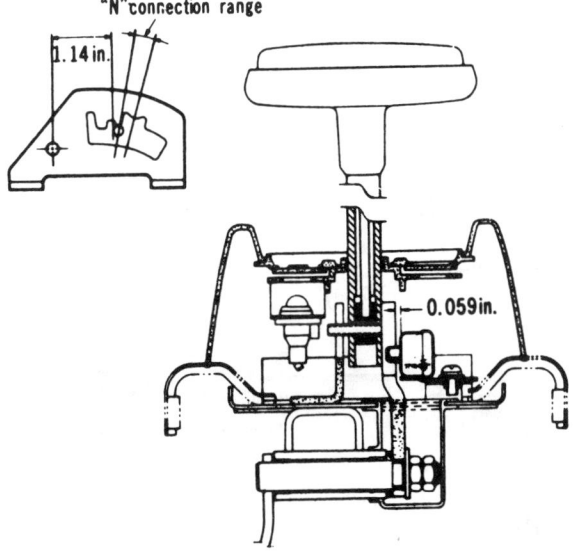

Fig. 6.23 Installation of inhibitor switch

Parking position until the vehicle is stationary or transmission damage may occur.

Starting

The engine will start with the selector lever in either the P (park) or N (neutral) positions. When starting in the neutral position, apply the footbrake or handbrake as a safety precaution.

The automatic transmission will not permit the vehicle to be started by pushing or towing for distances of greater than half a mile. The 2 (second) or L (lock up) position should be selected to reduce the possibility of overheating the transmission and converter. This also applies when towing, or carrying heavy loads which result in the vehicle needing a wide throttle opening at low speeds.

Vehicle being towed

If the vehicle has to be towed when the transmission is inoperative, it must be towed with either the rear wheels off the ground, or the propeller shaft must be removed before towing is started.

If the transmission is operating properly, the vehicle may be towed safely with its rear wheels on the ground if the transmission is in neutral and towing speed is less than 30 mph. Because the transmission is only lubricated when the engine is running, the propeller shaft should be removed if the vehicle needs to be towed more than 20 miles.

---

12 Transmission – removal and refitting

The transmission and torque converter must be removed as an assembly, otherwise the converter drive plate, pump bushing or oil seal may be damaged. The drive plate is not load bearing and none of the weight of the transmission should be allowed to rest on it during the removal operation

1 As a safety precaution, remove the battery leads.
2 Remove the cooler pipes at the transmission, then remove the starter motor and the cooling pipe bracket.
3 Place a container with a large opening under the transmission. Loosen the oil pan bolts and tap the pan at one corner to loosen it allowing fluid to drain into the container, then remove the pan.
4 Rotate the engine by means of a spanner attached to the crankshaft pulley, to gain access to the bolts attaching the torque converter to the drive plate. Remove the bolts.
5 Put mating marks on the two flanges of the propeller shaft to rear axle coupling. Remove the four fixing bolts then disconnect the shaft and carefully pull it out of the transmission.
6 Disconnect the throttle rod from the lever at the left-hand side of the transmission and remove the bellcrank from the transmission if fitted. Disconnect the gearshift rod and torque shaft assembly from the transmission.
7 Remove the oil filler tube and the speedometer cable.
8 Support the rear of the engine on a jack, or blocks. Place a jack under the transmission to support it over as large an area as possible, so that no high stress is induced in the oil pan.
9 Raise the transmission jack slightly to relieve the load on the supports. Remove the bolts securing the transmission mounting to the crossmember. Remove the bolts securing the crossmember to the chassis and take away the crossmember.
10 Remove the bellhousing bolts and carefully draw the transmission and converter assembly to the rear, to separate it from the cylinder block dowels and to disengage the converter hub from the end of the crankshaft. When this has been done, place a small G-clamp over the edge of the bellhousing to prevent the converter from falling out whilst the transmission is being removed.
11 Lower the transmission assembly and take it out from under the vehicle.
12 Remove the G-clamps from the bellhousing, then carefully slide the converter out of the housing.
13 When refitting the transmission, first check that the converter is fully engaged by placing a straight edge on the front of the case and measuring the distance to a front cover lug (Fig. 6.18). This dimension should be at least $\frac{1}{2}$ in (13 mm).
14 Inspect the converter drive plate for cracks and distortion, and renew if necessary. Ensure that the bolts securing it to the crankshaft are tightened to the torque wrench setting specified.
15 Smear some multi-purpose grease into the bore of the hub hole in the crankshaft, fit a G-clamp over the edge of the bellhousing to hold

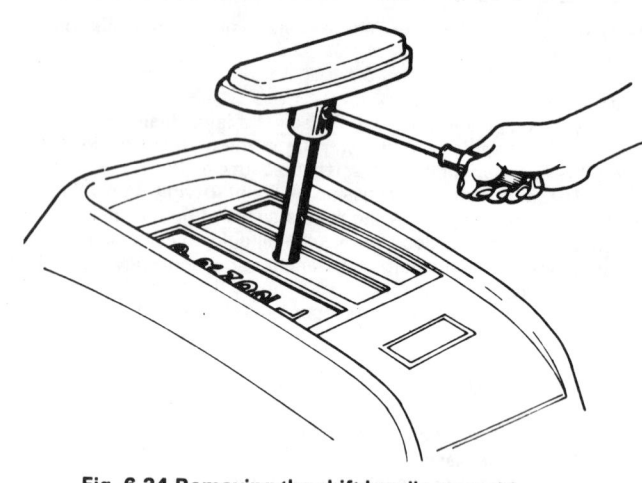

Fig. 6.24 Removing the shift handle assembly

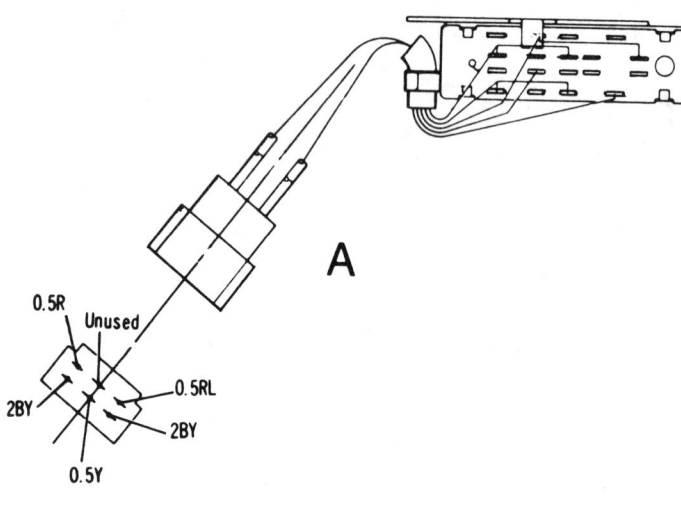

A

0.5R
Unused
2BY
0.5RL
2BY
0.5Y

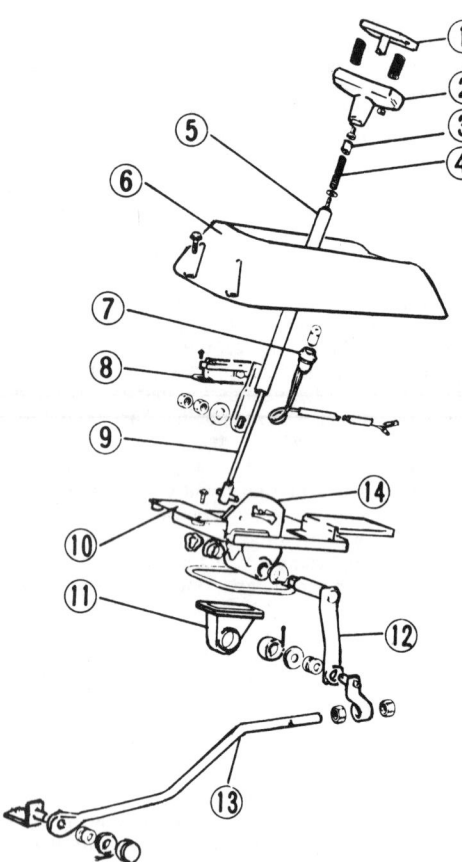

Fig. 6.26 Transmission control – exploded view

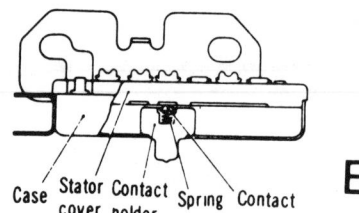

Case Stator Contact Spring Contact
cover holder

B

Fig. 6.25 Construction of inhibitor switch

1	Push button	8	Inhibitor switch
2	Shift handle	9	Shift lever rod
3	Rod adjusting nut	10	Shift lever bracket assembly
4	Rod return spring	11	Lever bracket cover
5	Selector lever assembly	12	Transmission control arm
6	Position indicator assembly	13	Transmission control rod
7	Indicator lamp socket assembly	14	Selector lever position plate

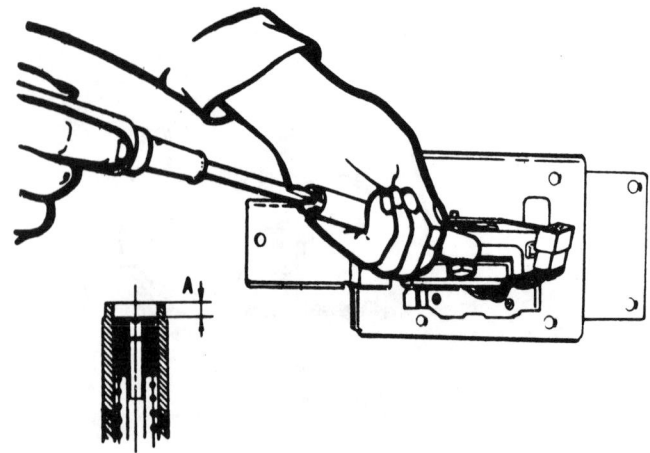

A

Fig. 6.27 Transmission control adjusting nut

the converter in place during the refitment of the transmission and proceed with refitting in the reverse order of removal. The converter housing and converter drive plate bolts should be tightened to the recommended torque wrench setting.

13 Throttle rod – adjustment

1 Run the engine until it reaches normal operating temperature.
2 With the carburetter automatic choke off the fast idle cam (see Chapter 3, Section 19) adjust the engine idling speed to 750 rpm, checking it with a tachometer.
3 With all linkages in place, loosen the clamp bolts so that rods B and C (Fig. 6.19) are free to slide. Lightly push rod A towards the idling stop and with the carburetter choke fully released tighten the bolt connecting rods B and C.
4 Check that when the carburetter throttle is wide open, the transmission throttle lever moves smoothly from the idling to the wide open position and that the lever has not moved its full stroke. The angle of operation of the transmission throttle lever is 45° to 54°.

14 Kickdown band – adjustment

*The kickdown band adjusting screw is on the left-hand side of the transmission case as shown in Fig. 6.20. (**Note**: Band adjustment is not normally required for average passenger car usage).*
1 Loosen the locknut and undo it about five turns then check that the adjusting screw turns freely.
2 Tighten the band adjusting screw to its specified torque. Unscrew the adjusting screw three complete turns and while holding the screw in this position, tighten the locknut to the recommended torque.

15 Low and reverse band – adjustment

Note: *Band adjustment is not normally required for average passenger car usage.*
1 Drain the transmission fluid and remove the oil pan (see Section 22, paragraph 3).
2 Adjustment is by means of a socket head screw at the servo end of the lever (Fig. 6 21). Release the locknut and unscrew it several turns. Tighten the screw to its torque then unscrew it $7\frac{1}{2}$ turns from this torque. Lock the screw in this position with the locknut tightened to the recommended torque.
3 Refit the oil pan, using a new gasket and tighten the fixing bolts to the correct torque.
4 Refill the transmission with Castrol TZ Dexron or an equivalent Dexron type (see following Section).

16 Refilling the transmission

Fluid and filter changes are not required for average passenger car usage, but under the following operating conditions the fluid and filter must be changed every 24 000 miles:

  (a) *More than 50% operation in heavy city traffic during hot weather (above 90°F)*
  (b) *Commercial type operation and towing*

If the transmission is dismantled for any reason, the filter should be changed and the bands adjusted.
1 After refitting and tightening the bolts of the oil pan, pour four quarts of Dexron type automatic transmission fluid through the filler tube.
2 Start the engine and allow it to idle for at least two minutes then, with the handbrake on, move the selector momentarily to each position, ending in the neutral position.
3 Hold sufficient fluid to bring the level to the '*Add 1 pint*' mark (Fig. 6.22). Recheck the level when the engine is at its normal operating temperature, when the level should be between the '*Full*' mark and the '*Add 1 pint*' mark.
4 **Caution**: *To prevent dirt from entering the transmission, make sure that the dipstick is clean and that the dipstick cap is properly seated on the dipstick tube.*

17 Inhibitor switch – checking and adjustment

1 In cases of a malfunction of the inhibitor switch, first check that the switch is operating correctly. Using a meter or battery and lamp with the selector in the P, R, N, D and L positions in turn, the switch connections should be in accordance with the following table.

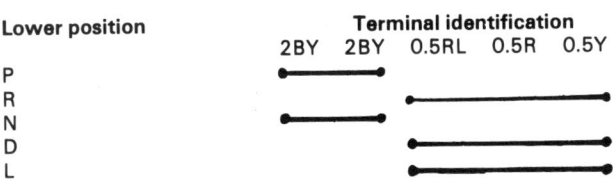

Lower position	Terminal identification				
	2BY	2BY	0.5RL	0.5R	0.5Y
P					
R					
N					
D					
L					

2 With the selector lever in the N position temporarily fix the switch with a single screw so that when the pin on the rod assembly is near the crest of the pawl on the detent plate (Fig. 6.15) the detent switch is at the forward end of the N connection range. Check that there is a clearance of 0.059 in between the selector lever and the switch and then tighten the fixing screws securely.

18 Transmission control – removal, refitting and adjustment

1 Remove the handle assembly from the lever by loosening the set screw (Fig. 6.26). Remove the attaching screws of the position indicator assembly and lift it off, then remove the indicator lamp.
2 Disconnect the control rod from the arm by loosening the nut from under the floor. Loosen the screws of the lever bracket assembly and remove it.
3 When refitting the transmission control arm to the selector lever assembly, apply grease to the sliding surfaces. Tighten the locknut, making sure that the arm is not loose and that a force of about 3 lbs (1.4 kg) applied to the knob will move the lever. If this value is not obtained, select an appropriate wave washer to achieve it.
4 Before refitting the control knob, adjust the screwed plug in the top of the selector lever when in the N position, so that the plug is flush with the bottom of the groove cut in the rod end (Fig. 6.27).
5 With the lever in the N position and the transmission also in neutral, connect the rod and the lever and tighten the locknut.

Fault diagnosis overleaf

19 Fault diagnosis – automatic transmission

The repair of an automatic transmission requires specialist knowledge and equipment and should not be attempted without these. The following faults, however, are within the capacity of the non-specialist.

Symptom	Reason/s
Starter does not operate in P and N positions	Inhibitor switch faulty or not adjusted correctly
Starter operates in all positions of selector lever	Inhibitor switch requires adjusting
Abnormal shock when D, L or R are selected	Engine idling speed too high Vacuum leak
Kickdown does not operate	Switch or solenoid faulty or broken wiring

Chapter 7 Propeller shaft

Contents

Specifications

Type	Tubular, one-piece, or two-piece. Necked or straight
Universal joints	Needle bearing – Hooke, sealed for life bearings
Journal outside diameter	0·5776 to 0·5783 in (14·671 to 14·689 mm)

Cars for Europe

	STD, GSR	EL, GL (M/T) Estate car	GL (A/T)
Shaft type	One-piece	Two-piece **Front**	Two-piece **Front**
LengthxODxID	44·84x2·76x2·63 in (1134x70x66·8 mm)	17·44x2·50x2·39 in (443x63·5 x60·7 mm) **Rear** 27·40x2·50x2·39 in (696x63·5 x60·7 mm)	13·90x2·50x2·39 in (353x63·5 60·7 mm) **Rear** 27·40x2·50x2·39 in (696x63·5 40·7 mm)

Except cars for Europe

	EL, GT (M/T) GSR, SL	GL (A/T)
Shaft type	One-piece	One-piece
LengthxODxID	44·84x2·76x2·63 in (1134x70x66·8 mm)	40·91x2·76x2·63 in (1039x70x66·8 mm)

Torque wrench settings

	lbf ft	kgf m
Flange coupling bolts	11 to 14	1·5 to 2·0
Damper bracket to damper	15 to 17	2·1 to 2·4
Damper bracket to extension housing	9 to 12	1·3 to 1·7
Damper bracket to damper arm	25 to 33	3·5 to 4·6
Damper arm to weight	43 to 51	6·0 to 7·1
Centre yoke attachment nut	120 to 160	16 to 22

1 General description

Drive is transmitted from the gearbox or automatic transmission to the rear axle by a balanced, tubular, propeller shaft. This may be in one piece, or may be in two pieces with a centre bearing. The two piece shaft is fitted to most cars for Europe to minimise propeller shaft vibration and noise. The balance weights on the shafts are fitted during assembly. A small degree of unbalance will have a large effect on the vibration and noise, propeller shafts should not be dismantled unless it is unavoidable.

To cater for axial misalignment of the gearbox and rear axle, a conventional Hooke's joint is fitted at each end of the shaft. When a two piece shaft with a centre bearing is fitted, there is an additional Hooke's joint at each side of the centre bearing. The propeller shaft is

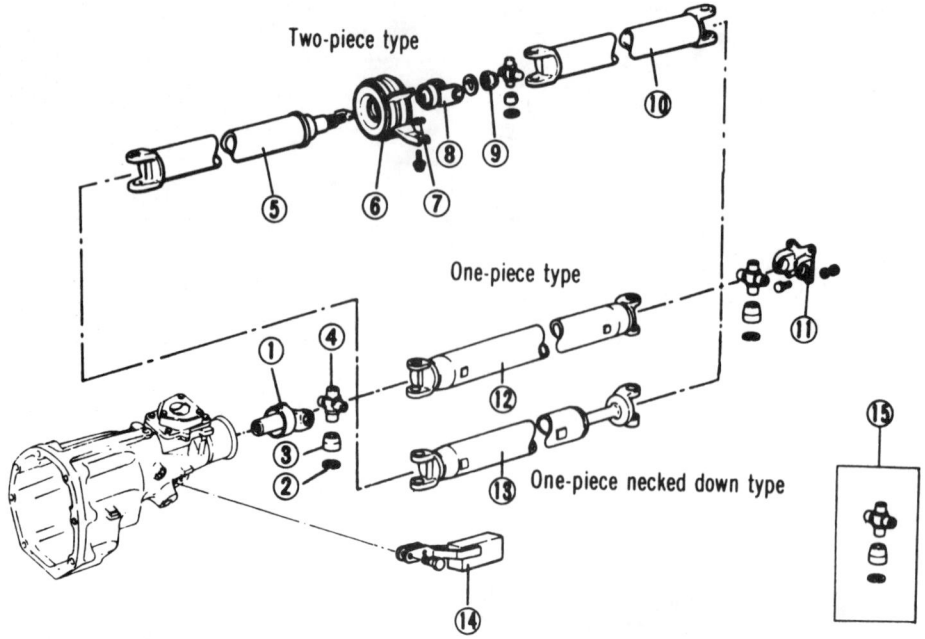

Fig. 7.1 Propeller shaft – exploded view

1	Sleeve yoke	*5	Propeller shaft (front)	*9	Centre yoke attachment nut	13	Propeller shaft (necked type)
2	Circlip	*6	Centre bearing	*10	Propeller shaft (rear)	14	Dynamic damper
3	Needle bearing	*7	Spacer	11	Flange yoke	15	Universal joint repair kit
4	Universal joint spider	*8	Centre yoke	12	Propeller shaft	*	two-piece type

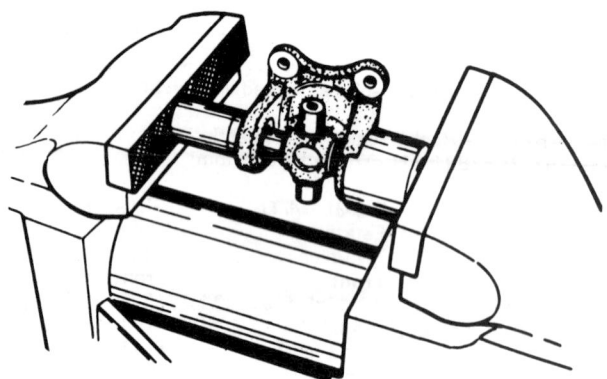

Fig. 7.2 Removing a needle bearing

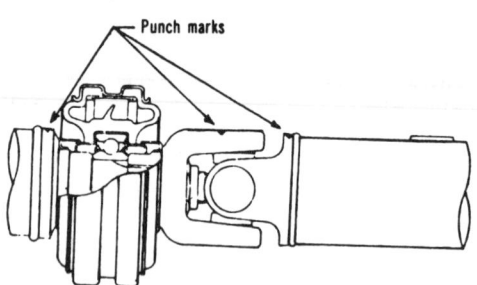

Fig. 7.3 Centre joint mating marks

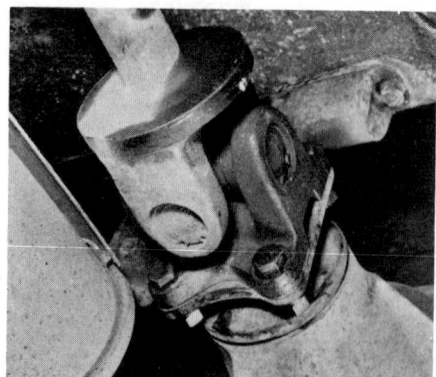

2.2 Propeller shaft rear attachment

2.3 Centre bearing attachment

2.4 Removing the propeller shaft sleeve yoke

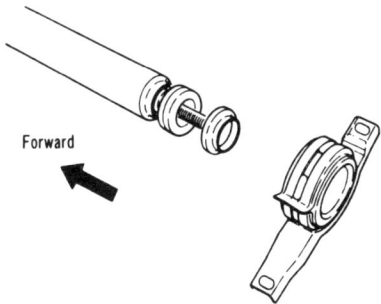

Fig. 7.4 Centre bearing assembly

attached to the rear axle by a flanged coupling and to the gearbox by a splined and sliding coupling. The shafts, for manual and automatic transmission, differ in length and have different sleeve yokes. There are also differences in the shafts for different models, giving a total of six variations. The bearings of the universal joints are of the needle type and are sealed for life, needing no lubrication unless they are removed.

On some shafts the universal joints cannot be dismantled and in the event of excessive wear, or damage, the complete shaft assembly must be renewed. These shafts can be identified by their bearings not being retained by circlips.

Vehicles with automatic transmission have a dynamic damper fitted to the rear of the transmission, to prevent resonance of the propeller shaft.

2 Propeller shaft – removal and refitting

1   Jack up the rear of the car to minimise the quantity of oil that runs out, when the transmission end of the shaft is removed.
2   Mark the two flanges of the rear axle, so that the coupling will be reassembled in exactly the same way. Then remove the four bolts from the flange (photo).
3   Push the shaft forward slightly to disengage the spigot of the flange coupling, then lower the rear axle end of the shaft. For a two piece shaft, remove the two bolts securing the centre bearing and lower the centre bearing (photo).
4   Place a container under the rear of the transmission, to catch any oil which runs out and then pull the shaft out from the transmission. When removing the sleeve yoke, take care not to damage the oil seal at the rear of the transmission (photo).
5   Before refitting the propeller shaft, clean the outside of the sleeve yoke very carefully, then smear it with gear oil.
6   Insert the sleeve yoke, taking care not to damage the oil seal. When a centre bearing is fitted, lift this up into place, then insert and tighten its fixing bolts.
7   Line up the mating marks on the two parts of the rear flange joint, insert the bolts and screw on the nuts to the specified torque.

3 Universal joints – dismantling, overhaul and reassembly

1   Support the driveshaft in a soft jawed vice and remove the circlips which retain the bearing yokes in the sleeve yoke and the driveshaft. If new bearings are not being fitted, it is important that each circlip and bearing is refitted to exactly the same position as the one from which it was removed.
2   Using a vice, a short piece of bar and a short piece of tube of suitable size, press the bearing out of the joint as far as possible (Fig. 7.2), then grip it with a pair of pliers and pull it off. Reverse the positions of

the bar and tube to remove the opposite bearing, then remove the other three pairs of bearings in the same manner.
3   After removing all the bearings of a joint, take out the spider, marking it so that it can be refitted in the same position.
4   Thoroughly clean the bearings and all other parts of the joint. Inspect them for damage and wear. If the journals of the spider show impressions of needle rollers, pitting, or rust, renew both the spider and the needle bearings. If the dust seals are damaged, renew the needle bearing assembly.
5   Check the sleeve yoke and the transmission mainshaft for wear and damage. Renew any part which is defective.
6   Fill the grease grooves of the journals with multi-purpose grease and apply a thin coat of grease evenly to the needle bearings and journals of the coupling halves. If too much grease is put in the grease grooves, the bearing outer track will not fit in position properly and will result in the selection of an incorrect circlip.
7   Press the bearings in, using the same method as for dismantling the joints. Fit a circlip over each bearing, selecting the circlip thickness so that the clearance between the needle bearing and the circlip does not exceed 0·001 in (0·025 mm).
8   Circlips are available in four thicknesses, coded as follows. If possible, fit the same thickness ring on each pair of yokes, to preserve the balance of the shaft.

Thickness	Colour code
0·0504 ± 0·0006 in	None
0·0516 ± 0·0006 in	Yellow
0·0528 ± 0·0006 in	Blue
0·0539 ± 0·0006 in	Purple

4 Centre bearing – removal and refitting

1   Remove the propeller shaft assembly from the vehicle.
2   Look for punch marks on the yoke and shaft (Fig. 7.3) and if not visible make some fresh ones to ensure correct reassembly.
3   Dismantle the centre universal joint, as described in the previous Section.
4   Remove the nut securing the centre yoke to the front end of the rear shaft and pull off the yoke.
5   Remove the housing assembly from the shaft, then pull out the bearing and remove the retainer.
6   When reassembling, make sure that the circlips, needle bearings and yokes are fitted to the same positions as before removal.
7   Fit the centre bearing to the front of the shaft and then fit the housing assembly, making sure that this is fitted the same way round as before removal.
8   Fit the centre yoke and tighten the nut to the specified torque. The unit is of the self-locking type and a new nut should be used on reassembly.
9   Reassemble the centre joint, taking care that the punch marks on the yoke and shaft are aligned.

5 Dynamic damper – removal, inspection and refitting

1   Remove the propeller shaft (Section 2).
2   Remove the two bolts securing the damper to its bracket. Remove the damper.
3   Remove the two nuts from the front fixings, and the two bolts from the rear fixings of the damper bracket. Remove the bracket.
4   Check the damper and its bracket for damage and renew or repair any defective part.
5   Refit the damper bracket, then the damper. Tighten the bolts to the recommended torque wrench setting.

6   Fault diagnosis – propeller shaft

Symptom	Reason/s
Propeller shaft noisy during high speed driving	Propeller shaft bent Propeller shaft unbalanced Axle flange bolts loose Excessive clearance between end of bearing and circlip Universal joint worn
Propeller shaft noisy, but not vibrating during medium speed and high speed driving	Dynamic damper attachment bolts loose

Chapter 8 Rear axle

Contents

Specifications

Type	Semi-floating live axle with hypoid bevel gears and two-pinion differential
Oil capacity	2·0 pints (1·1 litres)
Oil type	Hypoid gear oil to specification API GL4 or higher (SAE 90EP)

Torque wrench settings

	lbf ft	kgf m
Outer bearing retainer to brake backplate	25 to 29	3·5 to 4·0
Oil drain plug	50	7·0
Oil level plug	29	4·0
Differential assembly to axle housing mounting bolts	18 to 21	2·5 to 3

1 General description

The rear axle is of the hypoid, semi-floating type, supported by grease packed, hermetically sealed bearings. These are a variety of gears, which are used in different combinations. These are varied depending upon the size of engine and type of transmission used. A sticker indicating the ratio used is attached to the axle housing.

On all models except the estate car, the axle is attached to two asymetrical semi-elliptic leaf springs, that operate in combination with telescopic double-acting shock absorbers. On the estate car the suspension consists of coil springs and concentrically mounted shock absorbers carried on trailing arms.

The dismantling of the differential assembly and the refitting of parts, require special tools and the work should only be undertaken by an authorised dealer. As the differential is of the integral type it is preferable that the assembly is replaced as a complete unit and that no attempt is made at dismantling it.

2 Rear axle – removal and refitting

1 Loosen the rear wheel nuts and then raise the rear of the car by placing a jack beneath the differential case.
2 Remove the rear wheels and place a firmly based axle stand on each side of the vehicle, at a point forward of the rear suspension front attachment.
3 Lower the jack, under the differential, until it is only just supporting the rear axle.
4 Remove the propeller shaft (Chapter 7, Section 2).
5 Disconnect the main brake pipeline from the rear brake hose.
6 Disconnect the handbrake cable from each of the brake backplates and disconnect it from its fixing on top of the axle tube.

Leaf spring type

7 Loosen and remove the U-bolt nuts and then jack the rear axle housing so that it clears the spring seat. Remove the spring pad and spring. Also remove the shock absorber.
8 Remove the shackle pin nuts, take off the shackle plate and withdraw the shackle assembly. Take care not to knock the rear axle off the jack when the U-bolts have been removed.
9 With an assistant steadying the axle, lower the jack and then take the axle from beneath the vehicle.

Trailing arm type

10 Carry out the operations detailed in paragraphs 1 to 6, then remove the shock absorbers.
11 Lower the jack and remove the right and left coil springs.
12 Raise the jack a little and remove the lower control arm, assist link and upper arm (Chapter 11).
13 With an assistant steadying the axle, lower the jack and take the axle from beneath the vehicle.

Refitting

14 Refitting the rear axle is a reversal of the removal procedure, varying with the type of rear suspension fitted. After refitting the axle, bleed the braking system (Chapter 9, Section 14).

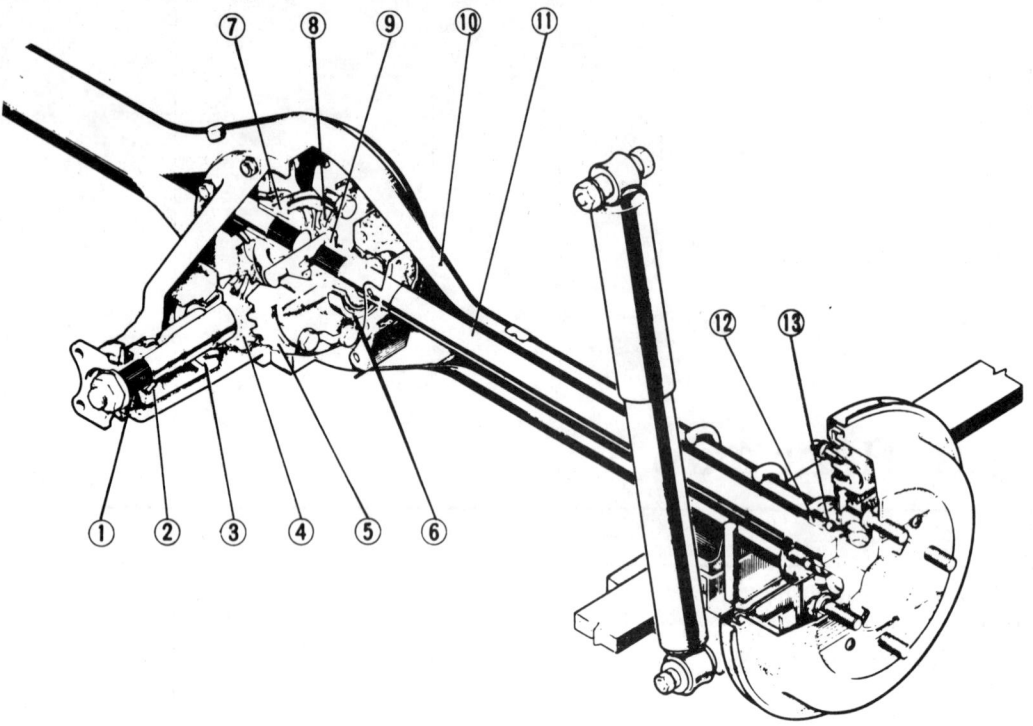

Fig. 8.1 Rear axle and differential construction

1	Drive pinion oil seal	5	Final drive gear
2	Drive pinion front bearing	6	Differential carrier side
3	Drive pinion rear bearing		bearing
4	Drive pinion	7	Differential case

8	Differential pinion
9	Differential side pinion
10	Rear axle housing

11	Rear axle shaft
12	Rear axle shaft oil seal
13	Rear axle shaft bearing

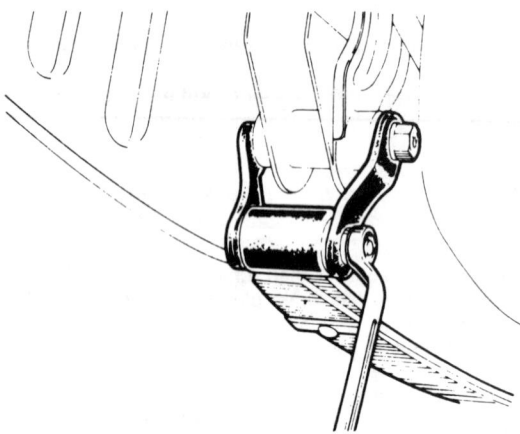

Fig. 8.2 Removing the shackle pin nuts

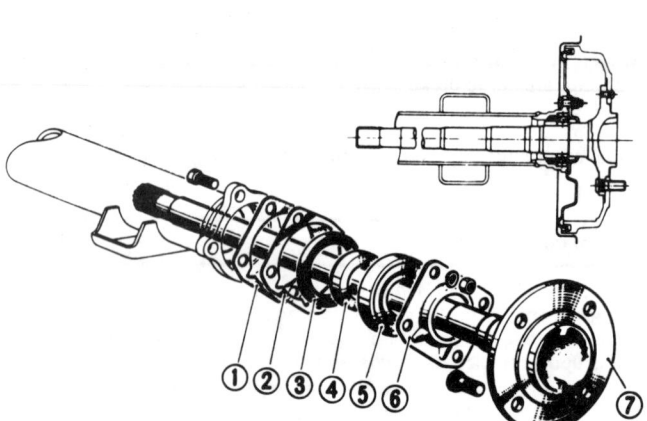

Fig. 8.3 Rear axle shaft – exploded view

1	Packing	5	Bearing
2	Shim	6	Bearing retainer, outer
3	Oil seal	7	Rear axle shaft
4	Bearing retainer, inner		

Fig. 8.4 Differential assembly removal

2.6 Handbrake fixing on axle tube

2.7 U-bolts and spring pad

4.9 Oil level and drain plugs

3   Rear axle – halfshaft removal

1   Loosen the wheel nuts, then jack up the rear axle so that the wheel is clear of the ground. Support the car on axle stands and then remove the wheel.
2   Remove the four nuts securing the brake backplate, then disconnect the brake pipe(s) from the wheel cylinder.
3   Remove the halfshaft using an impact puller. If one is not available the halfshaft can sometimes be prised off using a bar on each side of the hub. Secure the brake backplate by tying it to the rear spring, leaving the handbrake cable still attached to it. Dismantling the halfshaft assembly should be done by an authorised dealer.

4   Differential assembly – removal and refitting

1   Place a bowl under the rear axle, remove the drain plug and allow the oil to drain.
2   Remove the four bolts from the axle drive flange, disconnect the propeller shaft and allow its free end to rest on the ground, out of the way.
3   Disconnect both the left and the right-hand halfshafts as described in the previous Section. Withdraw each halfshaft at least two inches out of the axle tube, so that its splined end is free from its engagement in the side gear.
4   Remove the 8 nuts securing the differential gear carrier to the axle casing. The joint between the two faces is sealed with jointing compound and it may be necessary to tap the gear carrier with a soft-headed hammer to separate the joint.
5   When the joint faces have been separated, pull the gear carrier forward and out of the axle casing.
6   When refitting the differential assembly, clean all traces of the old jointing compound to both faces of a new gasket.
7   Fit the gasket to the axle housing studs, insert the differential carrier and fit the nuts finger tight.
8   Tighten the bolts in a diagonal sequence, until they have all been tightened to the torque given in the Specification.
9   Ensure that the drain plug has been fitted and tightened, then pour in the specified quantity of axle oil through the level plug hole. Replace the level plug (photo).
10   Reconnect the propeller shaft and tighten the flange bolts.

5   Halfshaft oil seal – renewal

1   The removal of the oil seal without damage requires a special tool, but if the oil seal is defective and a new one is required, the following method may be adopted.
2   Remove the halfshaft assembly as described in Section 3.
3   Break the flange of the oil seal with a chisel and then carefully drive a thin screwdriver between the rim of the oil seal and its housing at the point where the flange is broken and prise the rim up.
4   Use a pair of cutters to cut the rim of the seal and then pull the seal out with a pair of pliers.
5   Before fitting the new seal, carefully clean the oil seal housing in the rear axle and apply a thin coat of chassis grease. Taking great care to ensure that the seal is square with the bore of the axle, press the seal in by thumb pressure as far as possible. Then, using a block of wood which is just small enough to go into the axle bore, carefully tap the seal home.
6   Smear the lip of the oil seal with a bearing grease containing at least 50% molybdenum disulphide and also smear grease over the area of the shaft which is in contact with the seal.
7   Make sure that all the packing washers which were on the halfshaft when it was removed are still in place, then thread the halfshaft through the brake backing plate.
8   Carefully refit the halfshaft assembly, taking care not to damage the oil seal and engage the splined end in the side pinion of the differential.
9   Align the oil holes in the packing washers and the outer bearing retainer, fit the spring washers and nuts and do up the nuts finger tight.
10   Tighten the outer bearing nuts in diagonal sequence to the specified torque, then reconnect the brake pipe and bleed the brakes (Chapter 9, Section 13).
11   Check the level of oil in the rear axle, then refit the plugs and tighten to the specified torque wrench setting.

6   Fault diagnosis – rear axle

Symptom	Reason/s
Vibration	Worn halfshaft bearings
	Loose drive flange bolts
	Propeller shaft out-of-balance
	Wheels require balancing
Noise	Insufficient lubricant
	Worn differential gears
'Clunk' on acceleration or deceleration	Incorrect crownwheel and pinion mesh
	Excessive backlash due to wear in differential gears
	Worn halfshaft or differential side gear splines
	Loose drive flange bolts
	Worn drive pinion flange splines
Oil leakage	Faulty pinion or halfshaft seals
	Blocked axle housing breather

Chapter 9 Braking system

Contents

Specifications

Type of system . . . . Disc or drum at front, self-adjusting drum at rear. Dual line with tandem master cylinder and servo assistance

Footbrake . . . . Hydraulic on all four wheels

Handbrake . . . . Mechanical to rear wheels only

Brake dimensions

Front disc
Disc diameter . . . . 7 in (184 mm) mean diameter
Disc thickness (except estate car) . . . . 0·51 in (13 mm)
                estate car . . . . 0·49 in (11 mm)
Minimum disc thickness (except estate car) . . . . 0·45 in (11·4 mm)
                     estate car . . . . 0·43 in (11·0 mm)
Pad thickness (except estate car) . . . . 0·38 in (9·7 mm)
              estate car . . . . 0·41 in (10·5 mm)
Minimum pad thickness (all models) . . . . 0·08 in (2·0 mm)
Wheel cylinder diameter . . . . 2 in (51·1 mm)

Front drum
Drum diameter . . . . 8 in (203 mm) or 9 in (228·6 mm)
Lining width . . . . 1·38 in (35 mm) or 1·77 in (45 mm)
Lining thickness . . . . 0·169 in (4·3 mm) or 0·177 in (4·5 mm)
Minimum lining thickness . . . . 0·039 in (1·0 mm)
Wheel cylinder diameter . . . . 0·938 in (23·8 mm)

Rear drum
Drum diameter . . . . 8 in (203 mm) or 9 in (228·6 mm)

Lining width	1·38 in (35 mm) or 1·57 in (40 mm)	
Lining thickness	0·157 in (4·0 mm) or 0·169 in (4·3 mm)	
Minimum lining thickness	0·04 in (1·0 mm)	
Wheel cylinder diameter:		
(with drum brakes at front)	0·814 in (20·62 mm)	
(with disc brakes at front)	0·75 in (19·1 mm)	

Vacuum servo unit

	RHD	LHD
Effective diameter of power cylinder	4·5 in (114·3 mm)	6 in (152·4 mm)
Full stroke of operating rod	1·221 in (31 mm)	1·378 in (35 mm)
Master cylinder diameter	0·75 in (19·05 mm)	0·8126 in (20·64 mm)
Brake fluid specification	SAE J1703	SAE J1703

Handbrake adjustment

Handbrake lever stroke		
Models for Europe 8 in drums	4 to 6 notches	
9 in drums	5 to 7 notches	
Models except Europe	6 to 8 notches	
Extension lever to backplate clearance		
Models for Europe	0.008 to 0·08 in (0·2 to 2·0 mm)	
Models except Europe		
except estate car	0·008 to 0·08 in (0·2 to 2·0 mm)	
estate car only	0·1 in (2·5 mm) or less	

Brake pedal adjustment

Distance from top of pedal to toeboard		
Cars with manual transmission (except estate car)	6·4 in (163 mm)	
Cars with automatic transmission (except estate car)	6·5 in (165 mm)	
Estate car only	6·9 in (175 mm)	
Brake pedal play	0·4 to 0·6 in (10 to 15 mm)	
Minimum distance from depressed pedal to toeboard		
except estate car	At least 1·6 in (40 mm)	
estate car only	At least 1 in (25 mm)	

Torque wrench settings

	lbf ft	kgf m
Bleeder screw	5·1 to 6·4	0·7 to 0·9
Brake tube flare nuts and brake hoses	9·4 to 12·3	1·3 to 1·7
Brake booster holder and fixings	5·8 to 8·7	0·8 to 1·2
Check valve cap to master cylinder	18·1 to 23·5	2·5 to 3·5
Valve case to master cylinder	28·9 to 36·2	4·0 to 5·0
Master cylinder to joint	18·1 to 25·3	2·5 to 3·5
Reservoir tank band	1·8 to 2·9	0·25 to 0·4
Inner and outer caliper bridge bolts	58 to 69	8·0 to 9·5
Caliper assembly torque plate	58 to 72	8·0 to 10·0
Caliper adapter	29 to 36	4·0 to 5·0
Disc to hub	25 to 29	3·5 to 4·0

1 General description

Although most models have disc front brakes, there are some which have drum brakes of the two leading shoe type, which are manually adjusted. The front disc brakes are of the pin caliper type, with the exception of the estate car which has sliding caliper front brakes.

Rear brakes on all models are of the drum type, with leading/trailing shoes which are self-adjusting.

The mechanically operated handbrake works on the rear wheels only and is cable controlled from a lever situated centrally between the front seats.

The front brakes are of the rotating disc and static caliper type, with one piston per caliper and two friction pads. Application of the brakes causes the piston to move and pinch the rotating disc between the two pads. The front brakes are of the trailing caliper type, an arrangement which minimises the entry of water. As the friction pads wear, the caliper pistons move further out of their cylinders, maintaining the pads in a position just clear of the discs. This movement causes the level of fluid in the brake reservoir to drop. Disc pad wear is taken up automatically, eliminating the need for the owner to make adjustments.

All models have a centrally mounted handbrake lever between the front seats. A single cable from this is connected to an equalizer which is mounted beneath the vehicle floor above the propeller shaft, except on the estate car, when it is attached to the rear axle tube. From the equalizer, a separate cable runs to each of the two rear brakes.

The rear brakes contain a self-adjusting mechanism of the ratchet type, to take up the wear of the friction linings. The only adjustment required is on the handbrake lever assembly, or, in the case of the estate car on the rear axle. A screwed adjuster at these points permits any slack in the cable, due to stretching, and wear in the brake linkages to be taken up.

All models have a dual line braking system with a tandem master cylinder and separate hydraulic systems for the front and rear wheels. In the event of a failure of either a pipe, or one of the hydraulic seals, half the braking system will still operate and servo-assistance in this condition is still available.

Some models have a proportioning valve in the braking system, which regulates the fluid pressure to the front and rear wheels to prevent skidding in the event of the rear wheels locking and also to obtain a higher braking efficiency within the normal operating range of the brakes.

As an alternative to a proportioning valve, a combination valve may be fitted. This has the three functions of pressure control of the rear brakes, indicating the failure of a brake pipe and overriding the pressure control to the rear brakes if the front brakes fail.

2 Front disc pads – inspection and renewal

Always renew both the left and the right-hand sets when renewing the brake pads. Renew the pads when their thickness falls to the minimum value given in the Specifications.

Pin caliper type

1 Apply the handbrake, loosen the front wheel nuts and then raise

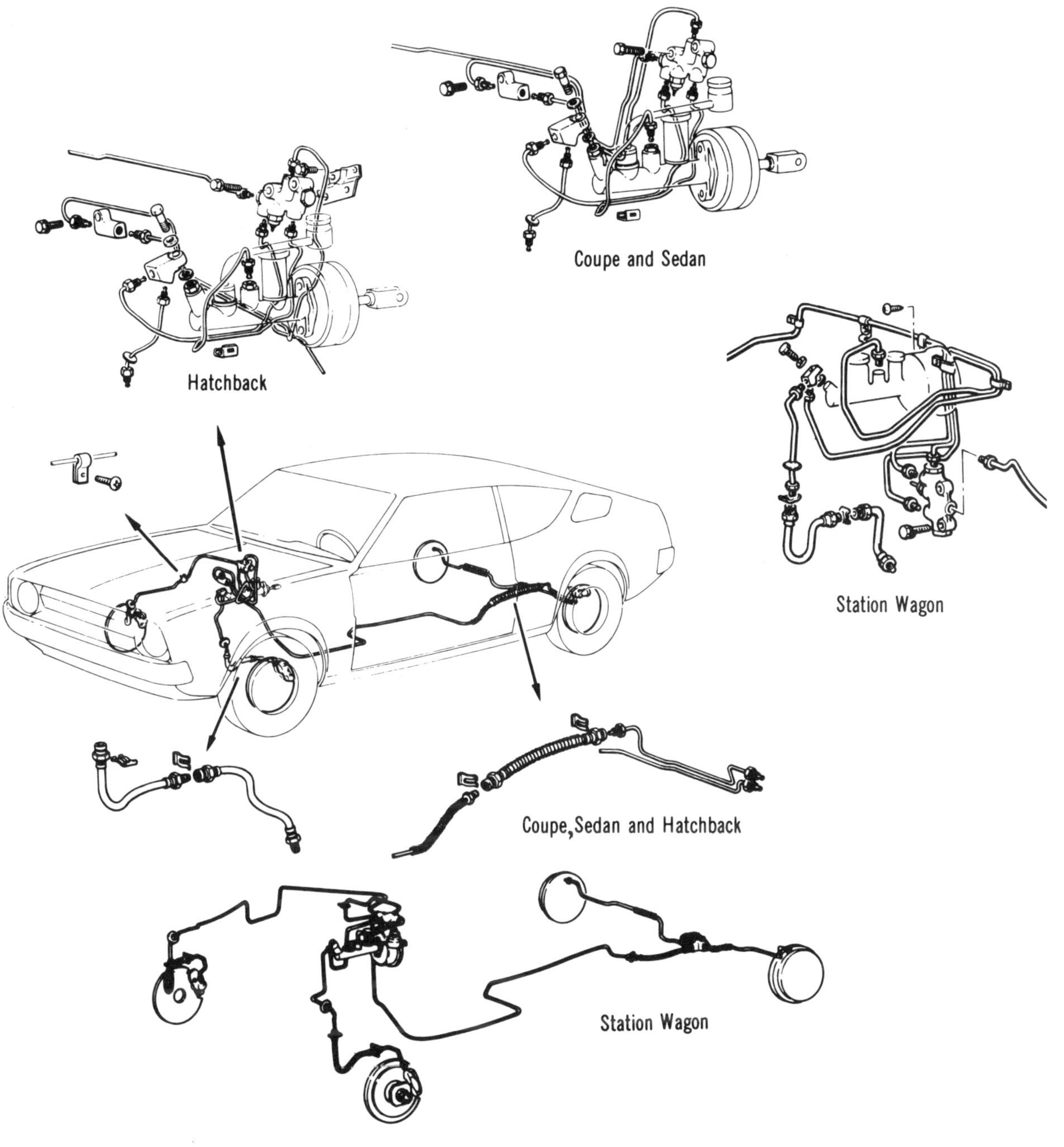

Coupe and Sedan

Hatchback

Station Wagon

Coupe, Sedan and Hatchback

Station Wagon

Fig. 9.1 Brake system layout

2.2a Brake pad protector

2.2b Caliper after removal of M clip

2.7a Friction pad against brake disc

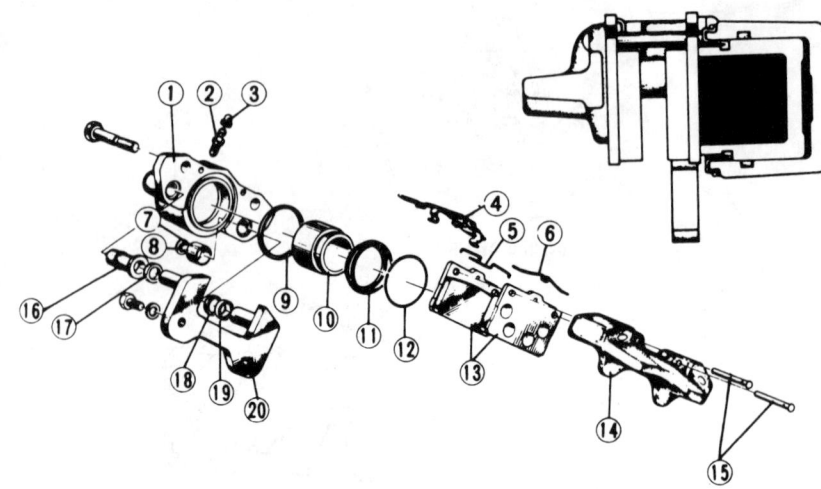

Fig. 9.2 Pin caliper brake – exploded view

1	Caliper, inner	11	Dust seal
2	Bleeder screw	12	Retaining ring
3	Bleeder screw cap	13	Pad assembly
4	Pad protector	14	Caliper, outer
5	K-spring	15	Pad retaining pin
6	M-clip	16	Torque plate pin bushing
7	Torque plate pin cap	17	Spacer
8	Cap plug	18	Wiper seal retainer
9	Piston seal	19	Wiper seal
10	Piston	20	Torque plate

2.7b Pins K spring and M clip in position

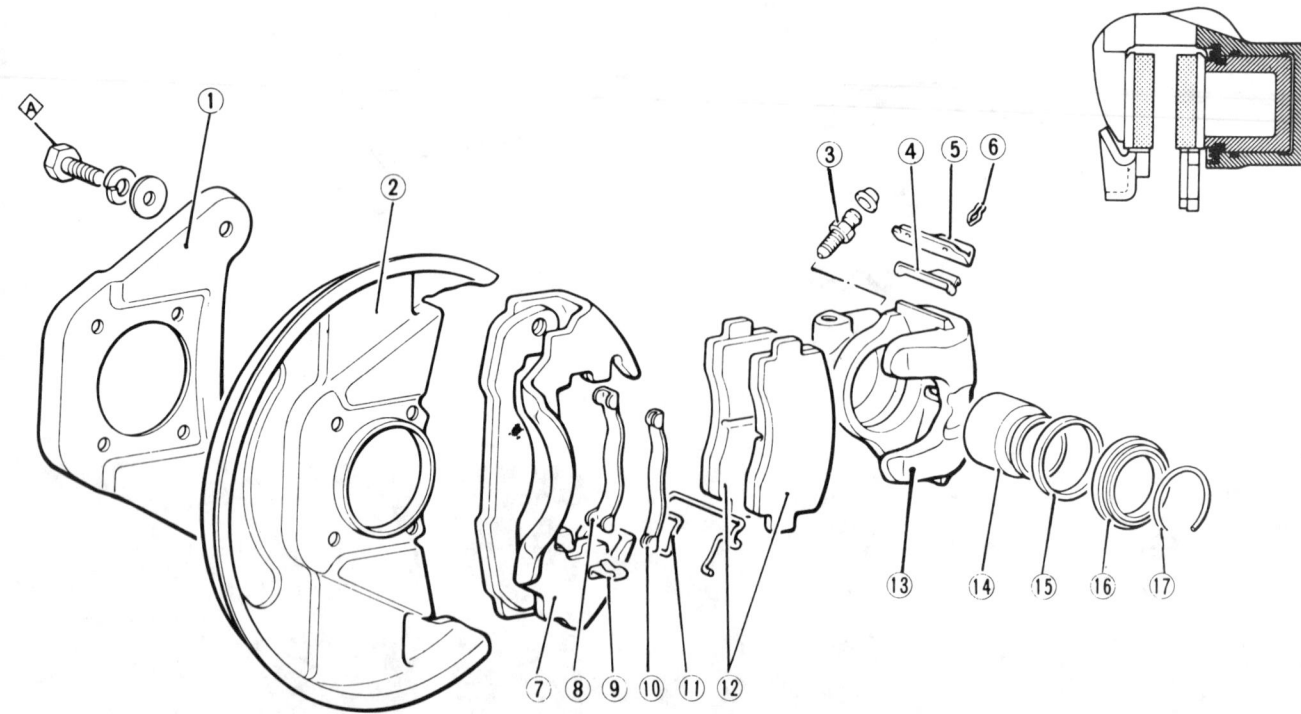

Fig. 9.3 Sliding caliper brake – exploded view

1	Disc brake adapter	6	Spigot pin	10	Outer pad clip	14	Piston
2	Dust cover	7	Caliper support	11	Anti-rattle spring	15	Piston seal
3	Bleed screw	8	Inner pad clip	12	Brake pad	16	Dust boot
4	Pad support plate	9	Pad clip B	13	Caliper body	17	Boot clip
5	Stopper plug						

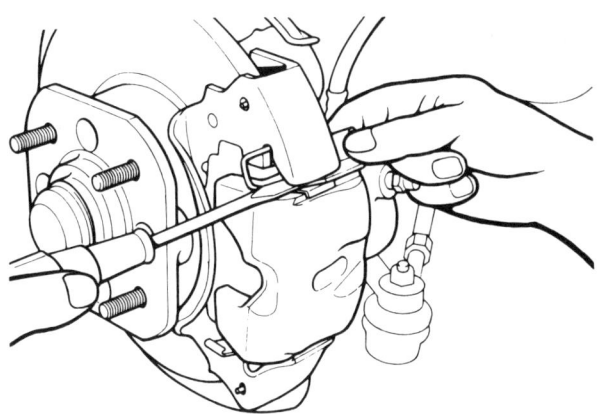

Fig. 9.4 Removing the stopper plug

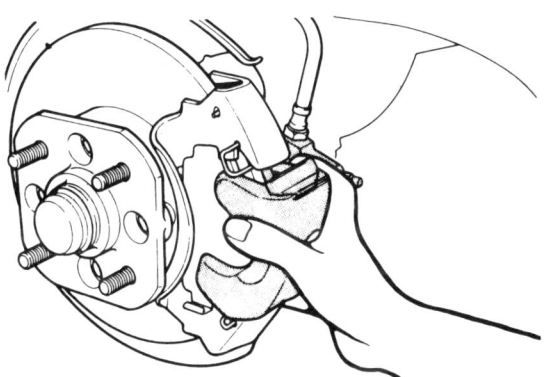

Fig. 9.5 Removing the caliper assembly

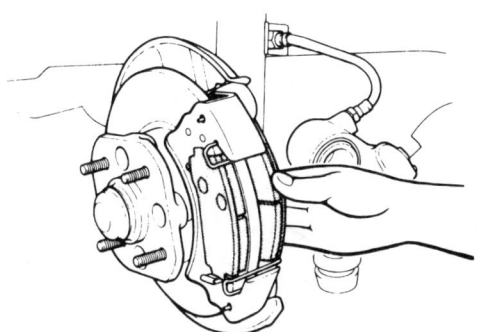

Fig. 9.6 Removing the brake pads

the front wheels and either support the car on firmly based axle stands, or on blocks. Remove the front wheels.

2   Remove the pad protector (photo) by prising up one end with a screwdriver. Remove the loop of the *M* clip from the hole in the outer brake pad, slide the clip to disengage it from one of the pad retaining pins and then pull its other end from the other pin (photo). Pull out the two pad retaining pins and then remove the *K* spring. In case of difficulty, the lower pin may be driven out from the back using a soft drift, but the upper pin goes into a blind hole.

3   Using a pair of locking pliers to grip the backing plate area, withdraw one of the brake pads.

4   If the level of fluid in the brake reservoir is high, syphon fluid until the reservoir is only half full, to prevent the reservoir overflowing when the caliper pistons are pushed back. Insert a piece of flat metal or hard wood between the piston and the disc and then insert a screwdriver to lever back the piston. Remove the second brake pad.

5   Clean the pads and check that the thickness of friction material is above $\frac{5}{64}$ in (2 mm). Clean the recesses in the calipers to remove dirt and corrosion and clean the pad retaining pads to ensure easy refitting.

6   Remove the two caliper fixing bolts and pull off the outer caliper. Remove the torque plate and clean it and its shaft. Because the caliper is of the floating type, this shaft must be kept clean to ensure effective operation. If the shaft is encrusted with dirt and mud, the caliper and bushing will wear prematurely. After cleaning, refit the torque plate, outer caliper and retaining bolts.

7   Insert the brake pads, ensuring that the friction pad is towards the brake disc (photo). Refit the two pad retaining pins, the *K* spring, the *M* clip (photo) and pad protector.

8   Refit the roadwheel and lower the car, then tighten the wheel nuts securely.

9   Top up the brake reservoir and operate the brake pedal to force the brake pads against the discs. Recheck the level of fluid in the reservoir and top up again if necessary.

10   Check that there is no excessive brake drag by rotating each wheel. A tangential force of 13 lb (6 kg) applied to a wheel nut should be sufficient to turn the wheel.

Sliding caliper type

11   Apply the handbrake, loosen the front wheel nuts and then raise the front wheels. Then support the car on firmly based axle stands, or on blocks. Remove the front wheels.

12   Remove the spigot pin from the caliper assembly and pull out the stopper plug (Fig. 9.4).

13   Loosen the caliper assembly mounting and then pull the caliper assembly diagonally upwards and downwards repeatedly until it can be pulled off (Fig. 9.5).

14   Remove the pads from the caliper support, clean them and check that the thickness of friction material is above $\frac{5}{64}$ in (2 mm). Also check that the friction pads are free of oil contamination.

15   After cleaning off the dirt and corrosion, refit the old pads if satisfactory, or new ones if necessary.

16   Clean the exposed part of the caliper piston and then use the handle of a hammer to push the piston right in, taking care to keep the piston square with its bore. If the piston cannot be pushed in with a hammer handle, loosen the bleeder screw and it will then go in easily. But, it will then be necessary to bleed the braking system (Section 17) after refitting the caliper.

17   Refitting the caliper is the reversal of the removal procedure, but it is necessary to ensure that pad clip B and the inner and outer pad clips are fitted correctly (Fig. 9.7).

18   Check that there is no excessive brake drag, by rotating the wheel. A tangential force of 13 lb (6 kg) applied to the wheel nut should be sufficient to turn the wheel.

19   On this type of brake it is not necessary to remove the caliper in order to check the remaining pad thickness. Pad thickness can be checked by removing the roadwheel and looking through the inspection hole (Fig. 9.8). The groove in the centre of the pad is not a pad wear indicator, but is there to assist in removing pad dust.

3   Front brake shoes – inspection and renewal

1   Apply the handbrake, loosen the front wheel nuts and then raise the front wheels. Either support the car on firmly based axle stands, or on blocks. Remove the front wheels.

2   Remove the brake drum securing screw and using a soft faced

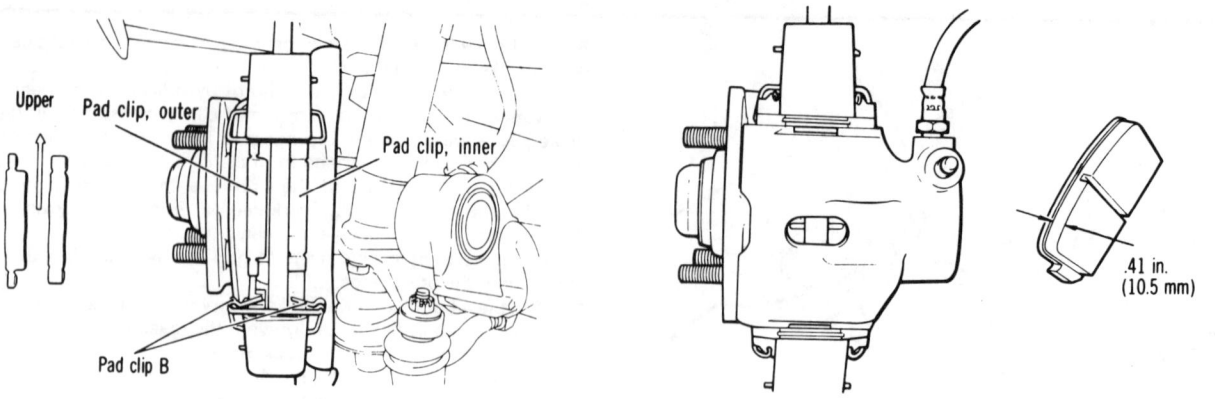

Fig. 9.7 Fitting the pad clips

Fig. 9.8 Checking pad wear

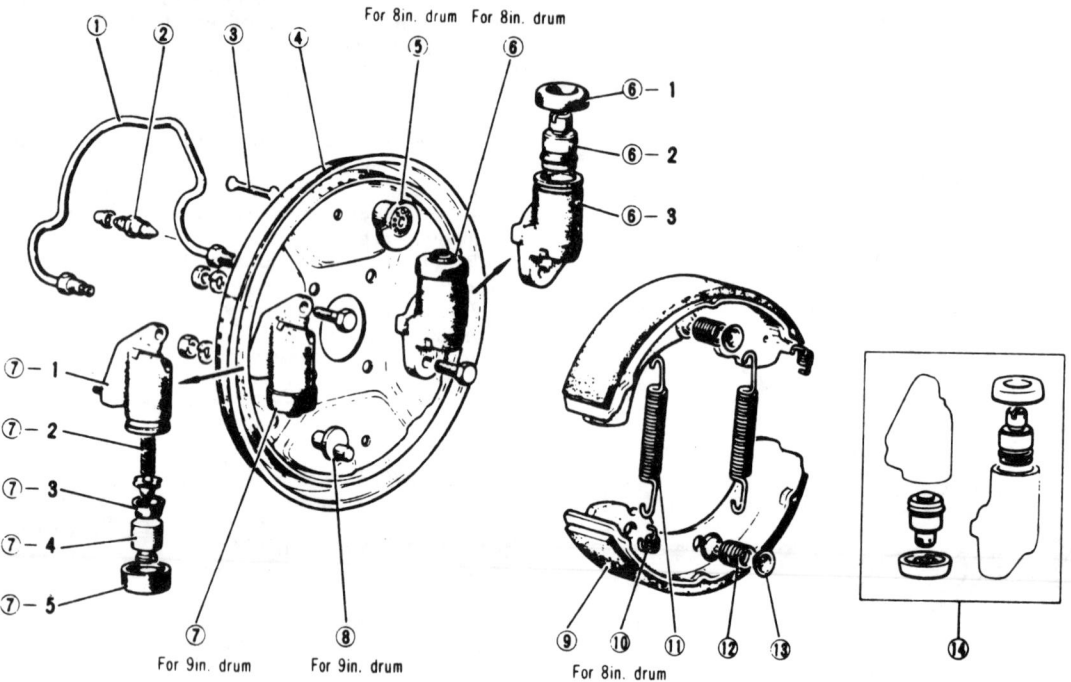

Fig. 9.9 Front drum brake – exploded view

1	Brake tube	6-1 Wheel cylinder boot	7-2 Wheel cylinder piston spring	10 Shoe-to-piston spring (8 in drum)
2	Bleed screw	6-2 Wheel cylinder piston assembly	7-3 Wheel cylinder piston cup	
3	Shoe hold-down spring pin		7-4 Wheel cylinder piston	11 Return spring
4	Backing plate	6-3 Wheel cylinder	7-5 Wheel cylinder boot	12 Shoe hold-down spring
5	Shoe adjusting cam (8 in drum)	7 Wheel cylinder assembly (9 in drum)	8 Shoe adjusting cam (9 in drum)	13 Shoe hold-down spring seat
6	Wheel cylinder assembly (8in drum)	7-1 Wheel cylinder	9 Brake shoe	14 Wheel cylinder kit

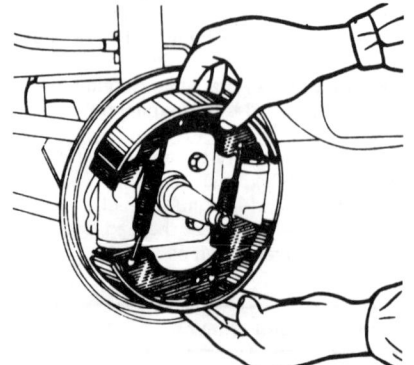

Fig. 9.10 Removing the brake shoes and return springs

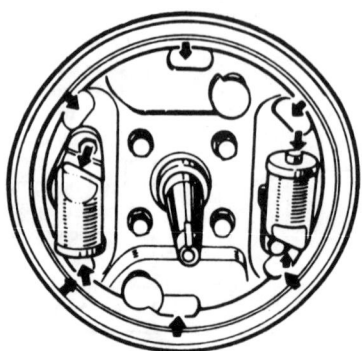

Fig. 9.11 Brake greasing points (arrowed)

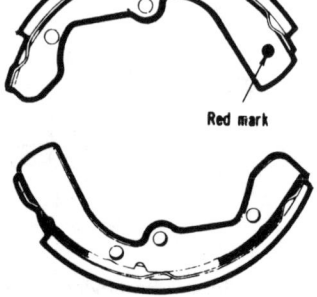

Fig. 9.12 Brake shoe identification

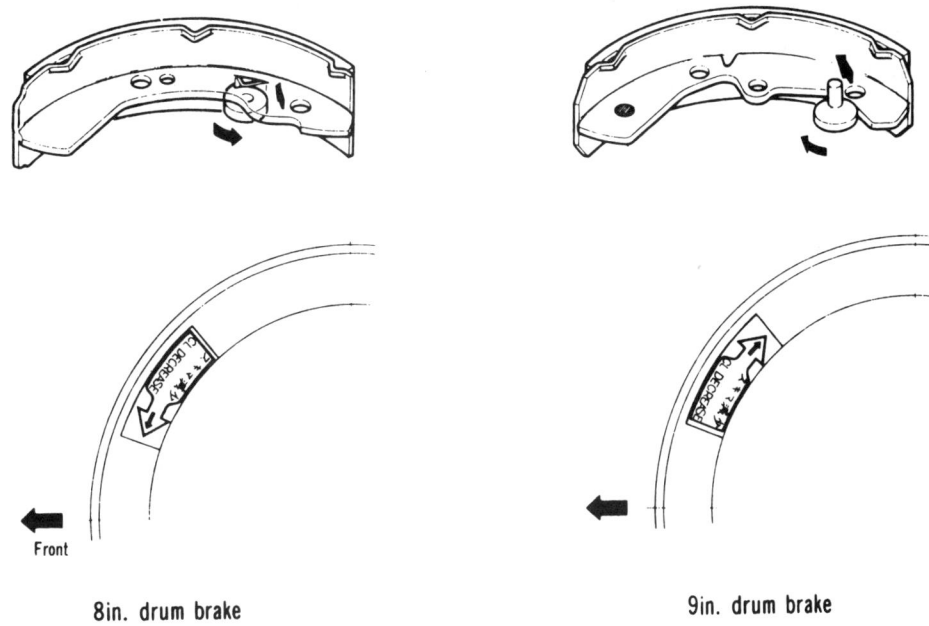

8in. drum brake   9in. drum brake

Fig. 9.13 Brake shoe adjustment

hammer on the outer circumference of the brake drum, remove the drum.

3   Remove the brake shoe hold down pins and springs. Remove the shoe to piston springs, if fitted.

4   Pull one brake shoe out of the slots in the brake cylinders and then lift away both brake shoes and their return springs as an assembly (Fig. 9.10). Mark the hole used to secure the springs in the brake shoes. It is not necessary to remove the front hub in order to remove the brake shoes, although the job is easier if the wheel hub has been removed.

5   Clean all the dust from inside the drum, from the brake backplate, brake cylinders and shoes.

6   Inspect the brake shoes and discard them if the friction linings are contaminated with oil, or if the linings are worn below the minimum thickness given in the Specifications.

7   Fit the return springs to the brakes, taking care that the springs are fitted against the outer face of the shoes and that the ends of the springs are fitted into the correct holes. Apply brake grease to the points indicated in Fig. 9.11.

8   When refitting the shoes of the 9 in diameter brakes, note that one of the shoes has a red paint mark on it (Fig. 9.12). Ensure that this shoe is in the upper position.

9   Refit the shoe retainer pins and springs, and the shoe to cylinder springs if appropriate.

10   Adjust the brake clearances as described in the following Section.

4   Front brake shoes – adjustment

1   Have an assistant sit in the car and depress the brake pedal firmly.

2   With the assistant keeping the pedal held down, turn the brake shoe adjusters in the direction of the arrow (Fig. 9.13) until the cam is just felt to come into contact with the brake shoe.

3   Release the brake pedal and while turning the wheel, back off the brake adjuster one sixth of a turn (60°).

4   Depress the brake pedal several times repeatedly and then turn the wheel to ensure that the brake lining is not rubbing against the drum.

5   Front brake caliper – removal, overhaul and refitting

Pin caliper type

Removal

1   Remove the brake pads as described in Section 2.

2   Pull off the brake hose clip from the strut area and then disconnect the brake hose at the caliper.

3   Remove the torque plate and adapter mounting bolts. Then remove the caliper assembly.

Dismantling and overhaul

4   Remove the caliper attachment bolts and separate the inner and outer calipers. Remove the cylinder dust seal and then apply air pressure to the brake hose fitting to blow the piston out.

5   Remove the piston seal, being careful not to damage the cylinder bore.

6   Clean all removed parts in methylated spirit, taking care that rubber parts are not in contact with the cleaning fluid for more than 30 seconds.

7   Inspect the cylinder and piston for wear, damage and corrosion and renew them if there is a significant amount of deterioration. It is preferable to renew the piston seal, dust seal and wiper seal whenever the cylinder is dismantled and in any case, to renew them every two years. The wiper seal retainer, plug cap, spacer and bushing should also be renewed whenever the unit is dismantled.

8   Service kits contain special lubricants as well as new parts. Smear a little of the rubber grease (red) on to the piston seal and carefully insert the seal into the recess in the piston bore. Smear the piston surface with the same grease and insert the piston into the bore, taking care not to dislodge or damage the seal. If it is necessary to lubricate the piston cylinder bore, brake fluid should be used.

9   Clean the torque plate shaft and the bores of the caliper. Smear the special grease (yellow) on to the rubber bushing, wiper seal inner surface and torque plate shafts and reassemble.

10   Insert and then tighten the inner and outer caliper bridge bolts to

9.3 Removing the hold-down spring

9.5a Brake adjusting lever and latch

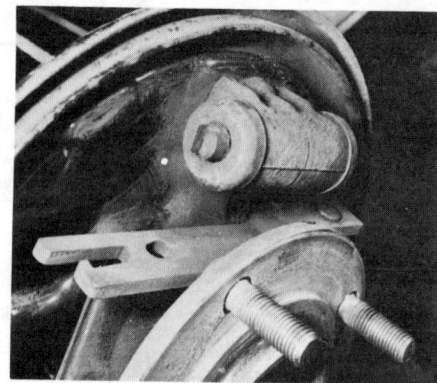
9.5b Parking brake strut hooked end

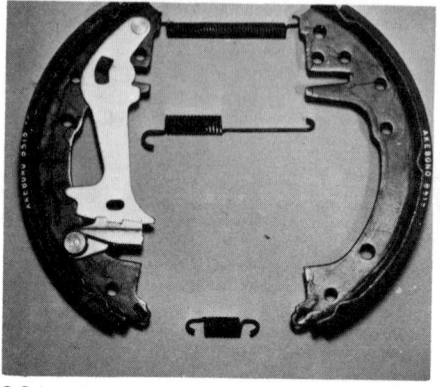
9.9 Leading shoe with adjusting lever fitted

9.12 Shoes joined by lower brake spring

9.13 Strut spring and shoe to strut spring fitted

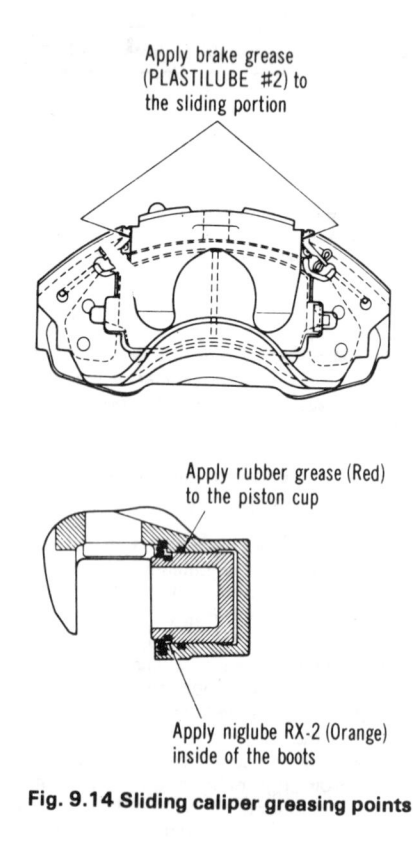

Apply brake grease (PLASTILUBE #2) to the sliding portion

Apply rubber grease (Red) to the piston cup

Apply niglube RX-2 (Orange) inside of the boots

Fig. 9.14 Sliding caliper greasing points

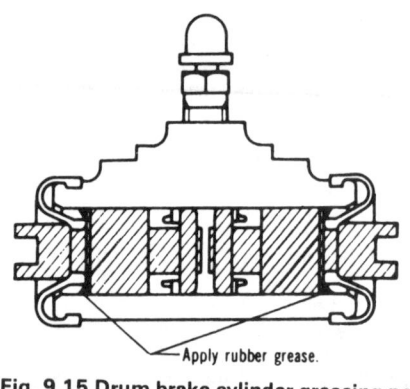

Apply rubber grease.

Fig. 9.15 Drum brake cylinder greasing points

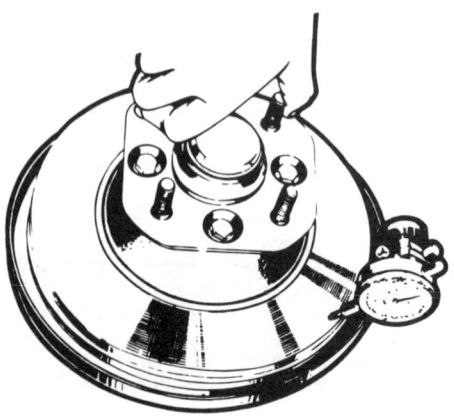

Fig. 9.16 Checking brake disc deflection

the recommended torque. Refit the caliper to the brake backplate then reconnect the brake hose.

11 Bleed the brake system as described in Section 17. Because the wheel cylinder has a large diameter piston, even a small amount of air will reduce brake performance seriously and bleeding should be done carefully and thoroughly.

Sliding caliper type
Removal
12 Refer to Section 2 and carry out the operations detailed in paragraphs 11 and 12.
13 Remove the brake pads.
14 Pull the brake hose from out of its clip and then disconnect the brake hose from the caliper assembly.

Dismantling and overhaul
Place a cap over the end of the brake hose, or plug its end to prevent loss of fluid and the entry of dirt.
15 Remove the clip securing the dust boot of the cylinder and pull off the dust boot. Cover the end of the piston with a cloth and apply air pressure into the brake hose fitting to push the piston out.
16 Remove the piston seal from the groove in the cylinder bore, taking care not to damage the cylinder bore.
17 Wash all the parts in methylated spirit, taking care that the piston seal and dust boot are not immersed in methylated spirit for longer than 30 seconds.
18 Check the piston and cylinder for wear, damage and corrosion and discard any defective parts.
19 If the piston seal and rubber boot are suspect, or if they are known to be more than two years old, discard and replace them.
20 Smear rubber grease over the piston seal and carefully fit it into the groove in the cylinder bore.
21 Push the piston in by hand after having first lubricated both the piston and the cylinder with brake fluid. Take care not to distort or displace the bore seal when inserting the piston.
22 Apply the special lubricant, supplied with the wheel cylinder repair kit, to the dust boot. After fitting the boot, fit the boot retaining clip.
23 Refit the brake hose to the brake cylinder and tighten it to the specified torque. Reassemble the caliper assembly as described in Section 2.
24 After completing the reassembly, bleed the braking system thoroughly. Because the caliper uses a large diameter piston, even a small amount of air will reduce brake performance seriously.

---

6 Front drum brake cylinders – removal, overhaul and refitting

1 Remove the front brake drum, as described in Section 3, paragraphs 1 and 2.
2 Remove the hub cap, split pin, lock cap and lock nut.
3 Pull off the hub assembly, taking care not to drop the wheel outer bearing cone.
4 Remove the brake shoe hold down pins and springs, and the shoe to piston springs, if fitted.
5 Pull off the brake shoes and lift away both brake shoes and their return springs as an assembly. Note the brake shoe holes that retain the return springs for correct reassembly.
6 Disconnect the flexible brake hose and seal the end of the brake pipe to prevent loss of fluid.
7 Remove the four bolts attaching the brake backplate to the stub axle and lift away the back plate assembly.
8 Remove the brake hose and the brake pipe connecting the two wheel cylinders. Then remove the brake cylinder attachment nuts and separate the brake cylinders from the backplate.
9 Remove the pistons from the brake cylinders and pull the seals from the pistons. Discard the cylinder boots and seals and wash the pistons and cylinders in methylated spirit.
10 Inspect the pistons and cylinders for signs of wear, damage and corrosion and discard any parts which are unsatisfactory.
11 Apply rubber grease to a new piston seal and fit the seal with its flat face towards the piston body.
12 Lubricate the piston and cylinder bore with brake fluid and insert the piston, taking care not to damage, or distort the seal.
13 Fit the dust boots to the piston. Apply rubber grease to the boot and piston joints on the side of the boots. Then fit the boot rims to the

grooves in the outer surface of the cylinders.
14 Complete reassembly is a reversal of removal procedure, applying brake grease to the points indicated in Fig. 9.15 before refitting the brake shoes.
15 After completing assembly, bleed the brakes as described in Section 17.

---

7 Brake disc – removal, inspection and refitting

1 Remove the wheel and brake caliper assembly as described in Section 5.
2 Remove the hub cap, split-pin and locking nut and prise off the washer.
3 Pull the brake disc and hub assembly off the stub axle, taking care that the wheel outer bearing cone does not fall off.
4 Inspect the disc for damage or obvious distortion then measure the disc thickness at several points around its circumference. If the disc thickness is less than 0.45 in (11.4mm) the disc should be renewed.

---

8 Brake disc – renewal

1 Remove the disc and hub assembly as described in Section 7.
2 Remove the four nuts and bolts securing the disc to the hub, hold the disc in a soft jawed vice or place a piece of soft metal on each side of the disc before gripping it and prise the hub away from the disc.
3 Fit the new disc, refit the four bolts and nuts and tighten them to the recommended torque wrench settings.
4 Refit the assembly on to the stub axle (see Chapter 11), Section 3) and with a dial gauge mounted on the brake backplate (Fig. 9.16) and set to zero, rotate the disc slowly and note the deflection of the dial gauge needle. If the deflection exceeds 0.006 in (0.15 mm), change the position of the disc on the hub and recheck.

---

9 Rear brakes – dismantling, inspection and renewal

After a high mileage, it will be necessary to fit new brake shoes, or new linings. Refitting new brake linings to shoes is not normally considered to be economic, or possible without special equipment. However, if the services of a local garage, or workshop having brake lining equipment are available, there is no reason why the original shoes cannot be relined satisfactorily. It is necessary to ensure that the new linings are of the correct specification.

1 Securely chock the front wheels, loosen the rear wheel hub nuts, jack up the rear wheel and support the axle with a firmly based axle stand, or blocks and remove the roadwheel.
2 Remove the brake drum securing screw and using a soft faced hammer on the outer circumference of the brake drum, remove the drum. Because the brakes are fitted with a wear compensating mechanism which limits the clearance between the shoes and the drum, removal may prove difficult. If this is the case, two screws should be inserted in the tapped holes in the brake drum and tightened alternately half a turn at a time.
3 Remove the shoe hold down spring and pin (photo).
4 Detach the strut-to-shoe spring and the end hook of the upper shoe return spring from the trailing brake shoe, then remove the trailing shoe with the lower shoe return spring attached to it.
5 Holding the adjusting latch down, pull the adjusting lever towards the centre of the brake (photo). Hold the parking brake strut at its pivot (photo), release the adjusting lever from the hooked end of the parking brake strut and remove the leading shoe, the upper return spring and strut-to-shoe spring.
6 Remove the upper return spring and the strut-to-shoe spring from the shoe. Pull off the retainer and separate the brake shoe and the adjusting lever. Also remove the adjusting latch.
7 Clean all the dust from the brake shoes, brake drum and other components, taking care not to inhale the dust.
8 Inspect the brake linings and fit new shoes if the lining thickness is less than 0.04 in (1 mm). Inspect the inside of the brake drum and renew it if it is excessively worn or is scored badly enough to damage the new brake linings. An 8 in diameter brake drum has a permissible wear limit of 8.071 in (205 mm) and a 9 in drum should not exceed 9.079

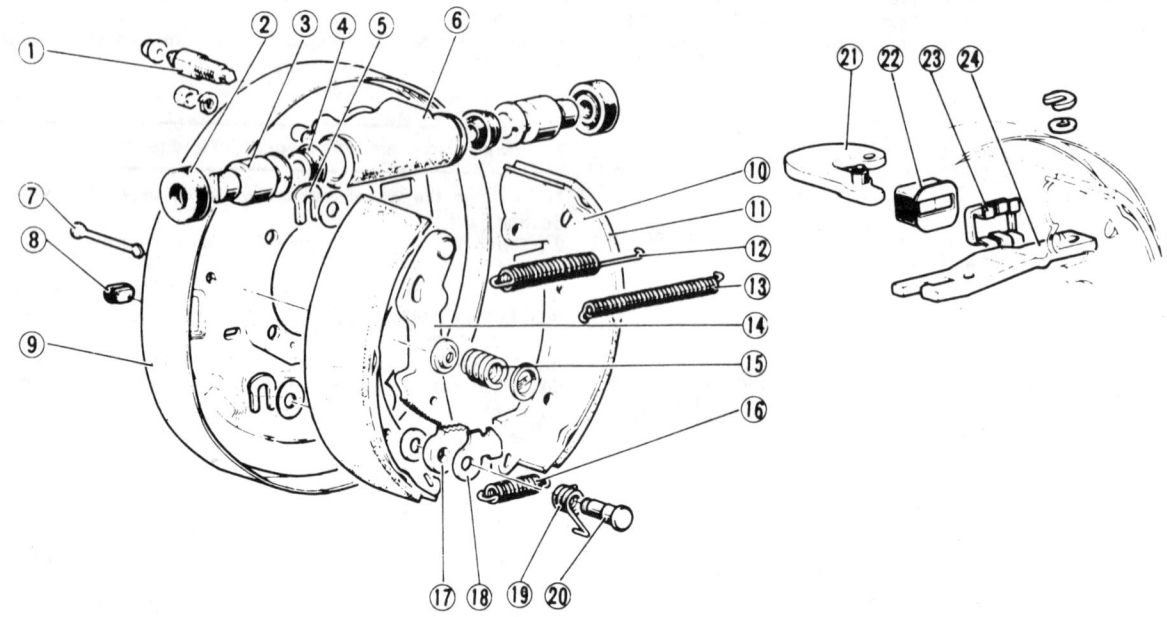

Fig. 9.17 Rear brake – exploded view

1 Bleeder screw	7 Shoe hold-down pin	13 Automatic adjusting spring	19 Return spring
2 Wheel cylinder boot	8 Adjusting wheel cover	14 Adjusting lever	20 Pin
3 Wheel cylinder piston	9 Backing plate	15 Shoe hold-down spring	21 Handbrake extension lever
4 Wheel cylinder cup	10 Brake shoes assembly	16 Shoe return spring (lower)	22 Handbrake extension lever cup
5 Retainer	11 Brake lining	17 Adjusting latch	23 Handbrake extension lever retainer
6 Wheel cylinder body	12 Shoe return spring (upper)	18 Stopper	24 Handbrake strut

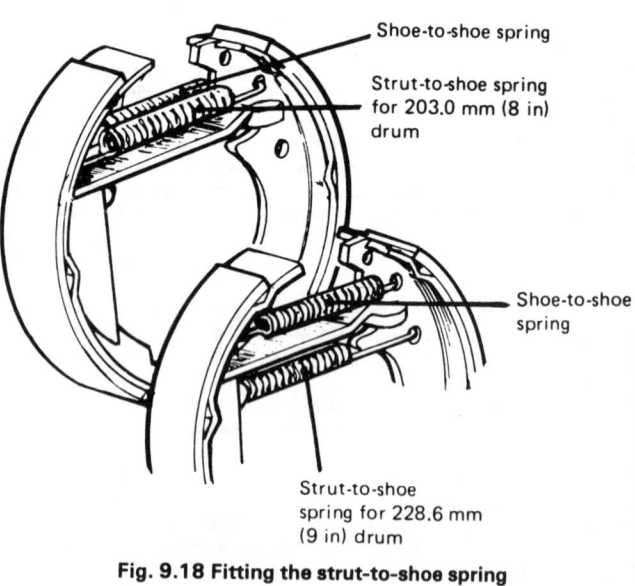

Fig. 9.18 Fitting the strut-to-shoe spring

Shoe-to-shoe spring

Strut-to-shoe spring
for 203.0 mm (8 in)
drum

Shoe-to-shoe
spring

Strut-to-shoe
spring for 228.6 mm
(9 in) drum

10.2 Rear brake cylinder

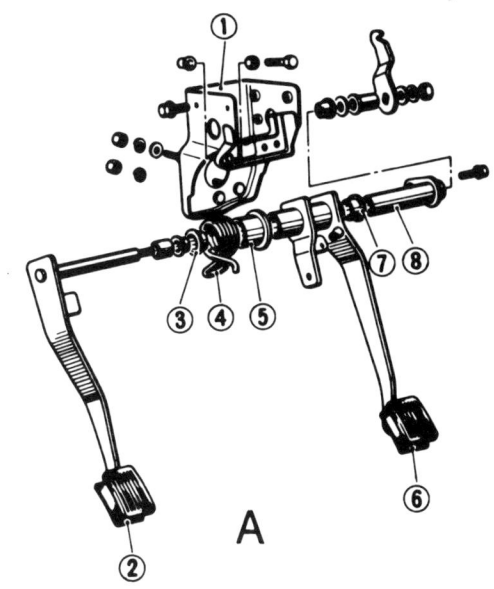

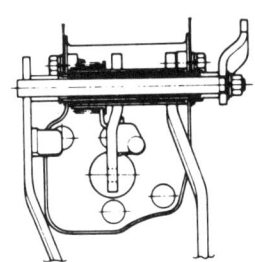

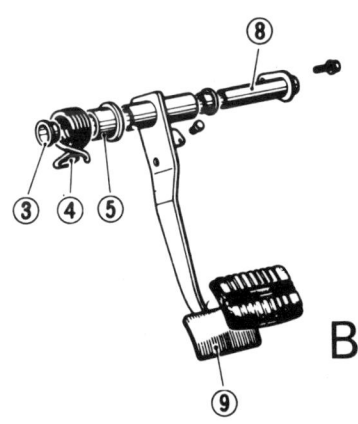

Fig. 9.19 Brake pedal control – exploded view

A *Manual gearbox models*	B *Automatic transmission*
1 *Pedal bracket*	*models*
2 *Clutch pedal*	6 *Brake pedal*
3 *Bushing*	7 *Bushing*
4 *Return spring*	8 *Pedal rod*
5 *Silencer*	9 *Brake pedal (automatic*
	transmission)

in (230·6 mm).

9   Fit the adjusting lever and latch to the leading brake shoe (photo).

10   Apply brake grease to the brake shoe contact surfaces of the backplate, to the wheel cylinder, adjuster plate and parking brake strut surfaces in contact with the shoes.

11   Disengage the adjusting lever from its latch, engage it with the parking brake strut. Re-engage the strut and latch, then fit the shoe into the slot of the brake cylinder piston.

12   Fit the upper brake spring and strut-to-shoe spring forward ends. Join the two shoes with the lower brake springs and fit the trailing brake shoe into the other brake cylinder piston. When fitting the shoes to the pistons, take care not to damage the wheel cylinder boots (photo).

13   Engage the rear ends of the upper shoe spring and strut-to-shoe spring in the trailing shoe (photo). There are differences in fitting the strut-to-shoe spring and upper return spring between the 8 in and 9 in brake drums (Fig. 9.18). There are also differences in the adjusting lever and latch spring of the left-hand side and right-hand side rear brakes. Correct fitting is as follows:

Description		Identification colour
Adjusting lever	*Left*	*White*
(colour of plating)	*Right*	*Yellow*
Latch spring	*Left*	*Black*
	Right	*Grey*

Note also that the right strut-to-shoe spring differs in colour from the left one.

Strut-to-shoe spring	*Left*	*White*
(colour of paint)	*Right*	—

10 Rear brake cylinder – removal and overhaul

1   Remove the brake drum and shoes as described in Section 9.

2   Disconnect and remove the flexible brake pipe at the wheel cylinder. Remove the two fixing nuts and washers behind the brake backplate and remove the cylinder (photo).

3   Remove the boots from the cylinder ends, withdraw the pistons and remove the wheel cylinder cups.

4   Clean all the brake cylinder parts in methylated spirit, but do not allow the cups or boots in contact with the spirit for more than 30 seconds.

5   Examine the cylinder bore and renew the cylinder if the bore is badly scored or corroded. Measure the piston-to-bore clearance, which must not exceed 0·006 in (0·15 mm).

6   Fit new cups to the piston, making sure that the flat end of the cup is against the shoulder of the piston.

7   Smear the cups with brake fluid, insert the pistons into the cylinder, taking care not to distort the cups, and refit the boots.

8   Refit the cylinder to the back plate, reconnect the brake pipe and after fitting the shoes and drum, bleed the system (see Section 17). Before refitting the brake drum, move the adjusting lever along the latch until the brake shoes are almost in contact with the inside of the drum when it is fitted; and after fitting and bleeding, depress the brake pedal several times to take up any unnecessary clearance which remains. The automatic adjuster is designed to operate about every 0·003 in (0·08 mm) wear of the linings.

11 Brake pedal adjustment

Effective operation of the braking system is dependent upon correct setting of the brake pedal position and travel. The dimensions given in the Specifications must be maintained. Pedal operating pressure should be approximately 110 lbs (50 kg).

1   Remove the pin connecting the brake booster operating rod to the pedal. Unscrew the pedal stopper a small amount and then screw it in until the specified dimension between the top of the pedal and the toeboard is achieved. Lock the pedal stopper in this position.

2   Ensure that the booster operating rod is not pushed in at all, line up the hole in the operating rod clevis with the hole in the brake pedal, insert the hinge pin and split cotter. If, after setting the brake pedal stop, the pedal travel is excessive, check the master cylinder to brake booster push rod clearance and the brake shoe-to-drum clearance.

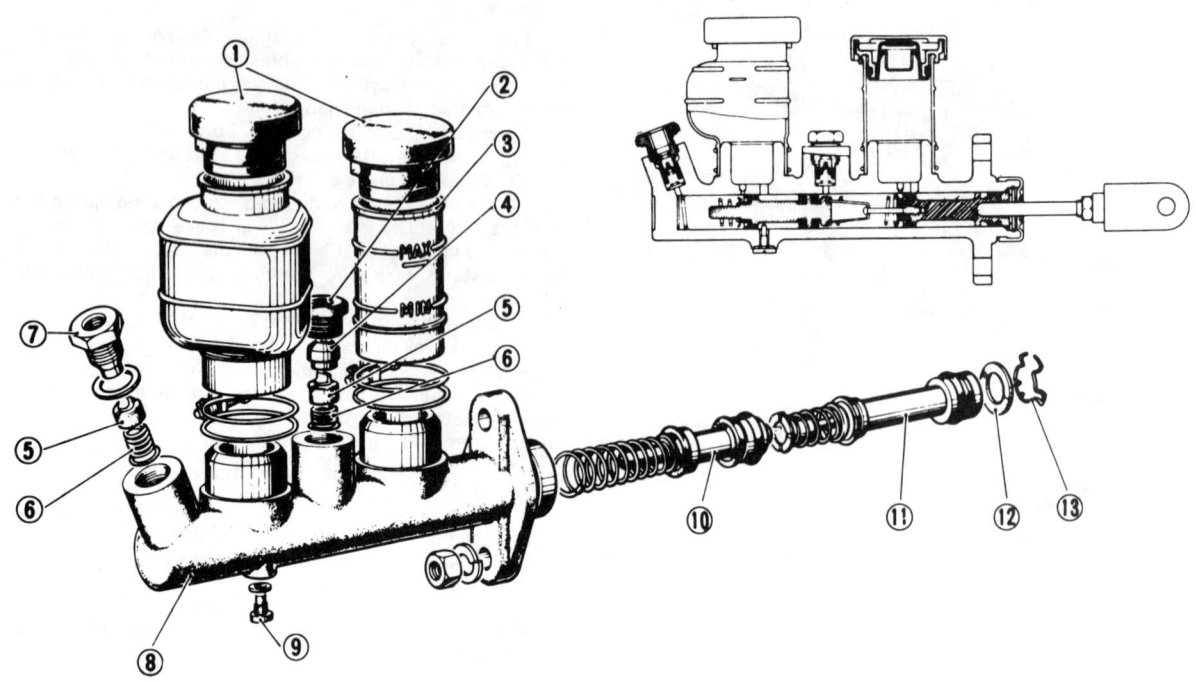

Fig. 9.20 Master cylinder – exploded view

1	Reservoir cap	5	Check valve	8	Master cylinder	11	Primary piston assembly
2	Check valve cap	6	Check valve spring	9	Piston stopper	12	Piston stopper
3	Fluid reservoir	7	Valve case	10	Secondary piston assembly	13	Stopper ring
4	Outer pipe seat						

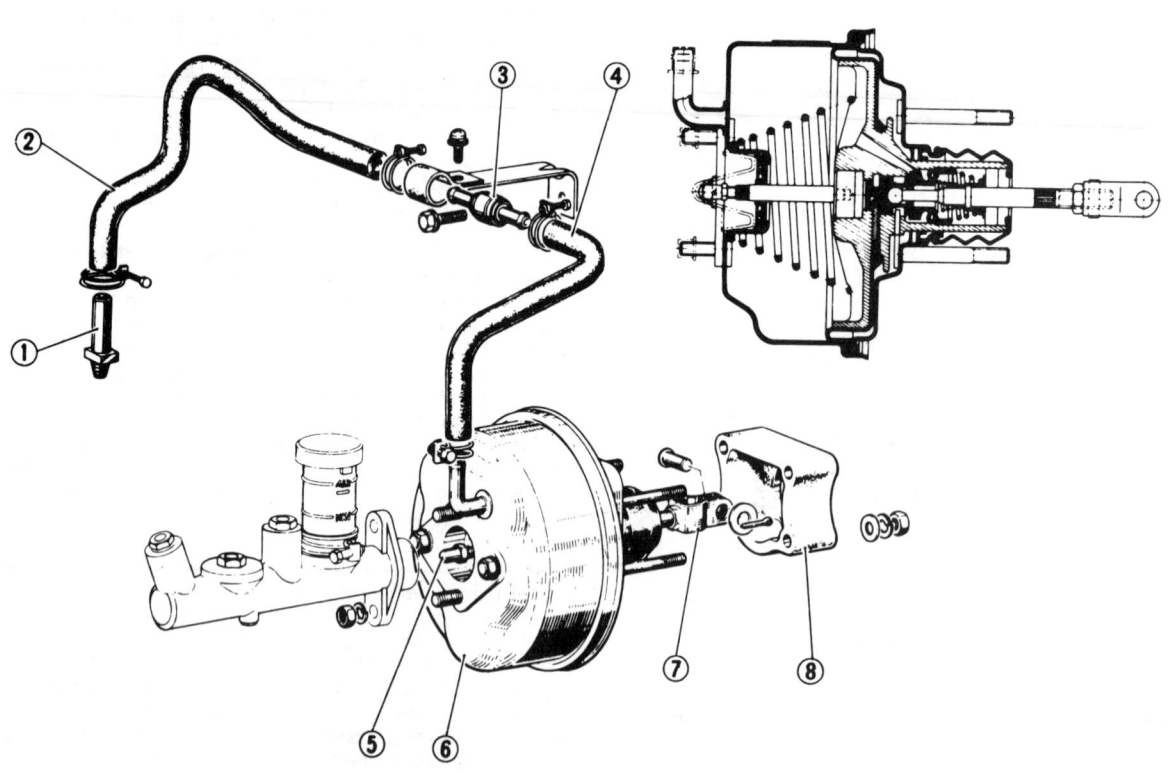

Fig. 9.21 Brake booster – exploded view

1	Fitting	4	Vacuum hose	6	Power brake (booster assembly)	7	Yoke
2	Vacuum hose	5	Push rod			8	Booster spacer
3	Check valve						

12 Master cylinder – removal and servicing

1   Disconnect the brake pipes from the master cylinder and then slowly depress the brake pedal to drain the fluid.
2   Remove the two nuts and washers attaching the master cylinder to the brake booster and remove the master cylinder.
3   Remove the boot and stopper ring, then withdraw the primary piston assembly, secondary piston assembly and secondary return spring, in that order.
4   Unscrew the check valve cases and remove the check valves and check valve springs.
5   Inspect the pistons and if worn or damaged, renew the complete piston assembly. Inspect the cylinder bore for corrosion and wear and renew the cylinder if the piston to cylinder clearance exceeds 0·006 in.
6   Wash all parts in methylated spirit, ensuring that non-metal parts are not in contact with spirit for longer than 30 seconds. Allow to dry and reassemble.
7   Refit the master cylinder and bleed the system (Section 14).

13 Brake booster – dismantling and overhaul

Although there are variations in dimensions and different models of brake booster, the following instructions are applicable generally. Failure in the check valve may be mistaken for a booster failure and the check valve in the vacuum line should always be tested before dismantling the brake booster. With the vacuum hose disconnected from the check valve at the booster side, spin the engine while holding a finger against the end of the check valve to see if a vacuum is produced and maintained. If there is no vacuum, renew the check valve. If a satisfactory vacuum is produced, proceed as follows.
1   Remove the master cylinder.
2   Disconnect the vacuum hose from the brake booster.
3   Remove the pin connecting the brake booster operating rod to the pedal.
4   Remove the brake booster attachment nuts (which also secure the pedal support bracket) and withdraw the brake booster assembly.
5   Before starting to dismantle the booster, clean all dirt from its outside and ensure that a repair kit is to hand, so that components subject to deterioration can be renewed.
6   Ensure that the work can be carried out in a clean, dry place. Hold the front shell flange in a vice, then remove the clevis and locknut.
7   Scribe mating marks on the front and rear shells and then, holding the rear shell clamped between two bars, unscrew it anti-clockwise (Fig. 9.22).
8   Remove the diaphragm spring and diaphragm plate, taking care not to damage the plate which is made of plastic and is fragile.
9   Remove the rear shell assembly and dismantle it by pulling off the retainer with a screwdriver and then removing the bearing and the valve body seal (Fig. 9.23).
10   Remove the diaphragm plate assembly, pull the diaphragm from the plate, remove the silencer retainer from the diaphragm plate with a screwdriver, then remove the silencer filter and the silencer. Remove

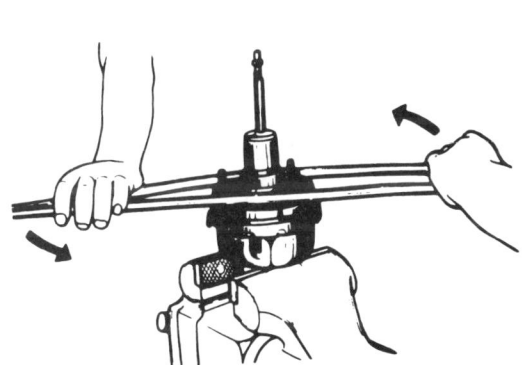

Fig. 9.22 Removing the rear shell

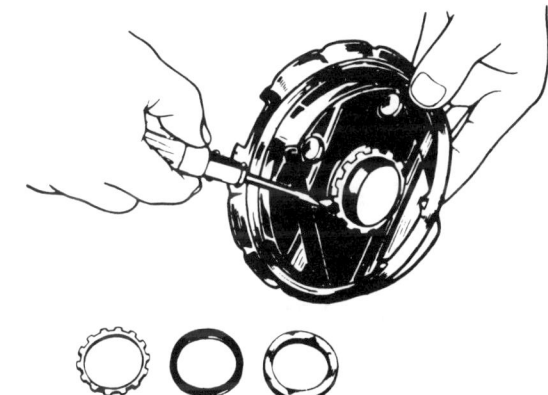

Fig. 9.23 Removing the rear shell seal

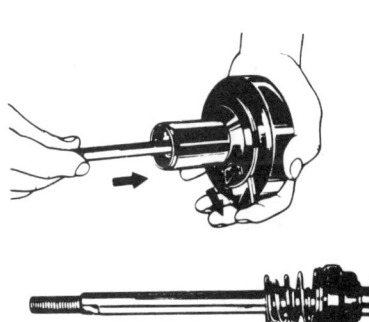

Fig. 9.24 Removing the valve rod plunger

13 Brake booster check valve

the valve plunger stop key and gently pull off the valve rod and plunger assembly (Fig. 9.24). To remove the key, hold the valve plunger with the key downwards and while pushing on the rod, gently tap the assembly against the bench. Finally, remove the reaction disc. Some valve rod plunger assemblies cannot be dismantled and the entire assembly has to be renewed.

11 When dismantling has been completed, clean all the parts carefully then check the diaphragm plate for damage and cracks and the front and rear shells for cracks and distortion. Check that the push rod is not bent or damaged and that there is no cracking or damage around the stud mountings.

14 Brake booster – assembly

Before starting assembly, apply silicone grease to the following places (Fig. 9.25).

(a) *Front shell seal and push rod sliding surfaces*
(b) *Push rod and seal contact surfaces*
(c) *Diaphragm lug, to rear shell, contact surfaces*
(d) *Outside surface of reaction disc (grease sparingly)*
(e) *Reaction disc inserting part of diaphragm plate*
(f) *Rear shell seal and diaphragm plate sliding surfaces*
(g) *Interior of piston plate into which plunger assembly is inserted; and seal sliding surfaces*

1   Insert the seal, bearing and retainer into the rear shell in that order, then lightly press in the retainer.
2   Carefully insert the valve rod and plunger assembly into the diaphragm plate.
3   Insert the valve plunger stop key (Fig. 9.26), with its chamfered face towards the piston and then pull the plunger assembly to make certain that the valve plunger is locked securely. If the valve key is inserted the wrong way round, it may be difficult to remove the next time that it is dismantled.
4   Fit the reaction disc and diaphragm to the diaphragm plate. After fitting make sure that the diaphragm has been inserted into the diaphragm plate securely. When fitting the diaphragm, care must be taken to ensure that it is not contaminated with oil.
5   Insert the urethane foam silencer filter (Fig. 9.27) and then the felt silencer into the rear of the diaphragm plate and then fit the retainer. Inserting the foam filter and felt silencer in the wrong order will adversely affect the operation of the diaphragm, due to fibres from the felt becoming stuck in the valve.
6   Fit the diaphragm plate in the rear shell and then fit the valve bodyguard to the rear shell, with the rear of the guard into the end of the retainer.
7   Fit the plate and seal assembly into the front shell, fit the push rod and then attach the flange to the front shell by pressing it in, as with the front shell seal.
8   Roughly align the mating marks on the front and rear shell, fit the front shell and turn it until the mating marks are in line and its notch is against the stop.
9   Measure the clearance between the brake booster pushrod and the back of the master cylinder (Fig. 9.28) and if necessary adjust the length of the push rod to obtain the recommended clearance of 0 to 0·03 in (0 to 7·6 mm).
10   Fit the yoke to the threaded end of the operating rod, with $0.512 ^{+0.08}_{-0.16}$ in ($13 ^{+2}_{-4}$ mm) of rod inserted into the yoke.
11   Apply sealing compound (Cemedine 366E) to the brake booster mounting surface and toeboard, install the booster, refit the master cylinder and tighten to the recommended torque wrench setting.
12   Connect the vacuum hose to the check valve, ensuring that the check valve is fitted the right way round (Fig. 9.29), with the arrow on its casing pointing towards the engine vacuum connection. Apply sealing compound (*THREE BOND No 4*) to the valve end before fitting the pipes. Then clamp the connections so that there are no air leaks.
13   Connect the brake booster operating rod to the brake pedal and check that the pedal is adjusted correctly (Section 11).
14   Bleed the brake system (Section 17). If braking performance is not satisfactory, check the brake booster and master cylinder for leaks.

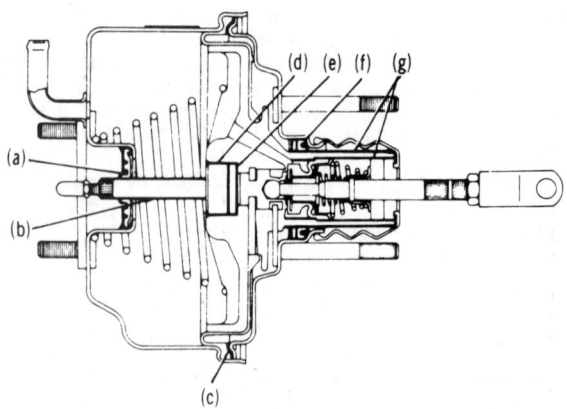

Fig. 9.25 Silicone grease lubrication points

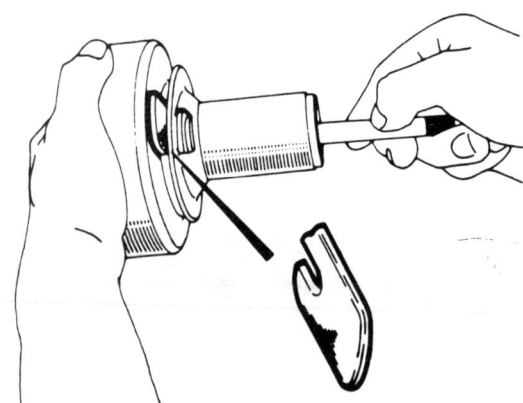

Fig. 9.26 Fitting the valve plunger stop key

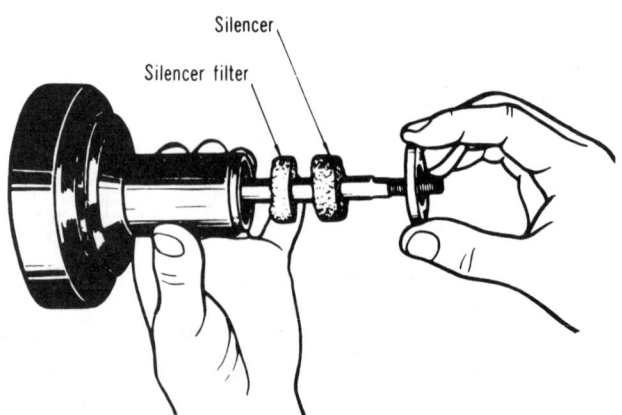

Silencer

Silencer filter

Fig. 9.27 Fitting the silencer and filter

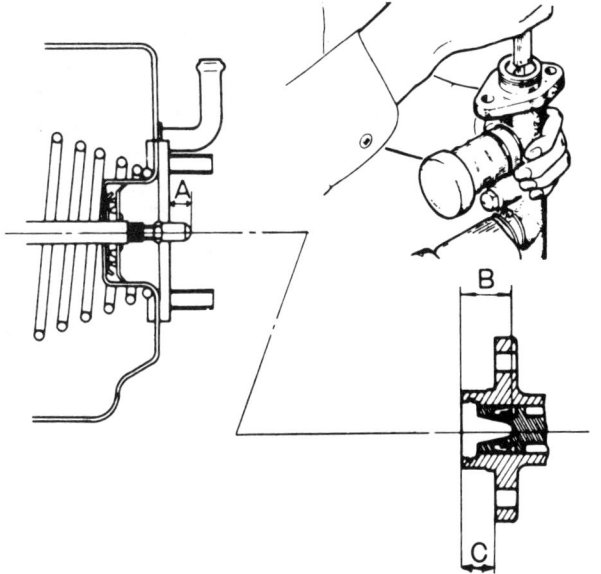

Fig. 9.28 Checking the clearance from pushrod to master cylinder piston

Pushrod length A $0.315 \begin{smallmatrix} + 0 \text{ in} \\ - 0.010 \end{smallmatrix}$

Master cylinder piston end gap B-C $0.315 \begin{smallmatrix} + 0.020 \\ - 0 \text{ in} \end{smallmatrix}$

Pushrod-to-master cylinder piston
end clearance (B-C)-A   0 to 0.03 in

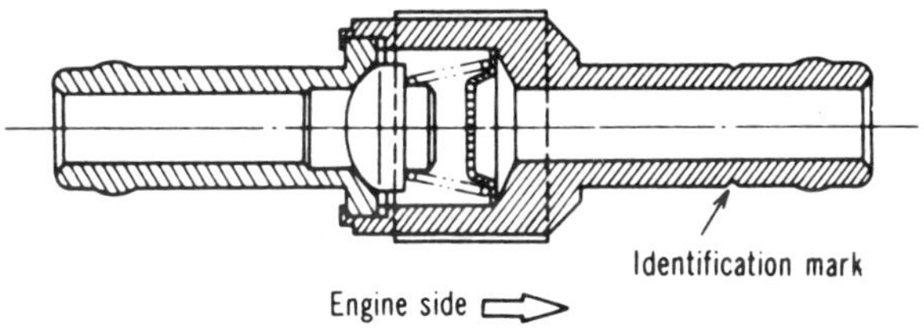

Identification mark

Engine side ⟹

Fig. 9.29 Correct fitting for check valve

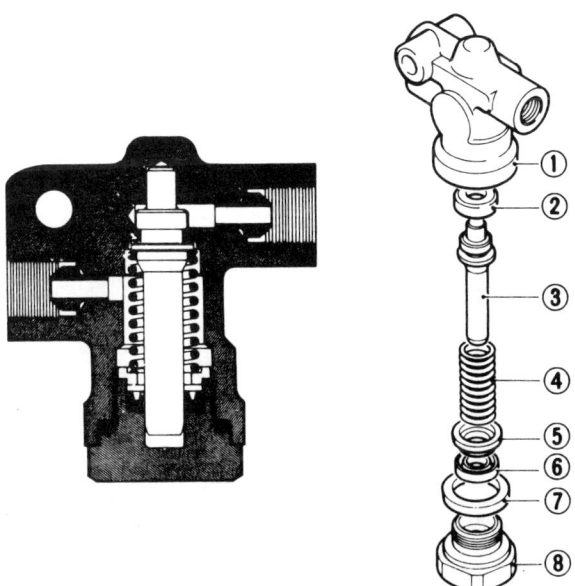

Fig. 9.30 Proportioning valve – exploded view

1	Valve body	5	Spring retainer
2	Lip seal	6	Pushrod seal
3	Plunger	7	O-ring
4	Spring	8	Plug

15 Proportioning valve – checking

A proportioning valve (Fig. 9.30) is fitted to some models and is mounted either on the front toeboard (photo) or on the rear axle. Its function is to make an ideal distribution of pressure between the front and rear brakes to give maximum braking efficiency and to prevent the rear wheels from locking under heavy braking conditions. The setting of the valve is done on assembly and under no circumstances should it be dismantled.

If you are in doubt about the valve functioning correctly, it is advisable to have it tested by your dealer, as specialized equipment is needed.

16 Combination valve – checking hydraulic and electrical functioning

The combination valve (Fig. 9.31) has the following three functions:

(1)   Pressure control of the rear brakes
(2)   Stopping control of rear brake pressure in case of failure of the front brakes
(3)   Providing a visual warning of brake failure

The valve is calibrated on assembly and under no circumstances should it be dismantled. Checking the hydraulic function of the valve requires specialized equipment and this job is best entrusted to your dealer.

1   To test the operation of the brake failure indicator, loosen the bleeder screw of a front brake and depress the brake pedal. If the lamp does not light, check the electrical circuit by shorting together the two switch connections to see if the lamp then lights. If this is so, renew the switch.

2   Having checked the switch operation on the front brakes, close the front brake bleed nipple. Unscrew one of the rear brake bleed nipples and depress the brake pedal to reset the switch. If the switch is tested by opening a rear brake bleed nipple, it must be reset by opening a front brake bleed nipple.

3   After completing the checks on the combination valve, bleed the hydraulic system.

17 Bleeding the hydraulic braking system

Have ready a tin of brake fluid conforming to SAE J1703 or SAE 70R3. The fluid should be clean and preferably fresh because brake fluid absorbs water which leads to corrosion of components. The brake system should be bled whenever any brake hose, brake pipe, master cylinder, brake valve or wheel cylinder has been disconnected. Bleeding the brakes should also be done whenever the brake pedal feels spongy when pressed. The sequence of bleeding should be: left rear wheel, right rear wheel, left front wheel, right front wheel.

1   Ensure that the brake fluid reservoir is full of fluid and make sure that the level is topped up frequently during bleeding. If the level is allowed to fall to the bottom of the reservoir, air is likely to enter the system and nullify all previous work (photos).

2   Remove the bleed nipple cap of a wheel cylinder (photos), slide a piece of plastic tubing over the nipple and place the other end of the tube in a clean container containing enough brake fluid to submerge the end of the pipe.

3   With an assistant to operate the brake pedal, open the bleed screw while the assistant slowly depresses the brake pedal the full length of its travel, keeping the pedal depressed until the bleed screw has been closed. Repeat this sequence as many times as is necessary until no air bubbles can be seen in the fluid coming out of the plastic pipe. Check the level of fluid in the reservoir at frequent intervals during bleeding.

4   On completion of bleeding, tighten the bleed screw to the recommended torque wrench setting, refit the bleed screw cap and top up the fluid reservoir.

5   Repeat operations 1 to 4 on each of the brake cylinders in turn.

18 Handbrake lever assembly – removal, refitting and adjustment

1   Remove the clevis pin and disconnect the clevis.

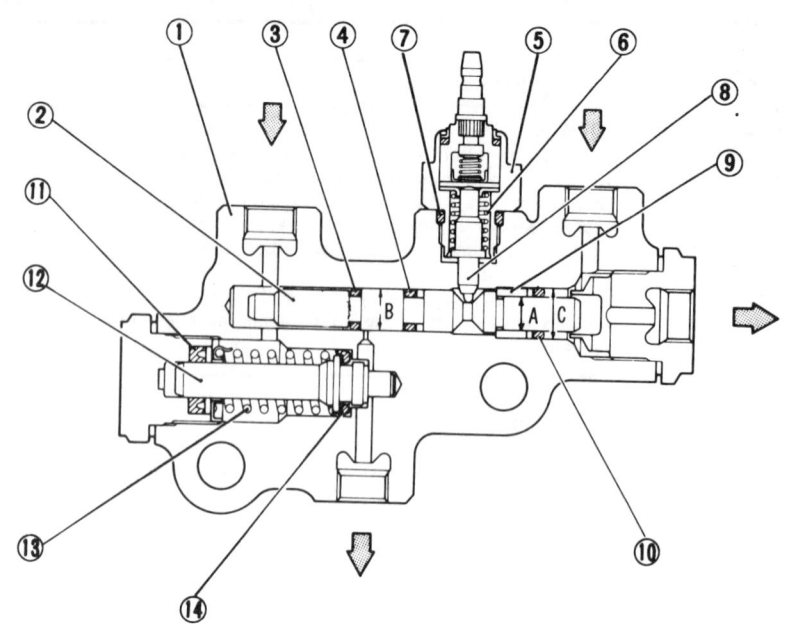

Fig. 9.31 Combination valve components

1	Combination valve body	6	Spring
2	Differential valve piston	7	O-ring
	(D valve)	8	Plunger switch
3	No 1 ring	9	Differential valve sleeve
4	No 2 ring	10	No 3 ring
5	Differential valve switch	11	Cylinder cup
	assembly	12	Proportioning valve piston

(P valve)
13 Spring
14 Valve seal
Identification colour
  Blue: for models except
  estate car
  Red: for estate car

15 Proportioning valve mounted on toeboard

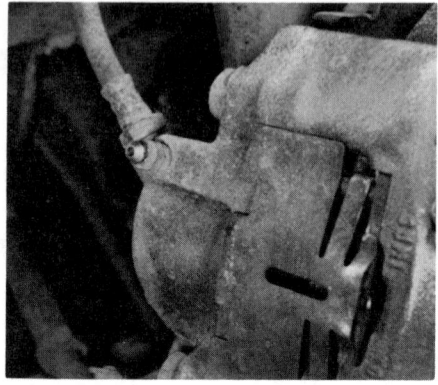

17.2a Front brake bleed nipple

17.2b Rear brake bleed nipple

19.1 Brake cable to extension lever connection

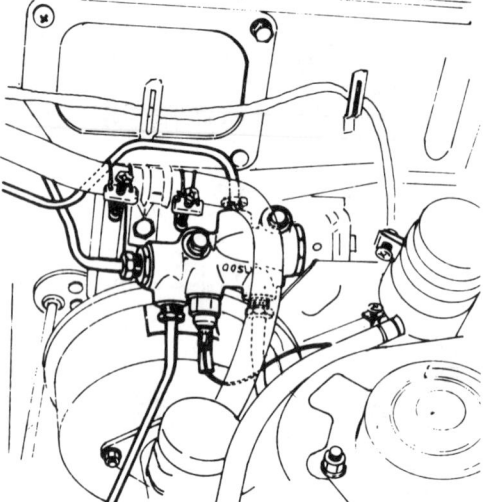

Coupe, Sedan and Hatchback

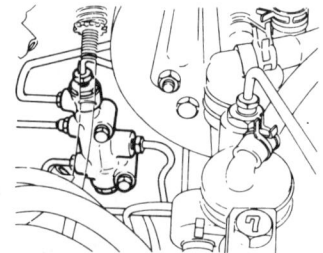

Station Wagon

Fig. 9.32 Combination valve location

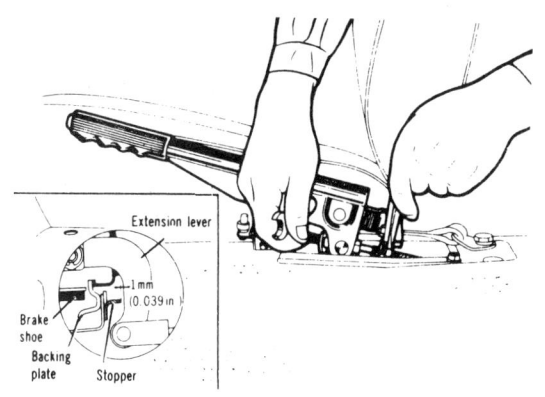

Fig. 9.33 Handbrake adjustment

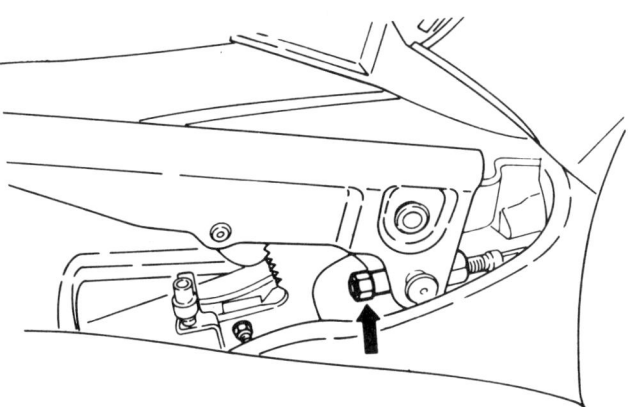

Fig. 9.34 Handbrake adjustment (models except estate car)

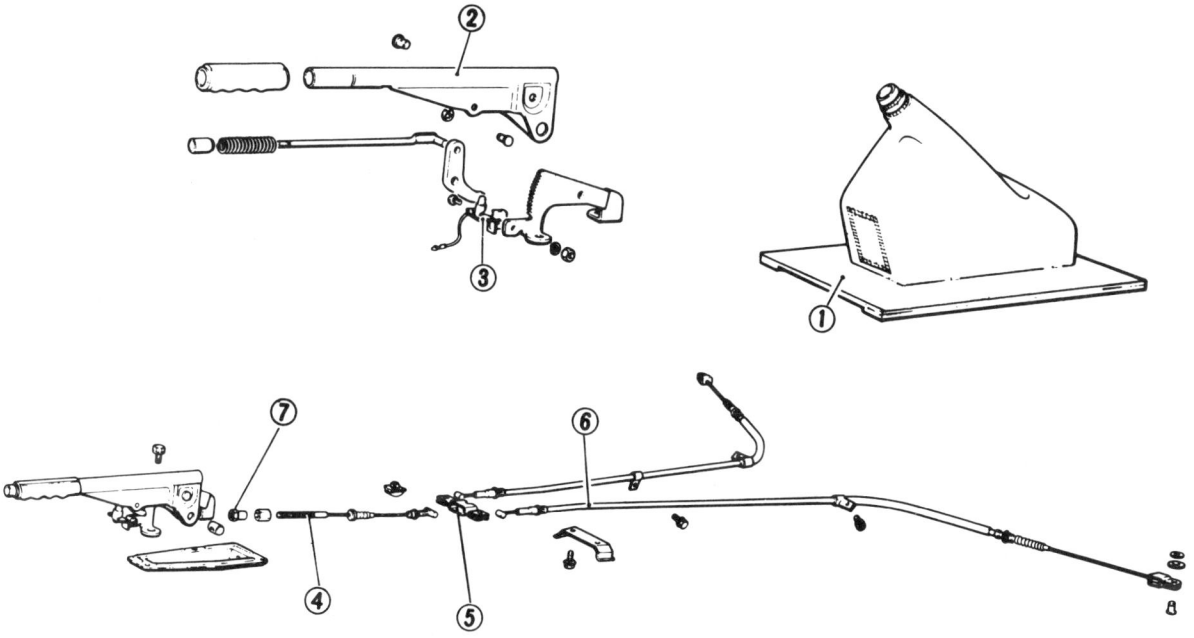

Fig. 9.35 Handbrake components (models except estate car)

1 Cover	3 Handbrake switch	5 Equalizer	7 Adjusting nut
2 Handbrake lever	4 Handbrake cable (front)	6 Handbrake cable (rear)	

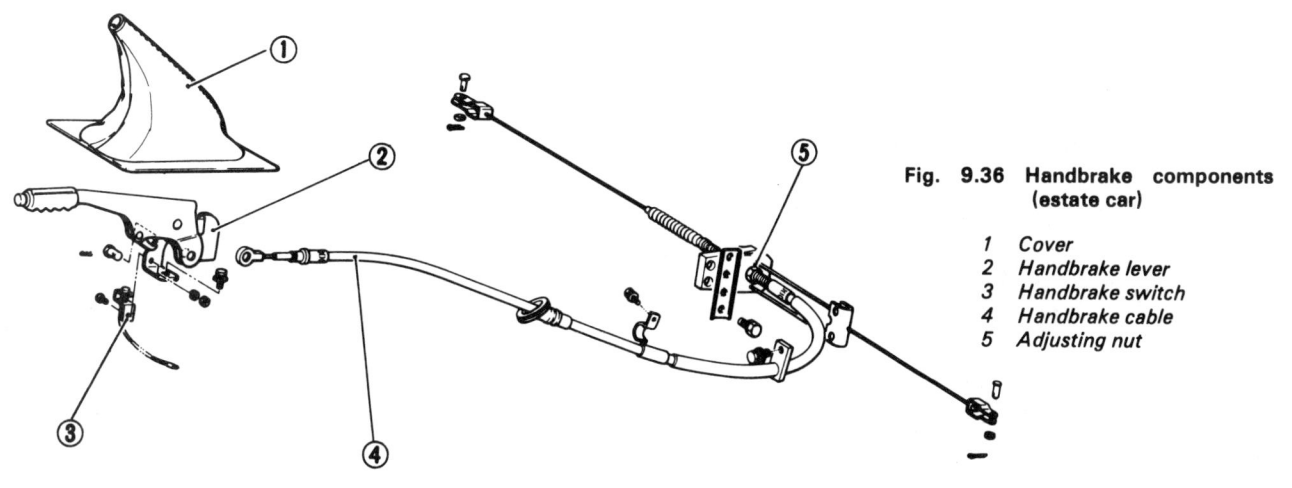

Fig. 9.36 Handbrake components (estate car)

1 Cover
2 Handbrake lever
3 Handbrake switch
4 Handbrake cable
5 Adjusting nut

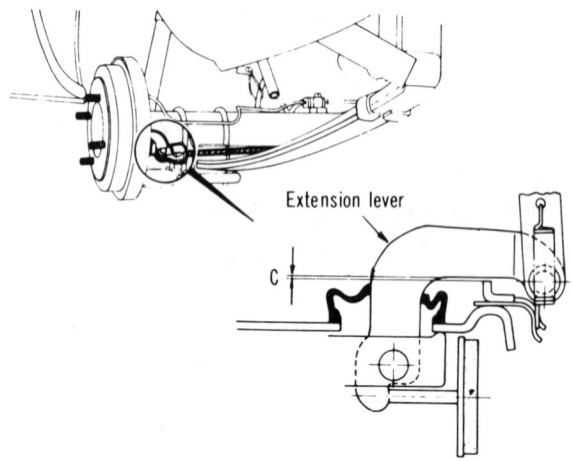

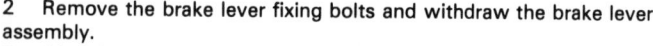

Fig. 9.37 Clearance between brake extension lever and stop

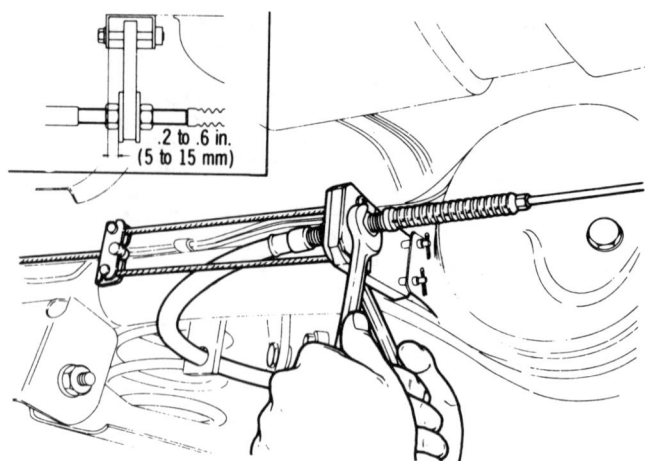

Fig. 9.38 Handbrake adjustment (estate car)

2   Remove the brake lever fixing bolts and withdraw the brake lever assembly.

3   After fitting check that there is a clearance of 0·04 in (1 mm) between the handbrake extension lever and its stop. Also check that the clearance between the extension lever and the stop on the rear brake assembly is 0·04 in (1 mm) and if necessary rotate the cable adjuster on the handbrake lever to obtain this dimension.

4   After making any necessary adjustments, check that the total travel of the handbrake lever is between 4 and 6 notches. If the stroke is larger than this, the rear brake automatic adjusters are malfunctioning. Dismantle and check the automatic adjusters.

---

19 Handbrake cables – removal, refitting and adjustment

Models other than estate car

1   Remove the clevis pin from each side of the rear brakes and disconnect the cables from the extension levers (photo).

2   Remove the bolts from the clips securing the cables to the body and remove the brake operating cables by disengaging them from the brake equalizer.

3   Detach the brake lever cable from the equalizer, then remove the cable by unscrewing the handbrake lever adjusting nut until the cable is free.

4   When refitting the cables, apply grease to all sliding surfaces. Fit the cable clips securely, ensuring that the cables are well away from any rotating part of the drive system.

5   Adjust the cable by turning the brake lever adjuster until the

specified clearance exists between the brake extension lever and its stop on the brake backplate. After this adjustment has been made, the stroke of the brake lever should be checked, to ensure that it also is within the specification.

Estate car

6   Remove the clevis pin from each side of the rear brakes and disconnect the cables from the extension levers.

7   Remove the rubber hanger from the centre of the rear axle housing.

8   Remove the two bolts securing the handbrake lever to the floor of the vehicle and lift the lever assembly.

9   Remove the clevis pin connecting the handbrake cable to the lever.

10 Remove the clips securing the cable to the underside of the vehicle and draw out the cable.

11 When refitting, lubricate all sliding parts with chassis grease. Fit the cable clips so that they secure the cable in a position clear of all rotating parts.

12 Ensure that the cable grommet is fitted in the floor properly and secure it with a drying adhesive.

13 Release the handbrake fully and then check that the rubber hanger to bracket clearance is as shown in Fig. 9.34.

14 Adjust the clearance between the extension levers and their stop to the specified dimension, using the cable adjusting nut. To do this, loosen both the cable lever attachment bolt and the adjusting nut, then move the cable to the right. First set the left cable and tighten the cable lever.

15 Subsequently, tighten the adjusting nut and set the right cable.

20 Fault diagnosis – braking system

Symptom	Reason/s
Pedal travels almost to floorboards before brakes operate	Brake fluid level too low Caliper leaking Master cylinder leaking (bubbles in master cylinder fluid) Brake flexible hose leaking Brake line fractured Brake system unions loose Rear automatic adjusters seized
Brake pedal feels springy	New linings not yet bedded in Brake discs or drums badly worn or cracked Master cylinder securing nuts loose
Brake pedal feels spongy and soggy	Caliper or wheel cylinder leaking Master cylinder leaking (bubbles in master cylinder reservoir) Brake pipe line or flexible hose leaking Unions in brake system loose Air in hydraulic system
Excessive effort required to brake car	Pad or shoe linings badly worn New pads or shoes recently fitted – not yet bedded-in Harder linings fitted than standard causing increase in pedal pressure Linings and brake drums contaminated with oil, grease or hydraulic fluid Servo unit inoperative or faulty One half of dual brake system inoperative
Brakes uneven and pulling to one side	Linings and discs or drums contaminated with oil grease or hydraulic fluid Tyre pressures unequal Radial ply tyres fitted at one end of the car only Brake caliper loose Brake pads or shoes fitted incorrectly Different type of linings fitted at each wheel Anchorages for front suspension or rear suspension loose Brake discs or drums badly worn, cracked or distorted
Brakes tend to bind, drag or lock-on	Air in hydraulic system Wheel cylinders seized Handbrake cables too tight

Chapter 10 Electrical system

Contents

Specifications

Battery

Voltage	12V	
Capacity (20 hour rate) and type		
Cars for Europe and GS model 2000 cc manual		
transmission except Canada	45Ah	NS60
1600 cc automatic transmission and Canada. All Sedan models		
2000 cc automatic transmission and Canada. All Estate cars		
except 2600 cc	60Ah	N50Z
2600 cc manual transmission and automatic transmission	65Ah	NS70

Alternator

Polarity	Negative earth

Rotation	Clockwise, viewed from pulley end

Model	Output
1200 cc and 1400 cc for Europe	AH2035K	35A
1600 cc for Europe	AH2035K1	45A
1600 cc except Europe	021000–6420	45A
2000 cc and 2600 cc	AH2050M1	50A

Voltage regulator

Type	Tirrie type, with temperature compensation
Range	14·5 to 15·3 V at 68°F
	Type
Models for Europe	RQB 2220D1
1600 cc except Europe	026000–1764
2000 cc and 2600 cc	RQB–2D1

Bulbs

Headlamps (all models except Type II Estate car)	50/40W
Type II Estate car	50/37·5W
Front turn signal and parking lights all models except	
Estate car	27/8W
Estate car only – turn signal	27W
–parking light	8W
Front side marker lights all models except Estate car	8W
Estate car only	3·8W
Stop, turn signal and tail lights	27/8W
Reversing lights	27W
Rear side marker lights all models except Estate car	8W
Estate car only	3·8W
Number plate lights	8W
Interior lights	10W
Meter illumination lights	3·4W or 3·8W
Heater panel light all models except Estate car	3·4W or 3·8W
Estate car only	1·4W
Ash tray lights	3·4W
Reading lights (Hatchback GT only)	3·4W or 3·8W
Combination gauge lights (Hatchback GT only)	3·4W

Note: *Where both 3·4W and 3·8W are denoted, either may be used, or the two may be used in combination.*

---

1 General description

All models have a 12 volt negative earth system consisting of an alternator, the necessary voltage control equipment and a battery. Fuse protection is provided on all circuits and in addition to this there is a fusible link which protects the entire system from excessive current.

A variety of electrical testing devices are required for the complete diagnosis and adjustment of the electrical system, but much preliminary work can be done with a multimeter and a test lamp. Electrical parts can be removed and taken to an automotive electrical specialist and it is recommended that this is done unless the reader is sufficiently knowledgeable and has the necessary testing facilities.

2 Battery – removal and refitting

1   Loosen the clamps and detach the battery leads from the battery terminals, negative lead first.
2   Remove the two nuts securing the battery clamp and lift the clamp off (photo).
3   Remove the battery from its tray.
4   Before refitting the battery, clean the tray, wash and dry the outside of the battery. Ensure that the battery terminals and cable connections are free from corrosion and smeared with petroleum jelly.
5   Fit the battery, refit the battery clamp and tighten the nuts until they are firm, but do not overtighten or bend the clamp. Refit the battery leads (negative lead last) and tighten the clamps.

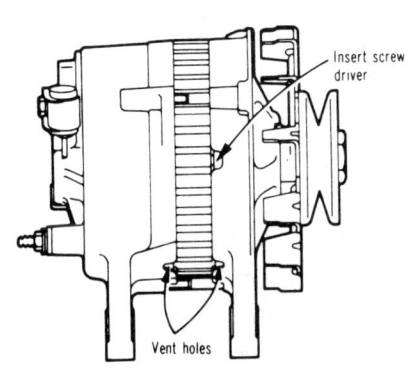

Fig. 10.1 Prising off the front bracket

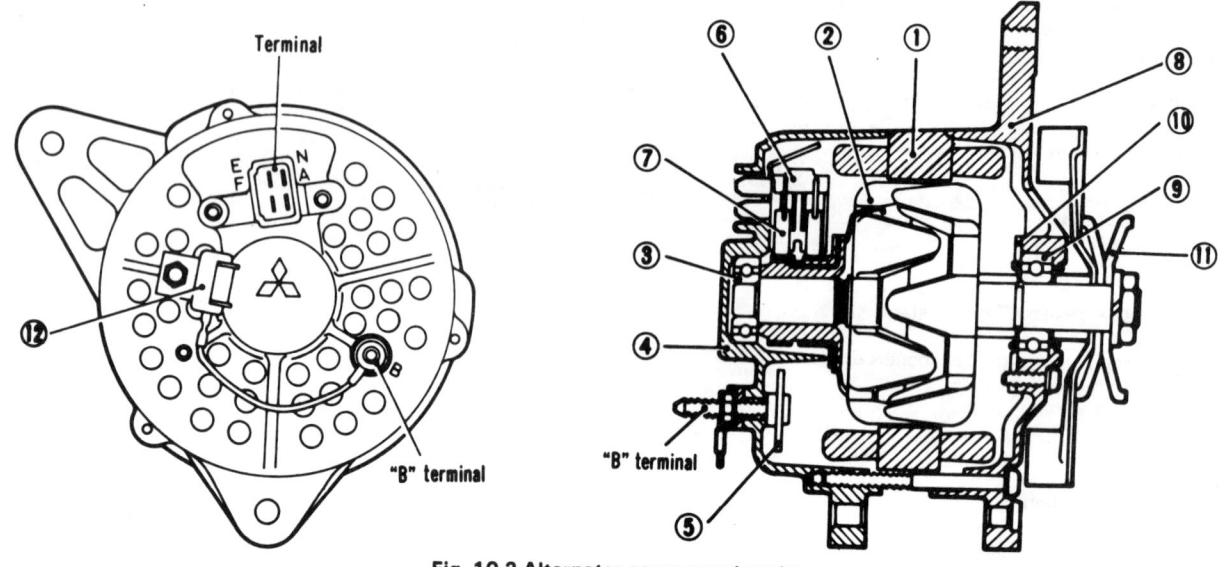

Fig. 10.2 Alternator component parts

1	Stator	4	Rear bracket
2	Rotor	5	Rectifier assembly
3	Ball bearing	6	Brush holder assembly

7	Brush	10	Bearing retainer
8	Front bracket	11	Pulley
9	Ball bearing	12	Capacitor

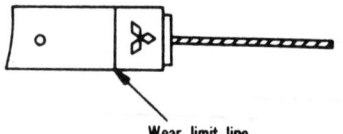

Fig. 10.3 Brush wear check

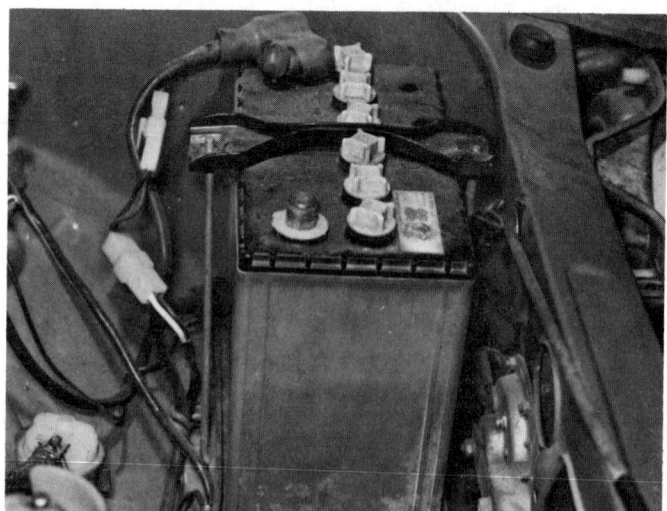

2.2 Battery and clamp

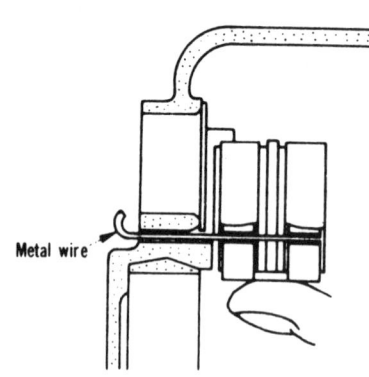

Fig. 10.4 Supporting the brushes clear of the rotor

3 Battery – maintenance

1   Make a weekly check of the level electrolyte and make sure that the separators are covered. Using distilled water, top-up the level to the full level mark, but do not overfill. If any electrolyte is spilled, wipe it up immediately to prevent corrosion.
2   After checking the electrolyte, refit the filler plugs securely.
3   Keep the top of the battery and the terminals clean and dry.
4   A long and reliable battery life depends upon the battery never being left for long in a discharged condition. During the winter when the normal load on the electrical system absorbs most of the alternator output, the battery should be charged occasionally.

4 Battery charging

1   When charging the battery on the car, connect the positive battery terminal first, then the negative and disconnect in the reverse order, taking care that neither the battery, nor the charger becomes short-circuited.
2   When charging the battery from an external charger first remove the positive and negative battery cables, otherwise the diodes in the alternator may be damaged.
3   Make sure that the charger is connected with the same polarity as the battery, ie. positive lead from the charger connected to the positive terminal of the battery, etc.
4   For normal charging, the charging current should be approximately $\frac{1}{10}$th of the ampere hour capacity of the battery. A 40Ah battery should not normally be charged at a current higher than 4 amps and during charging the temperature of the electrolyte should not exceed 113°F.

5 Alternator – general description

An alternator is an electrical generator which produces an alternating current which is changed into direct current by a rectifier inside the alternator. The advantage of an alternator over a direct current generator is that the output of an alternator is constant over a wide range of speeds, so that a high rate of charge can be produced at low speeds such as when driving in heavy traffic, thus reducing the drain on the battery.

6 Alternator – routine maintenance

1   The equipment has been designed for the minimum amount of maintenance in service, the only items subject to wear being the brushes and bearings.
2   Brushes should be examined after about 75 000 miles (120 000 km) and renewed if necessary. The bearings are prepacked with grease for life, and should not require further attention.
3   Check the fan belt every 3000 miles (5000 km) for correct adjustment which should be $\frac{1}{3}$ inch (8 mm) total movement at the centre of the run between the alternator and water pump pulleys.

7 Alternator – special precautions

Whenever the electrical system of the car is being attended to, and external means of starting the engine is used, there are certain precautions that must be taken otherwise serious and expensive damage can result.
1   Always make sure that the negative terminal of the battery is earthed. If the terminal connections are accidentally reversed or if the battery has been reverse charged the alternator diodes will be damaged.
2   The output terminal on the alternator marked *BAT* or *B+* must never be earthed but should always be connected directly to the positive terminal of the battery.
3   Whenever the alternator is to be removed or when disconnecting the terminals of the alternator circuit, always disconnect the battery earth terminal first.
4   The alternator must never be operated without the battery to alternator cable connected.
5   If the battery is to be charged by external means always disconnect both battery cables before the external charger is connected.
6   Should it be necessary to use a booster charger or booster battery to start the engine always double check that the negative cable is connected to the negative terminal and the positive cable to positive terminal.
7   When washing the car, take care not to get the alternator wet.
8   If the brushes are worn down to the wear limit line (Section 9) renew them with approved spares.
9   The bearings are sealed and lubricated for life but if there is any sign of leakage of lubricant, the bearings should be renewed with approved spares.

8 Alternator – removal and refitting

1   Disconnect the battery leads.
2   Remove the plug connections and also the wire from the screwed terminal on the alternator.
3   Undo and remove the adjustment arm bolt (photo), then slacken the mounting bolts until the alternator can be swung towards the engine and the fan belt removed.
4   Remove the nut of the mounting bolt and withdraw the bolt, being careful not to lose any shims which may be fitted. Hold the alternator while removing the bolt, so that the alternator does not fall.
5   When refitting the alternator, hold it with its mounting lugs in position and insert shims on the inside of each mounting lug until the shims are sufficiently tight to stay in on their own. Insert the mounting bolt and fit its nut loosely.
6   Refit the fan belt.
7   Insert the clamp bolt into the adjuster arm and tension the fan belt (Chapter 2, Section 7) then tighten the nut of the support bolt and the adjuster bolt to the specified torque.
8   Reconnect the alternator leads and then the battery leads.

9 Alternator – renewing brushes

1   Remove the alternator from the engine.
2   Remove the three through bolts between the front and rear housing.
3   Insert a screwdriver in the hole between the front housing and the stator assembly (Fig. 10.2) and prise off the front bracket and rotor assembly. Do not insert a screwdriver in the vent holes because this might damage the stator windings.
4   Unsolder the three stator leads from the diodes and the set of three neutral leads, noting carefully the terminals to which they are connected. Remove the stator assembly. Unsolder the leads to the diodes as quickly as possible, because the heat of a soldering iron on the diodes for more than about three seconds will damage them.
5   Unsolder the brush leads and remove the brushes.
6   If the brushes are worn down to the wear limit line (Fig. 10.3) fit new ones, soldering the brush leads on to the terminals and cutting off any surplus wire.
7   Refit the stator and solder the wires back on to the same terminals as the ones from which they were removed.
8   Push the brushes up into their holders and temporarily keep them in place with a piece of wire (Fig. 10.4).
9   Refit the rotor and front housing, then release the brushes.
10   Reconnect and refit the alternator.

10 Starter motor – general description

The starter motor incorporates a solenoid mounted on top of the starter body, the solenoid operating switch contacts and also a mechanical clutch.
When the starter switch is operated, the voltage coil of the solenoid is energised which operates the clutch and starts to engage the starter pinion in the flywheel ring gear, (or the torque converter on automatic transmission). After the pinion has engaged, the solenoid closes the contacts which connect the battery to the starter motor.

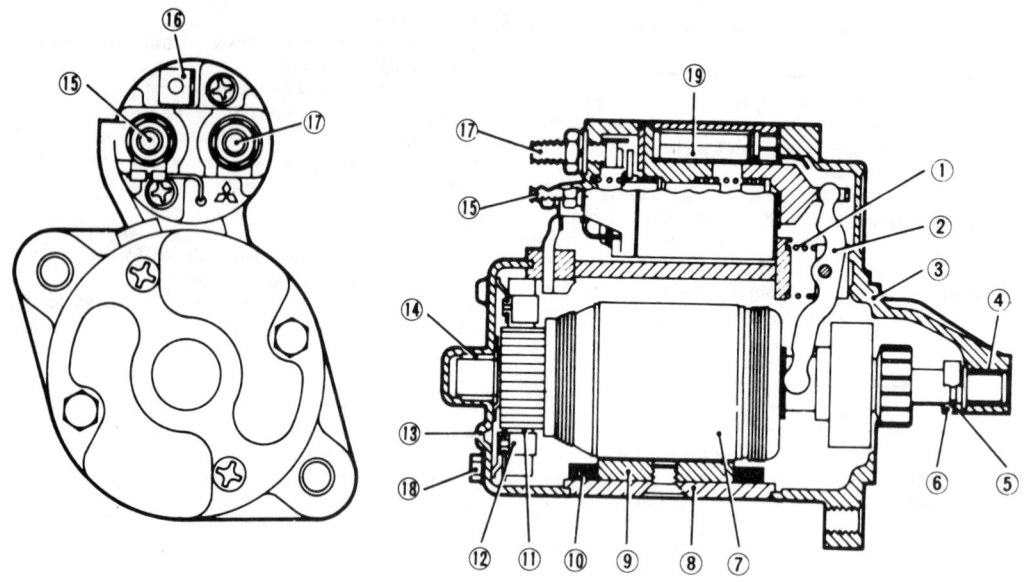

Fig. 10.5 Starter motor component parts (Manual transmission)

1	Spring	6	Stopper	11	Brush	16	S terminal
2	Lever	7	Armature	12	Brush holder	17	B terminal
3	Front bracket	8	Yoke	13	Rear bracket	18	Through bolt
4	Bearing	9	Pole	14	Bearing	19	Magnetic switch
5	Ring	10	Field coil	15	M terminal		

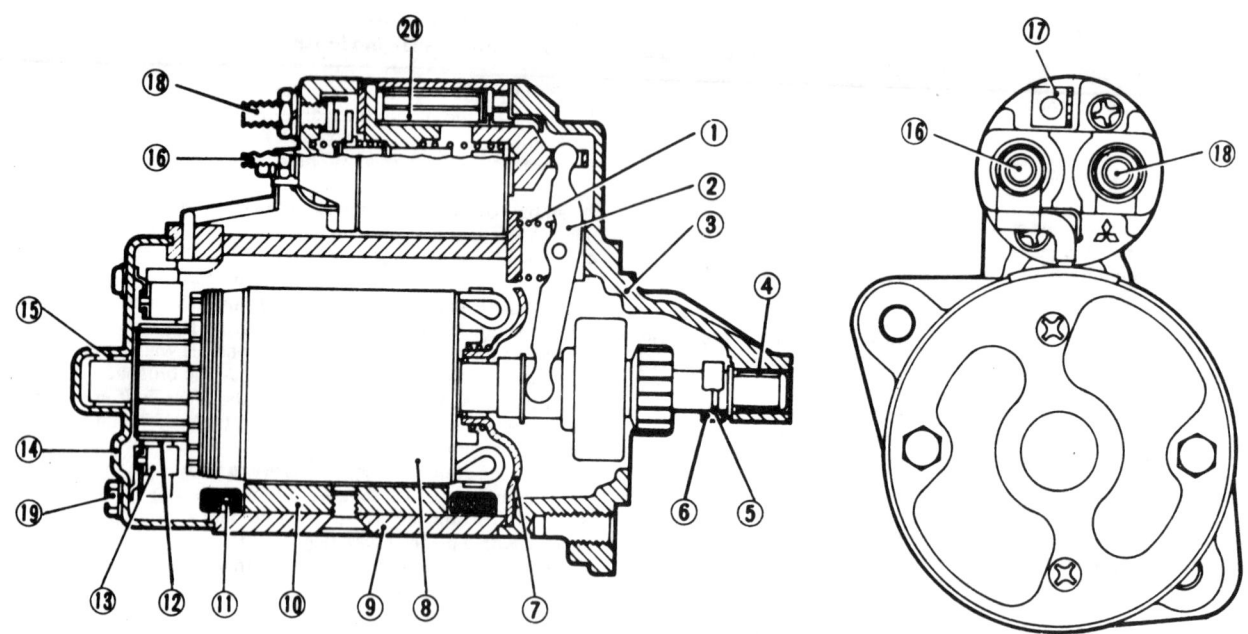

Fig. 10.6 Starter motor component parts (Automatic transmission)

1	Spring	6	Stopper	11	Field coil	16	M terminal
2	Lever	7	Centre bracket	12	Brush	17	S terminal
3	Front bracket	8	Armature	13	Brush holder	18	B terminal
4	Bearing	9	Yoke	14	Rear bracket	19	Through bolt
5	Ring	10	Pole	15	Bearing	20	Magnetic switch

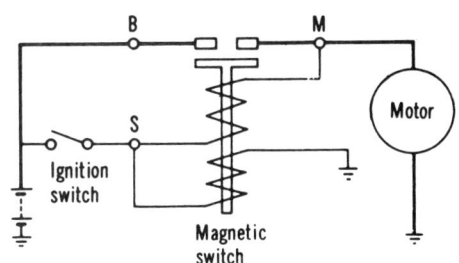

Fig. 10.7 Starter motor circuit diagram

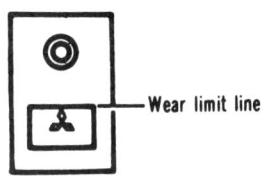

Fig. 10.8 Starter motor brush wear check

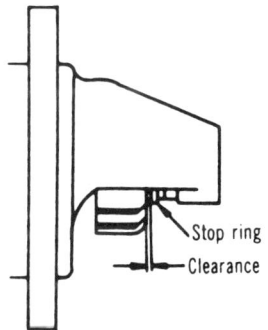

Fig. 10.9 Starter pinion to stop clearance

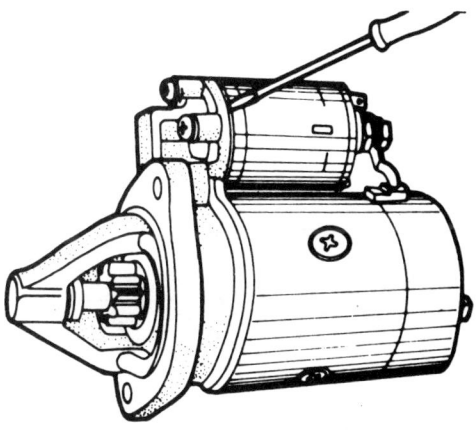

Fig. 10.10 Adjustment of pinion stop clearance

This also energises the solenoid hold on coil, so that the starter motor continues to spin until the engine starts, even if the starter switch is released. When the engine starts, the starter motor is no longer exerting a driving torque and the free running clutch of the starter motor comes into operation to break the starter motor circuit and disengage the pinion. Pre-engagement of the starter pinion reduces wear on the starter pinion and starter ring and it is unlikely that they will need to be renewed.

11 Starter motor – removal and refitting

1 Remove the battery leads.
2 Disconnect the cables from the three terminals of the starter motor.
3 Remove the starter mounting bolts, pull the starter motor back slightly to disengage the starter motor spigot and then remove the starter motor. If the vehicle is equipped with an air conditioner, or with a large steering box, disconnect the drop arm from the starter motor attachment bolts and then remove the motor from beneath the vehicle.
4 When refitting the motor, make sure that there is no misalignment between the motor and its mounting on the engine. Clean the mating surfaces between the motor and engine to ensure a good electrical contact and tighten the fixing bolts to the required torque.

12 Starter motor – dismantling, overhaul and reassembly

1 Remove the connection from the *M* terminal, take out the solenoid switch fixing screw and remove the solenoid switch.
2 Remove the two through bolts and separate the motor into the armature and yoke.
3 Remove the armature and the lever from the front housing, being careful to note which way round the lever is fitted and also the positions of the spring and spring holder.
4 Remove the small washer which is fitted to the pinion end of the armature. This may be adhering to the inside of the pinion housing.
5 Remove the two screws and pull off the rear housing, then pull out the brushes and remove the brush holder assembly.
6 To remove the clutch, tap the stop ring towards the pinion until the circlip is exposed, then remove the circlip and the pinion and clutch assembly off the shaft.
7 Thoroughly clean all parts, examine the brushes and fit new ones if the existing ones are down to the wear limit line (Fig. 10.8).
8 Reassemble by inserting the brushes, then screwing the brush holder in its position in the rear housing.
9 Smear silicone or white grease on the armature shaft then slide the pinion/clutch assembly on to the shaft. Fit the stop ring and circlip, then use a puller to pull the stop ring tight up to the circlip.
10 Grease the faces of the small washer and fit it over the shaft.
11 Fit the solenoid lever and spring into the pinion housing, being careful to refit them in the same positions as they were when removed, then fit the armature into the pinion housing.
12 Fit the yoke and starter housing to the armature and pinion housing. Fit and tighten the through bolts.
13 Fit the solenoid, tighten the three mounting screws and reconnect the wire on the rear solenoid terminal.
14 With the drive pinion at its outer limit of travel, measure the clearance (Fig. 10.9) between the pinion and the stop. If this is outside the limits 0·02 to 0·08 in (0·5 to 2·1 mm) correct the clearance by adding or removing packing washers between the solenoid assembly and the pinion housing (Fig. 10.10).

13 Voltage regulator – general description

The voltage regulator is mounted in the engine compartment on the right-hand side of the car (photo). It consists of two elements, a constant voltage relay and a pilot lamp relay, each relay comprising an electromagnet, armature, frame and contacts. The regulator has a temperature compensator which automatically adjusts the setting of the constant voltage relay to give a higher voltage and therefore a higher battery charging rate in cold weather and a lower voltage and lower charging rate in hot weather. The regulator is a sealed unit and should not be tampered with, but its setting can be checked as described in the following Section.

IG	F	L
A	N	E

Fig. 10.11 Voltage regulator connections
(viewed from front of coupler)

15.1 Fuse block

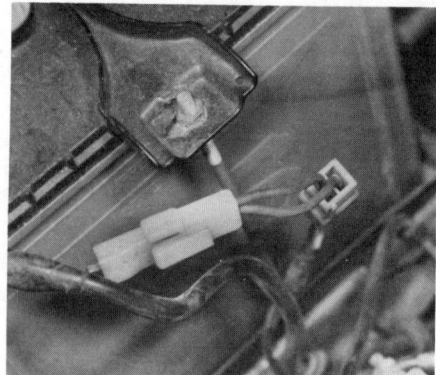

16.1 Fusible link

18.3 Headlamp with plug connection removed

18.4 Releasing the bulb

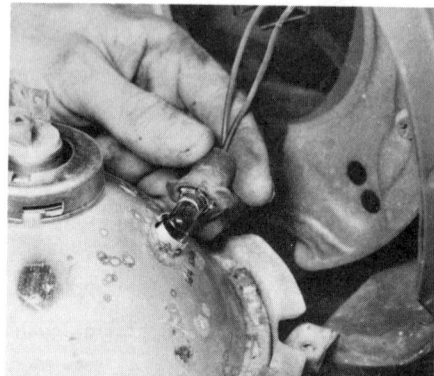

19.1 Parking light bulb (single headlamp)

Fuse No.	Rated capacity (A)	Working capacity (A)	Intermittent load (A)	Max. load (A)	Connection
1–11	10	4.5	–	4.5	Headlamp (R) U, indicator
2–12	10	4.3	–	4.3	Headlamp (L) U
3–13	10	3.4	–	3.4	Headlamp (R) L
4–14	10	3.4	–	3.4	Headlamp (L) L
5–15	15	6.3	–	6.3	Tail, number plate, parking, and instrument panel lamps
6–16	15	5.2 (16.3 when locked)	2.9	8.1 (18.9 when locked)	Wiper motor, washer, regulator, charging indicators
7–17	15	7.2	3.7	12.1	Turn, reversing, fuel, temperature, heater, etc.
8–18	15	–	8.4	8.4	Horn and stop
9–19	15	0.7	8.0	8.7	Cigar lighter and radio
10–20	15	2.0	7.3	11.7	Hazard, interior, door indicator, and clock

Fig. 10.12 Fuse capacity table

14 Voltage regulator – testing

1   Separate the two halves of the regulator connector just enough to be able to insert meter test probes, but do not disconnect the connector.

2   Connect a voltmeter with a range of 0 to 20 volts between terminals A and E, the voltmeter positive lead being connected to A (Fig. 10.11).

3   With the engine running at idling speed, disconnect one of the battery leads, then increase the engine speed to 2000 rpm. Do not exceed this speed, or the alternator diodes may be damaged.

4   The voltage indicated by the voltmeter should be between 14·3 and 15·8 volts for an ambient temperature of 68°F. If there is a serious deviation from this value, a new regulator should be fitted, or the existing one adjusted by an automotive electrical workshop.

15 Fuses

1   Fuses are mounted in a multi-way fuse block mounted below the instrument panel at the side of the driver (photo).

2   When a fuse has blown, locate the fault and correct it before fitting a new fuse.

3   Always use the correct fuse rating and never use heavier fuses than fitted originally, unless additional equipment has been connected to a circuit (see Table Fig. 10.12).

4   If a fuse holder becomes loose, it may become sufficiently hot to burn out the fuse and damage the holder. To prevent this, check the fuse holders for tightness of contact.

5   If a fuse holder becomes defective, it is necessary to renew the entire fuse block assembly.

16 Fusible link

1   A fusible link is fitted in the battery to give electrical protection to the electrical system which is not protected by the distribution fuses (Fig. 10.13 and photo).

2   A melted fusible link can be detected by a swelling or discolouration of the harness covering and should be renewed by one of the same rating, after the cause of failure has been found and corrected.

3   Because the melting of a fusible link means that a current of 100 or 150 amps has flowed, it is very important to locate and correct the fault.

4   The ratings and identifications of fusible links are as follows:

	Lighting circuit (green)	Other circuits (red)
Fusible link size	$0.00078 \ in^2 \ (0.5 \ mm^2)$	$0.00132 \ in^2 \ (0.85 \ mm^2)$
Continuous rating	27 amps	34 amps
Fusing current	100 amps	150 amps

17 Ignition switch – removal and refitting

1   The ignition switch is combined with the steering wheel lock, so that when the switch is turned to the *LOCK* position and the key is withdrawn, the lock pin automatically enters the steering wheel shaft.

2   The switch has three positions in which it actuates circuits, these being to control accessories, to control the ignition circuit and a spring back position for operating the starter motor.

3   The switch assembly is fixed by shear bolts, the heads of which break off when tightened to the correct torque. The assembly cannot easily be removed unless the bolts are sawn through.

4   The switch mechanism can be renewed, if faulty, by removing the fixing screw and pulling out the switch.

5   Refitting is a reversal of the removal procedure.

18 Headlamp – bulb renewal and sealed beam replacement

Bulb renewal

1   Lift the bonnet, remove the screws securing the headlamp trim

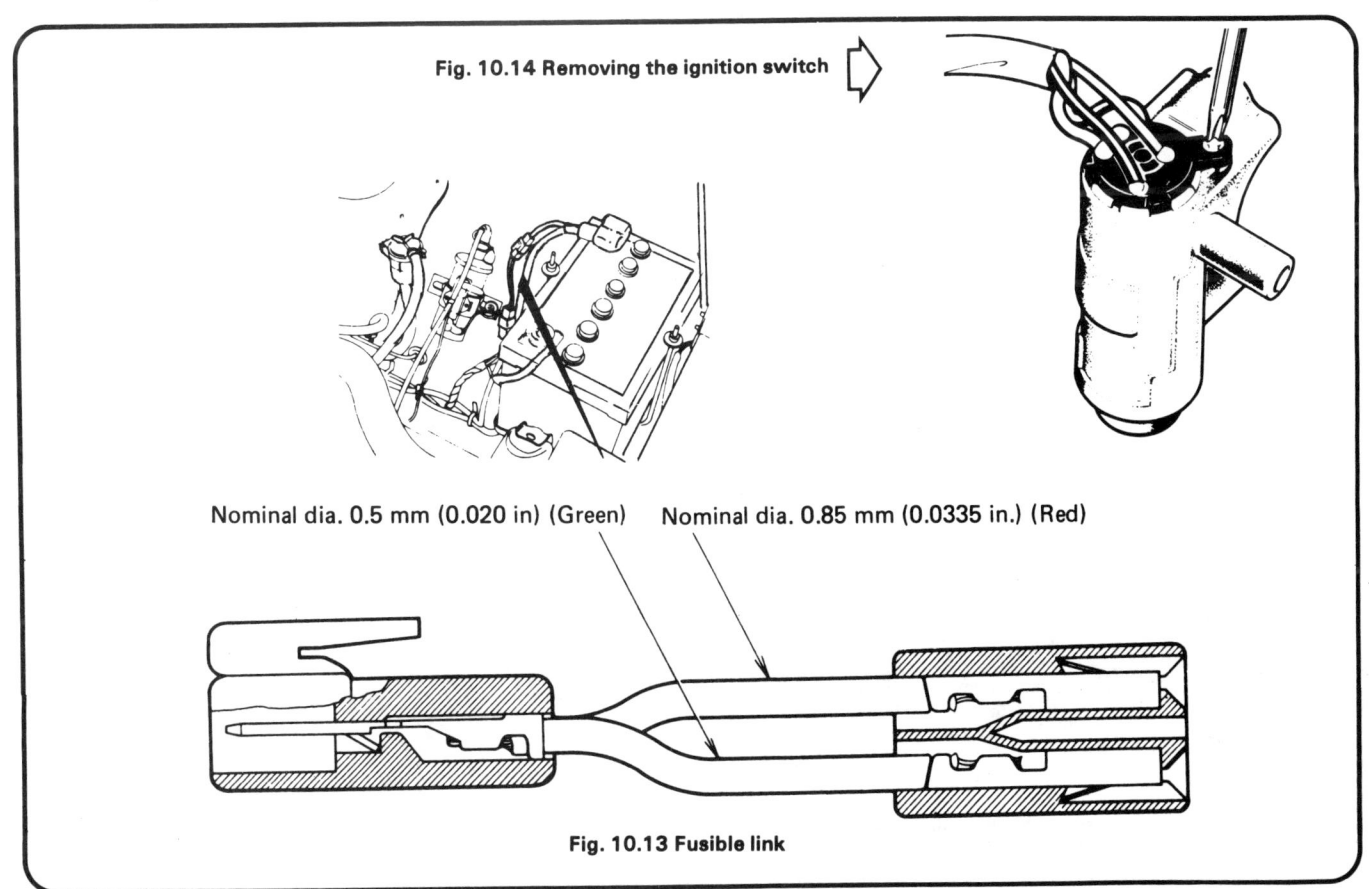

Fig. 10.14 Removing the ignition switch

Nominal dia. 0.5 mm (0.020 in) (Green)   Nominal dia. 0.85 mm (0.0335 in.) (Red)

Fig. 10.13 Fusible link

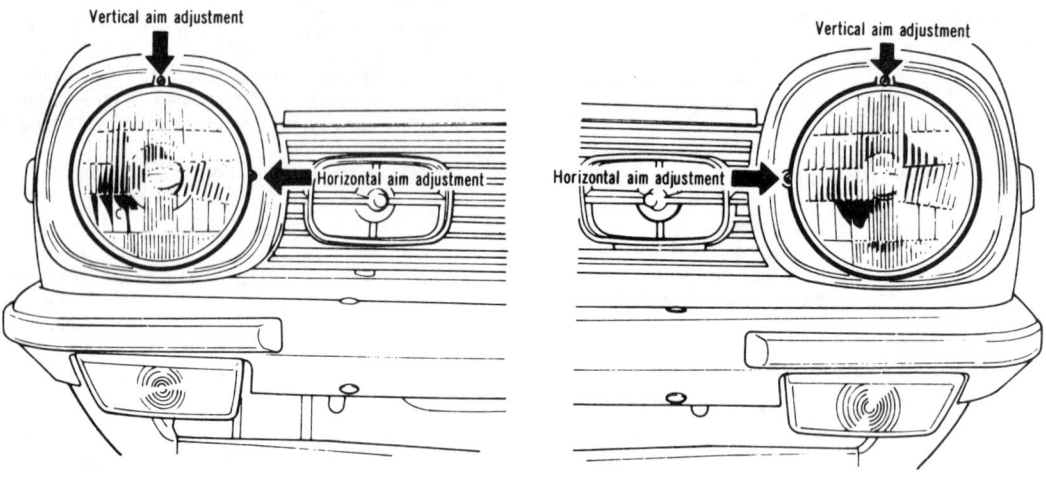

Fig. 10.15 Headlamp beam adjusting screws (single headlamps)

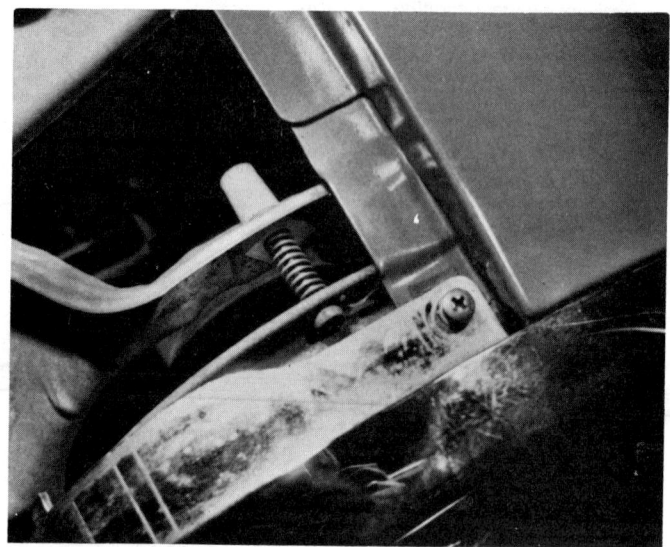

20 Headlamp adjusting screw

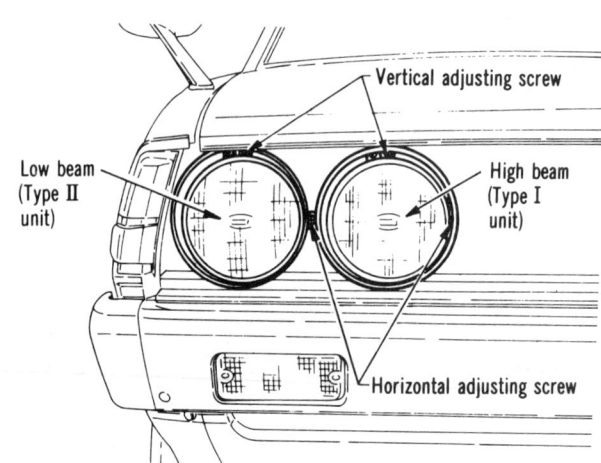

Fig. 10.16 Headlamp beam adjusting screws (dual headlamps)

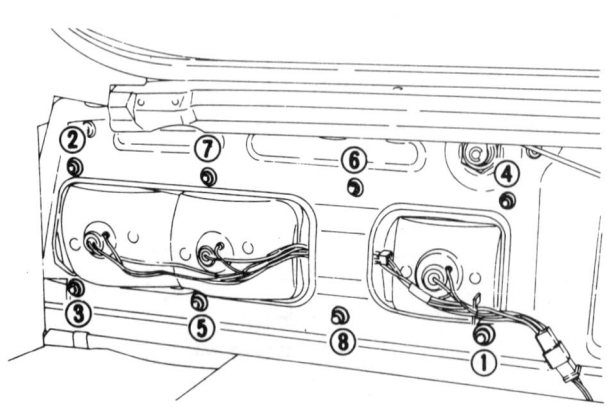

Fig. 10.17 Rear combination light (saloon)

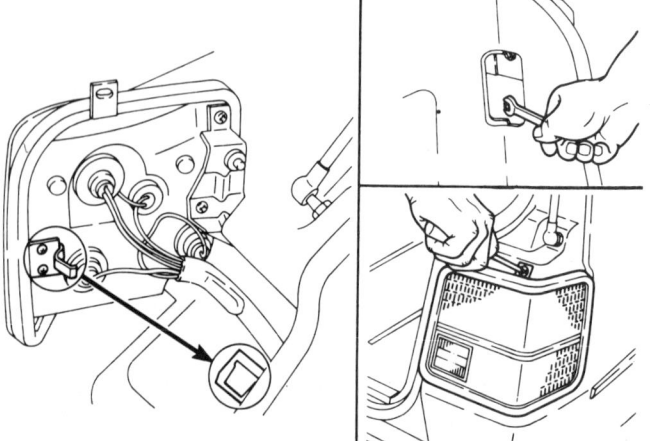

Fig. 10.18 Rear combination light (estate car)

and take the trim off to expose the headlamp bezel.
2   Remove the headlamp assembly by gripping its rim and twisting it to release the three mounting screws from the keyhole slots in the headlamp rim.
3   Allow the lamp to tip downwards to give access to the plug connection and pull off the plug connection (photo).
4   Unscrew and release the bayonet ring securing the bulb (photo). Remove the ring and take out the bulb.
5   Fit a new bulb and then replace the securing ring, the plug connection, headlamp assembly and headlamp trim.

Sealed beam unit replacement

6   When the headlight system is of the dual type, the outboard units are of the two filament type for low and high beam and are identified by having a figure 2 moulded on the lens. The single filament inner lamps have a figure 1 moulded on the lens. It is not possible to fit them incorrectly, because the mounting lugs are offset at different angles.
7   To change a unit, proceed as for changing a bulb, except that the plug connector on the rear of the unit is pulled off, the unit discarded and a new unit is fitted.
8   After renewing either a bulb, or a sealed beam unit, the headlamp beam alignment should be checked.

19 Front parking light – bulb renewal

Single headlamp vehicle

1   Remove the headlamp assembly as described in the previous Section and the parking light will be exposed (photo).
2   Twist the parking light to release its bayonet fitting to the reflector, and remove the bulb and its holder.
3   Withdraw the bulb from its holder and fit a new bulb.
4   Refit the bulb holder to the reflector and refit the headlamp assembly to the car.

Dual headlamp vehicle

5   On vehicles with dual headlights, the front parking light is combined with the front turn indicator in a fitting mounted below the front bumper.
6   Remove the two screws from the lens and pull out the lamp assembly.
7   Carefully prise off the lens, taking care not to damage its gasket. Renew the defective bulb, refit the lens and screw the unit back on to the vehicle.

20 Headlamp – beam alignment

Headlamp setting is achieved by a vertical adjustment screw which is above the headlamp and a horizontal adjustment screw on the horizontal centre line of the lamp, both screws being accessible without removing the grille. Approximate alignment may be carried out with the car standing on level ground, with the lamps shining on a vertical surface about ten feet in front, but it is recommended that the headlamps are aligned by a service station using optical beam setting equipment.

21 Front flasher – bulb replacement

1   From behind the flasher assembly, pull out the lampholder (photo).
2   Release the bayonet fitting bulb and fit a new one.
3   Push the lampholder assembly back into the flasher assembly firmly.
4   When the front flasher is combined with the front parking light, proceed as described in Section 19.

22 Side flasher – bulb renewal

1   Remove the two screws securing the lens and carefully prise off the lens.
2   Remove the defective bulb and fit a new one.
3   Ensure that the sealing gasket is in good condition. If not, fit a new one, then refit the lens and insert and tighten the two screws.

23 Rear lights – bulb renewal

1   The tail light, stop light and rear flashers are in a common cluster. To renew a bulb, remove the two screws from the rear of the fitting, access to which is obtained from inside the boot.
2   Pull off the back of the fitting and renew the bulbs as necessary (photo).

24 Number plate lamp – bulb renewal

1   Remove the two screws securing the lamp cover. Take off the cover and the lens (photo).
2   Renew the bulb and inspect the gasket to check that it has not allowed the ingress of water.
3   Fit a new gasket if necessary. Refit the lens and the lamp cover, then insert and tighten the fixing screws.

25 Interior light – bulb renewal

1   Grip the sides of the lens to release its fixing claws and take the lens off to expose the bulb (photo).
2   Renew the festoon bulb, making sure that it fits tightly, by bending the contacts inwards, before inserting the bulb.

26 Reversing lights – bulb renewal

1   The reversing lights may be separate units mounted under the rear bumper, or they may be in the rear combination light. This Section refers to the lights as a separate unit and the combination light is covered in the following Section.
2   Remove the two lens screws and remove the complete lamp unit from the panel (photo).
3   Carefully prise off the lens, taking care not to damage the lens, or the gasket.
4   Remove the defective bulb, fit a new one. Refit the lens to the lamp unit and the lamp unit to the panel.

27 Rear combination lights – bulb renewal

Except Estate car

1   The bulb carriers at the rear of the combination fitting are accessible from the interior of the boot.
2   Lift the boot lid, remove the rear trim panel to expose the combination light and pull out the appropriate bulb carrier.
3   Fit a new bulb and replace the bulb carrier and trim.

Estate car

4   The procedure is similar, except that it is necessary to remove the combination light mounting port cover by prising with a screwdriver between the trim and the cover (Fig. 10.18).

28 Instrument cluster – removal and refitting

1   Loosen the steering wheel clamp knob and lower the steering column to its fullest extent.
2   Remove the three screws from the tops of the instrument shrouds and the two screws at the bottom of the instrument cluster.
3   Pull the instrument cluster forward until its rear is accessible. Separate the two-pole and the multi-pole connectors at the back of the cluster.
4   Remove the speedometer drive bayonet connection to the rear of the speedometer and then lift the meter assembly clear.
5   When refitting the instrument cluster, take care that the speedometer cable is fitted correctly and that any spare cable is pulled through into the engine compartment. Also make sure that no cables are trapped, ensuring that nothing is obstructing the refitting of the

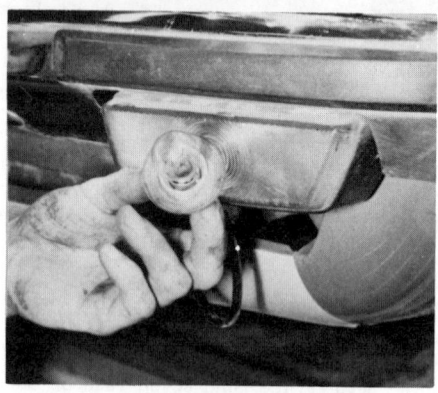

21.1 Front flasher bulb (separate flashers)

22.1 Side flasher bulb replacement

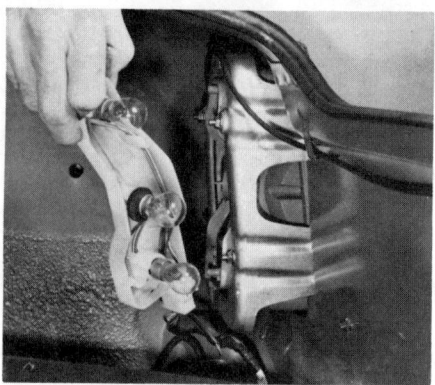

23.2 Rear combination unit bulb replacement

24.1 Number light bulb removal

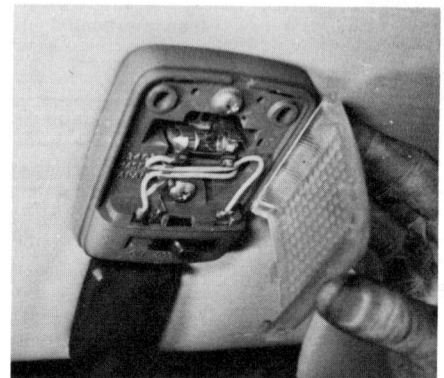

25.1 Interior light

26.2 Reversing light bulb renewal

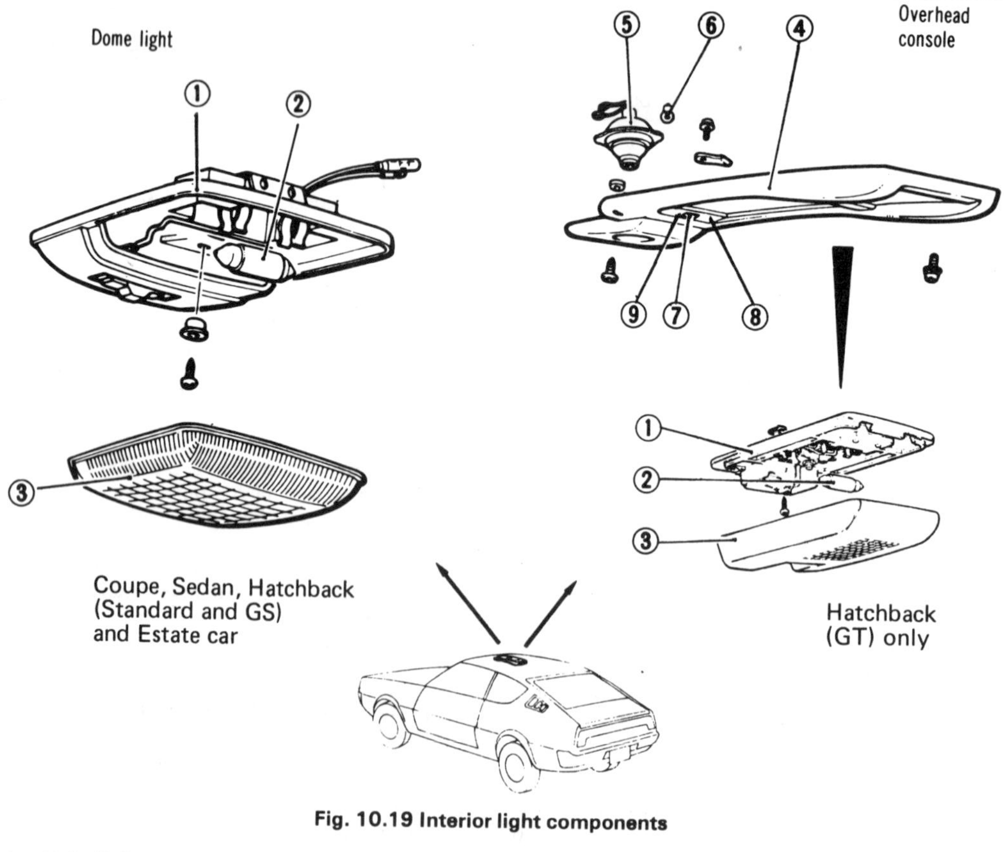

Dome light

Overhead console

Coupe, Sedan, Hatchback
(Standard and GS)
and Estate car

Hatchback
(GT) only

Fig. 10.19 Interior light components

1	Light fitting	4	Roof console body	6	Reading light bulb	8	Door indicator light
2	Festoon bulb	5	Reading light	7	Reading light switch	9	Washer liquid level warning
3	Lens					

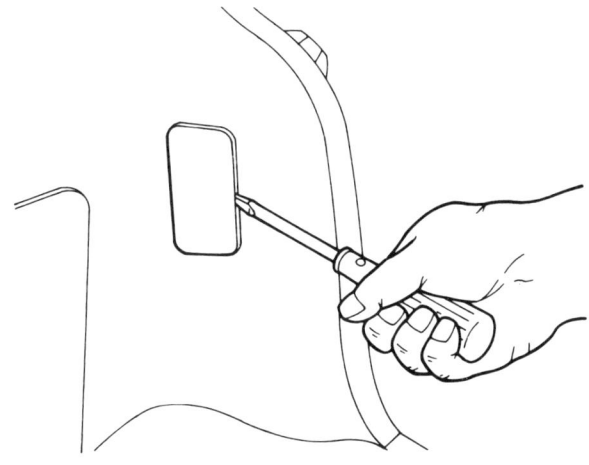

Fig. 10.20 Removing the trim cover

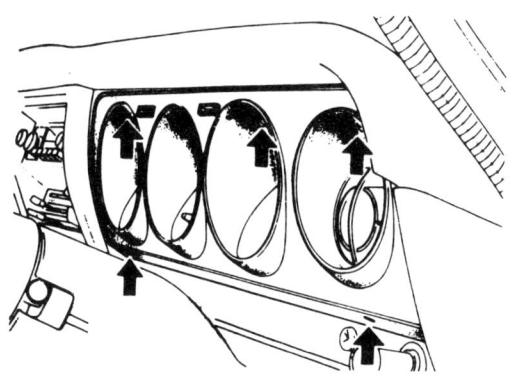

Fig. 10.21 Instrument cluster fixing points (arrowed)

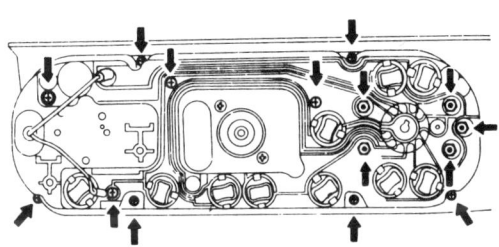

Fig. 10.22 Meter assembly fixing points (arrowed)

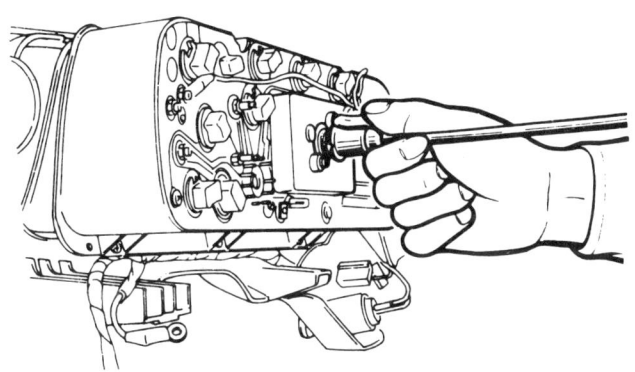

Fig. 10.23 Fitting the speedometer cable

cluster. If the cluster does not go back in easily, establish the reason. Do not try and force the assembly in.

29 Instrument cluster – bulb renewal

1   Remove the instrument cluster as described in the previous Section.
2   The bulbs are in bayonet fittings on the printed circuit board. Access to them is by twisting and pulling out the bulb holder.
3   Remove the bulb from the holder and fit a new one.

30 Instrument cluster – dismantling

1   Remove the 15 screws from the back of the instrument cluster assembly, after having removed the instrument cluster from the car.
2   Individual instruments may be removed by taking out their fixing screws, which become accessible after the panel has been dismantled.

31 Speedometer drive – refitting

1   When a speedometer drive needs renewing, it should be renewed as an assembly, and the correct one must be fitted. Drives are identified by different coloured cable tapes around the outer cable, the appropriate one for the models covered by this manual being yellow.
2   When connecting the cable to the speedometer, push it on until its

retainer engages in the groove in the speedometer. Then pull it to make sure that it is firmly engaged in its groove.
3   If the speedometer drive is not fitted carefully, it can give rise to a fluctuating pointer, noise and damage to the wiring harness of the instrument panel. Make sure that the cable is fitted securely at both ends, that it is not strained and that any bend radius is never less than 6 in (160 mm).
4   After fitting the speedometer end of the cable, pull the slack cable through into the engine compartment until the yellow tape cable marker is about 1·2 in (30 mm) out from the grommet in the toeboard.

32 Tachometer – testing

1   The tachometer is a DC instrument which receives its signal from a transistorized circuit, that counts the pulses produced by the switching action of the contact breaker points.
2   Connect a calibrated test meter to the engine and compare the readings at different engine speeds over the whole range of the meter. If there is a difference in reading between the test meter and the tachometer of more than 10% at the lower end of the scale and 5% at the upper end of the scale, fit a new tachometer.

33 Fuel gauge tank unit – testing

1   The tank unit may be tested with an ohmmeter, to measure the resistance between the two gauge terminals, which should be as follows:

Float position	E	½	F
Resistance	120± 6·5 ohms	45 ± 4·5 ohms	17 ± 2 ohms

To test the unit, remove the lining from the rear of the boot, which will give access to the wiring connectors of the tank unit.

2   The fuel gauge is of the bimetal type and the circuit (Fig. 10.26) has a constant voltage relay built into the gauge to prevent indication errors resulting from voltage fluctuations. The constant voltage on which the gauge operates is 7 volts.

3   To check the gauge, remove the wire to the tank unit and earth the tank unit terminal of the gauge. If the pointer indicates *F*, the gauge is satisfactory. If there is no indication, measure the resistance between the gauge terminals, which should be 30 ohms. A low resistance indicates a shorted coil and a resistance in excess of 100 ohms indicates a broken coil.

34 Temperature gauge – testing

1   The temperature gauge is of the bimetal type and the circuit has a constant voltage relay supply obtained from the fuel gauge. The constant voltage supply prevents indication errors resulting from voltage fluctuations. The operating voltage is 7 volts.

2   To test the gauge, disconnect the wire to the temperature sensor and connect the sensor terminal to earth through a 25 ohms resistor (Fig. 10.27). The gauge will be damaged if the terminal is connected directly to earth and not through a resistor. If the gauge is satisfactory it will indicate a temperature of about 250°F.

3   If the gauge is not satisfactory, check the resistance between the gauge terminals, which should be 25 ohms. A low resistance indicates a shorted coil and a high resistance (over 100 ohms) a broken coil.

4   The sensor may be tested by inserting it to the prescribed depth (Fig. 10.28) in hot water and measuring the resistance between the terminal and the sensor case, when the following readings should be obtained.

Thermometer temperature	176°F (80°C)	212°F (100°C)
Standard resistance	70 ohms	37 ohms
Tolerance	± 5 ohms	± 3 ohms

35 Oil pressure switch – testing and adjustment

1   The oil pressure switch is intended to operate at a pressure of about 5 lb/in².

2   Check the switch by connecting a lamp in series with a battery, or an ohmmeter between the terminal and the case, to see if the switch is *OFF* when no pressure is applied and *ON* when the pressure exceeds about 5 lb/in².

3   To adjust the switch operating pressure, remove the contact screw, insert a small screwdriver down the central hole and turn the adjuster screw (Fig. 10.29).

36 Handbrake switch – adjustment

1   The handbrake switch is of the push-to-*OFF* type, mounted below the handbrake lever (Fig. 10.30).

2   Pull the handbrake one notch up and after loosening the switch mounting screws, slide the switch up and down until it is in the *ON* position when in contact with the handbrake lever.

3   Tighten the fixing screws with the switch in this position.

4   On some models, an improved handbrake ratchet has been fitted and the handbrake switch is factory adjusted, requiring no further attention.

37 Headlamp switch – removal and refitting

1   The headlamp switch is of the single-pole, double-throw type and is mounted on the instrument panel. Its *T* contacts are rated at 11A and the *H* contacts at 12A.

2   To change the switch, unscrew and remove the bezel ring and push the switch through to the back of the panel.

3   Withdraw the switch from beneath the instrument panel and pull off its connector.

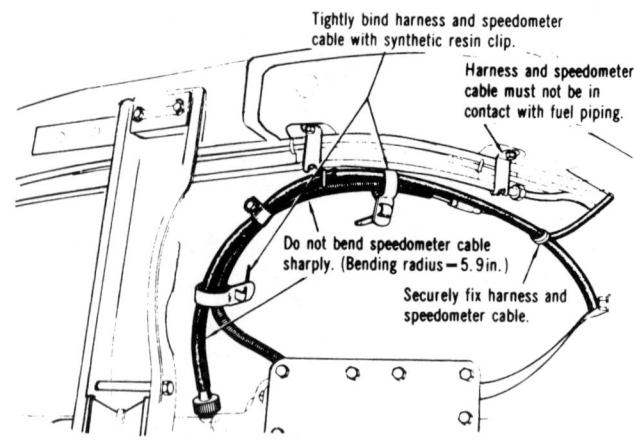

Fig. 10.24 Under floor installation of speedometer cable

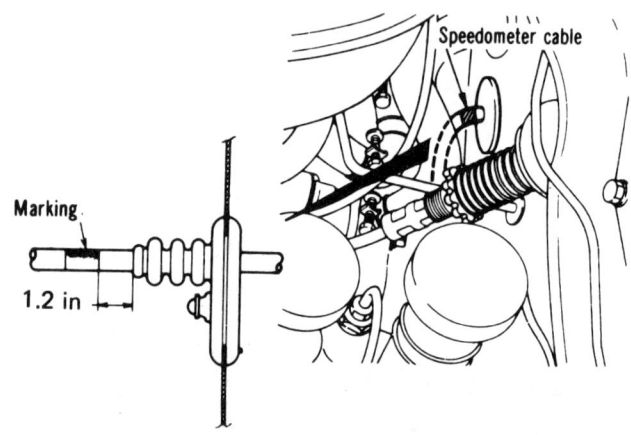

Fig. 10.25 Engine compartment installation of speedometer cable

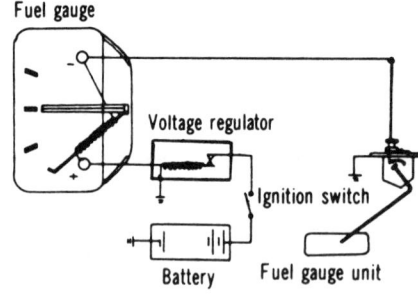

Fig. 10.26 Fuel gauge circuit

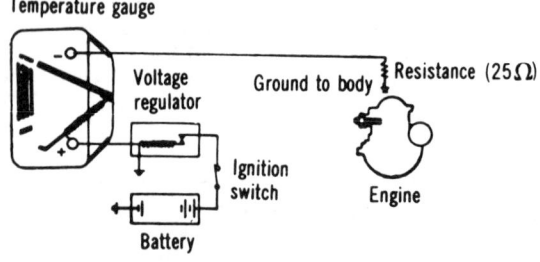

Fig. 10.27 Checking the temperature gauge

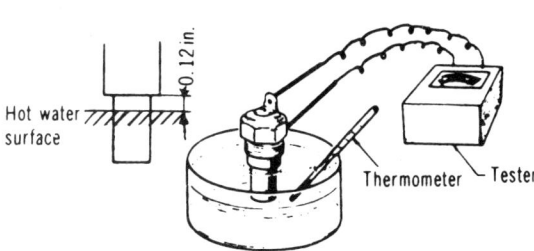

Fig. 10.28 Checking the temperature sensor

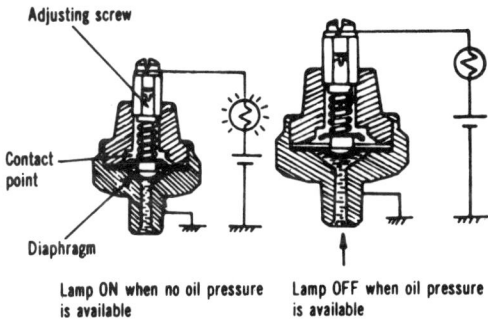

Fig. 10.29 Checking the oil pressure switch

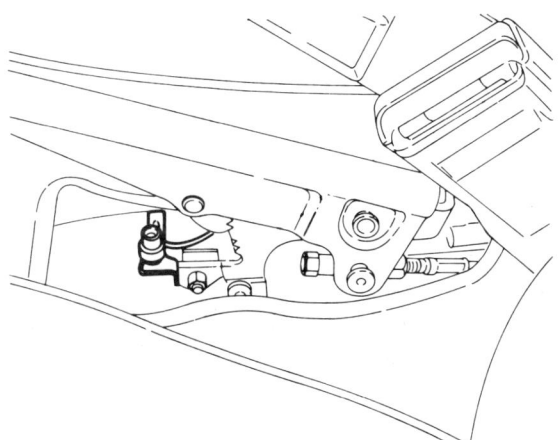

Fig. 10.30 Handbrake switch

4 When refitting, ensure that the switch is vertical and that the bezel ring is tightened so that the switch is firm, but take care not to damage the switch by overtightening.

38 Instrument panel rheostatic switch – removal and refitting

1 The rheostatic switch enables the brightness of the illumination of the instruments to be varied to reduce glare when driving at night.
2 To take out the switch, remove the knob then unscrew and remove the bezel ring.
3 Push the switch through the instrument panel and withdraw it from beneath the instrument panel, then pull off its connector.
4 Refitting is the reverse of the removal procedure.
5 The switch is designed for a load of five, 3·4 watt lamps and if this load is exceeded the switch will overheat and may burn out. Do not fit additional lamps, or renew the instrument lamps with any of a higher rating.

39 Headlamp switch and rheostat

1 On some models there is a combined switch, which is pulled to operate the head and tail lights and turned to change the brightness of the panel lights.
2 Switch removal is similar to the removal of the headlamp switch (Section 37).
3 The switches on the estate car are different from that on all other models, its rheostatic load being only 18·4W instead of 20·4W.
4 It is important that if a new switch is fitted, one of the correct rating is used and that the switch is not overloaded by fitting panel bulbs of a rating higher than that given in the Specifications.

40 Stop lamp switch

1 The stop lamp switch is also the limit stop of the footbrake pedal (photo) and its adjustment is described in Chapter 9, Section 11.
2 The rating of the switch is 12·5A.

41 Tailgate switch – adjustment

1 Two tailgate switches are fitted to the tailgate, one on each side. Both the cargo space light and also a warning light come on when either of the switches is operated.
2 Check that both switches operate when the gate opens and that the clearance between the lever and the switch is 0·08 to 0·12 in (2 to 3 mm). The adjustment is made by adjusting the clearance with shims when the tailgate is closed.

42 EGR warning lamp and reset switch

1 A visual signal warning incorporated in the speedometer assembly is activated when the EGR system is due for routine maintenance. The device has a mileage sensor which is interlocked with the mileometer. This operates a red warning light at every multiple of 15 000 miles.
2 After completion of the EGR maintenance work (Chapter 3, Section 18), the circuit must be reset by removing the instrument cluster and operating the reset switch on the rear of the instrument assembly.

43 Brake failure switch

1 The brake failure switch, when fitted, is part of the combination valve (Chapter 9, Section 16).
2 When a failure of the braking system causes the valve to operate, the switch illuminates the handbrake warning light. Resetting of the switch is described in Chapter 9.

40.1 Stop lamp switch

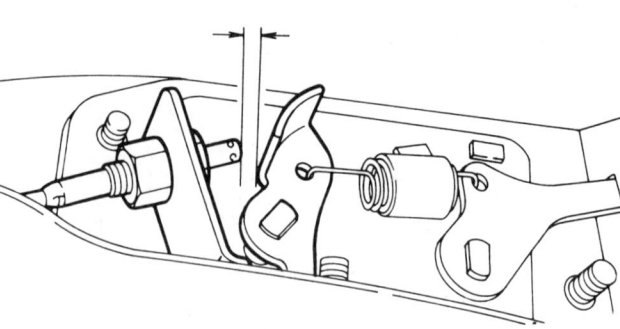

Fig. 10.31 Tailgate switch adjustment

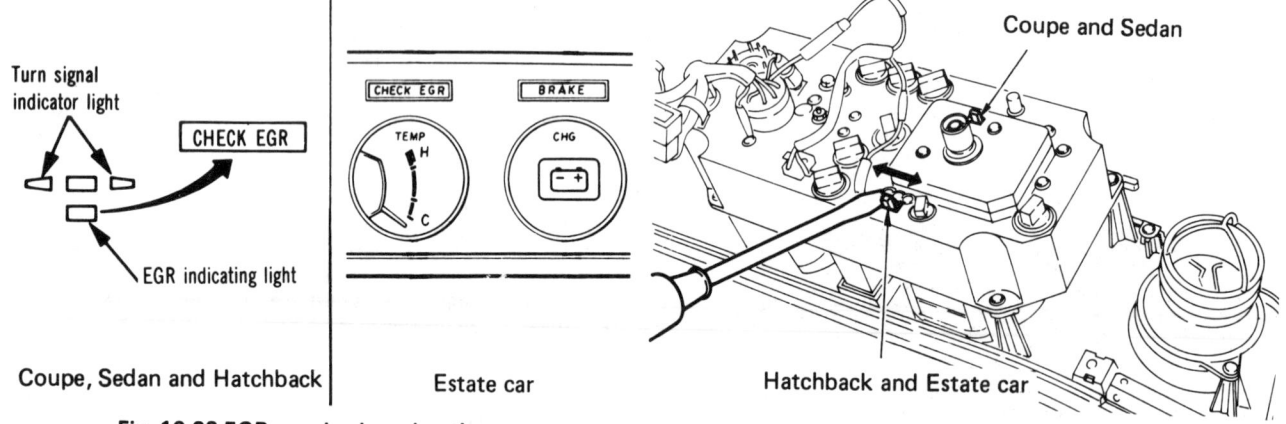

Turn signal
indicator light

CHECK EGR

EGR indicating light

Coupe, Sedan and Hatchback

Estate car

Fig. 10.32 EGR warning lamp location

Coupe and Sedan

Hatchback and Estate car

Fig. 10.33 EGR reset switch

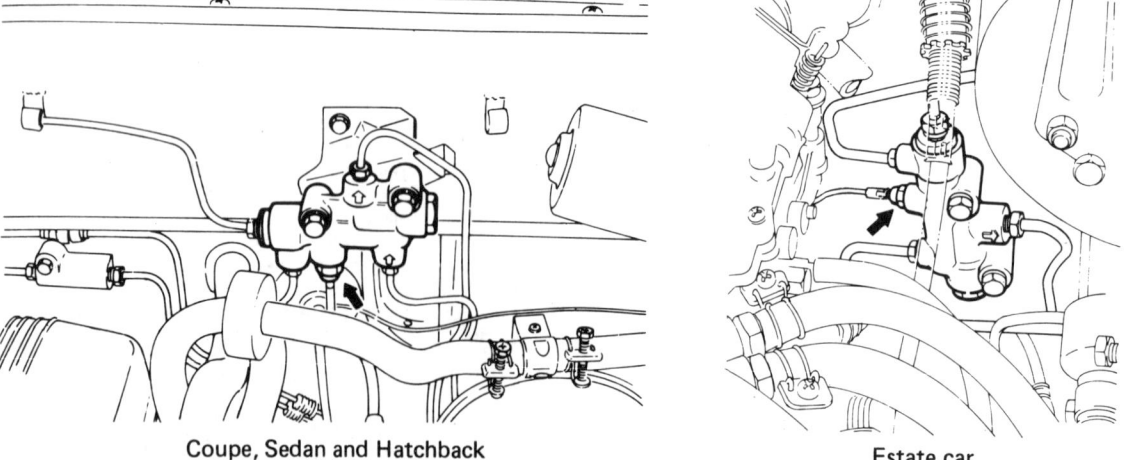

Coupe, Sedan and Hatchback

Estate car

Fig. 10.34 Brake failure switch location

44 Defogger switch and indicator light – removal

Coupe, Sedan and Estate car
1 Remove the instrument cluster (Section 28).
2 Remove the two fixing screws from the switch, separate the switch from the wiring harness and remove the switch.

Hatchback
3 Remove the instrument cluster.
4 Remove the heater fan switch and cigarette lighter, then remove the heater control panel from the instrument cluster.
5 Remove the defogger switch by pushing it from the back of the instrument cluster.

45 Steering column switch – removal and refitting

1 Remove the steering wheel as described in Chapter 11, Section 13.
2 Remove the steering column shroud to give access to the switch fixings and cableforms.
3 Remove the screws securing the column switch, remove the cable straps and separate the harness plugs and sockets, then remove the

switch assembly (photo).
4 When refitting the switch, make sure that it is concentric with the steering column.
5 Secure the cable harnesses, taking them as close as possible to the centre line of the column tube (Fig. 10.36).
6 Refit the steering column shroud and the steering wheel.

46 Door switches – removal and refitting

1 The door switches are mounted at the bottom of the door pillar, and give warning if any door is not fully closed.
2 To remove a switch, pull off the rubber gaiter, pull out the switch, which is a push-fit in the hole and disconnect the wiring connector.
3 Clean the switch if necessary, or renew it if it is badly corroded.
4 Push the wiring connectors into their sockets, push the switch into its mounting hole as far as it will go and refit the gaiter, using a new one if the one removed was perished or damaged.

47 Relays – renewal

1 The indicator flasher unit, hazard warning flasher and wiper relay of the Coupe, Sedan and Hatchback are located together on the underside of the instrument panel Fig. 10.38 and photo. If a demister

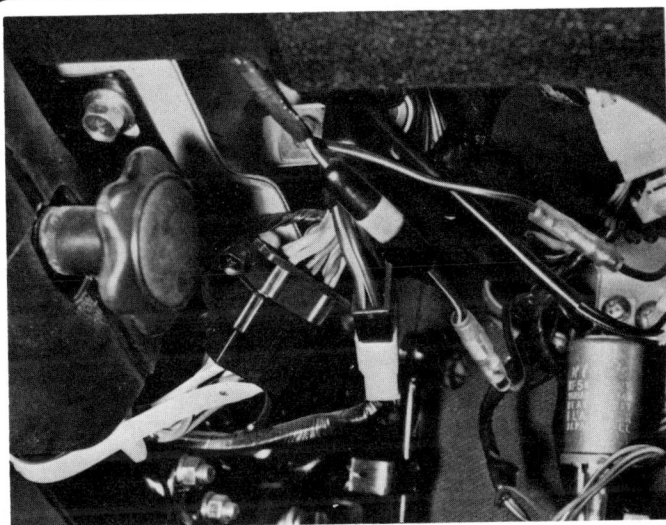

45.3 Steering column switch cable plugs

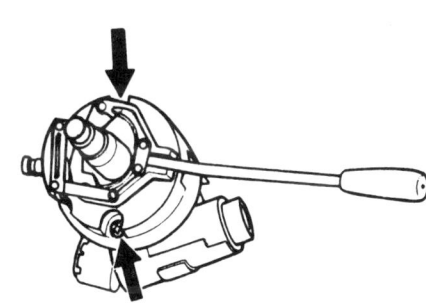

Fig. 10.35 Steering column switch fixing screws (arrowed)

Coupe, Sedan and Hatchback

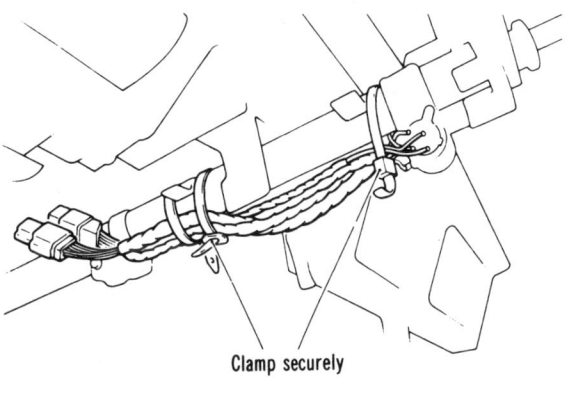

Clamp securely

Estate car

Fig. 10.36 Steering column switch wiring harness arrangement

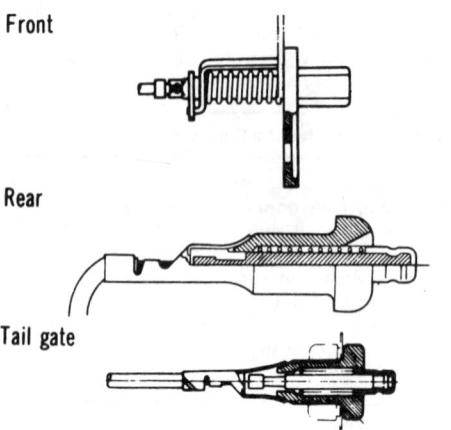

Front

Rear

Tail gate

Fig. 10.37 Types of door switch

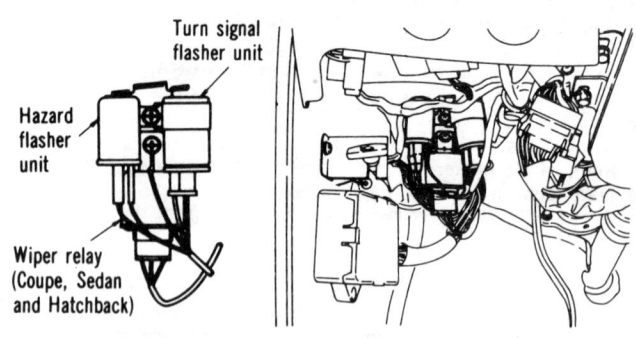

Turn signal flasher unit

Hazard flasher unit

Wiper relay (Coupe, Sedan and Hatchback)

Fig. 10.38 Relay positions (except Estate car)

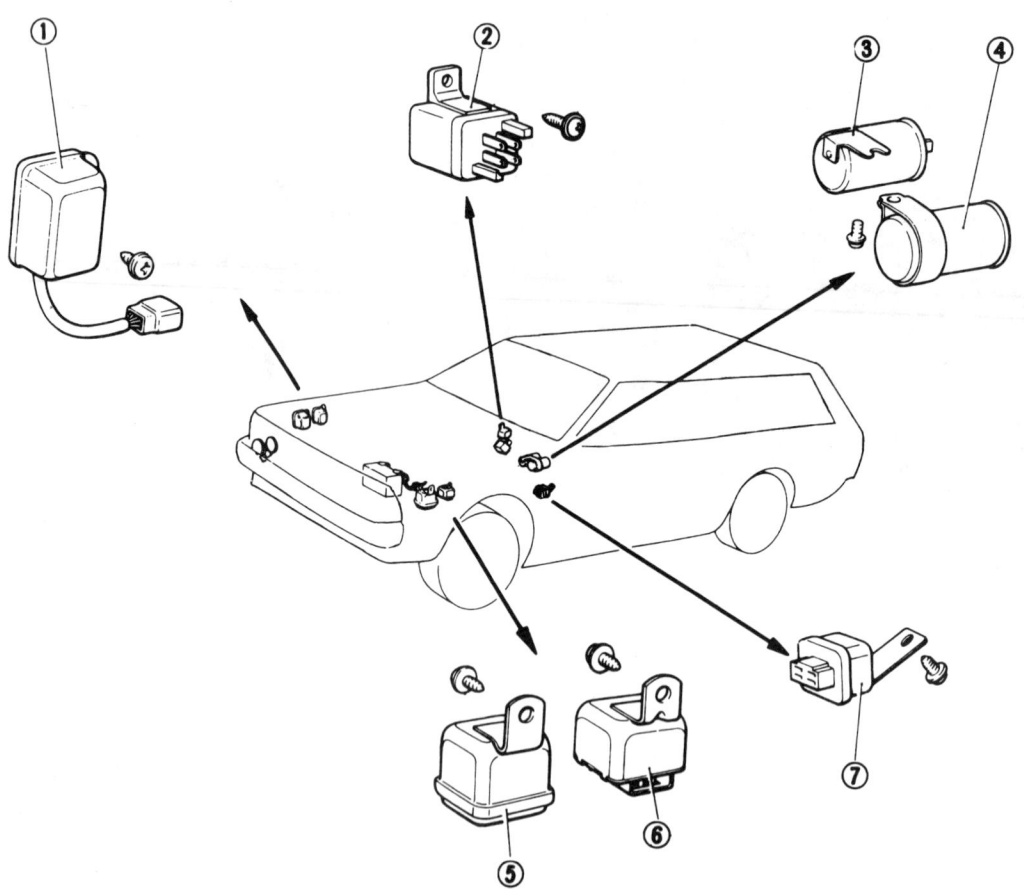

Fig. 10.39 Relay positions (Estate car)

1	Intermittent wiper relay (when fitted)		flasher unit
2	Seat belt chime drive	5	Light control relay
3	Hazard flasher relay	6	Windscreen wiper relay
4	Direction indicator	7	Seat belt warning relay

47.1 Relay location

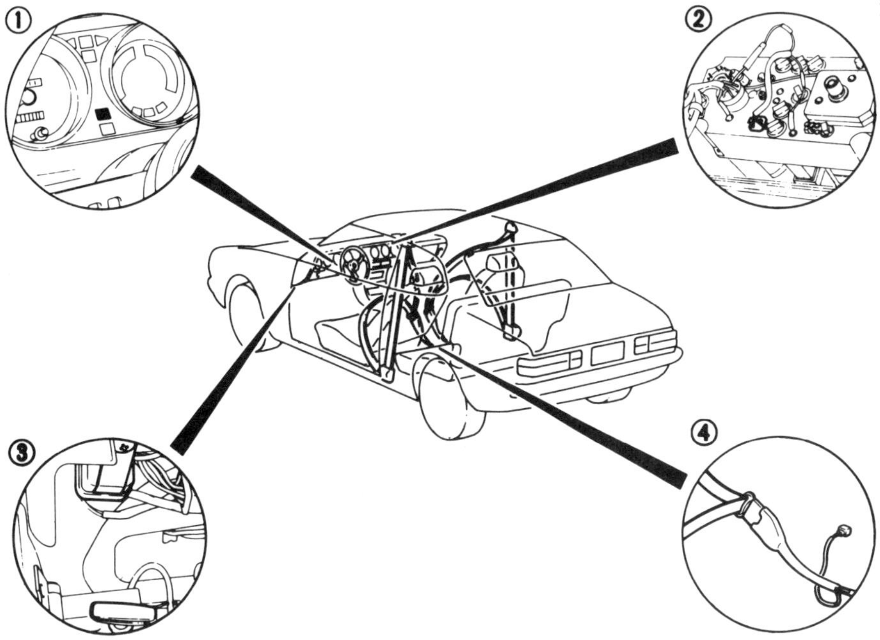

Fig. 10.41 Seat belt system component positions

1   *Warning light*   3   *Timer*
2   *Warning buzzer (except Estate car)*   4   *Belt switch*

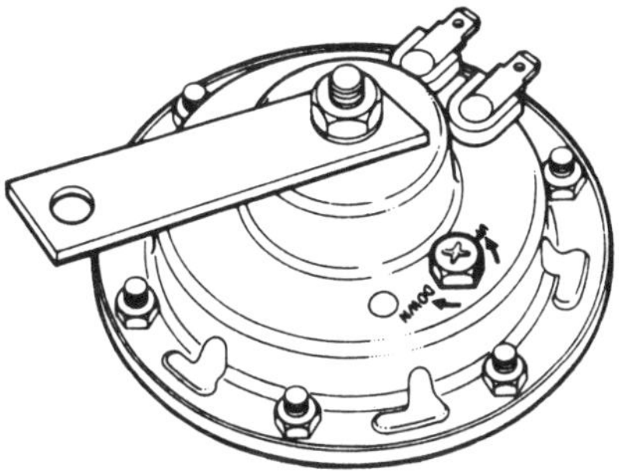

Fig. 10.40 Horn adjustment

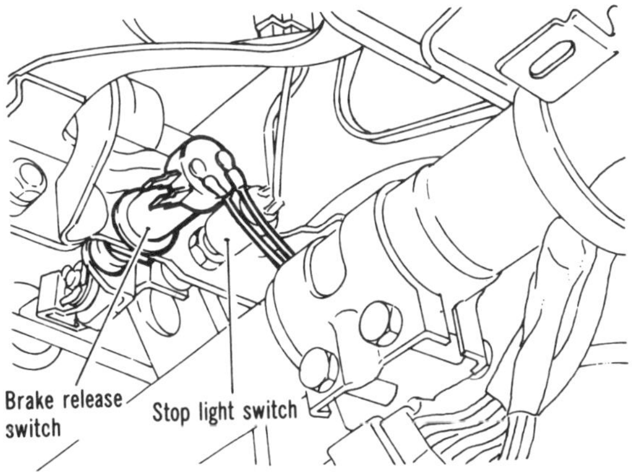

Hose from intake
manifold vacuum

Hose to power brake

Cable to carburetor
accelerator linkage

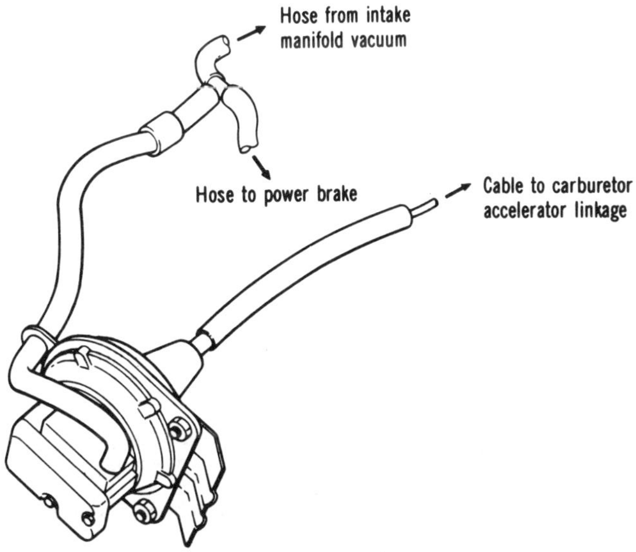

Fig. 10.42 The speed control unit

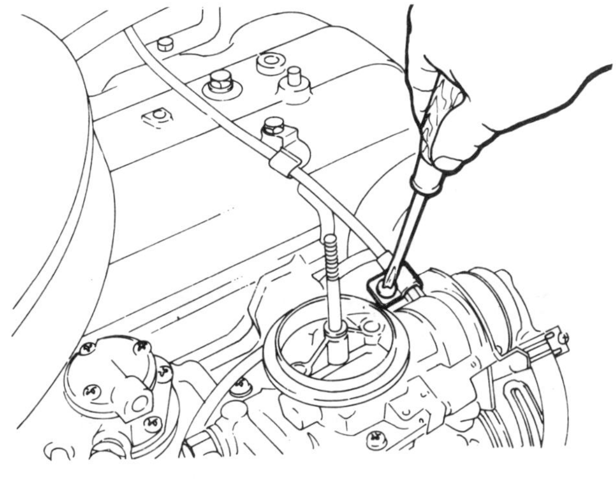

Brake release
switch   Stop light switch

Fig. 10.43 Brake release switch

Fig. 10.44 Throttle cable adjustment

is fitted, its relay is mounted alongside the other relays.
2   The position of the relays on the estate car is as shown in Fig. 10.39.
3   To renew a relay, separate its electrical connector, remove the fixing screws and fit the new relay.
4   Where a radio interference suppressor is fitted, this should be secured with the screw that holds the demister relay.
5   Ensure that the earth wire of the front harness is effectively bonded to the relay panel.

48 Horn – adjustment

1   Remove the horn from the car, fix its bracket in a vice and connect a battery of the correct voltage to the horn terminals.
2   Sound the horn and adjust its note by turning the adjuster screw (Fig. 10.40).
3   If the horn does not sound, turn the screw *UP* until a weak sound is heard, then continue turning up to a further 180 degrees to obtain the best tone.
4   If the horn makes a harsh low sound, turn the screw *UP* about half a turn to find the best tone.
5   If the horn makes a loud intermittent vibrating sound, turn the screw *DOWN* 20 to 30 degrees to find the best position.
6   Having found the best note, apply some clear lacquer to the screw to lock it.

49 Seat belt warning system

1   If the driver is seated and turns the ignition *ON* before fastening his seat belt, audible and visible alarms are activated.
2   The system consists of a belt switch, audible warning and indicator light. When the ignition is turned *ON*, the warning light is illuminated for between four and eight seconds regardless of whether the driver's seat belt is fastened and so serves as a reminder.
3   If the seat belt is not fastened when the ignition is turned *ON*, there is an audible warning and this warning continues for four to eight seconds, or until the belt is fastened.
4   The same audible warning is coupled to the door switches and steering wheel lock. It also sounds if the car door is opened without removing the ignition key.

50 Speed control system – adjustment

1   Some estate car models have an automatic speed control system as an optional extra.
2   It is electrically actuated and vacuum operated and is designed to maintain any preset speed in excess of 30 mph (48 kph).
3   A speed control lever on the steering column incorporates a slide switch with *OFF*, *ON* and *RESUME* positions as well as a *SET* button.
4   The speed control unit has a lock-in adjustment which may be used to make the necessary correction if the vehicle does not hold the speed at which the *SET* button was pressed. Before making this adjustment, check that the lock-in accuracy is not being affected by poor engine performance, excessive engine load, or incorrect throttle cable adjustment.
5   Optimum servo performance is obtained if the slack in the throttle cable is 0 to 0·04 in (0 to 1 mm) when the choke is fully open and the engine is running at idle speed.
6   Automatic speed control is cancelled by operating the brake pedal and there is an additional switch mounted on the foot brake pedal for this. This switch is adjusted in the same manner as the stop light switch (Chapter 9, Section 11).

51 Clock – adjustment

1   Access to the clock adjusting screw is gained by removing the instrument panel and pulling out the instrument cluster. The adjusting screw is on the back of the clock.
2   Determine how much the clock gains or loses in a period of 24 hours and adjust as follows.

Round type clock
3   One complete clockwise turn of the adjusting screw will cause the clock to gain 3 minutes in 24 hours (Fig. 10.45). A complete turn anti-clockwise will cause the clock to lose the same amount.

Estate car
4   Adjustment is similar, except that a complete clockwise turn causes the clock to gain 16 to 20 minutes a day and lose the same amount for a complete turn anti-clockwise (Fig. 10.46).

52 Radio – removal

Coupe, Sedan and Hatchback
1   Remove the instrument cluster (Section 28).
2   Pull off the station selector and volume control knobs and remove the two nuts then exposed behind them.
3   Remove the screw from the support bracket and withdraw the radio after disconnecting the aerial, power supply and speaker.

Estate car
4   Remove the side cover of the centre panel.
5   Disconnect the aerial, power supply and speaker leads.
6   Remove the knobs from the radio and remove the radio fixing screws on the sides, then withdraw the radio from underneath the tray.

Speaker removal
7   Remove the instrument cluster, if it has not already been removed for the removal of the radio.
8   On the estate car also remove the glove box.
9   Remove the two nuts attaching the speaker and lift the speaker out, downwards.

53 Windscreen wiper arms and blades – removal and refitting

1   Unscrew and remove the cap nut from the wiper arm and pull the arm off its splines (photo).
2   To remove the blade, grip the arm and the blade and pull apart.
3   Fit new blades if the existing ones are damaged, or do not wipe clearly.
4   Fit the arms on the splines so that, in the park position, the blades are about ¾ in (19 mm) above the bottom of the windscreen then refit and tighten the cap nuts.

54 Windscreen wiper motor – removal

1   Remove the windscreen wiper arms. Remove the arm shaft locknuts and push the shafts through their mounting holes.
2   Remove the four bolts securing the wiper motor mounting to the bodywork.
3   Hold the motor shaft firmly and with the crank arm and linkage held parallel, push the crank arm bush off.
4   If necessary, the linkage may be removed by threading it through the hole left by the removal of the motor.

55 Rear wiper motor – removal

1   Remove the wiper arm. Remove the arm shaft locknut and push the shaft through the panel.
2   Remove the four bolts securing the motor assembly mounting bracket to the vehicle body and pull the wiper motor assembly towards you.
3   Hold the motor, so that its shaft is at right-angles to the linkage and while holding the motor shaft tightly, take off the linkage.
4   *Do not separate the motor and crank arm, because these have been assembled to ensure that the wiper blade stops automatically in its correct parked position.*

56 Windscreen wiper motor – dismantling

1   Do not separate the motor and crank arm unless necessary

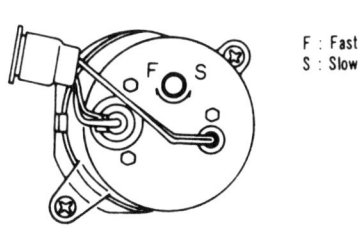

F : Fast
S : Slow

Fig. 10.45 Clock adjustment (except Estate car)

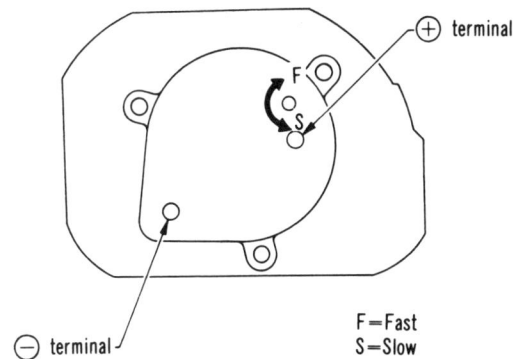

⊕ terminal

⊖ terminal

F = Fast
S = Slow

Fig. 10.46 Clock adjustment (Estate car)

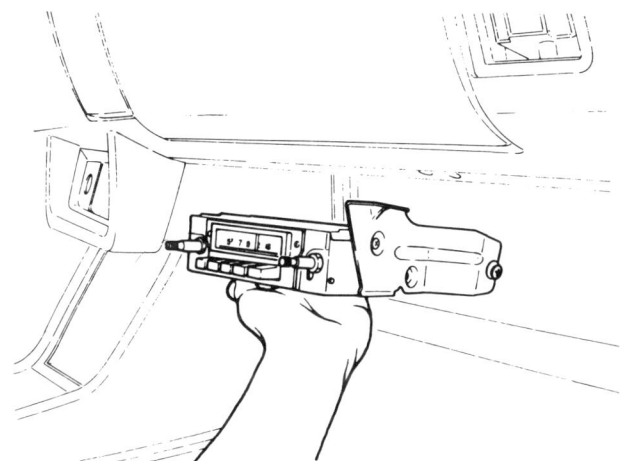

Fig. 10.47 Removing the radio

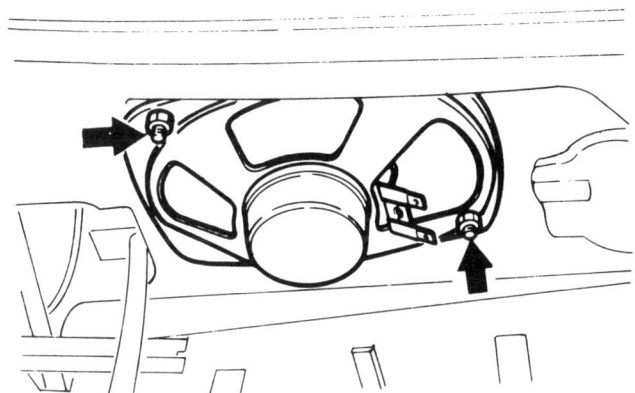

Fig. 10.48 Removing the speaker

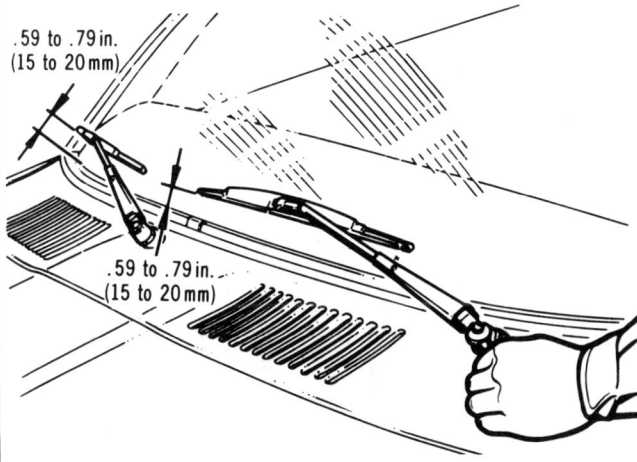

.59 to .79 in.
(15 to 20 mm)

.59 to .79 in.
(15 to 20 mm)

Fig. 10.49 Windscreen wiper blade adjustment

53.1 Windscreen wiper arm removal

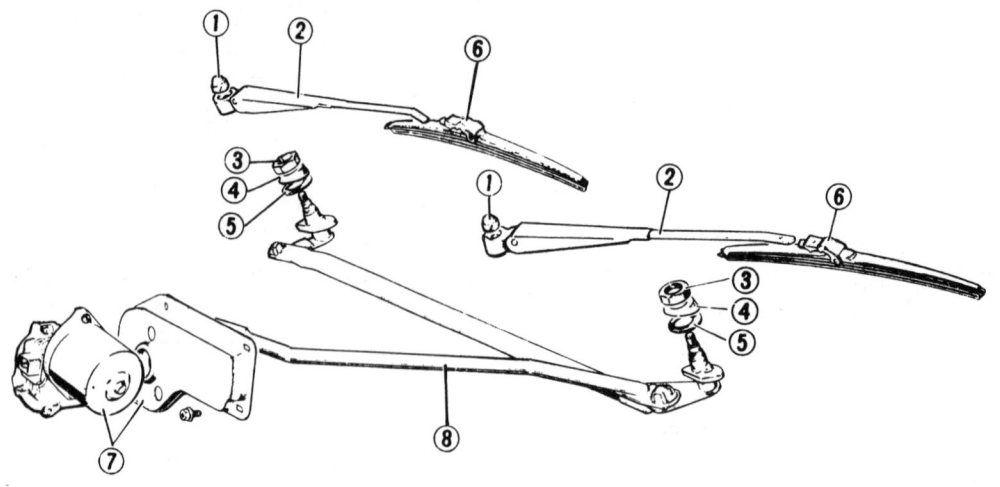

Fig. 10.50 Windscreen wiper (exploded view)

1	Nut	3	Lock nut	5	Washer	7	Motor and bracket assembly
2	Wiper arm	4	Spacer	6	Wiper blade	8	Wiper link

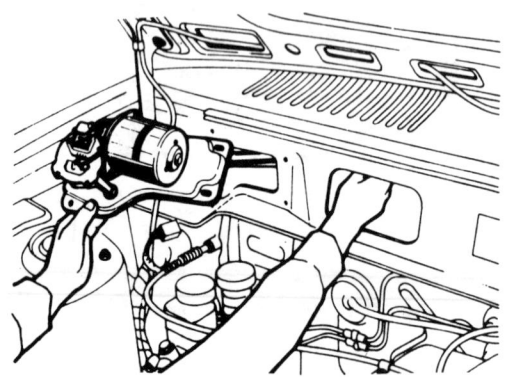

Fig. 10.51 Removing the motor and linkage

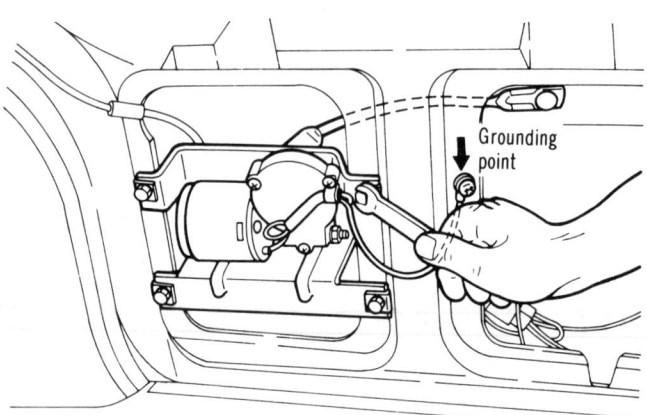

Fig. 10.52 Removing the rear window wiper motor

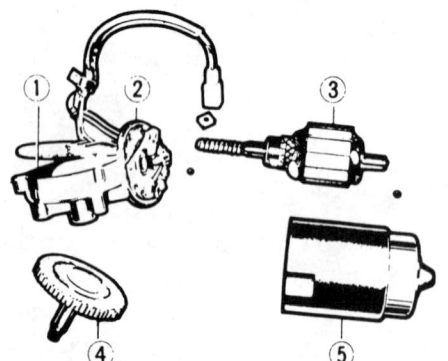

Fig. 10.53 Windscreen wiper motor components

1   Gearbox   4   Driven gear
2   Brush assembly   5   Motor case
3   Armature

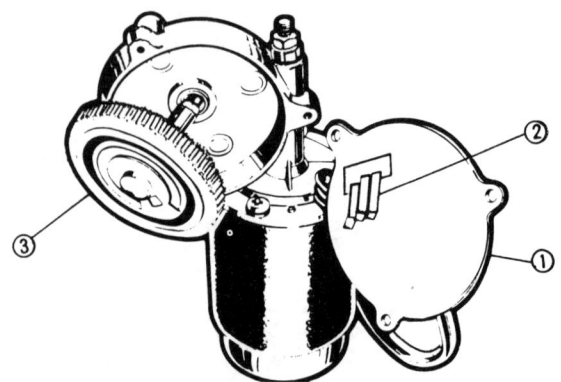

Fig. 10.54 Windscreen wiper motor gearbox

1   Gearbox cover
2   Contact point
3   Driven gear

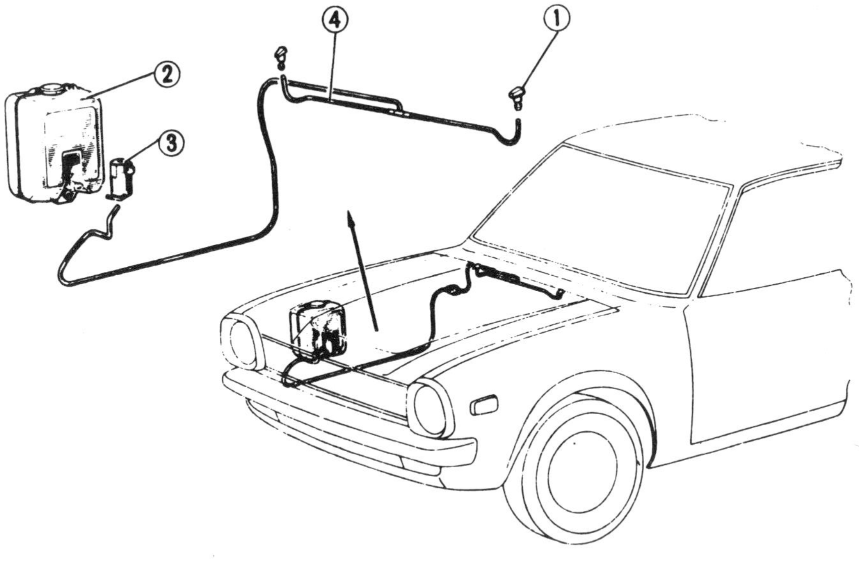

Fig. 10.55 Windscreen washer components

1 Washer nozzle
2 Reservoir tank
3 Washer pump
4 Tube

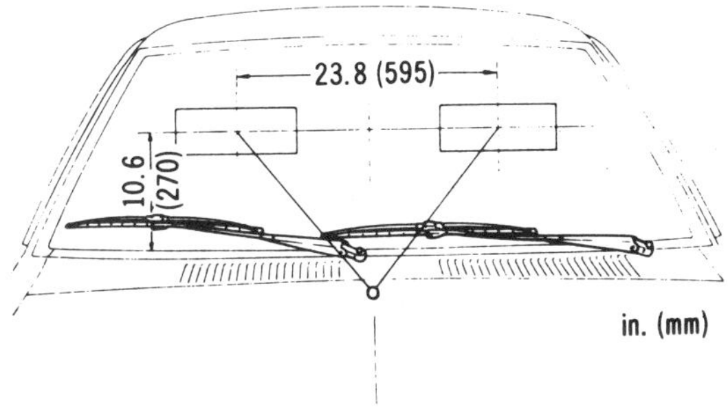

23.8 (595)

10.6 (270)

Coupe, Sedan and Hatchback

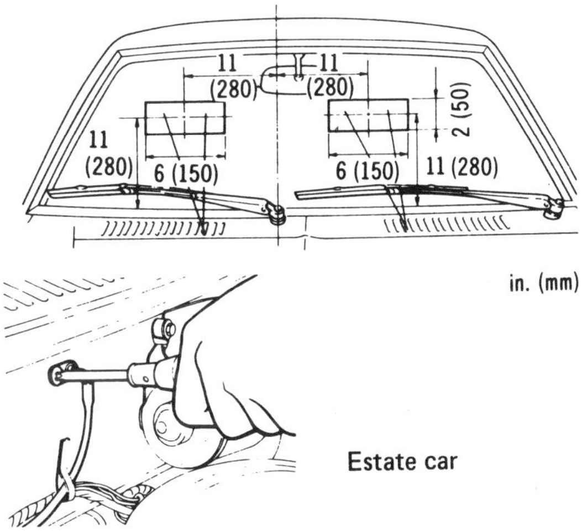

11 (280)   11 (280)   2 (50)

11 (280)   6 (150)   6 (150)   11 (280)

in. (mm)

Estate car

in. (mm)

Fig. 10.56 Washer jet settings (windscreen)

6.7 (170)

2 (50)

4 (100)

in. (mm)

Fig. 10.57 Washer jet setting (rear window)

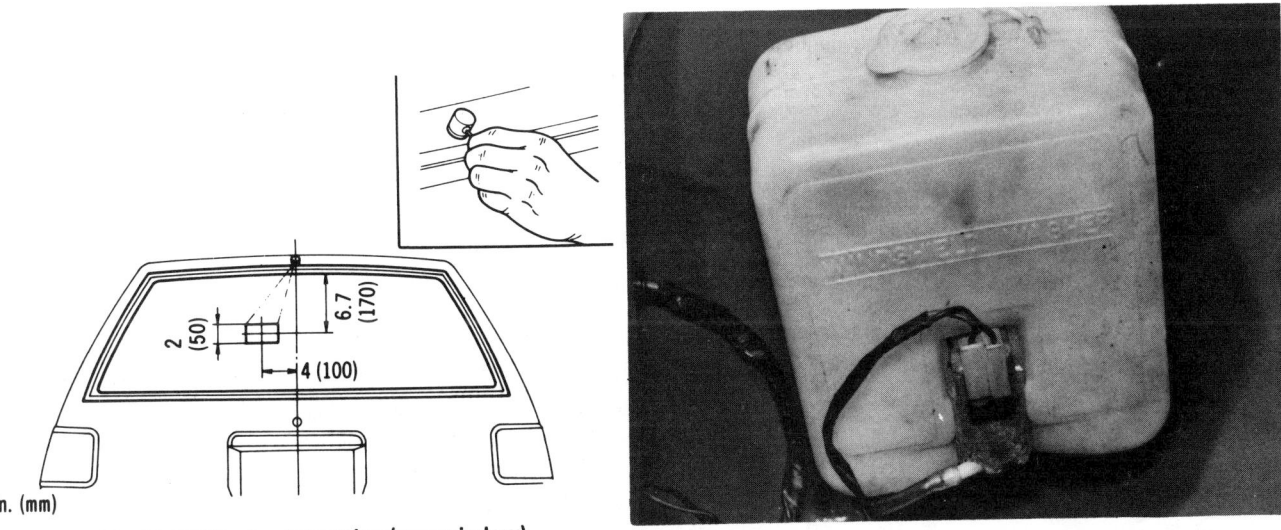

57.1 Windscreen washer reservoir

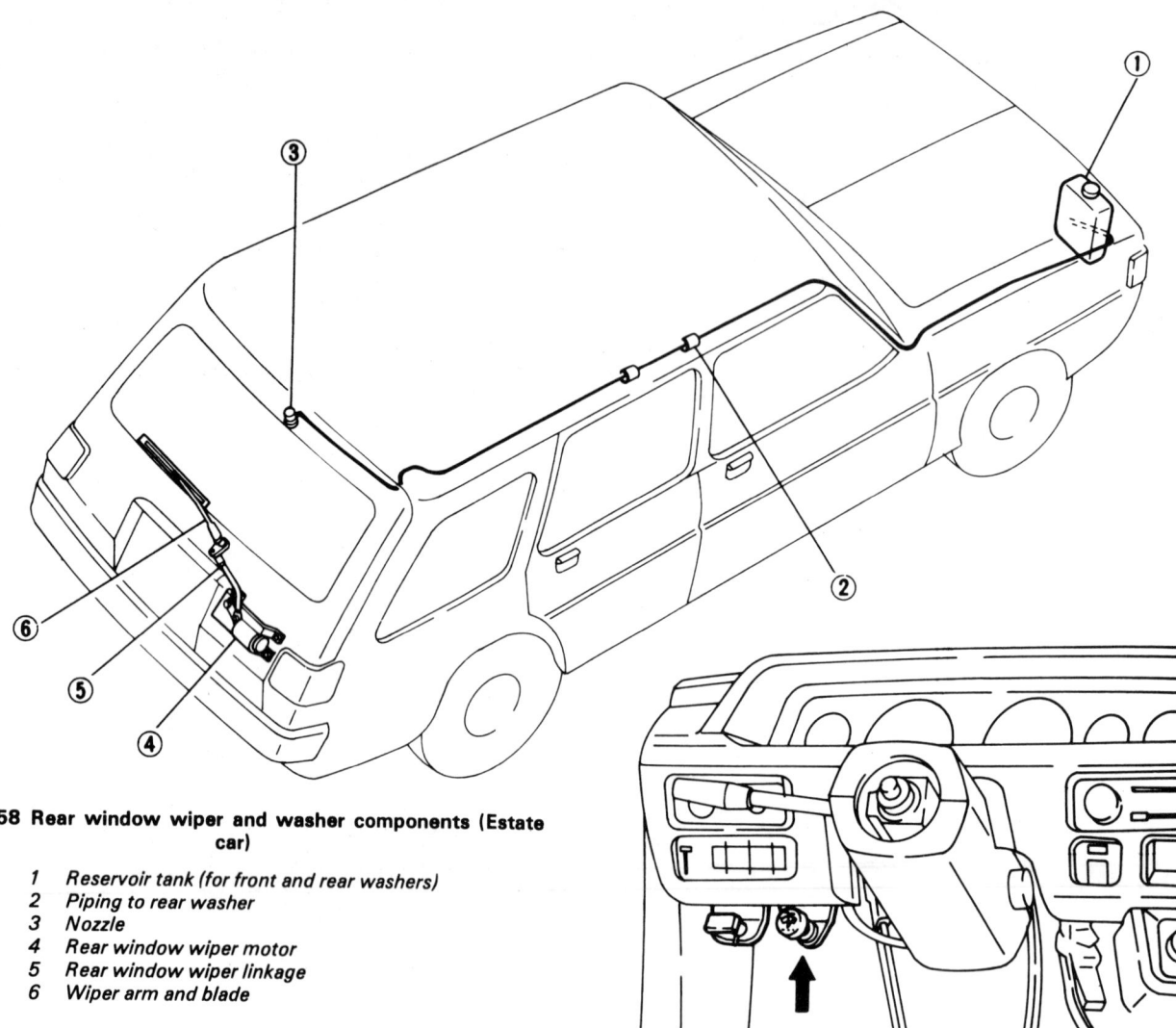

Fig. 10.58 Rear window wiper and washer components (Estate car)

1   *Reservoir tank (for front and rear washers)*
2   *Piping to rear washer*
3   *Nozzle*
4   *Rear window wiper motor*
5   *Rear window wiper linkage*
6   *Wiper arm and blade*

Fig. 10.59 Location of rear washer/wiper switch

because they have been assembled to give the correct parking position. If it is necessary to separate them, put mating marks to ensure correct reassembly.
2   Remove the crank arm and remove the gearbox cover.
3   Remove the driven gear, take off the motor cover and remove the armature assembly, being careful not to lose the steel ball which is fitted to each end of the shaft.
4   Check the brushes for wear, the brush springs for loss of tension and also check that the brush lead is soldered securely.
5   Check the contact point for signs of bad contact or burning, check the driven gear for damage and wear. Ensure that the commutator is clean and undamaged.
6   When reassembling the motor, grease the teeth of the driven gear and fix the ball to each end of the shaft with grease before refitting the armature.
7   After assembling the motor, run it under no load conditions before refitting it and check that the current is less than 3A at both low and high speed.
8   Refitting the motor is the reverse of removing it. Adjust the blades to give the correct parking position.

57 Windscreen washer – servicing

1   Normally, the windscreen washer requires no maintenance other

than keeping the reservoir topped up with water, to which a proprietary screen wash fluid has been added (photo).
2   On the Hatchback GT model a reed switch and float are incorporated in the reservoir and a warning light is illuminated on the console when the level of liquid in the reservoir is too low.
3   The nozzles should be adjusted so that their jets strike the screen symmetrically and in the area indicated in Fig. 10.56.
4   If the washer discharge is unsatisfactory, check that the tube is not clogged, kinked or crushed.

Coupe, Sedan and Hatchback

5   Adjust the path of the jet by inserting a piece of stiff wire, or a sewing needle into the nozzle and moving the ball horizontally and vertically until the aiming of the jet is satisfactory.

Estate car

6   Adjust the aiming of the jet by carefully bending the nozzle bracket until a satisfactory result is achieved.

58 Rear window washer

1   When a rear window washer is fitted it is fed by a pipe from the same reservoir as the windscreen washer. It has its own independent pump within the reservoir and a switch which is combined with the rear wiper control.

59 Fault diagnosis – electrical system

Symptom	Reason/s
Starter motor fails to turn engine	
No electricity at starter motor	Battery discharged
	Battery defective internally
	Battery terminal leads loose or earth lead not securely attached to body
	Loose or broken connections in starter motor circuit
	Starter motor switch or solenoid faulty
Electricity at starter motor: faulty motor	Starter motor pinion jammed in mesh with the flywheel gear ring
	Starter brushes badly worn, sticking, or brush wires loose
	Commutator dirty, worn or burnt
	Starter motor armature faulty
	Field coils earthed
Starter motor turns engine very slowly	Battery in discharged condition
Electrical defects	Starter brushes badly worn, sticking, or brush wires loose
	Loose wires in starter motor circuit
Starter motor operates without turning engine	Pinion or flywheel gear teeth broken or worn
Mechanical damage	Battery in discharged condition
Starter motor noisy or excessively rough engagement	
Lack of attention or mechanical damage	Pinion or flywheel gear teeth broken or worn
	Starter motor retaining bolts loose
Battery will not hold charge for more than a few days	
Wear or damage	Battery defective internally
	Electrolyte level too low or electrolyte too weak due to leakage
	Plate separators no longer fully effective
	Battery plates severely sulphated
Insufficient current flow to keep battery charged	Battery plates severely sulphated
	Alternator drivebelt slipping
	Battery terminal connections loose or corroded
	Alternator not charging
	Short in lighting circuit causing continual battery drain
	Regulator unit not working correctly
Ignition light fails to go out, battery runs flat in a few days	
Alternator not charging	Alternator drivebelt loose and slipping or broken
	Brushes worn, sticking, broken or dirty
	Brush springs worn or broken
	Commutator dirty, greasy, worn or burnt
	Alternator field coils burnt, open, or shorted
	Commutator worn
	Pole pieces very loose
Regulator or cut-out fails to work correctly	Regulator incorrectly set
	Cut-out incorrectly set
	Open circuit in wiring of cut-out and regulator unit
Horn	
Horn operates all the time	Horn push either earthed or stuck down
	Horn cable to horn push earthed
Horn fails to operate	Blown fuse
	Cable or cable connection loose, broken or disconnected
	Horn has an internal fault
Horn emits intermittent or unsatisfactory noise	Cable connections loose
	Horn incorrectly adjusted
Lights	
Lights do not come on	If engine not running, battery discharged
	Sealed beam filament burnt out or bulbs broken
	Wire connections loose, disconnected or broken
	Light switch shorting or otherwise faulty
Lights come on but fade out	If engine not running, battery discharged
	Light bulb filament burnt out or bulbs or sealed beam units broken

	Wire connections loose, disconnected or broken
	Light switch shorting or otherwise faulty
Lights give very poor illumination	Lamp glasses dirty
	Lamp badly out of adjustment
Lights work erratically – flashing on and off, especially over bumps	Battery terminals or earth connection loose
	Light not earthing properly
	Contacts in light switch faulty

Wipers

Wiper motor fails to work	Blown fuse
	Wire connection loose, disconnected, or broken
	Brushes badly worn
	Armature worn or faulty
	Field coils faulty
Wiper motor works very slowly and takes excessive current	Commutator dirty, greasy or burnt
	Armature bearings dirty or unaligned
	Armature badly worn or faulty
Wiper motor works slowly and takes little current	Brushes badly worn
	Commutator dirty, greasy or burnt
	Armature badly worn or faulty
Wiper motor works but wiper blades remain static	Wiper motor gearbox parts badly worn
Wipers do not stop when switched off or stop in wrong place	Auto-stop device faulty

COUPE AND SEDAN

Cable Coloring Identifications by Circuits

Symbol	Coloring
B	Black
BW	Black/white
BY	Black/yellow
BR	Black/red
W	White
WR	White/red
R	Red
RW	Red/white
RB	Red/black
RL	Red/blue
RG	Red/green
G	Green
GW	Green/white
GR	Green/red
GY	Green/yellow
GB	Green/black
GL	Green/blue
GO	Green/orange
Y	Yellow
YR	Yellow/red
YB	Yellow/black
YG	Yellow/green
YL	Yellow/blue
YW	Yellow/white
L	Blue
LW	Blue/white
LR	Blue/red
LB	Blue/black

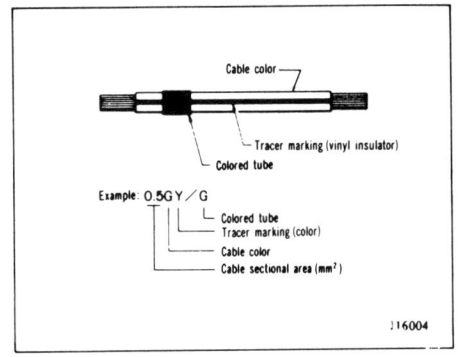

Example: 0.5GY ⁄ G
- Colored tube
- Tracer marking (color)
- Cable color
- Cable sectional area (mm²)

116004

Nominal size (designated by sectional area in mm² of wire)	SAE gauge No.	Permissible current	
		Within engine compartment	Other areas
0.5	20	7A	13A
0.85	18	9A	17A
1.25	16	12A	22A
2.0	14	16A	30A
3.0	12	21A	40A
5.0	10	31A	54A

NOTE: The symbols shown in parentheses denote the locations of the parts, ground, etc. as shown in the following table. CB, CE and CI in the symbols indicate body, engine compartment and instrument panel, respectively.

Symbol	Part name	Location
CB-1	Reversing light switch	Transmission
CB-2	Wiper motor	Front deck
CB 3	Stop light switch	Brake pedal bracket
CB-4	Fuse block	Lower part of left front pillar
CB-5	Connector	Lower part of left front pillar
CB-6	Inhibitor switch connector and shift indicator light connector	Inside the shift lever bracket
CB-7	Interior light connector	7.87 in. (200 mm) away from dome light
CB-8	Belt switch	Inside the buckle
CB-9	Hand brake switch	Under parking brake
CB-10	Door switch FR. R.H.	Lower part of R.H. center pillar
CB-11	Door switch FR. L.H.	Lower part of L.H. center pillar
CB-12	Door switch RR. R.H.	Upper side of R.H. rear wheel house
CB-13	Door switch RR. L.H.	Upper side of L.H. rear wheel house
CB-14	Fuel gauge unit connector	Front of fuel tank
CB-15	Fuel gauge unit	Fuel tank
CB-16	Body earth	Front of spare tire house
CE-1	Earth	Battery seat
CE-2	Engine earth	Left side of cylinder block under temperature gauge unit
CE-3	Earth	Tightened together with voltage regulator
CE-4	Brake failure indicator switch	Rear section of engine compartment
CI-1	Micro switch, Reset switch and Buzzer	Back of instrument cluster
CI-2	Hazard flasher unit, Turn signal flasher unit, Belt warning timer and Wiper relay	Underside of instrument panel
CI-3	Earth	Tightened together with wiper relay
CI-4	Connector	Lower left side of steering column

Fig. 10.60 Key to wiring diagram – Coupe – Sedan

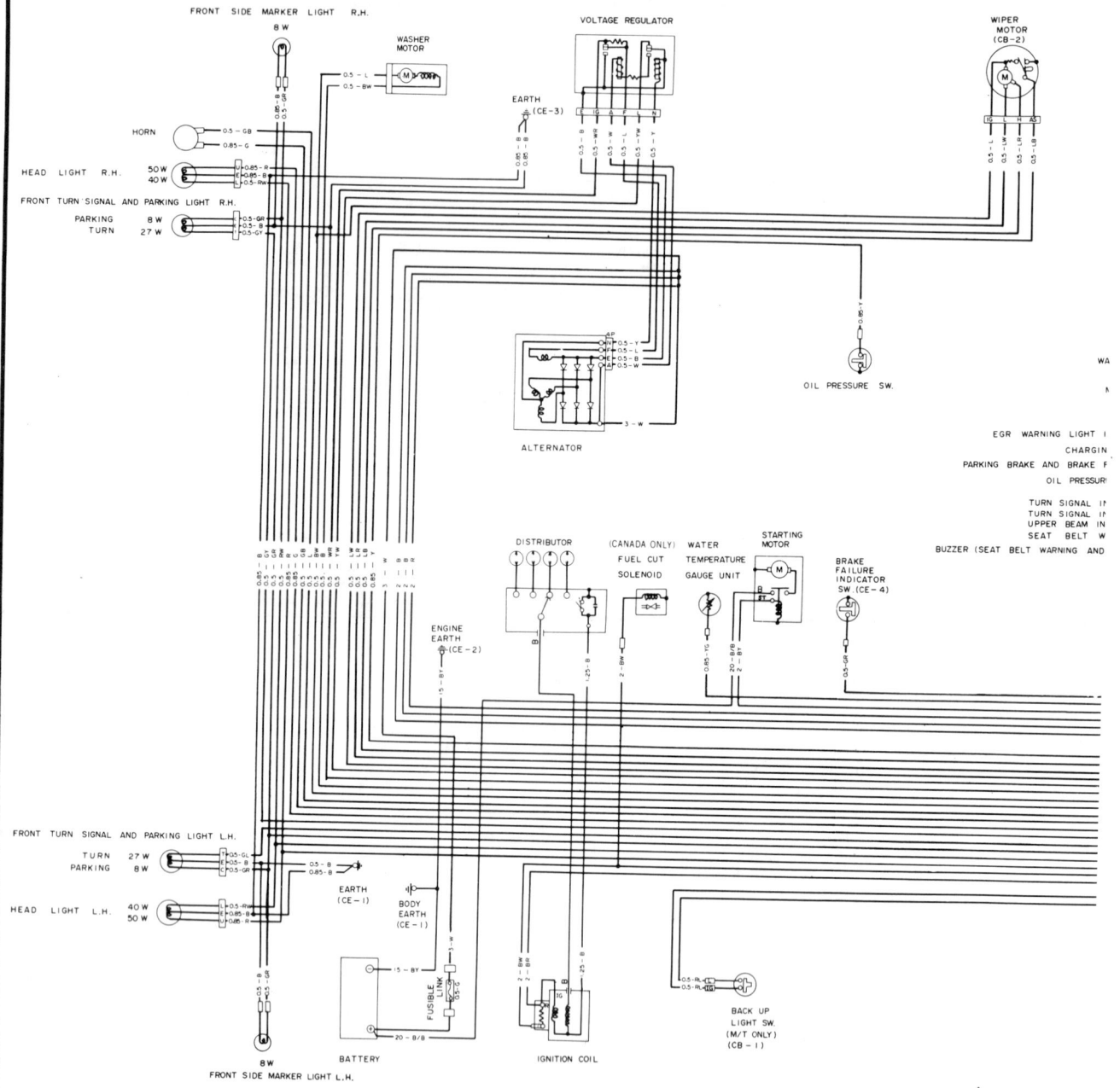

Fig. 10.60 Wiring diagram – Coupe – Sedan

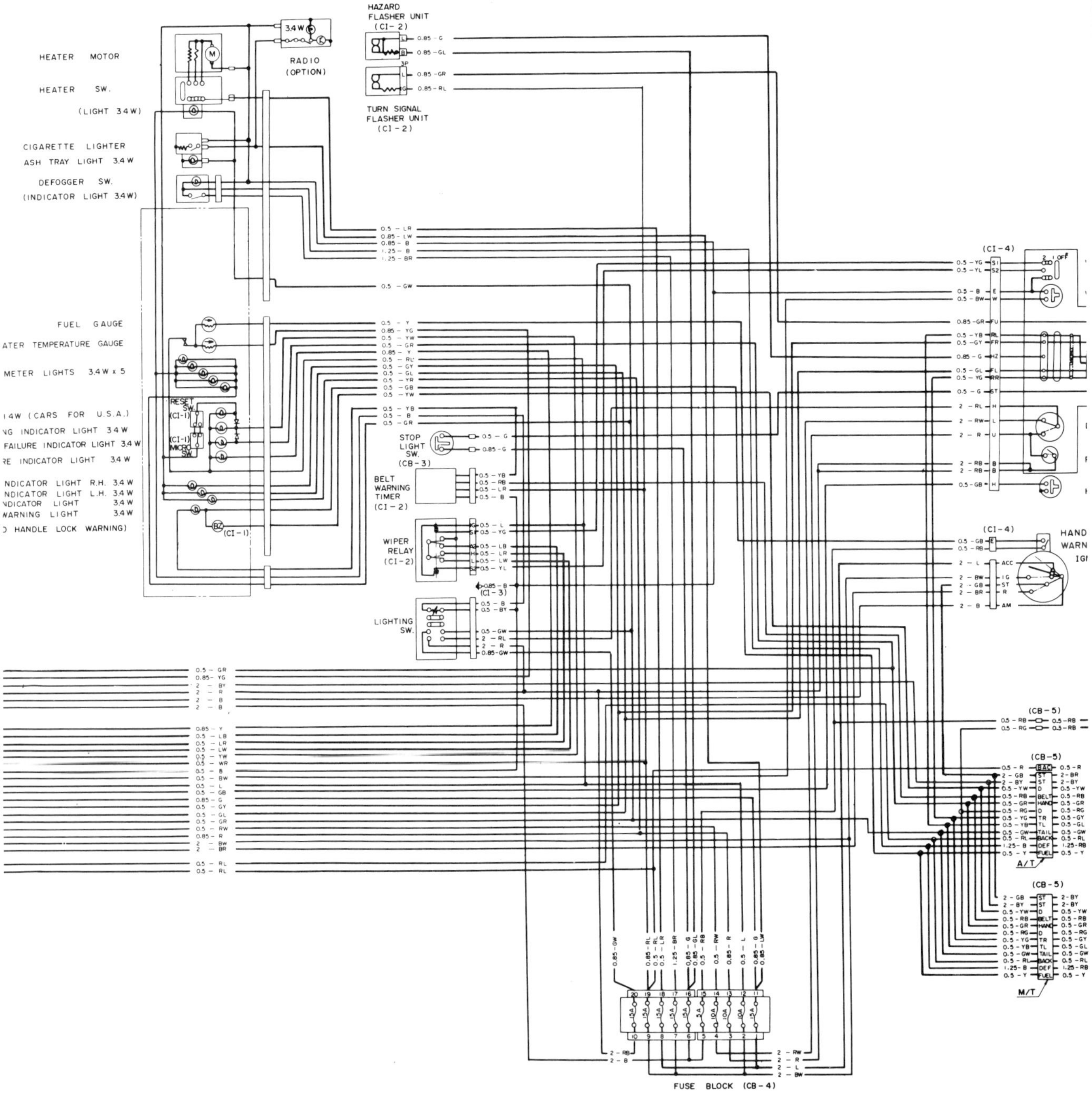

Fig. 10.60 Wiring diagram – Coupe – Sedan – continued

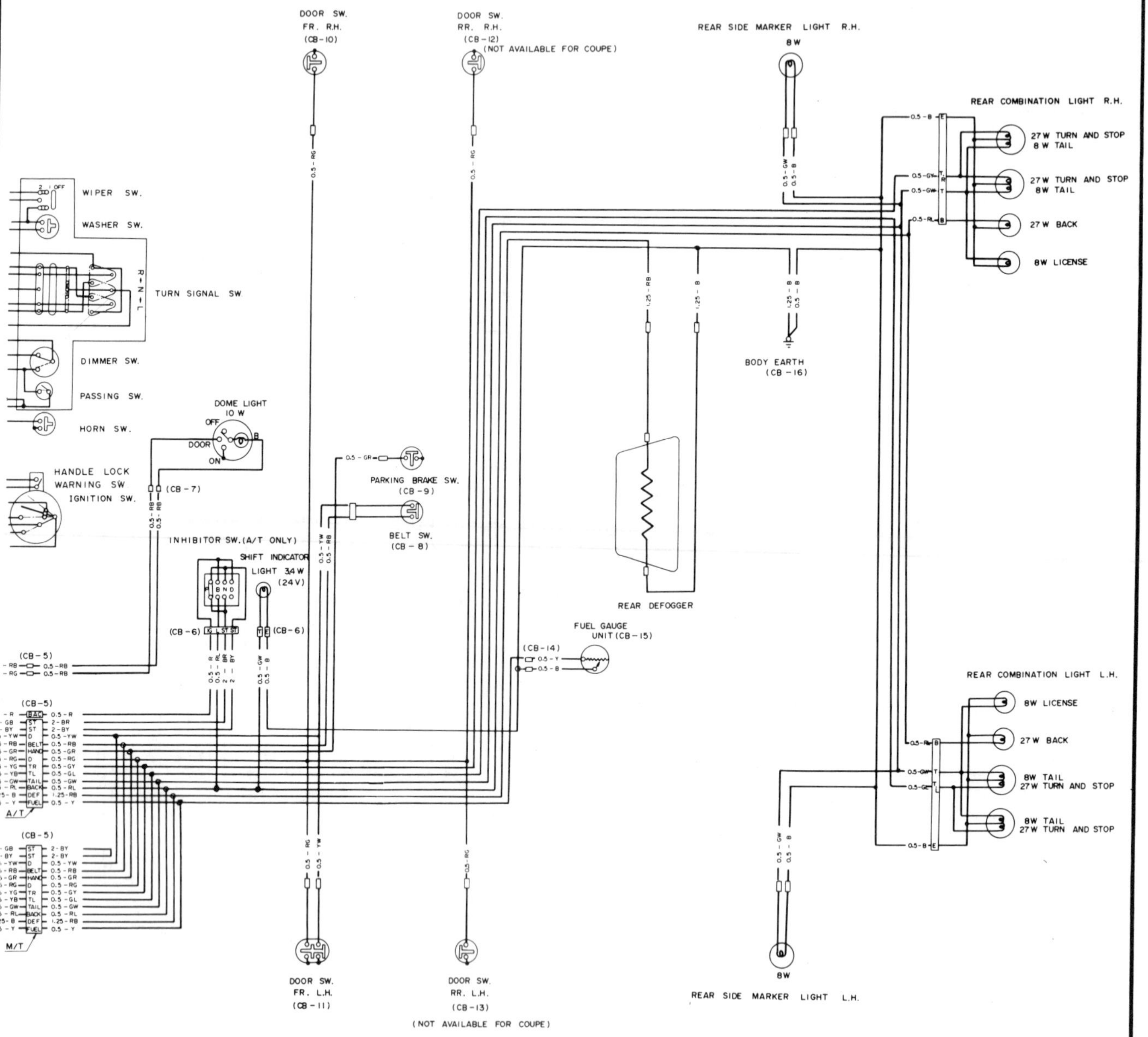

DOOR SW.
FR. R.H.
(CB-10)

DOOR SW.
RR. R.H.
(CB-12)
(NOT AVAILABLE FOR COUPE)

REAR SIDE MARKER LIGHT R.H.
8W

REAR COMBINATION LIGHT R.H.

27 W TURN AND STOP
8 W TAIL

27 W TURN AND STOP
8W TAIL

27 W BACK

8W LICENSE

WIPER SW.

WASHER SW.

TURN SIGNAL SW

DIMMER SW.

PASSING SW.

HORN SW.

HANDLE LOCK
WARNING SW
IGNITION SW.

DOME LIGHT
10 W
OFF
DOOR
ON

PARKING BRAKE SW.
(CB-9)

BELT SW.
(CB-8)

REAR DEFOGGER

BODY EARTH
(CB-16)

FUEL GAUGE
UNIT (CB-15)

(CB-7)

INHIBITOR SW.(A/T ONLY)
SHIFT INDICATOR
LIGHT 3.4 W
(24 V)

(CB-6)

(CB-6)

(CB-14)

(CB-5)

(CB-5)
A/T

(CB-5)
M/T

REAR COMBINATION LIGHT L.H.

8W LICENSE

27 W BACK

8W TAIL
27 W TURN AND STOP

8W TAIL
27 W TURN AND STOP

DOOR SW.
FR. L.H.
(CB-11)

DOOR SW.
RR. L.H.
(CB-13)
(NOT AVAILABLE FOR COUPE)

REAR SIDE MARKER LIGHT L.H.
8W

Fig. 10.60 Wiring diagram – Coupe – Sedan – continued

ESTATE CAR

Cable Coloring Identifications by Circuits

Symbol	Coloring
B	Black
BW	Black/white
BY	Black/yellow
BR	Black/red
W	White
R	Red
RW	Red/white
RB	Red/black
RL	Red/blue
RG	Red/green
G	Green
GW	Green/white
GR	Green/red
GY	Green/yellow
GB	Green/black
GL	Green/blue
GO	Green/orange
Y	Yellow
YR	Yellow/red
YB	Yellow/black
YG	Yellow/green
YL	Yellow/blue
YW	Yellow/white
L	Blue
LW	Blue/white
LR	Blue/red
LB	Blue/black
LY	Blue/yellow
LO	Blue/orange

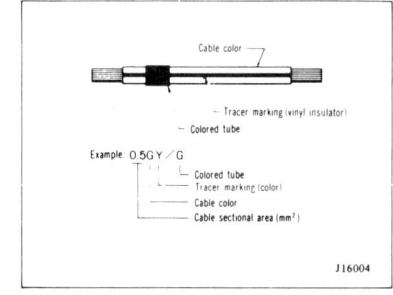

J16004

Nominal size (designated by sectional area in mm² of wire)	SAE gauge No.	Permissible current	
		Within engine compartment	Other areas
0.5	20	7A	13A
0.85	18	9A	17A
1.25	16	12A	22A
2.0	14	16A	30A
3.0	12	21A	40A
5.0	10	31A	54A

NOTE: The symbols shown in parentheses denote the locations of the parts, ground, etc. as shown in the following table. CB, CE and CI in the symbols indicate body, engine compartment and instrument panel, respectively.

Symbol	Part name	Location
CB-1	Earth, Intermittent wiper relay	R.H. side of front harness
CB-2	Wiper motor	Front deck
CB-3	Earth	L.H. side of front harness
CB-4	Backup light switch	Transmission
CB-5	Stop light switch	Brake pedal bracket
CB-6	Connector	Lower part of left front pillar
CB-7	Inhibitor switch connector, Shift indicator light connector	Inside the shift lever bracket
CB-8	Seat belt switch	Inside driver's seat belt buckle
CB-9	Parking brake switch	Under parking brake
CB-10	Door switch F.L.	Lower part of L.H. center pillar
CB-11	Door switch F.R.	Lower part of R.H. center pillar
CB-12	Door switch R.L.	Upper side of L.H. rear wheel house
CB-13	Door switch R.R.	Upper side of R.H. rear wheel house
CB-14	Gate switch L.H.	L.H. inside of tail gate
CB-15	Gate switch R.H.	R.H. inside of tail gate
CB-16	Earth	Middle inside of tail gate
CB-17	Earth	L.H. side of quarter inner panel
CB-18	Fuel gauge unit	Fuel tank
CB-19	Earth	Middle part of roof panel
CE-1	Earth	Battery seat
CE-2	Earth	Left side of cylinder block under temperature gauge unit
CE-3	Brake failure indicator switch	Rear section of engine compartment
CI-1	Earth	On steering support bracket
CI-2	Hazard flasher unit, Turn signal flasher unit, Belt warning timer	Under side of instrument panel
CI-3	Chime driver	Reinforcement at center panel
CI-4	Chime	Back of instrument cluster

Fig. 10.61 Key to wiring diagram – Estate car

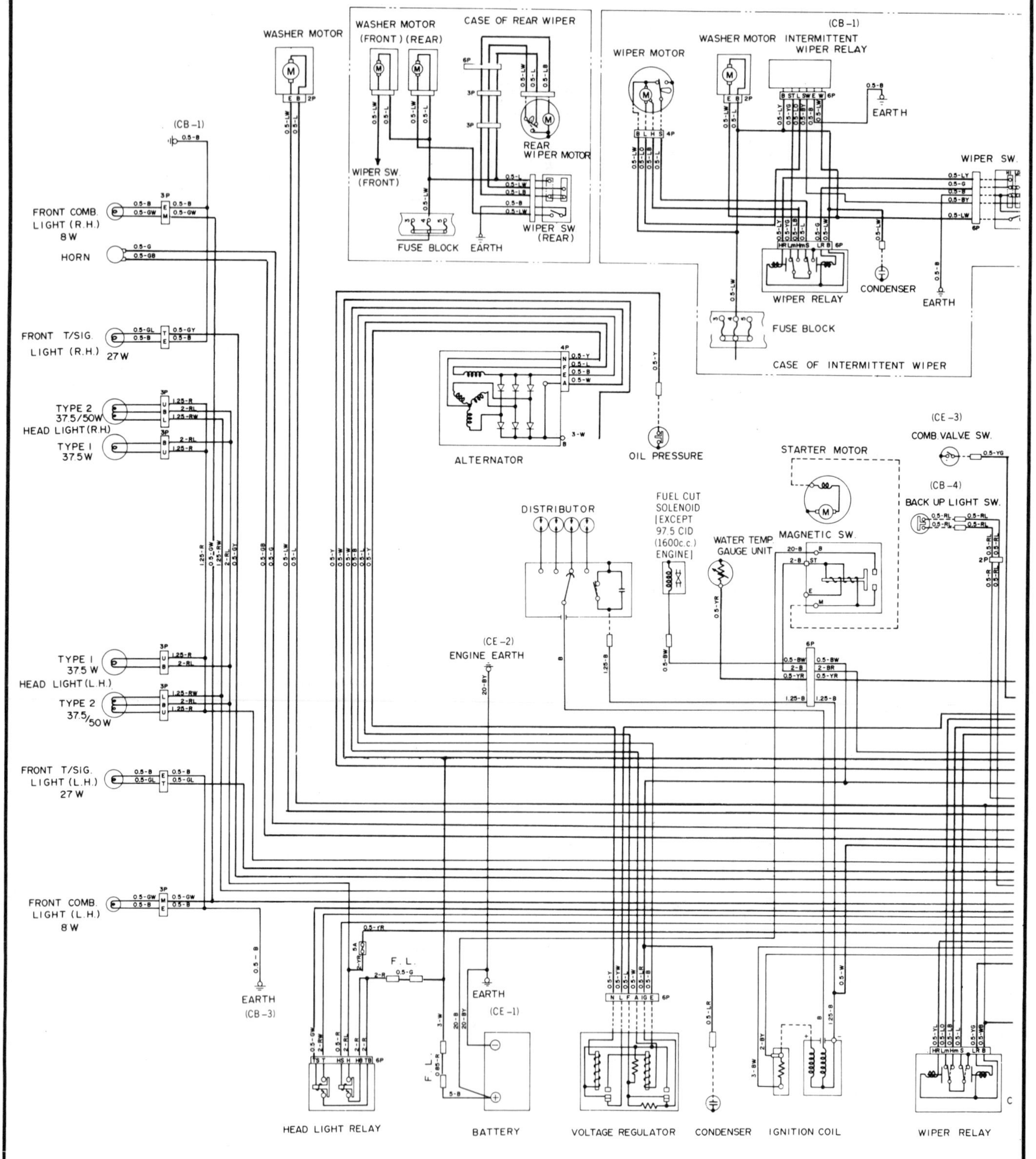

Fig. 10.61 Wiring diagram – Estate car

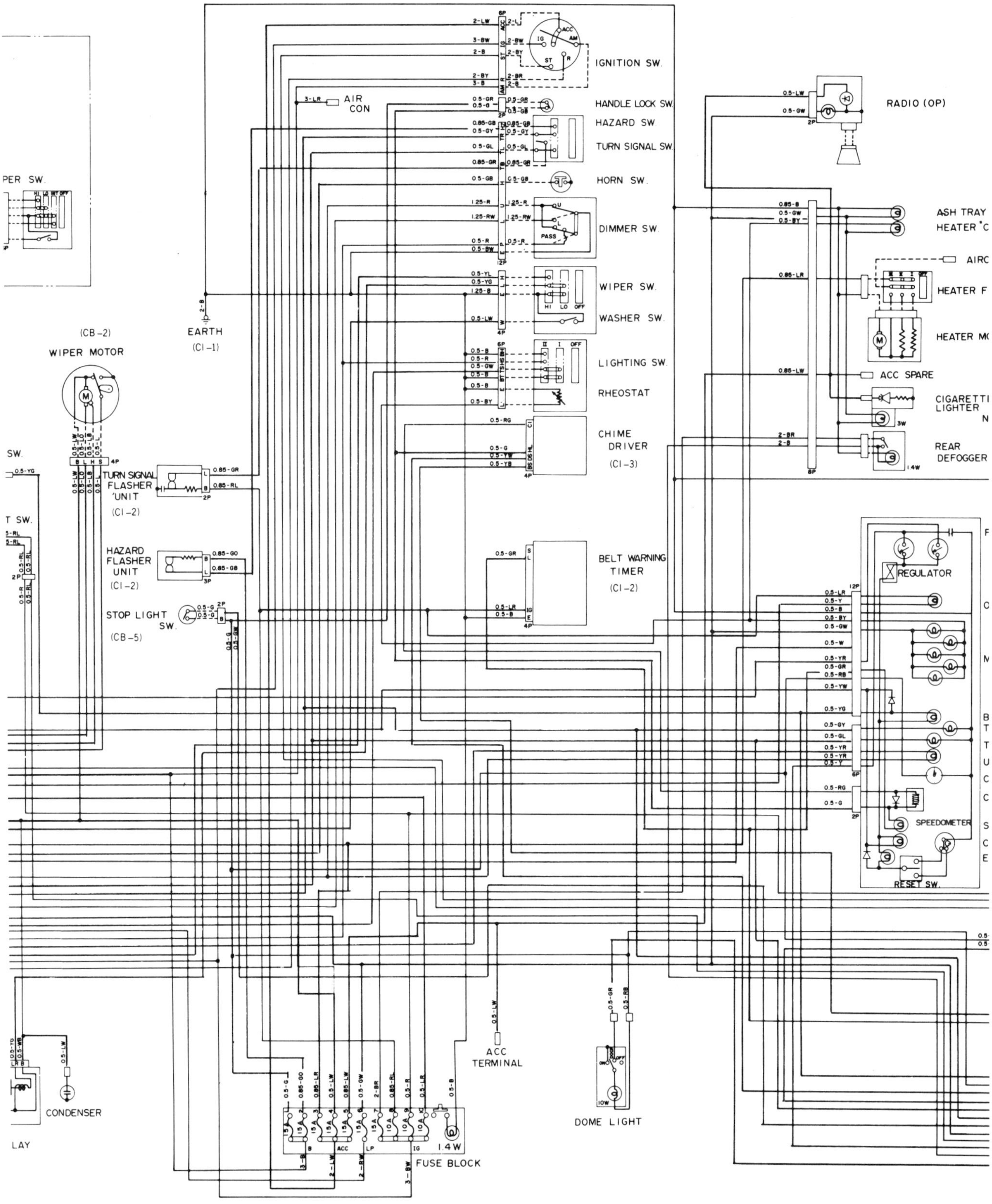

Fig. 10.61 Wiring diagram – Estate car – continued

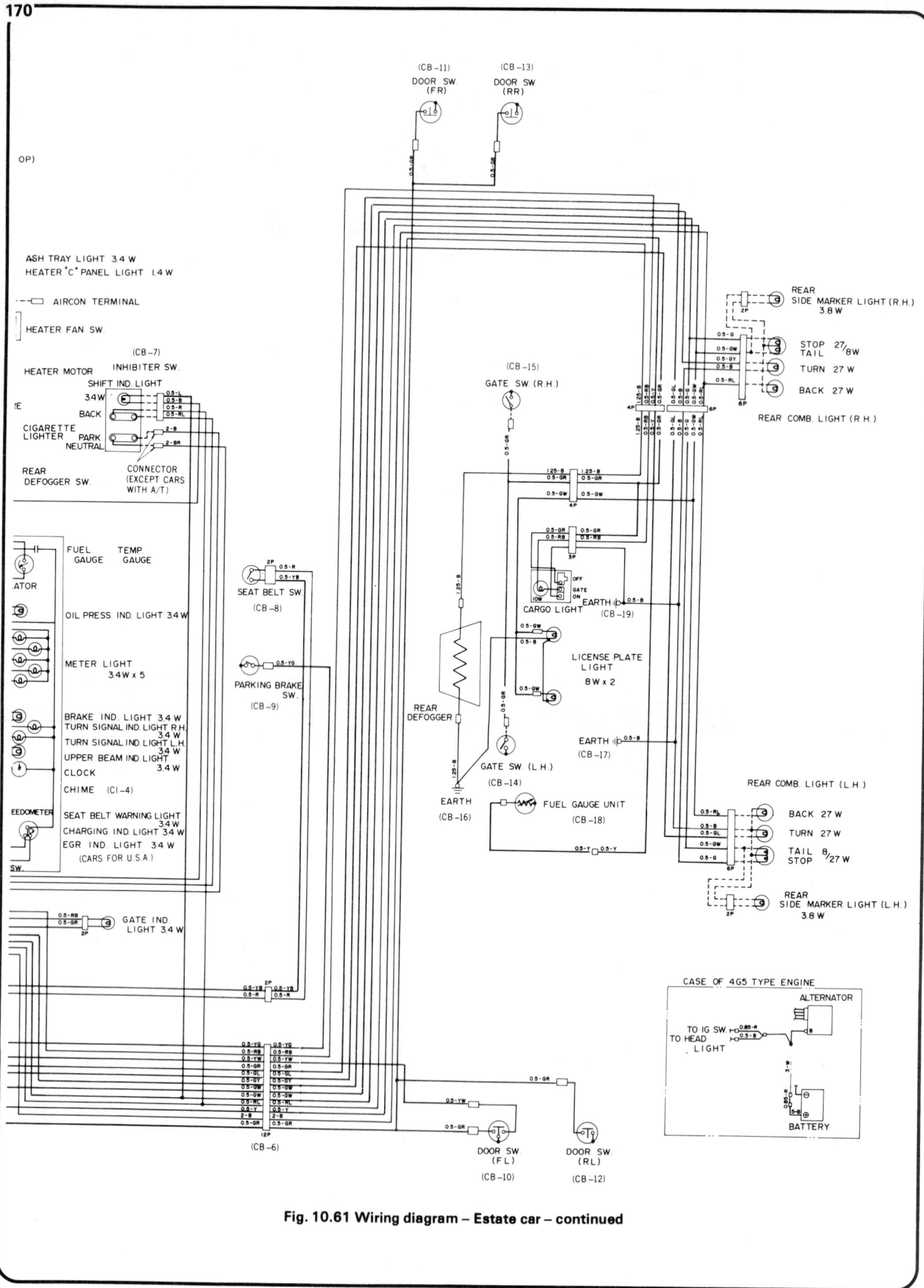

Fig. 10.61 Wiring diagram – Estate car – continued

HATCHBACK

Cable Coloring Identifications by Circuits

Symbol	Coloring
B	Black
BW	Black/white
BY	Black/yellow
BR	Black/red
W	White
WR	White/red
WB	White/black
R	Red
RW	Red/white
RB	Red/black
RY	Red/yellow
RL	Red/blue
RG	Red/green
G	Green
GW	Green/white
GR	Green/red
GY	Green/yellow
GB	Green/black
GL	Green/blue
Y	Yellow
YR	Yellow/red
YB	Yellow/black
YG	Yellow/green
YL	Yellow/blue
YW	Yellow/white
L	Blue
LW	Blue/white
LR	Blue/red
LB	Blue/black

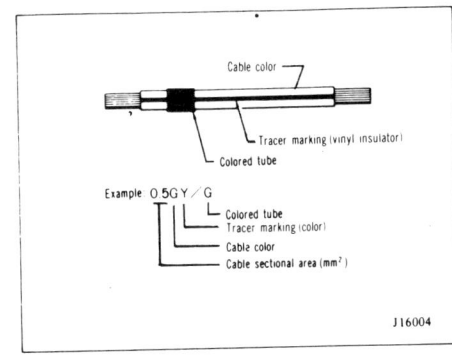

Nominal size (designated by sectional area in mm² of wire)	SAE gauge No.	Permissible current	
		Within engine compartment	Other areas
0.5	20	7 A	13 A
0.85	18	9 A	17 A
1.25	16	12 A	22 A
2.0	14	16 A	30 A
3.0	12	21 A	40 A
5.0	10	31 A	54 A

NOTE: The symbols shown in parentheses denote the locations of the parts, ground, etc. as shown in the following table. CB, CE and CI in the symbols indicate body, engine compartment and instrument panel, respectively.

Symbol	Part name	Location
CB-1	Backup light switch	Transmission
CB-2	Wiper motor	Front deck
CB-3	Stop light switch	Brake pedal bracket
CB-4	Fuse block	Lower part of left front pillar
CB-5	Connector	Lower part of left front pillar
CB-6	Inhibitor switch connector and Shift indicator light connector	Inside the shift lever bracket
CB-7	Dome light connector	7.87 in. (200 mm) away from dome light
CB-8	Belt switch	Inside the buckle
CB-9	Parking brake switch	Under parking brake
CB-10	Door switch R.H.	Lower part of R.H. center pillar
CB-11	Door switch L.H.	Lower part of L.H. center pillar
CB-12	Fuel gauge unit connector	Front of fuel tank
CB-13	Fuel gauge unit	Fuel tank
CB-14	Earth	Behind rear seat
CB-15	Earth	Tightened together with left rear door strut
CB-16	Stay switch	Hatchback stopper
CB-17	Earth	Front roof rail
CE-1	Earth	Battery seat
CE-2	Engine earth	Left side of cylinder block under temperature gauge unit
CE-3	Earth	Tightened together with voltage regulator
CE-4	Brake failure indicator switch	Rear section of engine compartment
CE-5	Earth	Tightened together with ignition coil
CI-1	Micro switch, Reset switch and Buzzer	Back of instrument cluster
CI-2	Hazard flasher unit, Turn signal flasher unit, Belt warning timer and Wiper relay	Underside of instrument panel
CI-3	Earth	Tightened together with turn signal flasher unit
CI-4	Connector	Lower left side of steering column
CI-5	Connector	Under instrument panel to the right of steering column
CI-6	Earth	Heater motor cover

Fig. 10.62 Key to wiring diagram – Hatchback

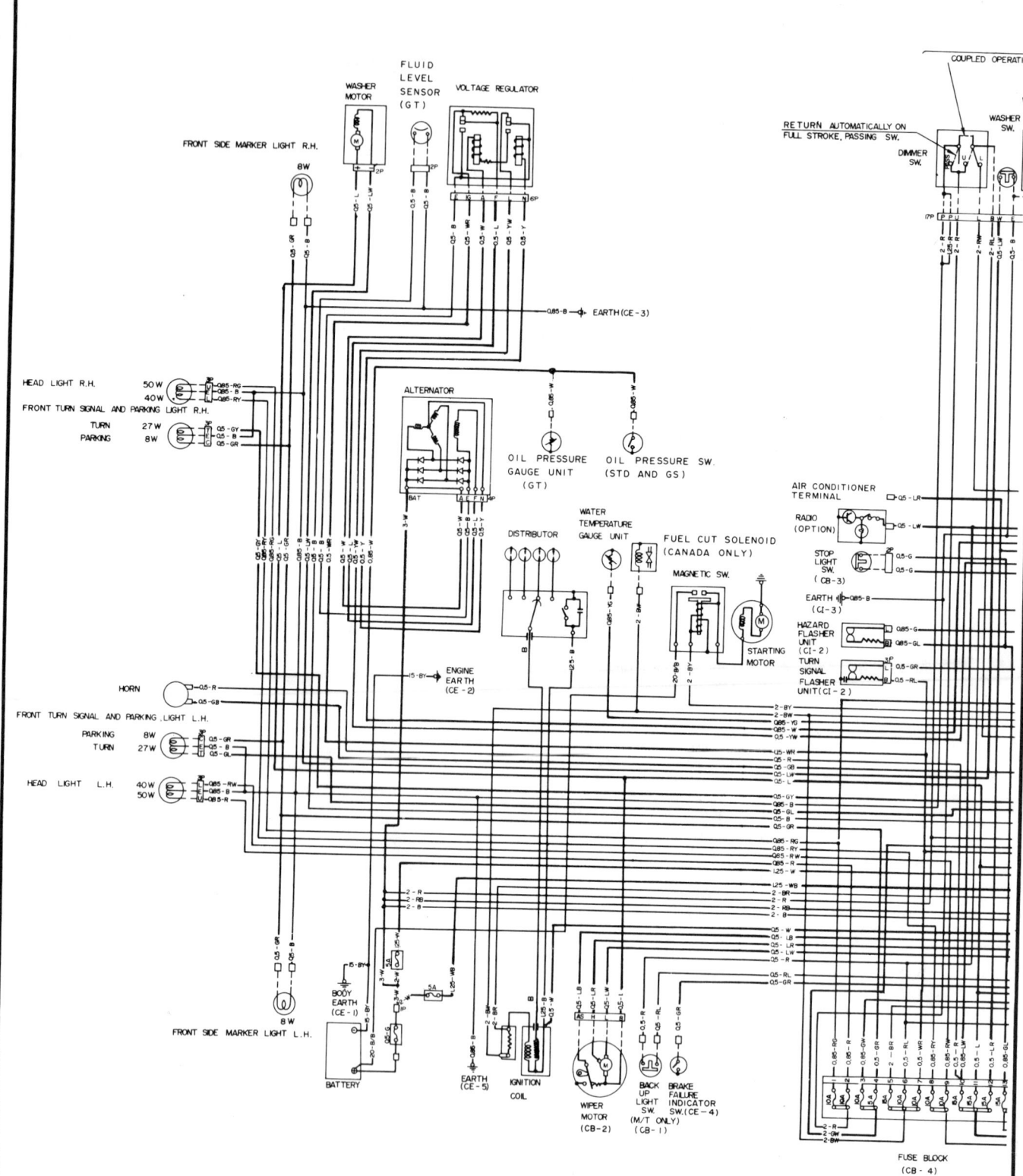

Fig. 10.62 Wiring diagram – Hatchback

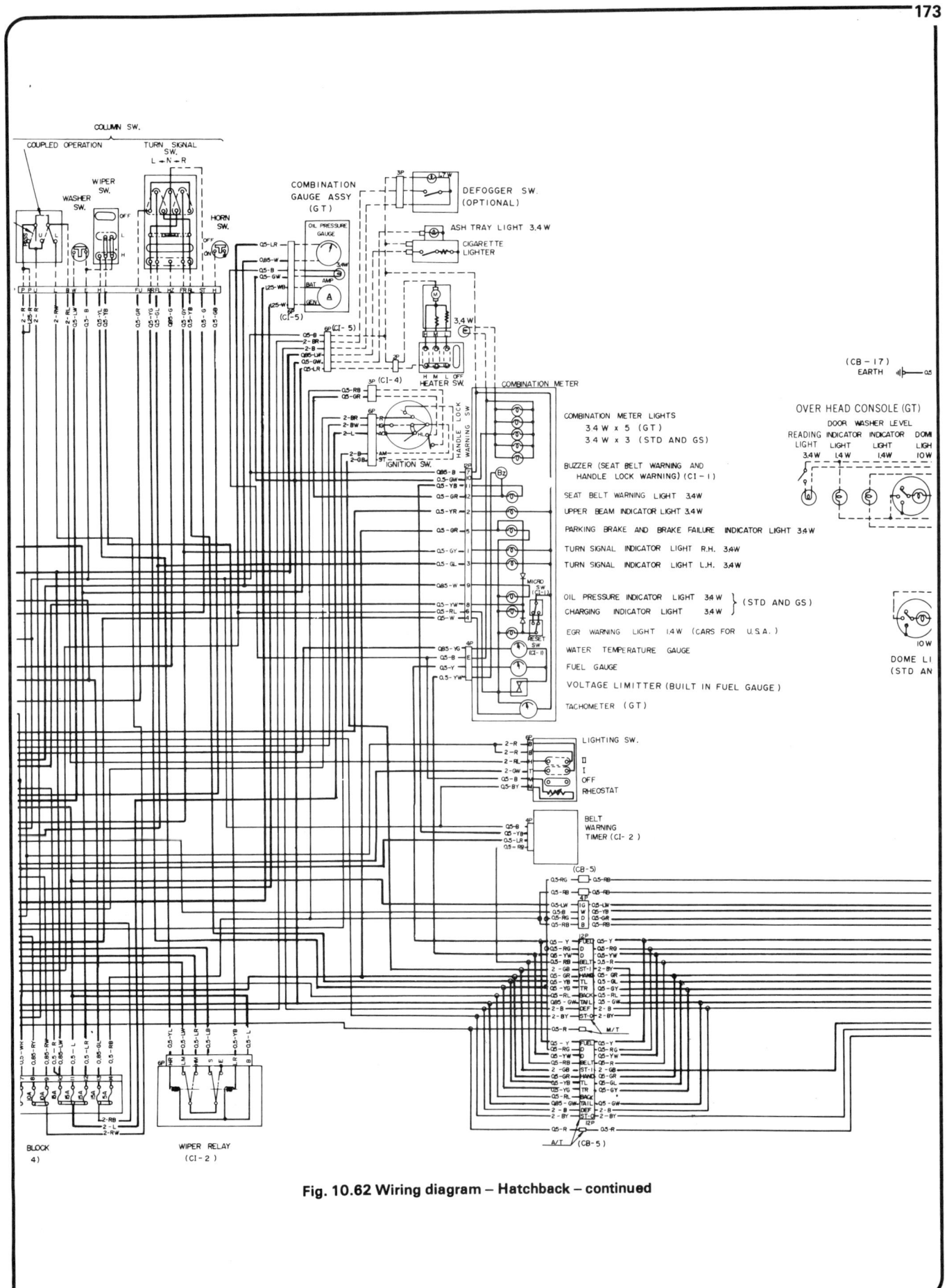

Fig. 10.62 Wiring diagram – Hatchback – continued

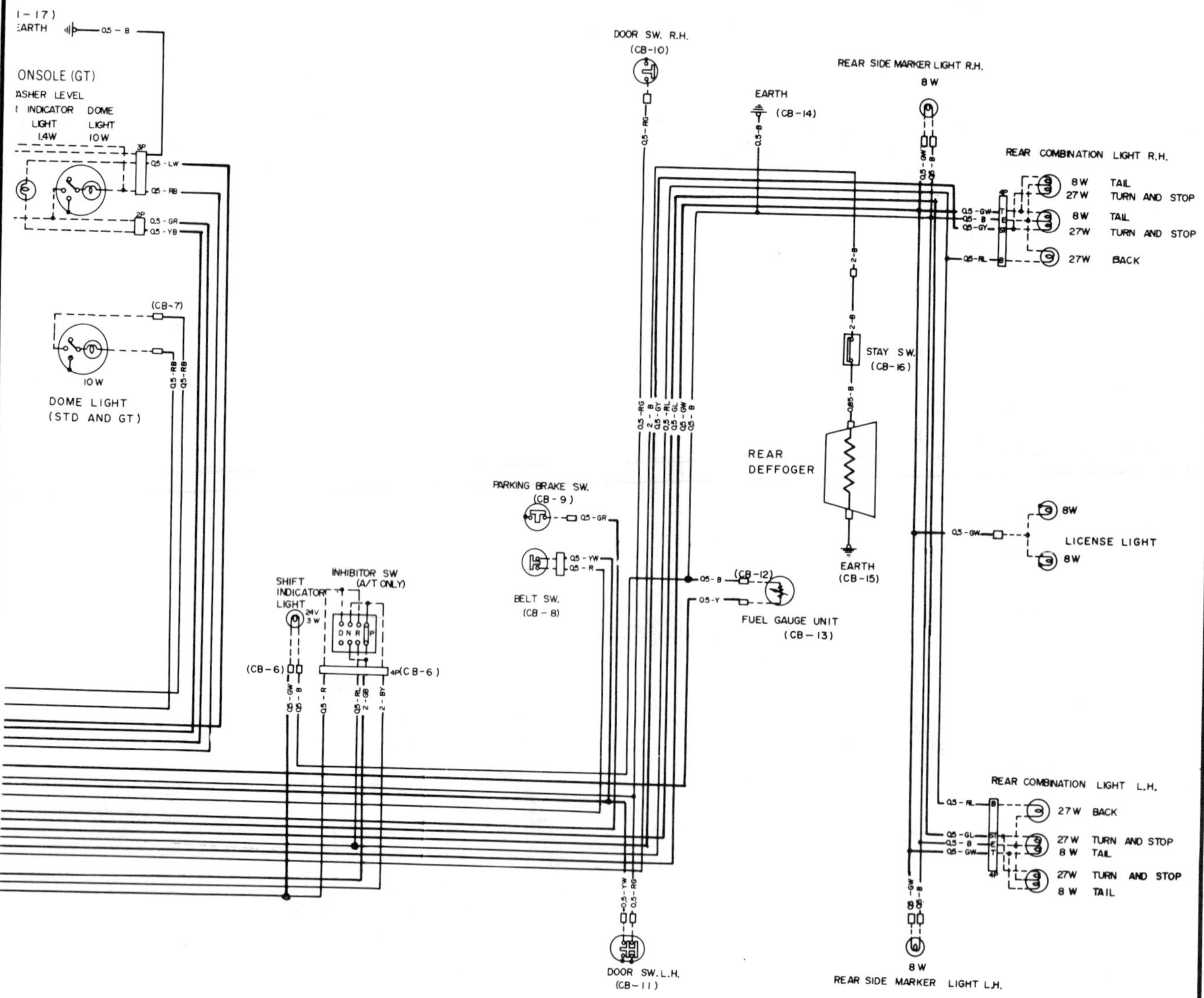

I – 17)
EARTH

0.5 – B

ONSOLE (GT)
ASHER LEVEL
INDICATOR   DOME
LIGHT   LIGHT
1.4W   10W

0.5 – LW

0.5 – RB

0.5 – GR
0.5 – YB

(CB~7)

0.5 – RB
0.5 – RB

10 W

DOME LIGHT
(STD AND GT)

SHIFT
INDICATOR
LIGHT

24V
3 W

INHIBITOR SW.
(A/T ONLY)

D N R 1 2

(CB – 6)

4P (CB – 6)

DOOR SW. R.H.
(CB – 10)

0.5 – RG

PARKING BRAKE SW.
(CB – 9)

0.5 – GR

0.5 – YW
0.5 – R

BELT SW.
(CB – 8)

0.5 – B

0.5 – Y

(CB–12)

FUEL GAUGE UNIT
(CB – 13)

0.5 – RG
2 – BY
0.5 – GY
0.5 – RL
0.5 – I
0.5 – GL
0.5 – GW
0.5 – B

0.5-0.5 – YW
0.5 – RG

DOOR SW. L.H.
(CB – 11)

EARTH
(CB – 14)

0.5 – B

STAY SW.
(CB – 16)

REAR
DEFFOGER

EARTH
(CB – 15)

REAR SIDE MARKER LIGHT R.H.
8 W

REAR COMBINATION LIGHT R.H.

8W   TAIL
27W   TURN AND STOP

8W   TAIL
27W   TURN AND STOP

27W   BACK

0.5 – GW

LICENSE LIGHT

REAR COMBINATION LIGHT L.H.

27 W   BACK

27 W   TURN AND STOP
8 W   TAIL

27W   TURN AND STOP
8 W   TAIL

8 W
REAR SIDE MARKER LIGHT L.H.

Fig. 10.62 Wiring diagram – Hatchback – continued

Chapter 11 Suspension and steering

Contents

Specifications

Front suspension
Type . . . .   MacPherson strut with telescopic dampers, co-axial coil springs and torsion bar
Coil spring free length . . . .   13·228 in (336 mm)
Wire diameter . . . .   0·445 in (11·3 mm)
Spring rate . . . .   108·8 lb in (1·94 kg mm)

Rear suspension
Type (except Estate car) . . . .   Semi-elliptical leaf springs with double acting dampers
Estate car . . . .   Drop arms with damper-assisted coil springs

Steering
Type . . . .   Recirculating ball nut, variable ratio
Gear ratio . . . .   15·58 to 18·18
Steering angle:
    Inside wheel . . . .   35° to 40°
    Outside wheel . . . .   33°

Steering geometry
Camber . . . .   1° ± 30′
Castor . . . .   1°45′ ± 30′
Toe-in . . . .   0·079 to 0·236 in (2 to 6 mm)
King pin inclination . . . .   8° 53′

Wheels
Size . . . .   4 J 13

Tyres . . . .   155 SR 13

Inflation pressure
  Front . . . .   20 lb in² (1·4 kg cm²)
  Rear . . . .   20 lb in² (1·4 kg cm²)

Torque wrench settings

	lbf ft	kgf m
Front suspension		
Strut bar adjusting nut and locknut	65	9
Lower arm balljoint to knuckle arm nuts	28·9 to 43·4	4·0 to 6·0
Strut assembly to knuckle arm bolts	39	5·4
Lower arm shaft to flange bolts	7·2	1·0
Lower arm shaft lock nuts	43·4	6·0
Stabilizer bar link attachment bolts	21·7	3·0
Knuckle arm to tie-rod end connecting bolts	28·9 to 36·2	4·0 to 5·0
Strut bar attachment bolts	36·2	5·0
Strut to wheel arch attachment nuts	7·2	1·0
Strut to knuckle arm connecting bolts	39·0	5·4
Front brake backing plate attachment bolts	28·9 to 36·2	4·0 to 5·0
Crossmember to body nuts and bolts	28·9	4·0
Strut bar bracket attachment bolts	28·9	4·0
Stabilizer bar bushing attachment bolts	7·2	1·0
Strut bar to lower arm attachment bolts	36·2	5·0
Stabilizer bar to lower arm attachment bolts	21·7	3·0
Hub nut	3·6	0.5
Rear suspension		
Spring pin assembly mounting bolt	10·8 to 14·5	1·5 to 2·0
U-bolt nuts	32·5 to 36·2	4·5 to 5·0
Spring pin nut	36·2 to 43·4	5·0 to 6·0
Shock absorber upper and lower mounting nuts	11·6 to 14·5	1·6 to 2·0
Shackle pin nut	36·2 to 43·4	5·0 to 6·0
Steering		
Steering box end cover bolts	10·8 to 14·5	1·5 to 2·0
Upper cover attachment bolts	10·8 to 14·5	1·5 to 2·0
Drop arm locknut	94·0 to 108·5	13·0 to 15·0
Tie-rod socket to relay rod nut	28·9 to 36·2	4·0 to 5·0
Tie-rod end castellated nut	28·9 to 36·2	4·0 to 5·0
Tie-rod locknut	36·2 to 39·8	5·0 to 5·5
Relay rod to drop arm locknut	28·9 to 36·2	4·0 to 5·0
Relay rod to idler arm locknut	28·9 to 36·2	4·0 to 5·0
Idler arm locknut	28·9 to 43·4	4·0 to 6·0
Idler arm bracket	25·3 to 28·9	3·5 to 4·0
Idler arm to relay rod	28·9 to 36·2	4·0 to 5·0

1 General description

The front suspension is of the MacPherson strut type with shock absorbers integral with the steering knuckle spindle. The shock absorbers, which have concentric springs are fixed to the wheel arch with an insulator assembly and are attached to the lower control arm through an oil-less balljoint at their lower ends. The single lower links are pivoted at their inner ends in rubber bushes set in the subframe assembly. Front camber is preset on manufacture, but there is provision for the adjustment of toe-in and camber.

A stabilizer bar is used to minimise the rolling angle of the car body and the lower arms are strut braced against longitudinal loads.

The steering system uses a recirculating ball steering box and variable ratio, a height adjustable, tilting steering wheel and a collapsible steering tube for safety in the event of an accident. The balljoints in the steering linkage have non-metallic bearings and do not require any lubrication.

The rear suspension is conventional, with semi-elliptical leaf springs and double-acting shock absorbers.

2 Wheel alignment

Camber
1   Wheel camber is preset on manufacture and no further adjustment is possible.

Toe-in
2   Toe-in adjustment is made by means of the tie-rod turnbuckle.
3   Release the locknuts at the ends of the tie-rod turnbuckle.

4   To reduce toe-in, turn the turnbuckle of the left-hand wheel in the direction of advance of the car. Turn that of the right-hand wheel in the opposite direction. Be careful to turn both rods by exactly the same amount and check that the difference in length of the two rods is not greater than 0·118 in (3 mm).
5   After making the adjustment, tighten the turnbuckle locknuts.

Castor
6   Castor is the inclination to the vertical of the steering axle. This may be altered by releasing the locknut at the threaded end of the steering strut, adjusting the strut length and then tightening the locknut.

3 Front hub – dismantling and reassembly

1   Jack-up the car, support the axle on a stand and remove the wheel.
2   Remove the brake caliper assembly (Chapter 9, Section 5) and support it on the lower arm. It should not be necessary to remove the brake hose from the caliper.
3   Remove the hub cap, split pin and nut.
4   Pull off the front hub with the brake disc attached, taking care not to drop the outer bearing track and washer.
5   Remove the grease from inside the wheel hub then use a drift to drive out the track of the outer bearing.
6   Drive out the inner bearing outer track and oil seal.
7   Clean the stub axle and inspect it for damage and wear. Check the shock absorber mounting area of the stub axle for cracks and if it is damaged, fit a new strut assembly.
8   Check the bearings for damage, wear and roughness and fit a new

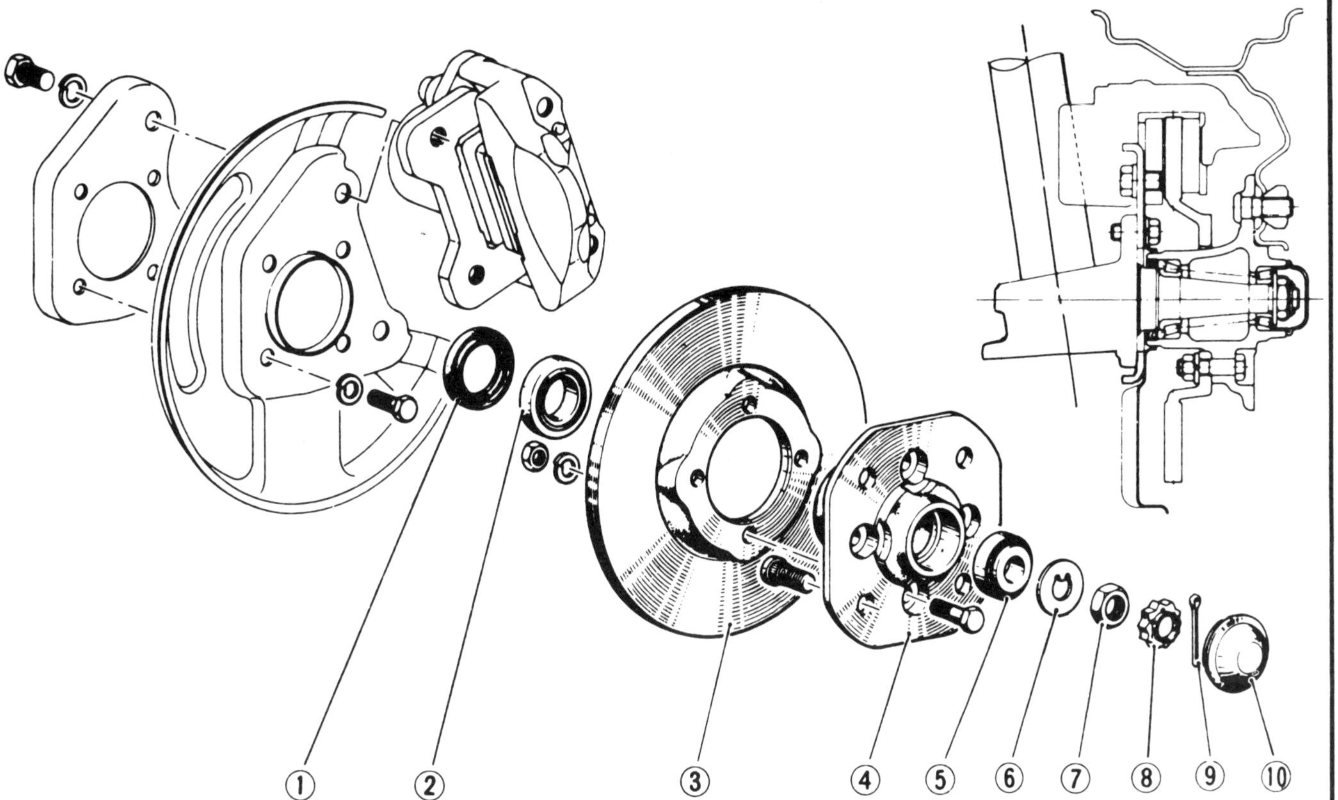

Fig. 11.1 Front axle hub – exploded view

1	Oil seal	3	Brake disc		(outer)
2	Front wheel bearing	4	Front wheel hub	6	Washer
	(inner)	5	Front wheel bearing	7	Slotted nut

8	Lock cap
9	Split-pin
10	Hub cap

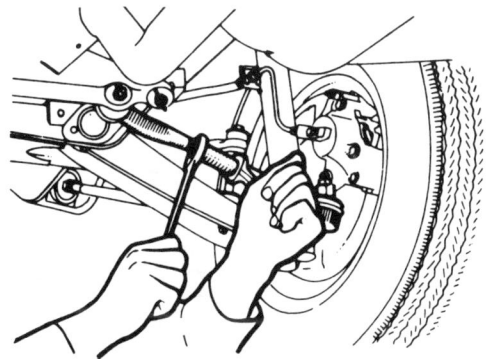

Fig. 11.2 Toe-in adjustment

4.3 Strut to knuckle arm attachment bolts

bearing if required.

9   Grease the bearings, oil seal and lip, and bore of the wheel hub. Pack the wheel hub cap with grease.

10 If the brake disc and hub are separated the nuts must be tightened evenly to a torque wrench setting as specified. On reassembly the disc should be checked for deflection (Chapter 9, Section 8).

11 Insert the inner bearing into the hub, carefully press in the oil seal with the lip inwards, until the back of the seal is flush with the end of the hub. Take great care not to distort the oil seal.

12 Fit the hub assembly on to the stub axle, taking care not to damage the oil seal.

13 Fit the outer bearing, plain washer and nut, then tighten the nut to 14.5 lbf ft (2.0 kgf m) to bed all the assembled parts.

14 Unscrew the nut to release all the pressure and then tighten it to its specified torque setting. Fit the lock cap and split pin, dividing and bending back the free ends of the pin. If the holes in the stub axle and lock cap cannot be aligned in any position, unscrew the nut slightly until the pin can be inserted, but do not unscrew the nut more than 15°.

15 Refit the brake caliper and tighten it to the recommended torque wrench setting.

---

4   Front suspension strut – removal and refitting

1   Jack-up the car, support it on firm stands and remove the wheel.

2   Remove the brake caliper (Chapter 9, Section 3) and wheel hub.

3   Disconnect the torsion bar from the lower arm and remove the three steering knuckle to strut attachment bolts (photo).

4   Carefully force down the lower arm and separate the strut assembly from the steering knuckle.

5   Unscrew the three retaining nuts at the top of the strut and with-draw the strut assembly (Fig. 11.4).

6   When refitting the strut, first position the top of the strut and screw on the retaining nuts finger tight.

7   Apply sealer to the bottom flange and fasten the strut assembly to the steering knuckle with the three bolts.

8   Tighten the upper retaining nuts to the specified torque wrench setting. Then tighten the knuckle arm bolts to their recommended torque.

9   Refit the torsion arm, the hub assembly and brake caliper.

10 Refit the roadwheel and lower the car.

11 Bounce the suspension up and down a few times, then tighten the torsion arm bolt to the correct torque wrench setting.

---

5   Front suspension strut – dismantling and overhaul

The dismantling and overhaul of the struts requires special tools and facilities. If a strut is not working satisfactorily, fit an exchange unit comprising strut and spring.

---

6   Front suspension strut – spring removal and refitting

1   If a coil spring compressor is available, the spring may be removed as follows, but the operation requires great care because of the large amount of energy stored in the compressed spring.

2   Clamp the lower end of the strut assembly in a soft jawed vice.

3   Fit a compressor to the spring, compress the spring and remove the dust cover, nut and insulator.

4   Slowly release the pressure on the spring and remove the spring and its seating.

5   When refitting the spring, first compress it and then fit it over the strut.

6   Extend the shock absorber piston rod to its limit then fit the upper spring seat.

7   Fit the insulator assembly and washer, then fit and partially tighten the self-locking nut.

8   Gradually release the pressure on the spring, taking care to seat both the upper and lower ends of the spring in their retainers, then fully release and remove the spring compressor.

9   While preventing the upper spring seat from rotating, tighten the retaining nut to its proper torque wrench setting.

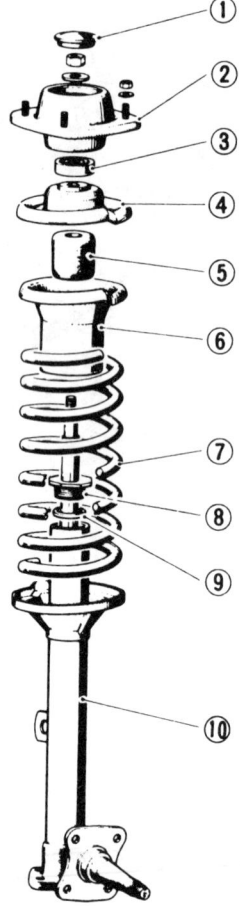

Fig. 11.3 Strut assembly – exploded view

1	Insulator cap	6	Dust cover
2	Strut insulator	7	Coil spring
3	Bearing	8	Oil seal assembly
4	Spring upper seat	9	Square ring
5	Bumper rubber	10	Strut sub-assembly

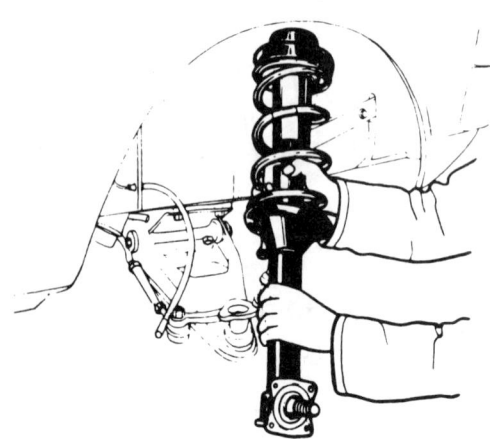

Fig. 11.4 Removing the strut assembly

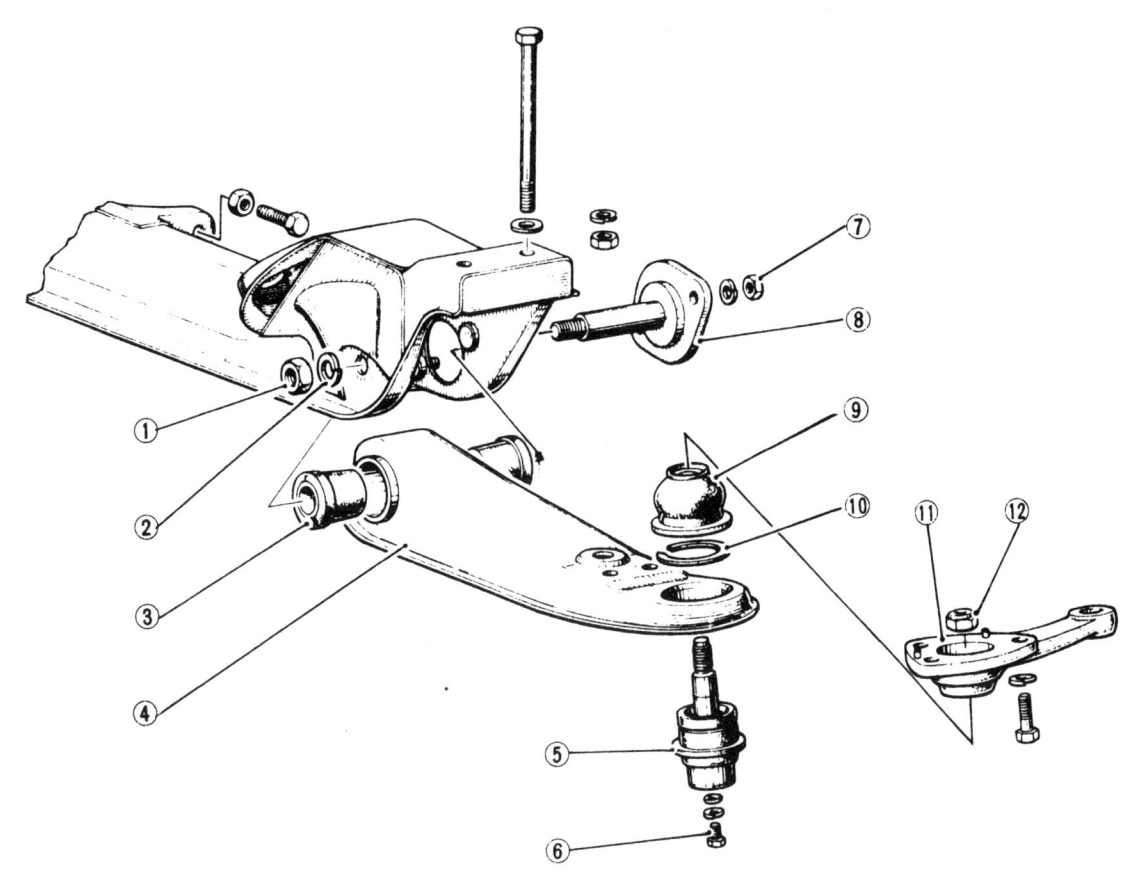

Fig. 11.5 Lower arm – exploded view

1	Nut	4 Lower arm	7 Nut	10	Snap-ring
2	Washer	5 Balljoint	8 Lower arm shaft	11	Knuckle arm
3	Lower arm shaft bushing	6 Screw	9 Dust cover	12	Nut

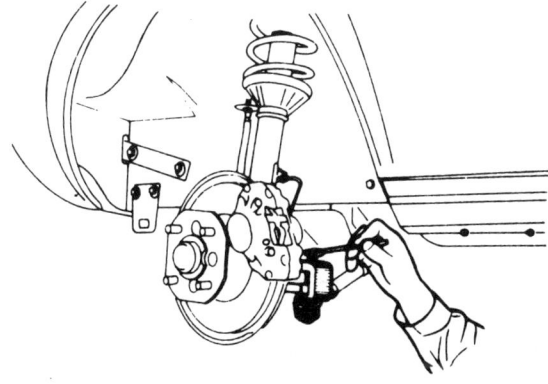

Fig. 11.6 Disconnecting the tie rod and knuckle arm

Fig. 11.7 Removing the knuckle arm

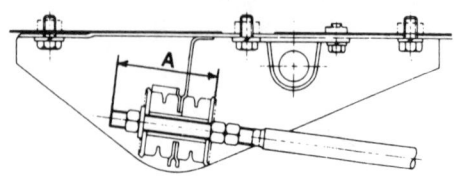

Fig. 11.8 Dimension of strut bar end when fitted

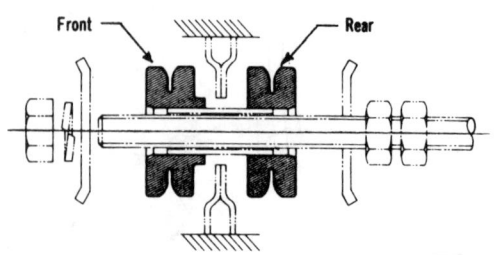

Fig. 11.9 Correct positions of strut rubber bushes

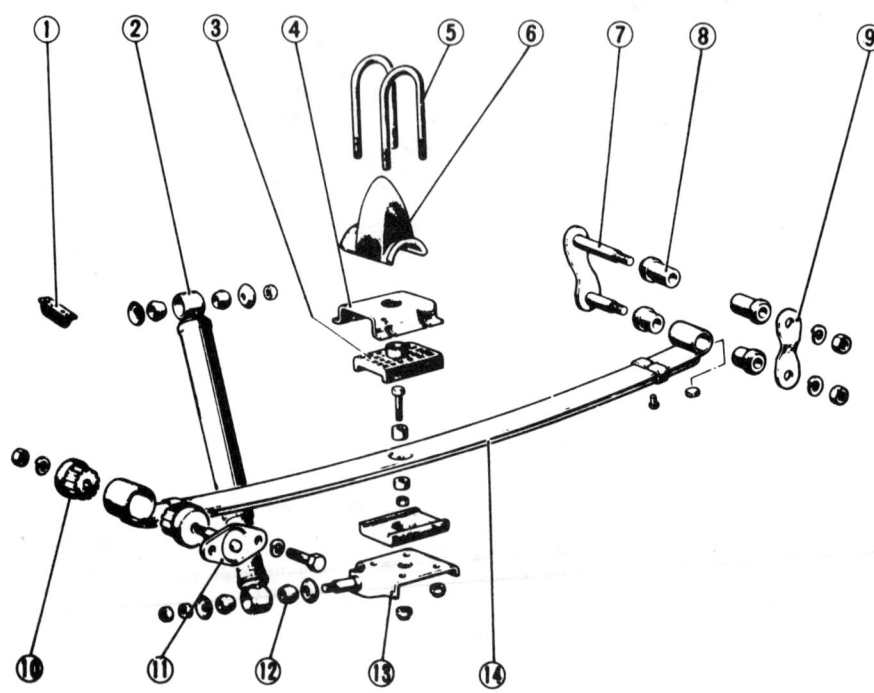

Fig. 11.10 Leaf spring rear suspension (exploded view)

1	Carrier bumper	5	U-bolt	9	Spring shackle		bushing
2	Shock absorber	6	Bump stop	10	Spring pin assembly	13	Spring U-bolt seat
3	Pad	7	Shackle plate	11	Front eye bushing	14	Leaf spring assembly
4	Spring seat	8	Rear eye bushing	12	Shock absorber eye		

7 Front suspension – lower arm removal

1   Jack-up the centre of the crossmember and support the front of the car on stands or blocks placed under the front jacking points. Lower the car slowly on to the supports.
2   Disconnect the torsion bar and the strut from the lower arm.
3   Using a knuckle breaker, disconnect the knuckle arm from the balljoint at the end of the tie-rod.
4   Remove the bolt attaching the strut to the knuckle arm and disconnect the knuckle arm from the strut by tapping the arm with a wooden mallet, or soft-headed hammer.
5   Move the steering linkage aside and remove the lower arm shaft from the crossmember, then remove the lower arm from the car body.

8 Lower arm balljoint – removal and refitting

1   After removing the lower arm assembly from the car, use a plate puller to remove the knuckle arm.
2   Remove the balljoint dust seal by levering it off with a screwdriver.
3   Remove the circlip and press, or drive out the balljoint.
4   Press, or drive in a new joint assembly and fit a new circlip and dust cover.

5   Apply sealing compound to the inside of the dust seal metal ring, after putting enough grease in the seal to half fill it.
6   Using a suitable sized piece of tube, hammer the dust seal over the circlip.

9 Front suspension – torsion bar removal and refitting

1   Disconnect both the torsion bar and the strut from the lower arm.
2   Remove the strut bracket from the body of the car.
3   Remove the torsion bar and the strut from the strut bracket.
4   Refitting is the reverse of removal, but the following points should be noted.
5   The distance from the front end of the strut to the front face of the locknut (Fig. 11.8) should be 30·071 in (78 cm).
6   The front and rear bushes are different, the front bush having a spigot to fit the hole in the strut bracket (Fig. 11.9 and photo).

10 Rear suspension – removal and refitting

Leaf spring type
1   Loosen the wheel nuts, jack the car with a jack placed under the

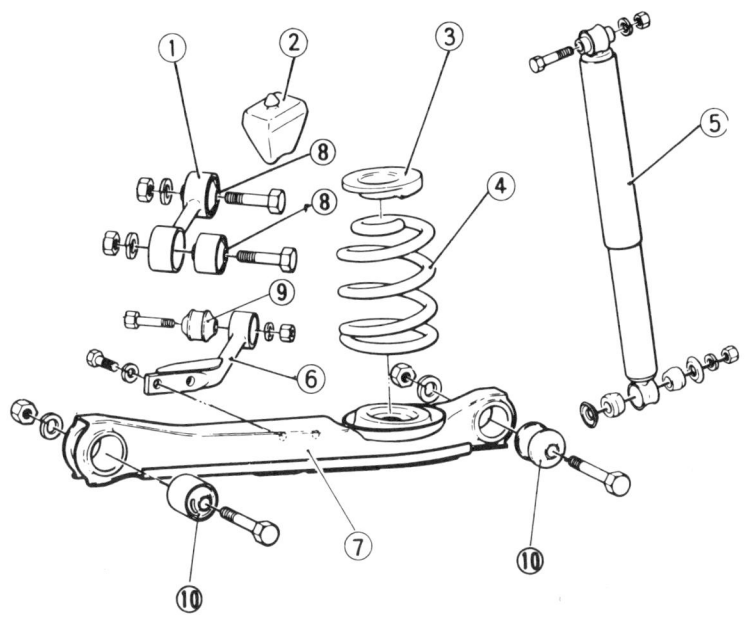

Fig. 11.11 Coil spring rear suspension (exploded view)

1 Upper control arm	5 Shock absorber	8 Upper control arm bush
2 Rear axle bump stop	6 Assist link	9 Assist link bush
3 Spring pad	7 Lower control arm	10 Lower control arm bush
4 Spring		

9.6 Strut end and strut bracket

10.3 U-bolt nuts and shock absorber lower mounting

10.4 Rear shackle bolts

10.5 Front spring pin assembly fixings

Fig. 11.12 Removing a coil spring

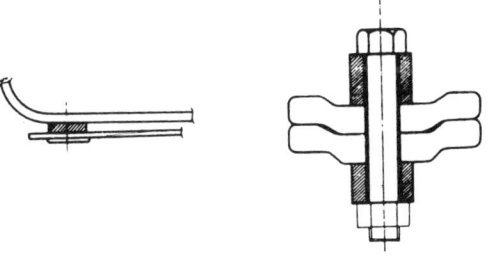

Fig. 11.13 Spring centre bolt and silencer

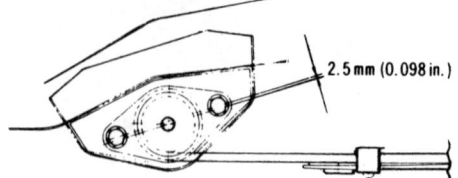

2.5 mm (0.098 in.)

Fig. 11.14 Asymmetry of spring pin assembly bolts

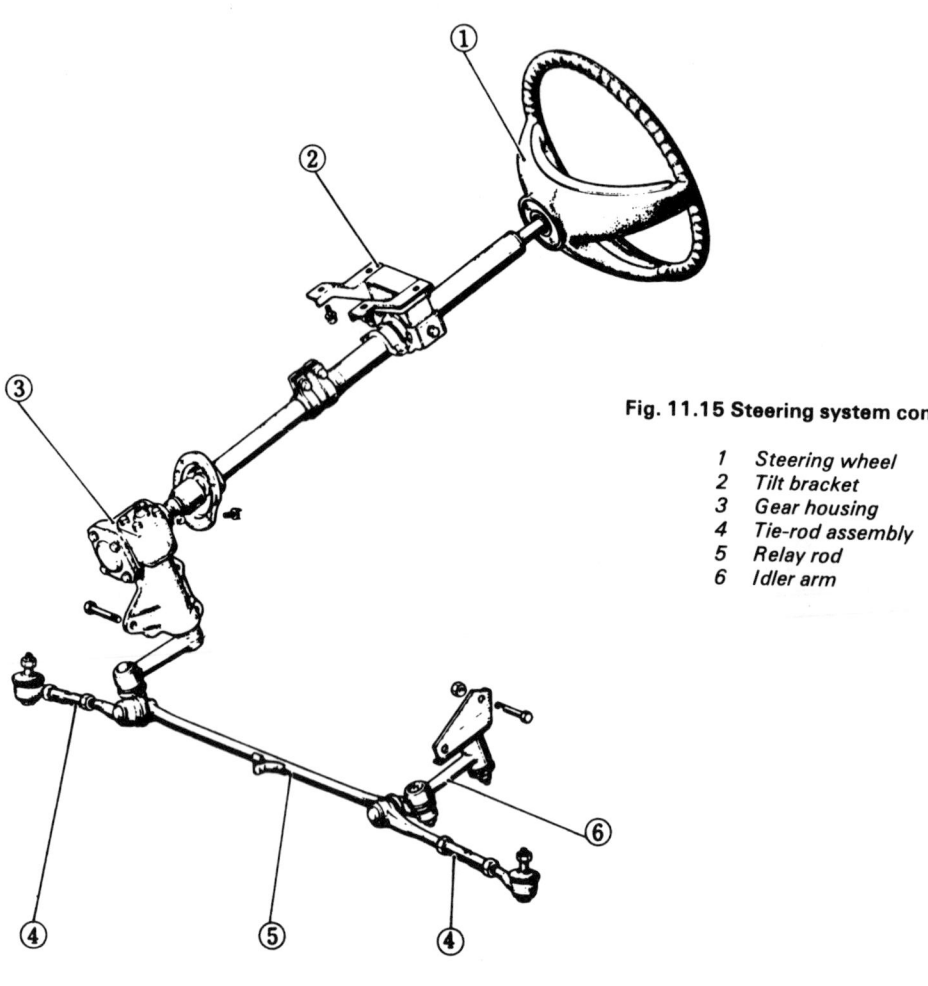

Fig. 11.15 Steering system components

1   Steering wheel
2   Tilt bracket
3   Gear housing
4   Tie-rod assembly
5   Relay rod
6   Idler arm

13.2 Removing the horn pad

13.4 Tilt lock knob

centre of the rear axle, support the car on stands placed under the side frames, lower the jack slowly and remove the roadwheels.

2   Disconnect the upper end of the shock absorber. If the shock absorber is to be removed, then remove the lower shock absorber fixing from the U-bolt seat, otherwise leave the shock absorber in place.

3   Loosen the U-bolt nuts then jack-up the rear axle until it separates from the spring seat. Remove the U-bolt nuts and take off the spring pad and spring seat (photo).

4   Remove the two nuts from the rear shackle and take off the shackle plate (photo).

5   Remove the two bolts from the front spring pin assembly and then remove the spring assembly (photo).

Coil spring type

6   Remove the wheels as in paragraph 1, and then disconnect the handbrake cable from the extension levers, leaving the rear axle supported by the jack.

7   Disconnect the two fixings of the shock absorber. Remove the shock absorber.

8   Lower the jack under the axle and then remove the left and right coil springs.

9   Raise the axle jack slightly and remove the lower control arm, assist link and upper arm. Take care not to knock the axle off the jack while the suspension is being removed. Lower the axle as soon as it has been disconnected.

10 Do not remove the bushes from the links unnecessarily. If they are removed, discard them and fit new ones.

11 When refitting the rear suspension, raise the rear axle on a jack. Support the axle securely before completing refitting as the reverse process of removal.

11 Rear leaf springs – dismantling, inspection and reassembly

1   Open and remove the spring leaf clamp bands and remove the centre bolt to dismantle the leaves.

2   Check each leaf for cracks and wear, looking to see whether it has acquired a permanent set.

3   Examine the rubber bushes and silencers to see if they have hardened or are distorted.

4   Clean the spring leaves with a wire brush and coat them with chassis black. Fit new silencers unless the ones which were removed are in good condition.

5   Fit the centre bolt (Fig. 11.13), with a collar at each end of it. Fit

and securely tighten the nut, then centre punch the thread of the bolt to prevent the nut from rotating.

6   Fit the leaf clips and bend them over securely, then fit the front and rear eye bushings, using new ones if necessary. Smear the bushes with brake fluid to make insertion easier.

7   Press the shackle assembly in so that when the spring is fitted to the car, the assembly will be on the outside. Fit the shackle plate and screw on the nuts to press the bushes fully home, then remove the nuts and plate.

8   Fit the front eye bushings with their flanges outwards, then insert the spring pin assembly and tighten the nut.

9   Fit the spring to the car with the bolts of the spring pin assembly and shackle plate nuts slack, noting that the fixings of the spring pin assembly are not symmetrical (Fig. 11.14).

10 Fit the upper spring pad and its bracket over the spring centre bolt and lower the axle until it is in contact with it.

11 Fit the lower spring bracket and U-bolt seat, fit the U-bolts through the holes in the U-bolt seat and then fit and tighten the nuts. After tightening the nuts, make sure that the pad bracket and U-bolt seat are firmly in contact with each other.

12 Refit the upper end of the shock absorber then lower the car to the ground so that the rear springs are under their normal load.

13 Tighten the spring pin bolts and shcakle pin nuts to the torque wrench setting specified.

12 Rear shock absorbers – inspection and testing

1   The testing of shock absorbers is best left to a service station having specialised equipment, but a general idea of whether or not a shock absorber is defective can be gained by bouncing the appropriate suspension unit to see whether the movement is damped out quickly.

2   Inspect the shock absorbers visually, looking for signs of damage, leakage of oil or deterioration of the rubber mounting bushes and fixings.

13 Steering column – removal and refitting

1   Remove the air cleaner and remove the bolt from the clamp, coupling the steering shaft to the steering box shaft. For cars fitted with air conditioning, this clamp is only accessible from beneath the car.

2   Remove the three horn pad fixing screws from the back of the steering wheel and take off the horn pad (photo).

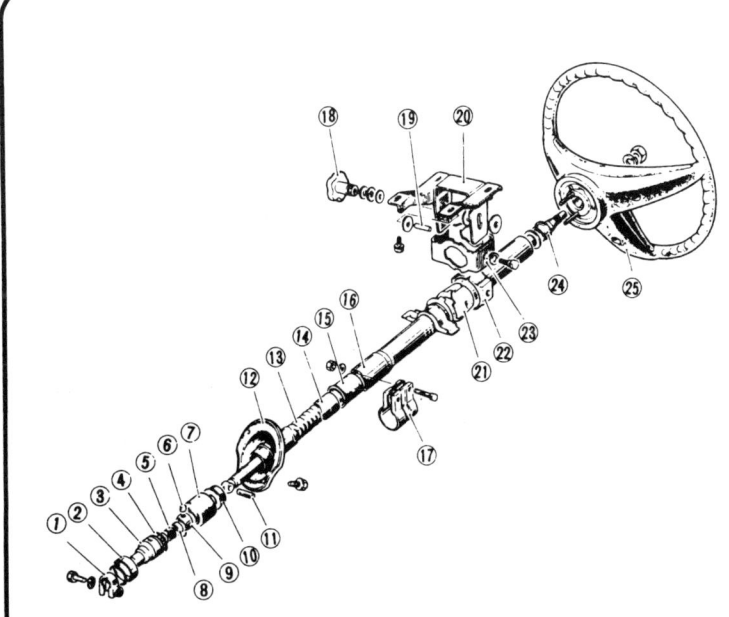

Fig. 11.16 Steering column assembly – exploded view

1 Clamp	(lower)
2 Joint pin retainer	15 Column tube bushing
3 Joint socket	16 Column tube assembly
4 Joint pin retainer stopper	(upper)
5 Spring	17 Column tube clamp
6 Joint pin (A)	18 Tilt lock knob
7 Joint cover	19 Tilt bracket support pin
8 Spring seat	20 Tilt bracket assembly
9 Joint bearing	21 Tilt bracket bearing
10 Bearing (lower)	22 Tilt bracket support
11 Joint pin (B)	23 Tilt bracket holder
12 Dust cover	24 Bearing (upper)
13 Steering shaft (collapsible)	25 Steering wheel
14 Column tube assembly	

Fig. 11.17 Steering box — exploded view

1 Gear housing end cover
2 Mainshaft adjusting shim
3 Mainshaft bearing
4 Mainshaft assembly
5 Gear adjusting bolt
6 Cross shaft adjusting shim
7 Mainshaft bearing
8 Gear housing upper cover
9 Packing
10 Mainshaft oil seal
11 Gear housing
12 Cross shaft
13 Cross shaft oil seal
14 Drop arm

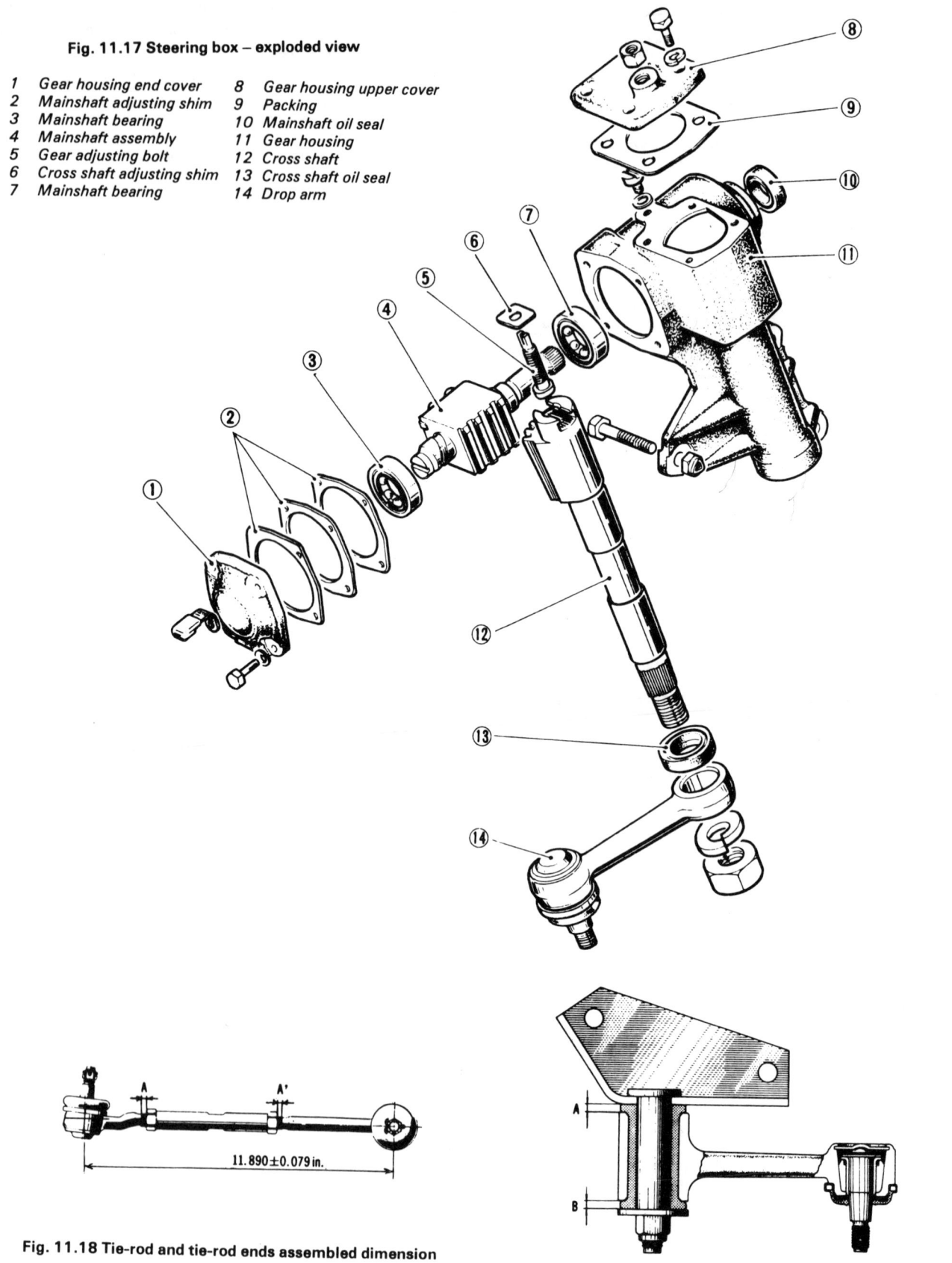

11.890 ±0.079 in.

Fig. 11.18 Tie-rod and tie-rod ends assembled dimension

Fig. 11.19 Dimensional relationship between bracket and arm

Chapter 11 Suspension and steering

Fig. 11.20 Steering play adjustment

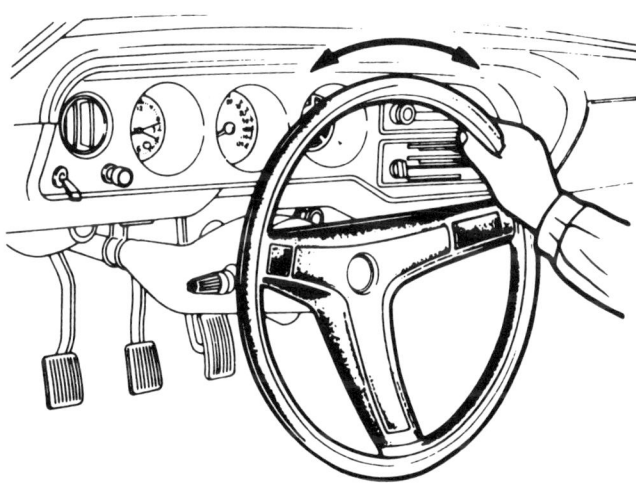

Fig. 11.21 Steering play

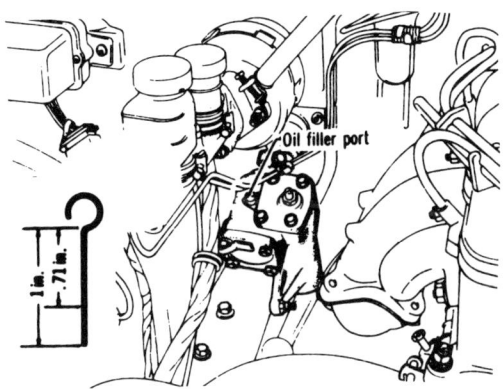

Fig. 11.22 Steering box oil level check

3   Lower the steering column to its lowest position, remove the steering wheel retaining nut and use a puller to draw the steering wheel off its shaft.

4   Remove the tilt lock knob (photo) and the steering column shroud. Disconnect the cables from the steering column switch, remove the ignition switch, remove the switch assembly mounting screws and pull the switch assembly off.

5   Remove the dust cover fixing bolts and lift the cover, then remove the tilt bracket assembly fixing bolts and pull out the steering column assembly.

6   Refit the steering column assembly from inside the car, couple it to the steering box and tighten the clamp with the clamp pointing downwards when the steering is in the straight ahead position.

7   Refit the tilt bracket, ensuring that there is projection of 3·70 to 3·74 in from the end of the steering rod to the upper end of the steering tube.

8   Refit the steering column switch assembly and the column shroud.

9   Ensure that the steering is in the straight ahead position, then fit the steering wheel so that it is symmetrical. Fit the lock nut and tighten it to its recommended torque. Refit the horn pad.

14 Steering box – removal

1   Remove the clamp bolt connecting the steering column shaft and the steering box shaft.

2   Using a balljoint separator, disconnect the drop arm from the relay rod.

3   Remove the fixing bolts and detach the steering box from the chassis, then use a balljoint separator to take the drop arm off the cross shaft.

15 Tie-rods – removal and refitting

1   Use a balljoint separator to disconnect the tie-rod ends. If the brake pads are worn down to near their limit, it may be difficult to fit the balljoint separator without first removing the brake pads and moving the caliper outwards.

2   Remove the tie-rod ends from the tie-rod, noting that the outer end has a left-hand thread and the inner end has a right-hand thread. The balljoints cannot be removed from the tie-rod ends.

3   Check the tie-rod ends for damage and wear and the balljoints for play and discard any unit which is defective.

4   Check the dust covers for cracks and damage and fit new ones if necessary. Fill the inside of the dust cover with grease before fitting it and apply a joint sealer to the tie-rod dust seal mounting surface.

5   Reassemble the tie-rods with a standard distance of 12·250 ± 0·08 in (311·15 ± 2·03 mm), between the ends (Figs. 11.18) making sure that dimension 'A' is the same at both ends of the rod.

6   Connect the tie-rod to the knuckle arm, tighten the nuts to their recommended torque wrench setting, insert a split pin and bend it over.

7   Make any necessary toe-in adjustment (Section 2) then tighten the lock nuts to their specified torque wrench setting.

16 Relay rod – removal and refitting

1   Use a balljoint separator to disconnect the tie-rod ends and then in the same manner disconnect the drop arm and idler arm joints.

2   Remove the relay rod, examine it for damage and the joints for excessive looseness. Examine the dust covers for damage and cracks, fitting new ones if necessary.

3   Refit the relay rod, tighten the drop arm and idler arm joints to their correct torque wrench setting. Check that the clearance between the relay arm and the drop arm at one end and the idler arm at the other is 0·146 to 0·169 in (3·71 to 4·29 mm).

17 Idler arm – removal, dismantling and reassembly

1   Use a balljoint separator to disconnect the relay rod from the idler arm.

2   Remove the idler arm fixing bolts and remove the idler assembly.

3   Remove the nut and washer from the idler arm assembly, pull off

the idler arm and inspect the rubber bushes for damage and wear. Renew if necessary.

4   To fit new bushes, apply soapy water to the idler arm and bushes, fit the bushes into the bore from both ends and press them in until their flanges are in contact with the idler arm.

5   Apply soapy water to the bracket shaft and use a vice to force the bracket into the bushes until the dimensions A and B (Fig. 11.19) are less than 0·08 in (2·03 mm) then tighten the locknut to the recommended torque wrench setting.

6   Insert and lock the split-pin.

7   Fit the idler bracket to the frame, tightening the bolts to their correct torque wrench setting, then reconnect the relay rod and tighten the joint to the specified torque wrench setting.

18 Steering play adjustment

1   Jack-up the front wheels clear of the ground and set the steering in the straight-ahead position. It is important that adjustment is only made when the steering is in the straight-ahead position, because the steering if of variable ratio type and otherwise the gear backlash would be too small, resulting in a damaged gear.

2   Loosen the locknut on the top of the steering box (Fig. 11.20), and adjust the screw to give a steering wheel play (Fig. 11.21) of not less than 1 in (25·4 mm). If the play cannot be reduced below 2 in (50·8 mm), the steering box is worn excessively and a new one should be fitted.

19 Steering box – oil level check

1   Remove the bolt at the lower inboard corner (Fig. 11.22).

2   Using a gauge, or thin screwdriver check that the oil is about 0·71 in (18 mm) from the outside surface of the top cover if the box has a square cover and 0·87 in (22 mm) if the box has a heart-shaped cover.

20 Fault diagnosis – suspension and steering

Before diagnosing faults from the following chart, check that any irregularities are not caused by:

1   *Binding brakes*
2   *Incorrect 'mix' of radial and crossply tyres*
3   *Incorrect tyre pressures*
4   *Misalignment of the body frame*

Symptom	Reason(s)
Steering wheel can be moved considerably before any movement of the roadwheels is apparent	Wear in the steering linkage, gear and column coupling
Vehicle difficult to steer in a consistent straight line – wandering	As above Wheel alignment incorrect (indicated by excessive or uneven tyre wear) Front wheel hub bearings loose or worn Worn balljoints
Steering stiff and heavy	Incorrect wheel alignment (indicated by excessive or uneven tyre wear) Excessive wear or seizure in one or more of the joints in the steering linkage or suspension Excessive wear in the steering gear unit
Wheel wobble and vibration	Roadwheels out of balance Roadwheels buckled Wheel alignment incorrect Wear in the steering linkage, suspension balljoints or track

Chapter 12 Bodywork and fittings

Contents

Specifications

Torque wrench settings

	lbf ft	kgf m
Front bumper stay to front frame panel	16 to 26	2·2 to 3·6
Front shock absorber to stay	12 to 14	1·7 to 2·0
Front bumper to shock absorber	12 to 14	1·7 to 2·0
Rear shock absorber to body	12 to 14	1·7 to 2·0
Rear bumper to shock isolator	12 to 14	1·7 to 2·0
Front safety belt inertia reel	17 to 21	2·4 to 3·0
Front safety belt shoulder anchor	More than 17	More than 2·4
Front safety belt buckle stalk	More than 17	More than 2·4

1 General description

The body and underframe are a unitary welded construction in a 2 door and 4 door version with saloon, hatchback and estate bodies. The doors are forward hinged, with anti-burst locks and flush door handles. The body is designed to reduce road shocks and vibratory noise, while providing a high degree of protection to the occupants because of high energy absorption characteristics at the front and rear of the body.

A laminated glass windscreen is fitted as standard equipment and the rear window is of heat absorbing glass. All the glass is tinted, and with the exception of the windscreen, is of the toughened, safety type.

The windscreen of the hatchback and estate car, the rear quarterlight glass on the hatchback and the hatchback rear window, are attached to the window frame by urethane adhesive. This method of fixing gives improved glass holding and sealing, as well as increased structural strength of the body openings, but the removal and refixing of the glass should be entrusted to a Colt agent, or windscreen specialist.

2 Maintenance – bodywork and underframe

1 The general condition of a car's bodywork is the one thing that significantly affects its value. Maintenance is easy but needs to be regular. Neglect, particularly after minor damage can lead quickly to further deterioration and costly repair bills. It is important also to keep

watch on those parts of the car not immediately visible, for instance, the underframe, inside all the wheel arches and the lower part of the engine compartment.

2   The basic maintenance routine for the bodywork is washing – preferably with a lot of water, from a hose. This will remove all the loose solids which may have stuck to the car. It is important to flush these off in such a way as to prevent grit from scratching the finish. The wheel arches and underframe need washing in the same way to remove any accumulated mud which will retain moisture and tend to encourage rust. Paradoxically enough, the best time to clean the underframe and wheel arches is in wet weather when the mud is thoroughly wet and soft. In very wet weather the underframe is usually cleaned of large accumulations automatically and this is a good time for inspection.

3   Periodically, it is a good idea to have the whole of the underframe of the car steam cleaned, engine compartment included so that a thorough inspection can be carried out to see what minor repairs and renovations are necessary. Steam cleaning is available at many garages and is necessary for removal of the accumulation of oily grime which sometimes is allowed to cake thick in certain areas near the engine, gearbox and back axle. If steam cleaning facilities are not available, there are one or two excellent grease solvents available which can be brush applied. The dirt can then be simply hosed off.

4   After washing paintwork, wipe off with a chamois leather to give an unspotted clear finish. A coat of clear protective wax polish will give added protection against chemical pollutants in the air. If the paintwork sheen has dulled or oxidised, use a cleaner/polisher combination to restore the brilliance of the shine. This requires a little effort, but is usually caused because regular washing has been neglected. Always check that the door and ventilator opening drain holes and pipes are completely clear so that water can be drained out. Bright work should be treated the same way as paintwork. Windscreens and windows can be kept clear of the smeary film which often appears if a little ammonia is added to the water. If they are scratched, a good rub with a proprietary metal polish will often clear them. Never use any form of wax or other body or chromium polish on glass.

3   Maintenance – upholstery and carpets

1   Mats and carpets should be brushed or vacuum cleaned regularly to keep them free of grit. If they are badly stained remove them from the car for scrubbing or sponging and make quite sure they are dry before refitting. Seats and interior trim panels can be kept clean by a wipe over with a damp cloth. If they do become stained (which can be more apparent on light coloured upholstery) use a little liquid detergent and a soft nail brush to scour the grime out of the grain of the material. Do not forget to keep the head lining clean in the same way as the upholstery. When using liquid cleaners inside the car do not over-wet the surfaces being cleaned. Excessive damp could get into the seams and padded interior causing stains, offensive odours or even rot. If the inside of the car gets wet accidentally it is worthwhile taking some trouble to dry it out properly, particularly where carpets are involved. *Do not leave oil or electric heaters inside the car for this purpose.*

4   Minor body damage – repair

The photographic sequence on pages 190 and 191 illustrates the operations detailed in the following sub-sections.

Repair of minor scratches in the car's bodywork

If the scratch is very superficial, and does not penetrate to the metal of the bodywork, repair is very simple. Lightly rub the area of the scratch with a paintwork renovator, or a very fine cutting paste, to remove loose paint from the scratch and to clear the surrounding bodywork of wax polish. Rinse the area with clean water.

Apply touch-up paint to the scratch using a thin paint brush; continue to apply thin layers of paint until the surface of the paint in the scratch is level with the surrounding paintwork. Allow the new paint at least two weeks to harden: then blend it into the surrounding paintwork by rubbing the paintwork, in the scratch area, with a paintwork renovator or a very fine cutting paste. Finally, apply wax polish.

An alternative to painting over the scratch is to use a paint transfer. Use the same preparation for the affected area, then simply pick a patch of a suitable size to cover the scratch completely. Hold the patch against the scratch and burnish its backing paper; the paper will adhere to the paintwork, freeing itself from the backing paper at the same time. Polish the affected area to blend the patch into the surrounding paintwork. Where the scratch has penetrated right through to the metal of the bodywork, causing the metal to rust, a different repair technique is required. Remove any loose rust from the bottom of the scratch with a penknife, then apply rust inhibiting paint to prevent the formation of rust in the future. Using a rubber or nylon applicator fill the scratch with bodystopper paste. If required, this paste can be mixed with cellulose thinners to provide a very thin paste which is ideal for filling narrow scratches. Before the stopper-paste in the scratch hardens, wrap a piece of smooth cotton rag around the top of a finger. Dip the finger in cellulose thinners and then quickly sweep it across the surface of the stopper-paste in the scratch; this will ensure that the surface of the stopper-paste is slightly hollowed. The scratch can now be painted over as described earlier in this Section.

Repair of dents in the car's bodywork

When deep denting of the car's bodywork has taken place, the first task is to pull the dent out, until the affected bodywork almost attains its original shape. There is little point in trying to restore the original shape completely, as the metal in the damaged area will have stretched on impact and cannot be reshaped fully to its original contour. It is better to bring the level of the dent up to a point which is about $\frac{1}{8}$ in (3 mm) below the level of the surrounding bodywork. In cases where the dent is very shallow anyway, it is not worth trying to pull it out at all. If the underside of the dent is accessible, it can be hammered out gently from behind, using a mallet with a wooden or plastic head. Whilst doing this, hold a suitable block of wood firmly against the impact from the hammer blows and thus prevent a large area of the bodywork from being 'belled-out'.

Should the dent be in a section of the bodywork which has double skin or some other factor making it inaccessible from behind, a different technique is called for. Drill several small holes through the metal inside the area – particularly in the deeper section. Then screw long self-tapping screws into the holes just sufficiently for them to gain a good purchase in the metal. Now the dent can be pulled out by pulling on the protruding heads of the screws with a pair of pliers.

The next stage of the repair is the removal of the paint from the damaged area, and from an inch or so of the surrounding 'sound' bodywork. This is accomplished most easily by using a wire brush or abrasive pad on a power drill, although it can be done just as effectively by hand using sheets of abrasive paper. To complete the preparation for filling, score the surface of the bare metal with a screwdriver or the tang of a file, or alternatively, drill small holes in the affected area. This will provide a really good 'key' for the filler paste.

To complete the repair see the Section on filling and respraying.

Repair of rust holes or gashes in the car's bodywork

Remove all paint from the affected area and from an inch or so of the surrounding 'sound' bodywork, using an abrasive pad or a wire brush on a power drill. If these are not available a few sheets of abrasive paper will do the job just as effectively. With the paint removed you will be able to gauge the severity of the corrosion and therefore decide whether to renew the whole panel (if this is possible) or to repair the affected area. New body panels are not as expensive as most people think and it is often quicker and more satisfactory to fit a new panel than to attempt to repair large areas of corrosion.

Remove all fittings from the affected area except those which will act as a guide to the original shape of the damaged bodywork (eg headlamp shells etc). Then, using tin snips or a hacksaw blade, remove all loose metal and any other metal badly affected by corrosion. Hammer the edges of the hole inwards in order to create a slight depression for the filler paste.

Wire brush the affected area to remove the powdery rust from the surface of the remaining metal. Paint the affected area with rust inhibiting paint; if the back of the rusted area is accessible treat this also.

Before filling can take place it will be necessary to block the hole in some way. This can be achieved by the use of one of the following materials: Zinc gauze, Aluminium tape or Polyurethane foam.

Zinc gauze is probably the best material to use for a large hole. Cut a piece to the approximate size and shape of the hole to be filled, then position it in the hole so that its edges are below the level of the surrounding bodywork. It can be retained in position by several blobs of filler paste around its periphery.

Aluminium tape should be used for small or very narrow holes. Pull a piece off the roll and trim it to the approximate size and shape required, then pull off the backing paper (if used) and stick the tape over the hole; it can be overlapped if the thickness of one piece is insufficient. Burnish down the edges of the tape with the handle of a screwdriver or similar, to ensure that the tape is securely attached to the metal underneath.

Polyurethane foam is best used where the hole is situated in a section of bodywork of complex shape, backed by a small box section (eg where the sill panel meets the rear wheel arch – most cars). The usual mixing procedure for this foam is as follows: put equal amounts of fluid from each of the two cans provided in the kit, into one container. Stir until the mixture begins to thicken, then quickly pour this mixture into the hole, and hold a piece of cardboard over the larger apertures. Almost immediately the polyurethane will begin to expand, gushing out of any small holes left unblocked. When the foam hardens it can be cut back to just below the level of the surrounding bodywork with a hacksaw blade.

Bodywork repairs – filling and respraying

Before using this Section, see the Sections on dent, deep scratch, rust holes and gash repairs.

Many types of bodyfiller are available, but generally speaking those proprietary kits which contain a tin of filler paste and a tube of resin hardener are best for this type of repair. A wide, flexible plastic or nylon applicator will be found invaluable for imparting a smooth and well contoured finish to the surface of the filler.

Mix up a little filler on a clean piece of card or board – use the hardener sparingly (follow the maker's instructions on the pack) otherwise the filler will set too rapidly or too slowly.

Using the applicator apply the filler paste to the prepared area: draw the applicator across the surface of the filler to achieve the correct contour and to level the filler surface. As soon as a contour that approximates the correct one is achieved, stop working the paste – if you carry on too long the paste will become sticky and begin to 'pick up' on the applicator. Continue to add thin layers of filler paste at twenty-minute intervals until the level of the filler is just proud of the surrounding bodywork.

Once the filler has hardened, excess can be removed using a metal plane or file. From then on, progressively finer grades of abrasive paper should be used, starting with a 40 grade production paper and finishing with 400 grade wet-and-dry paper. Always wrap the abrasive paper around a flat rubber, cork, or wooden block – otherwise the surface of the filler will not be completely flat. During the smoothing of the filler surface the wet-and-dry paper should be periodically rinsed in water. This will ensure that a very smooth finish is imparted to the filler at the final stage.

At this stage the 'dent' should be surrounded by a ring of bare metal, which in turn should be encircled by the finely 'feathered' edge of the good paintwork. Rinse the repair area with clean water, until all of the dust produced by the rubbing-down operation has gone.

Spray the whole repair area with a light coat of primer – this will show up any imperfections in the surface of the filler. Repair these imperfections with fresh filler paste or bodystopper, and once more smooth the surface with abrasive paper. If bodystopper is used, it can be mixed with cellulose thinners to form a really thin paste which is ideal for filling small holes. Repeat this spray and repair procedure until you are satisfied that the surface of the filler, and the feathered edge of the paintwork are perfect. Clean the repair area with clean water and allow to dry fully.

The repair area is now ready for final spraying. Paint spraying must be carried out in a warm, dry, windless and dust free atmosphere. This condition can be created artificially if you have access to a large indoor working area, but if you are forced to work in the open, you will have to pick your day very carefully. If you are working indoors, dousing the floor in the work area with water will help settle the dust which would otherwise be in the atmosphere. If the repair area is confined to one body panel, mask off the surrounding panels; this will help to minimise the effects of a slight mis-match in paint colours. Bodywork fittings (eg chrome strips, door handles etc) will also need to be masked off. Use genuine masking tape and several thicknesses of newspaper for the masking operations.

Before commencing to spray, agitate the aerosol can thoroughly, then spray a test area (an old tin, or similar) until the technique is mastered. Cover the repair area with a thick coat of primer; the thickness should be built up using several thin layers of paint rather than one thick one. Using 400 grade wet-and-dry paper, rub down the surface of the primer until it is really smooth. While doing this, the work area should be thoroughly doused with water, and the wet-and-dry paper periodically rinsed in water. Allow to dry before spraying on more paint.

Spray on the top coat, again building up the thickness by using several thin layers of paint. Start spraying in the centre of the repair area and then using a circular motion, work outwards until the whole repair area and about 2 inches of the surrounding original paintwork is covered. Remove all masking material 10 to 15 minutes after spraying on the final coat of paint.

Allow the new paint at least two weeks to harden, then, using a paintwork renovator or a very fine cutting paste, blend the edges of the paint into the existing paintwork. Finally, apply wax polish.

5 Major body damage – repair

Where serious damage has occurred or large areas need renewal due to neglect, it means certainly that completely new sections or panels will need welding in and this is best left to professionals. If the damage is due to impact it will also be necessary to completely check the alignment of the body shell structure. Due to the principle of construction the strength and shape of the whole car can be affected by damage to a part. In such instances the services of a workshop with specialist checking jigs are essential. If a body is left misaligned it is first of all dangerous as the car will not handle properly and secondly uneven stresses will be imposed on the steering, engine and transmission, causing abnormal wear or complete failure. Tyre wear may also be excessive.

6 Bumpers – general description

The bumpers of saloons and estate cars are fitted with two solid-media shock absorbers which are telescopic. Each consists of a piston rod with a metering orifice which is hermetically sealed inside a pressure cylinder filled with silicone rubber (Fig. 12.3). Under an impact load, the silicone rubber is compressed and is caused to flow through the metering orifice, the combined effect of the compression and flow being to absorb energy.

7 Bumpers – removal and refitting

Front bumper assembly
1 Remove the bumper to shock isolator locking nuts (or bolts on the estate car), to disconnect the bumper from the isolator, and lift the bumper off.
2 Remove the bolts (or nuts and bolts on the estate car) which secure the shock isolator to the front body frame and then remove the isolator.

Rear bumper assembly
3 The removal of the rear bumper assembly is the same as the removal of the front bumper assembly.
4 When refitting the bumper assemblies, leave all the fixings loose until the bumpers have been aligned, and then tighten the fixings to the specified torque.

8 Windscreen – removal and refitting (except hatchback)

The following procedure is only applicable to windscreens which are fitted in rubber mouldings. The hatchback has a windscreen which is bonded to the body and windscreen removal should be entrusted to a Colt agent, or windscreen specialist.
1 Remove the windscreen wiper arms, interior mirror and sun visor.
2 From inside the car, prise out the weatherstrip, using a screwdriver (Fig. 12.4), then remove the weatherstrip from the body flange.

This sequence of photographs deals with the repair of the dent and paintwork damage shown in this photo. The procedure will be similar for the repair of a hole. It should be noted that the procedures given here are simplified – more explicit instructions will be found in the text

In the case of a dent the first job – after removing surrounding trim – is to hammer out the dent where access is possible. This will minimise filling. Here, the large dent having been hammered out, the damaged area is being made slightly concave

Now all paint must be removed from the damaged area, by rubbing with coarse abrasive paper. Alternatively, a wire brush or abrasive pad can be used in a power drill. Where the repair area meets good paintwork, the edge of the paintwork should be 'feathered', using a finer grade of abrasive paper

In the case of a hole caused by rusting, all damaged sheet-metal should be cut away before proceeding to this stage. Here, the damaged area is being treated with rust remover and inhibitor before being filled

Mix the body filler according to its manufacturer's instructions. In the case of corrosion damage, it will be necessary to block off any large holes before filling – this can be done with aluminium or plastic mesh, or aluminium tape. Make sure the area is absolutely clean before ...

... applying the filler. Filler should be applied with a flexible applicator, as shown, for best results; the wooden spatula being used for confined areas. Apply thin layers of filler at 20-minute intervals, until the surface of the filler is slightly proud of the surrounding bodywork

Initial shaping can be done with a Surform plane or Dreadnought file. Then, using progressively finer grades of wet-and-dry paper, wrapped around a sanding block, and copious amounts of clean water, rub down the filler until really smooth and flat. Again, feather the edges of adjoining paintwork

The whole repair area can now be sprayed or brush-painted with primer. If spraying, ensure adjoining areas are protected from over-spray. Note that at least one inch of the surrounding sound paintwork should be coated with primer. Primer has a 'thick' consistency, so will find small imperfections

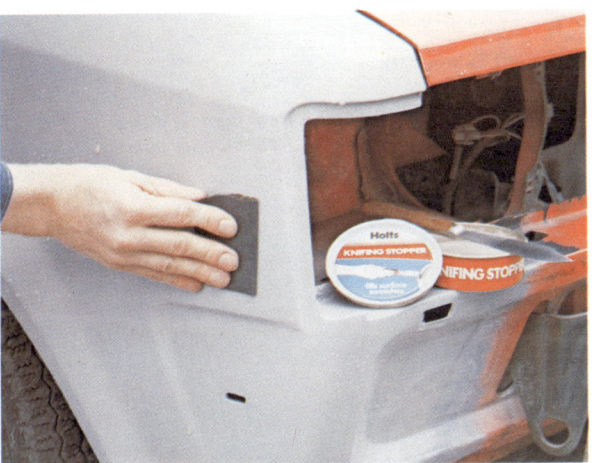

Again, using plenty of water, rub down the primer with a fine grade wet-and-dry paper (400 grade is probably best) until it is really smooth and well blended into the surrounding paintwork. Any remaining imperfections can now be filled by carefully applied knifing stopper paste

When the stopper has hardened, rub down the repair area again before applying the final coat of primer. Before rubbing down this last coat of primer, ensure the repair area is blemish-free – use more stopper if necessary. To ensure that the surface of the primer is really smooth use some finishing compound

The top coat can now be applied. When working out of doors, pick a dry, warm and wind-free day. Ensure surrounding areas are protected from over-spray. Agitate the aerosol thoroughly, then spray the centre of the repair area, working outwards with a circular motion. Apply the paint as several thin coats

After a period of about two weeks, which the paint needs to harden fully, the surface of the repaired area can be 'cut' with a mild cutting compound prior to wax polishing. When carrying out bodywork repairs, remember that the quality of the finished job is proportional to the time and effort expended

Front

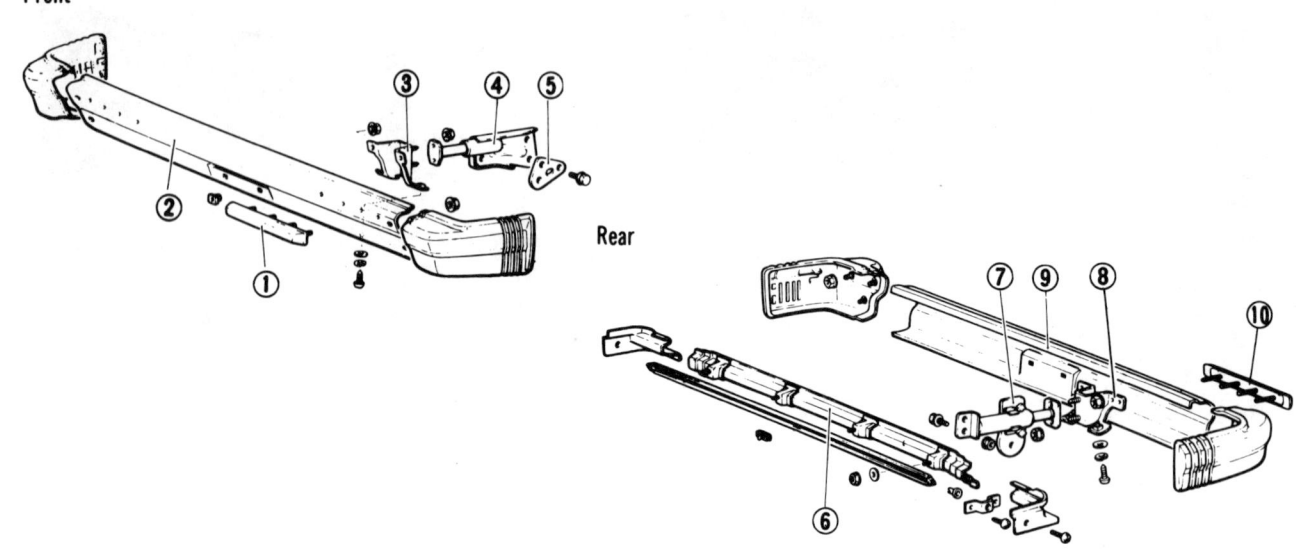

Rear

Fig. 12.1 Details of bumpers (except Estate car)

1	Front bumper guard	4	Shock absorber (front)	7	Shock absorber (rear)	9	Rear bumper guard
2	Front bumper	5	Fillet plate	8	Rear bumper	10	Rear bumper guard
3	Bracket	6	Filler piece				

Front

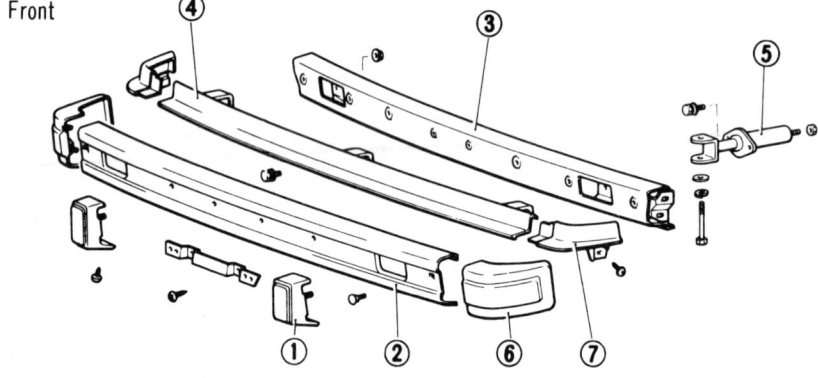

Rear

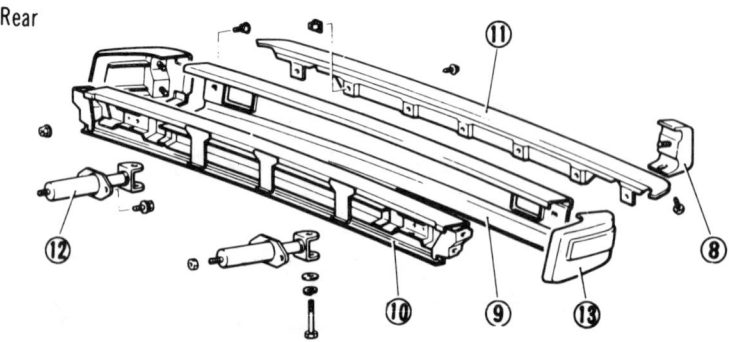

Fig. 12.2 Details of bumpers (Estate car)

1	Front bumper guard	5	Shock absorber (front)	8	Rear bumper guard	11	Rear filler
2	Front bumper	6	Front bumper corner	9	Rear bumper	12	Shock absorber (rear)
3	Front bumper reinforcement	7	Front filler corner	10	Rear bumper reinforcement	13	Rear bumper
4	Filler piece						

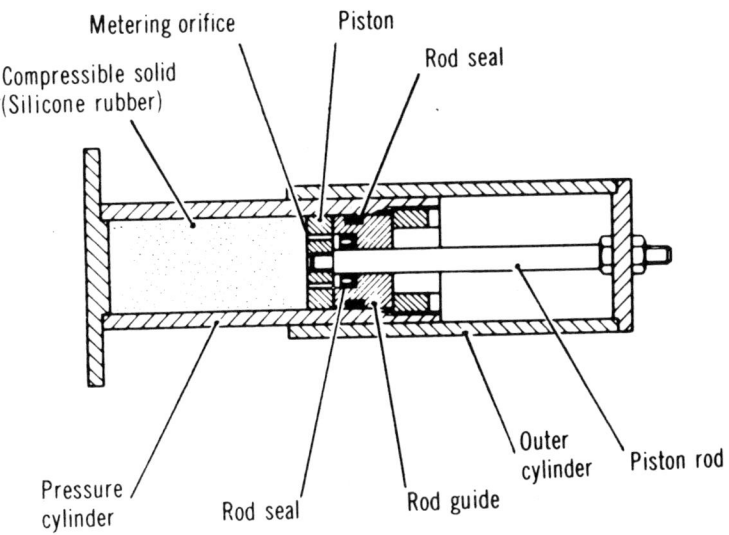

Compressible solid
(Silicone rubber)

Metering orifice

Piston

Rod seal

Pressure
cylinder

Rod seal

Rod guide

Outer
cylinder

Piston rod

Fig. 12.3 Solid medium shock absorber

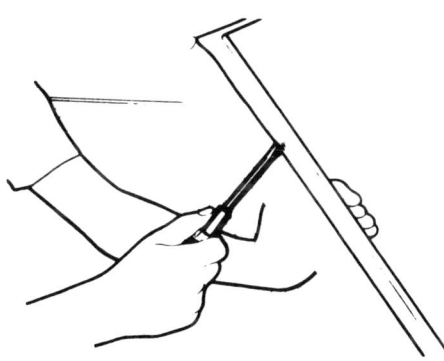

Fig. 12.4 Removing the windscreen

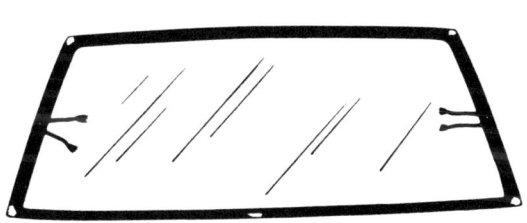

Fig. 12.5 Pull cords fitted in weatherstrip

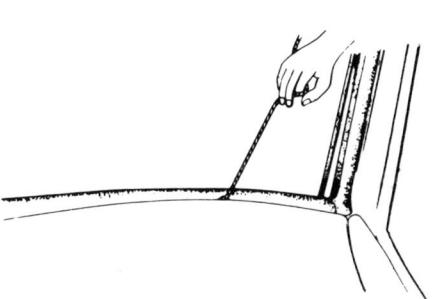

Fig. 12.6 Fitting the windscreen

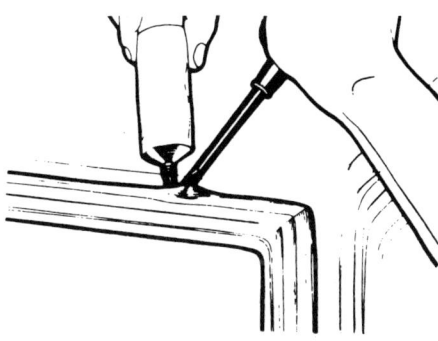

Fig. 12.7 Weatherproofing the windscreen

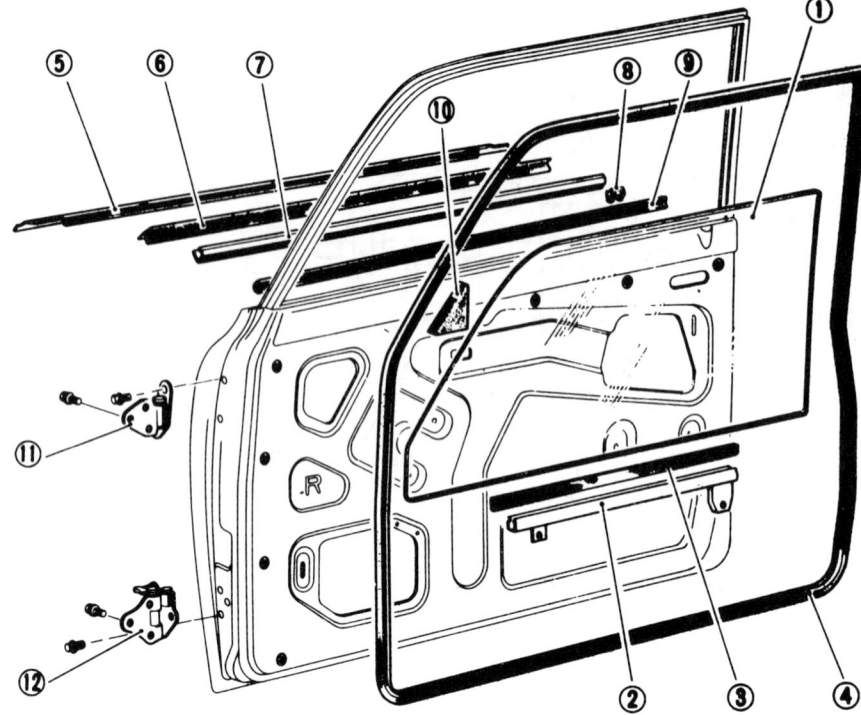

Fig. 12.8 Front door assembly – exploded view

1   Front door window glass
2   Glass holder
3   Glass holder pad
4   Door opening weatherstrip
5   Outside moulding
6   Outer weatherstrip
7   Weatherstrip holder
8   Clip
9   Inner weatherstrip
10 Packing
11 Upper hinge
12 Lower hinge

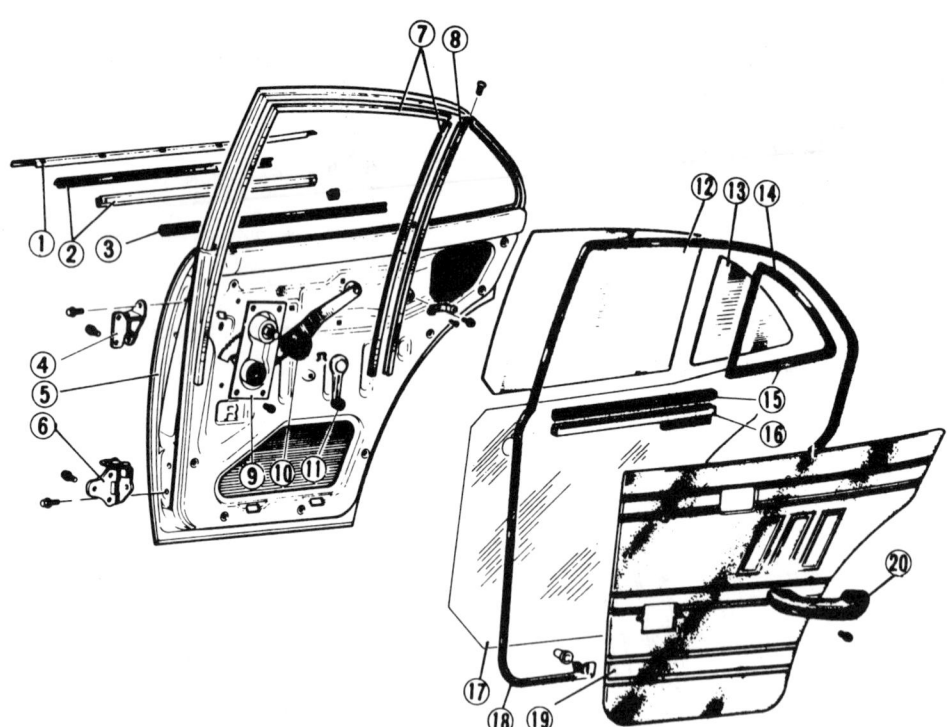

Fig. 12.9 Rear door assembly – exploded view

1 Outside moulding	6 Rear door lower hinge	11 Regulator handle	16 Glass holder
2 Outer weatherstrip and holder	7 Run channel	12 Rear door glass	17 Water-proof film
	8 Centre sash	13 Stationary glass	18 Opening weatherstrip
3 Inner weatherstrip	9 Window glass regulator	14 Stationary weatherstrip	19 Door trim board
4 Rear door upper hinge	10 Escutcheon	15 Glass holder pad	20 Arm rest
5 Rear door panel assembly			

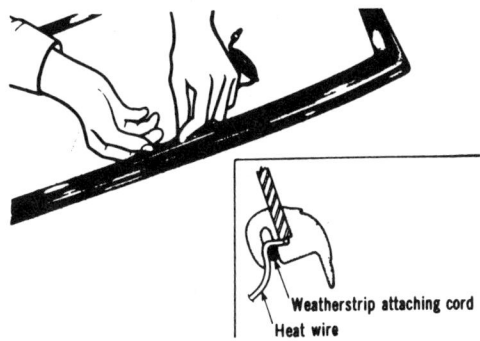

Fig. 12.10 Position of pull-cord for heated rear window

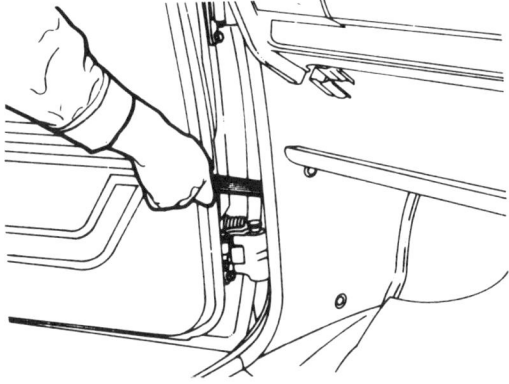

Fig. 12.11 Door hinge adjustment

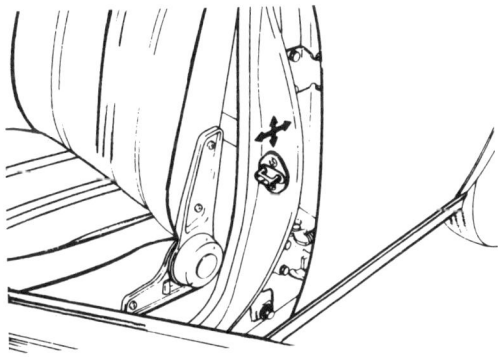

Fig. 12.12 Door striker adjustment

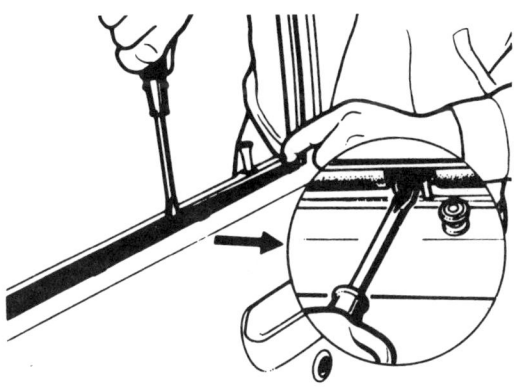

Fig. 12.13 Removing the outer weatherstrip and holder

3   Remove the windscreen by pushing it outwards.
4   When refitting the glass, fit the weatherstrip to the glass and insert pull cords in the weatherstrip so that the ends overlap at each side of the glass, (Fig. 12.5), then fit the moulding to the weatherstrip.
5   Clean the body flange with solvent, (taking precautions appropriate when handling inflammable liquids) and rectify any damage to the flange.
6   Apply soap solution to all the car surfaces which are in contact with the weatherstrip.
7   With an assistant holding the glass in its proper position against the outside of the car, pull the cords from the inside (Fig. 12.6) while the assistant presses the glass. Pull each cord at right angles to the glass, starting at the side and working towards the centre.
8   Tap the glass until it is hard against the body flange then seal the flange to the weatherstrip and the weatherstrip to the glass, with a windscreen sealer of approved specification.
9   Refit the windscreen wiper arms, interior mirror and sun visor.

9   Rear window – removal and refitting (except hatchback)

1   The rear window can be removed and fitted in exactly the same way as the windscreen. If the glass is fitted with a demister panel, take care to insert the pull cords on top of the cable (Fig. 12.10) otherwise the cable may be broken when the cord is pulled.
2   The hatchback rear window is bonded to the body shell and its removal and refitting should only be undertaken by a Colt agent, or windscreen specialist.

10   Doors – removal and refitting

1   Mark the position of the door hinges so that the door can be refitted in the same position, then remove the wing if a front door is to be removed.
2   With an assistant holding the door, remove the bolts from the upper and lower hinges.
3   Before refitting the door, paint primer or body sealer on to the back of the hinge and their mating surfaces on the door.
4   Tighten the hinge bolts to a torque wrench setting as stated in the Specifications.

11   Doors – adjustment

1   Loosen the hinge attachment bolts on the body and then adjust the longitudinal and vertical positions of the door to give a uniform gap between the door and the car body.
2   Alter the vertical and horizontal position by sliding the hinges up and down and obtain longitudinal adjustment by fitting shims behind the hinges.

12   Door striker – adjustment

1   Adjust the vertical and horizontal positions of the striker by loosening the attachment screws and sliding the striker plate (Fig. 12.12).
2   Adjust the longitudinal position by packing shims behind the striker plate.

13   Front door glass and window regulator – removal and refitting

1   Remove the arm rest and the inside handle cover, then separate the door trim and the regulator handle escutcheon with a screwdriver. Pull off the handle fixing clip and handle (photos).
2   Unscrew the door inside locking knob, then insert a flat screwdriver between the door and the trim and prise off the trim.
3   Carefully peel the weather film from the inside of the door.
4   Lower the glass to its fullest extent and remove the outer door moulding and weatherstrip by levering out the clip with a screwdriver. After removing them as an assembly it is not necessary to separate the clip, weatherstrip and moulding.
5   Remove the inner weatherstrip by prising it off.
6   Remove the two screws attaching the glass holder to the door

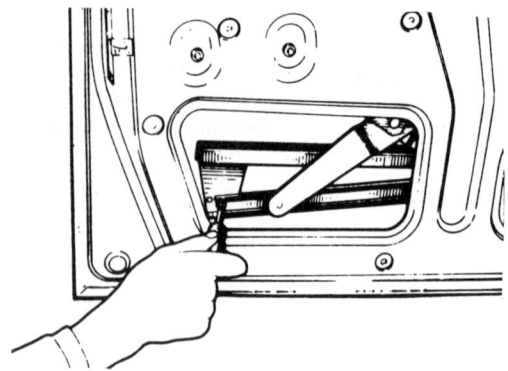

Fig. 12.14 Removing the glass holder attachment screws

13.1a Removing the arm rest

13.1b ... inside handle cover

13.1c ... and handle fixing clip and handle

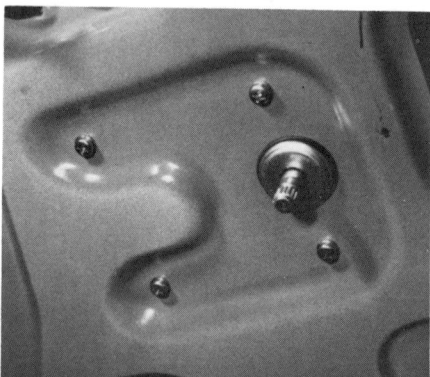

13.8a Regulator fixing screws

13.8b Roller arm and guide

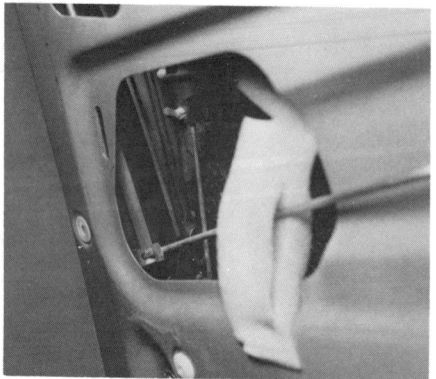

14.3a Door lock remote control connection

14.3b Inside handle fixing screw

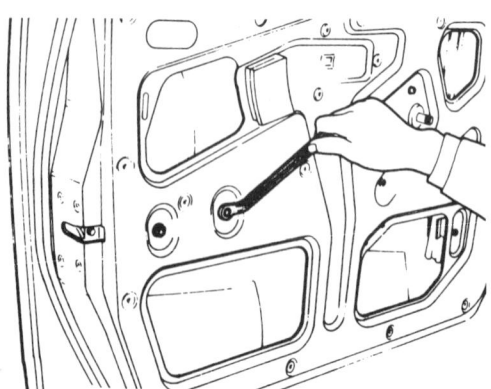

Fig. 12.15 Removing the door regulator

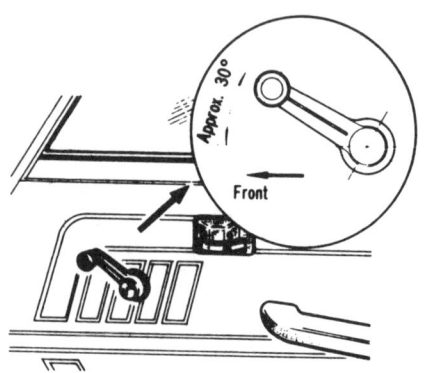

Fig. 12.16 Correct position for installation of regulator handle

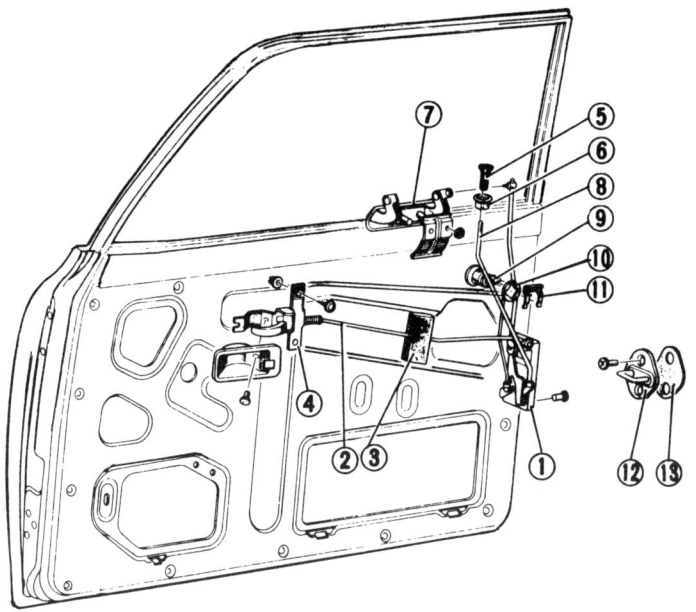

Fig. 12.17 Front door lock components

1 Door latch
2 Inside handle rod
3 Cushion
4 Inside handle
5 Inside lock knob
6 Knob bushing
7 Outer handle
8 Inside lock rod
9 Lock cylinder
10 Lock cylinder pad
11 Retainer
12 Striker
13 Striker shim

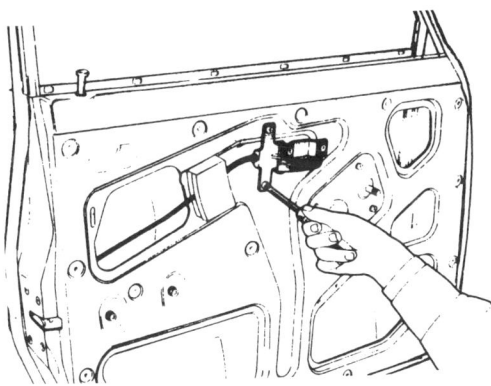

Fig. 12.18 Removing the door inside handle

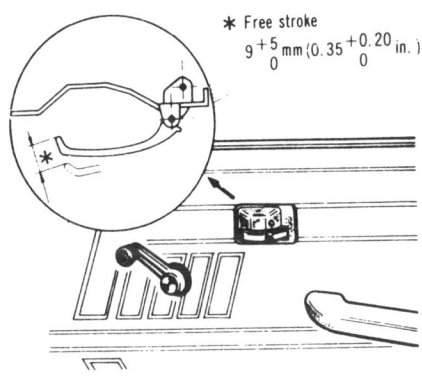

* Free stroke
$9 ^{+5}_{0}$ mm $(0.35 ^{+0.20}_{0}$ in. $)$

Fig. 12.19 Door handle free travel setting

regulator roller channel guide.

7 Hold the top edge of the window glass, and lift it out with the rear of the glass tilted higher than the front.

8 After removing the glass, remove the regulator assembly by removing the two screws securing the regulator roller guide and the four screws securing the regulator. The regulator assembly can then be withdrawn through the large hole at the bottom of the door inner panel (photos).

9 After fittting the regulator and glass by reversing the removal operations, take great care to ensure that the weather film is sealed to the door effectively.

10 When the window glass is in the fully raised position, fit the regulator handle so that it faces forward and is at an angle about 30° higher than the horizontal.

11 If not adequately lubricated already, apply grease to the gear, spring and sliding surfaces of the regulator mechanism before refitting them.

14 Front door handles and lock – removal and refitting

Door inside handle

1 Remove the arm rest and the inside handle cover, then separate the door trim and the regulator handle escutcheon with a screwdriver. Pull off the handle fixing clip and handle.

2 Unscrew and remove the door inside locking knob, then insert a flat screwdriver between the door and the trim, then prise off the trim.

3 Disconnect the remote control rod at the door lock end. Remove the screws securing the inside handle and remove the door handle and operating rod (photos).

4 After refitting the inside handle, check to see that the door lock operates correctly and ensure that the handle has a free movement of 0·35 in (9 mm) before the door lock begins to operate. The amount of free travel can be adjusted by utilising the slotted fixing holes of the inside handle.

15 Rear door glass and regulator – removal

1 Remove the arm rest, regulator handle and door inside lock knob.

2 Insert a flat screwdriver between the trim and the door panel, prise off and remove the trim, then remove the weather film from the inside panel.

3 Disconnect the inside handle from the door lock and remove the inside handle.

4 Lower the window, remove the quarter sash retaining screws, take out the quarter light (Fig. 12.20) and then its sash.

5 Tilt the glass to disconnect it from the regulator arm roller, then gently push it out, rear edge first.

6 Remove the four screws securing the regulator and take the regulator out through the hole near the bottom of the panel.

7 Before refitting the quarter light, apply soap solution all over the quarter light weatherstrip and sash.

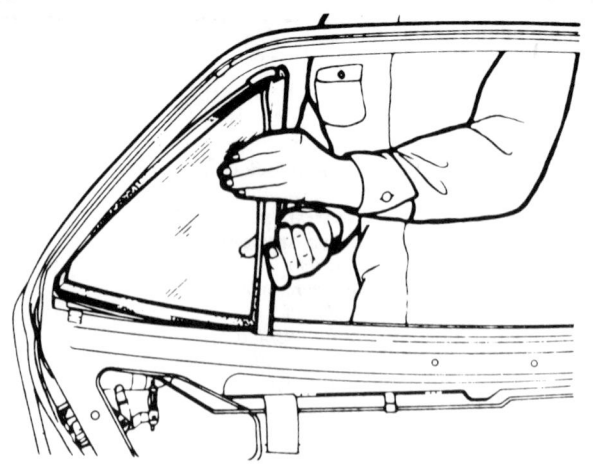

Fig. 12.20 Removing the quarter light and sash

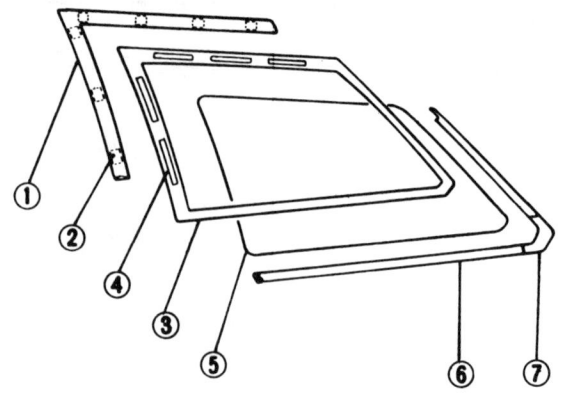

Fig. 12.21 Rear quarter window components

1	Sash	5	Window glass
2	Sash clip	6	Moulding
3	Weatherstrip	7	Joint
4	Clip holder		

Fig. 12.22 Side window – exploded view

1 Hinge
2 Link
3 Spacer
4 Weatherstrip
5 Side window glass
6 Bracket (alternative to hinge)

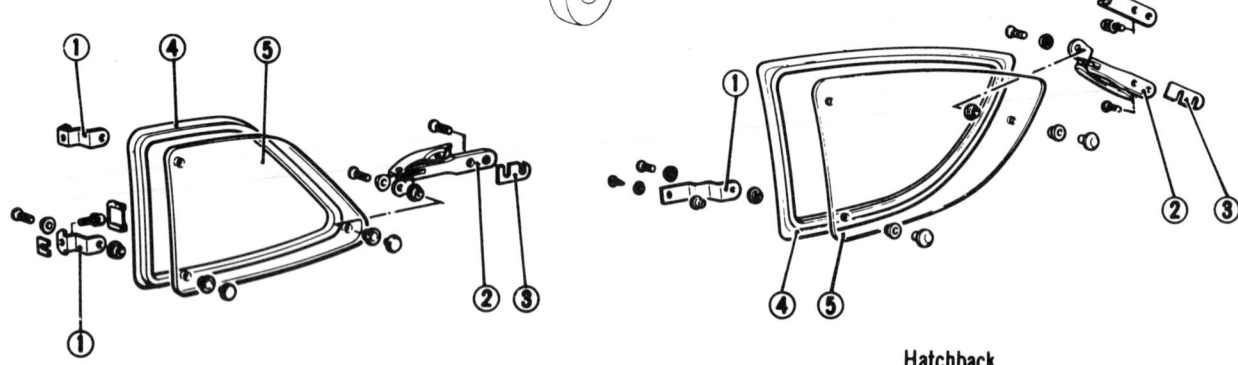

Coupe

Hatchback

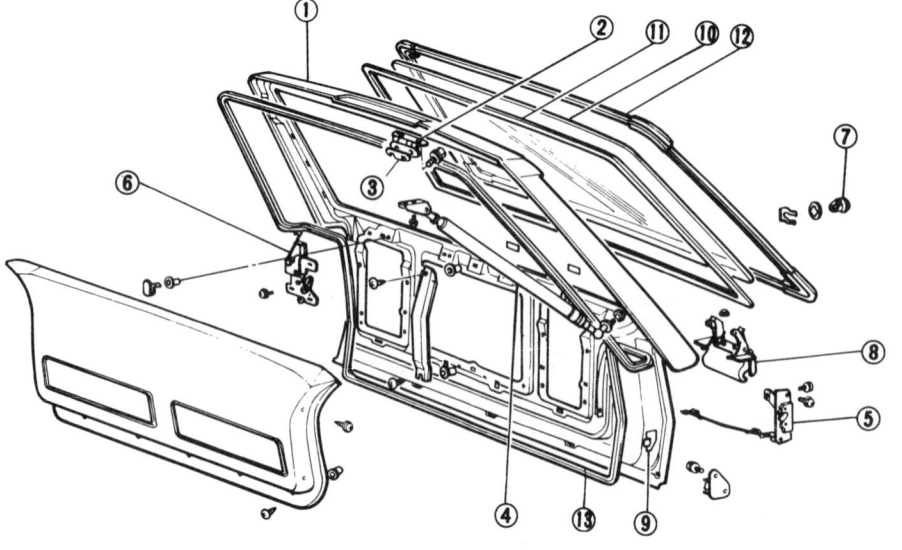

Fig. 12.23 Tailgate – exploded view

1 Tailgate panel
2 Tailgate hinge
3 Shim
4 Stay
5 Latch
6 Link assembly
7 Lock barrel
8 Handle
9 Damper
10 Window glass
11 Window weatherstrip
12 Window moulding
13 Gate opening weatherstrip

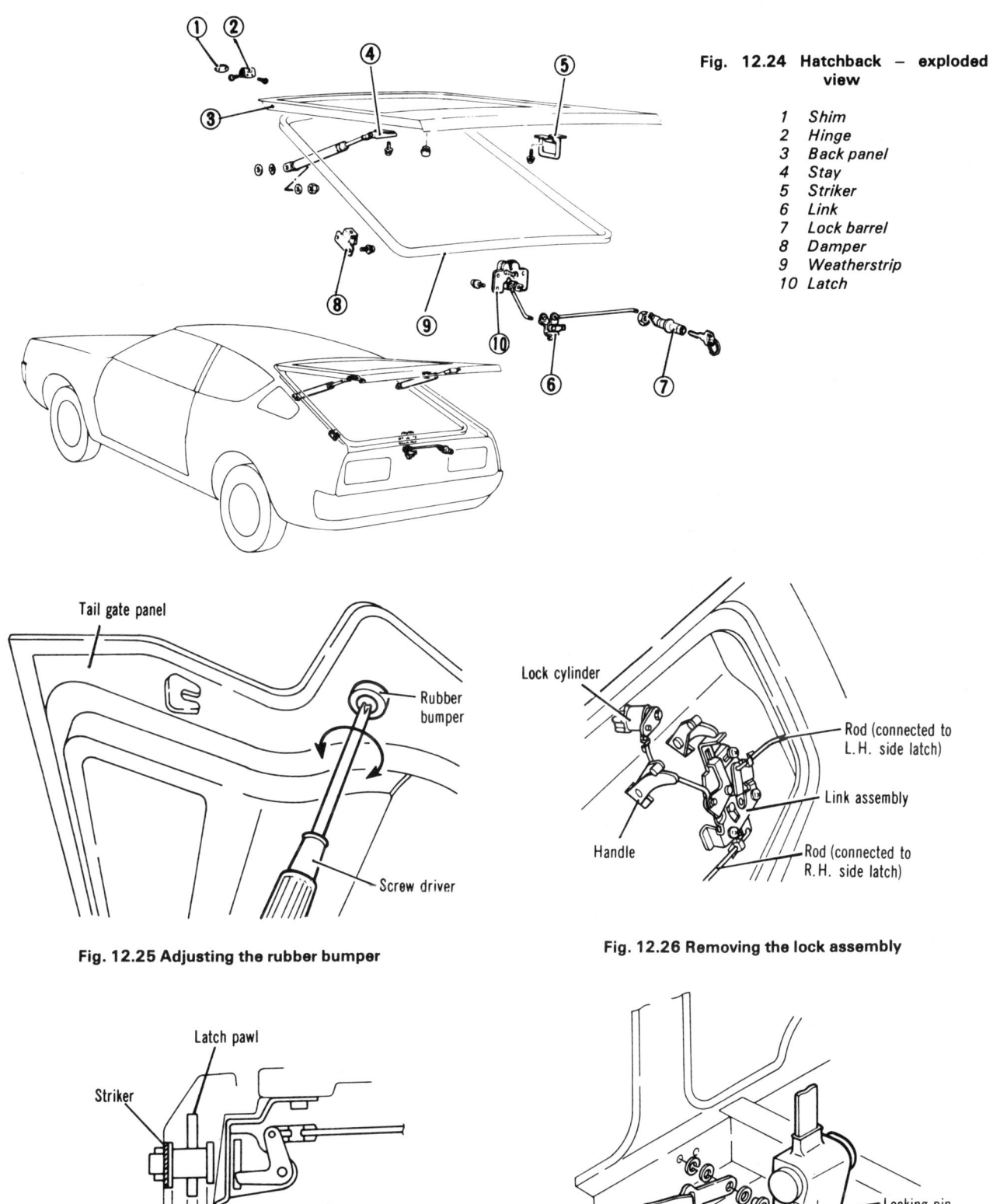

Fig. 12.24 Hatchback — exploded view

1 Shim
2 Hinge
3 Back panel
4 Stay
5 Striker
6 Link
7 Lock barrel
8 Damper
9 Weatherstrip
10 Latch

Tail gate panel

Rubber bumper

Screw driver

Fig. 12.25 Adjusting the rubber bumper

Lock cylinder

Rod (connected to L.H. side latch)

Link assembly

Handle

Rod (connected to R.H. side latch)

Fig. 12.26 Removing the lock assembly

Latch pawl

Striker

.3±.04in.
(7±1mm)

.16±.04in.
(4±1mm)

Fig. 12.27 Tailgate striker adjustment

Forward

Locking pin

Bolt

Fig. 12.28 Inertia reel installation (Coupe and Hatchback)

16 Side window – removal and refitting (coupe and hatchback)

1   Remove part of the door opening trim and also remove the centre pillar trim to expose the window frame.
2   Remove the screws attaching the stay link to the body, or the screws attaching the side window bracket to the body.
3   Remove the screws attaching the hinge to the body, then remove the window with the hinges and bracket attached.

17 Rear quarter window – removal and refitting (estate car)

1   Lever the sash off its fixing clips and remove the sash.
2   Prise up the edge of the weatherstrip flange and progressively pull the flange over the window frame until the window and weatherstrip can be removed.
3   Refit the window using the same procedure as for refitting the windscreen (Section 8), using sealer (Fig. 12.21) to attach the weatherstrip to the window frame.
4   Refit the sash.

18 Hatchback – removal, refitting and adjustment

1   Remove the screws attaching the hatchback stops to the sides of the hatchback.
2   With an assistant supporting the hatchback, mark the position of the hinges and remove the screws attaching the hinges to the body, then lift off the hatchback.
3   Before refitting the hatchback, apply a small amount of sealer to the hinge seating surfaces and to the countersunk surfaces of the hinges.
4   Do not alter the adjustment of the stops. If it is necessary to turn the outer tubes and rod in order to align them, compress the stop slightly before trying to turn it. If the stop is turned without being compressed, the packings will be damaged, the stops will begin leaking and their operation will be impaired.
5   To adjust the hatchback in both the horizontal and vertical directions, loosen the retaining nuts on the car body. Adjust the longitudinal position, by fitting shims between the hinge and the body.

19 Hatchback lock – removal, refitting and adjustment

1   Remove the luggage compartment trim.
2   Disconnect the link rod from the lock barrel. This can then be removed by removing its fixing nut.
3   Remove the screws attaching the latch assembly. Take off the latch assembly with the link rod attached.
4   Before refitting the latch, smear grease on the revolving and sliding surfaces of the assembly.
5   To adjust the horizontal position of the lock use the slotted holes in the striker.
6   Adjust the vertical position of the lock by means of the slotted holes in the latch assembly.

20 Tailgate – removal, refitting and adjustment

1   Remove the clips securing the rear end of the headlining and remove the screws securing the light fitting of the cargo space.
2   Disconnect the tailgate wiring harness and pull the pipe off the washer nozzle.
3   Unscrew and disconnect the tailgate stopper from its fixing to the body.
4   With an assistant supporting the tailgate, mark the position of the hinge. Remove the bolts securing the hinges to the body and lift away the tailgate.
5   Refitting is the reverse of removal, but the hinges should be lubricated with oil, or grease, before refitting.
6   The tailgate can be adjusted in both the horizontal and vertical directions by loosening the bolts attaching the hinges to the body, positioning the tailgate in its best position and then tightening the bolts. Adjustment longitudinally is achieved by fitting shims beneath the hinge.

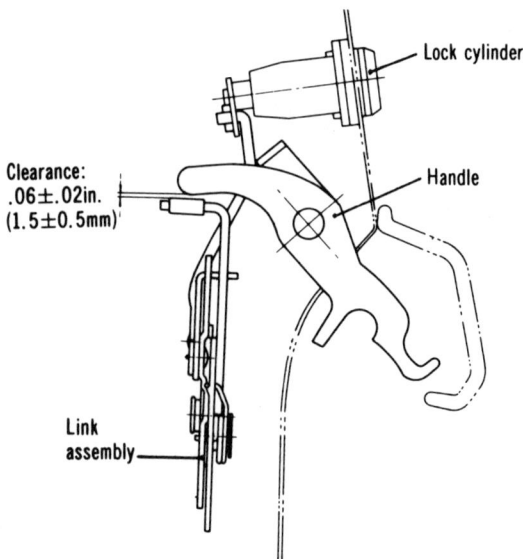

Fig. 12.29 Tailgate handle to link adjustment

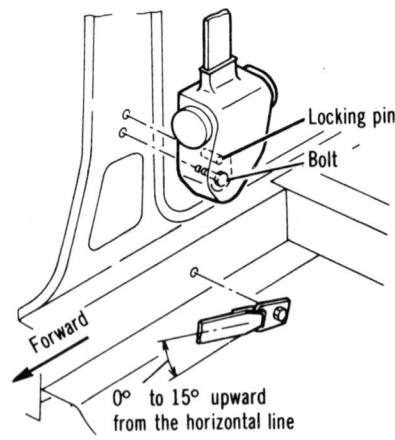

Fig. 12.30 Inertia reel installation (Saloon)

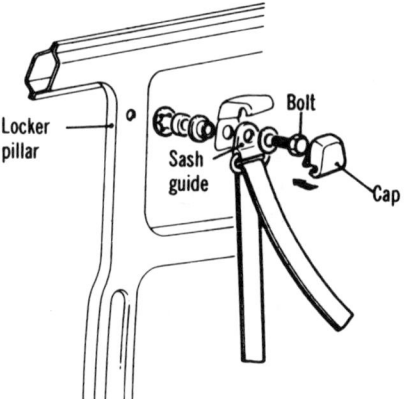

Fig. 12.31 Door pillar fixing

201

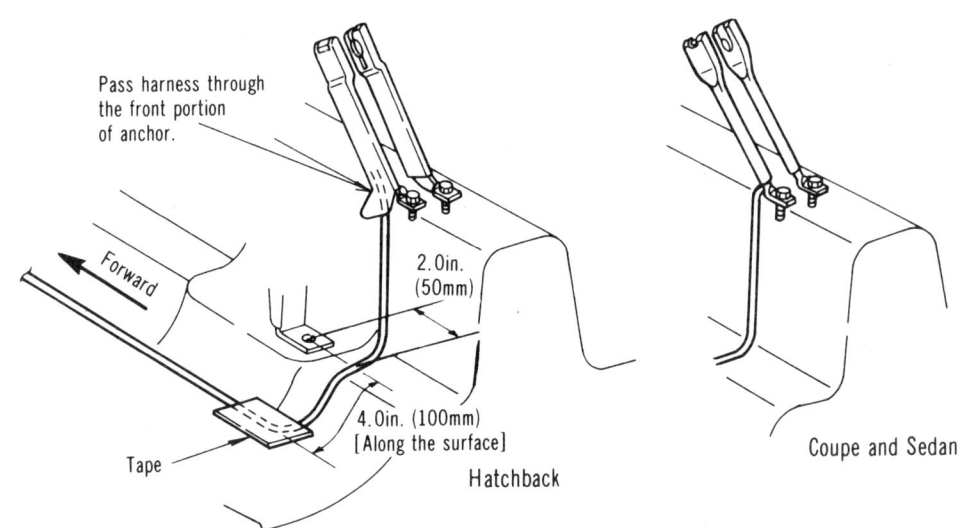

Pass harness through the front portion of anchor.

Forward

2.0in. (50mm)

4.0in. (100mm) [Along the surface]

Tape

Hatchback

Coupe and Sedan

Fig. 12.32 Buckle stalk installation

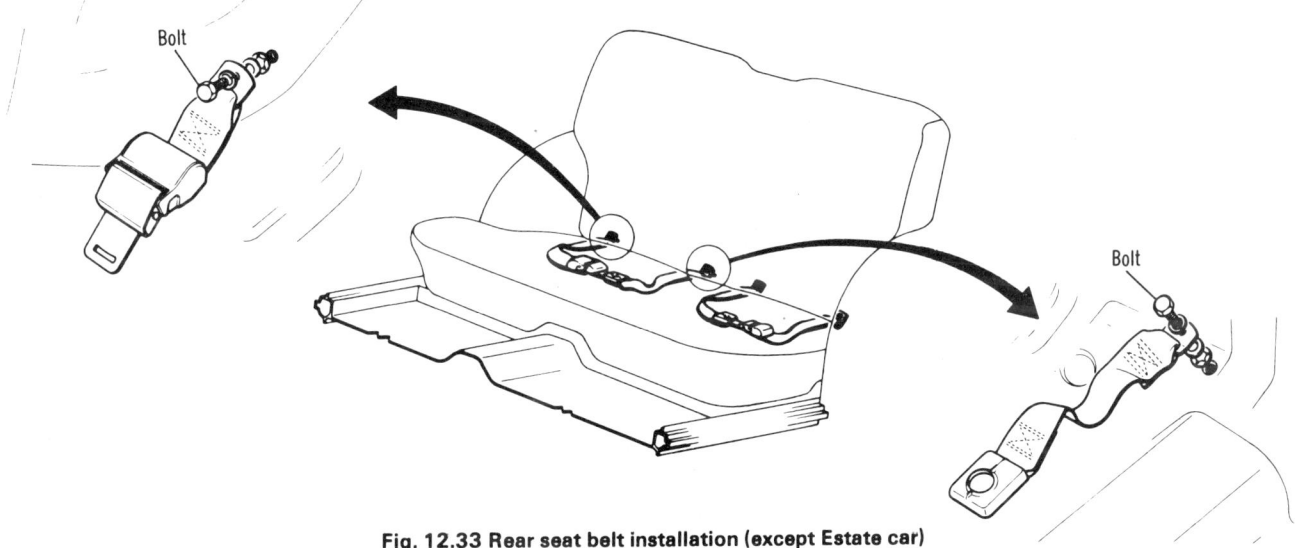

Bolt

Bolt

Fig. 12.33 Rear seat belt installation (except Estate car)

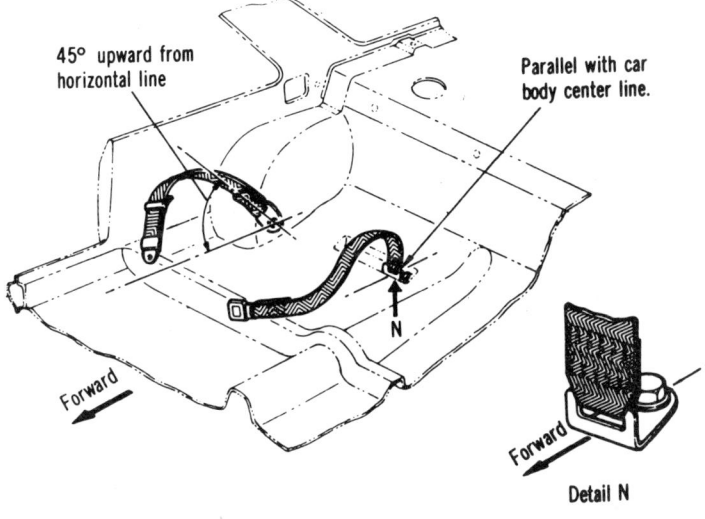

45° upward from horizontal line

Parallel with car body center line.

N

Forward

Forward

Detail N

Fig. 12.34 Rear seat belt installation (Estate car)

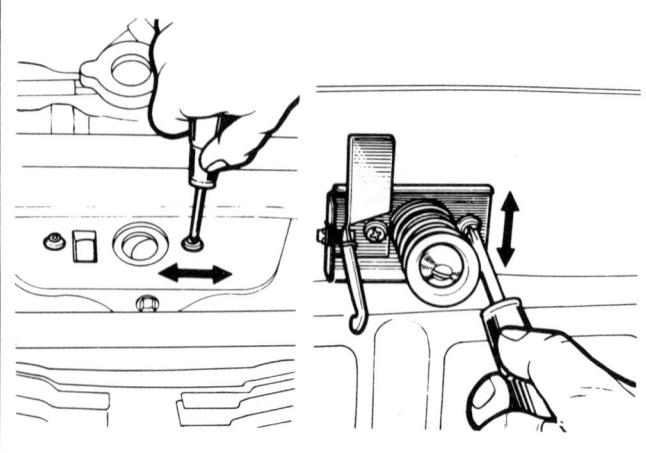

Fig. 12.35 Adjusting the bonnet lock

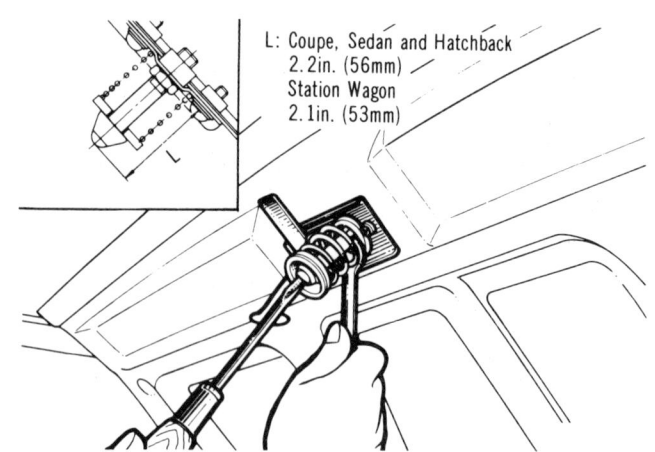

L: Coupe, Sedan and Hatchback
2.2in. (56mm)
Station Wagon
2.1in. (53mm)

Fig. 12.36 Adjusting the length of the bonnet lock bolt

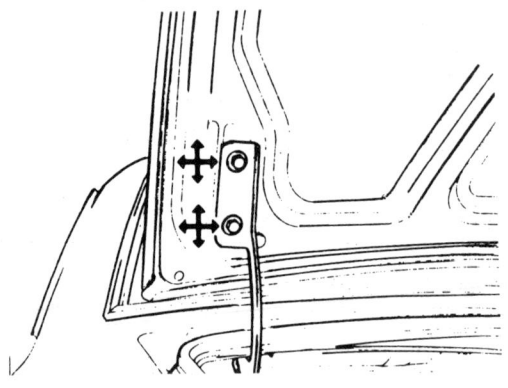

Fig. 12.37 Boot lid adjustment

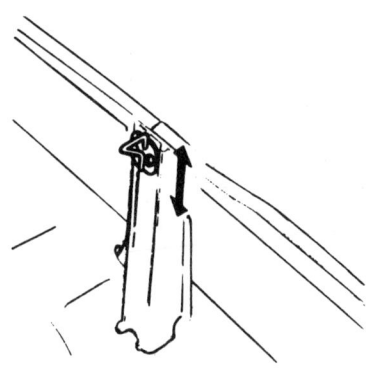

Fig. 12.38 Striker adjustment

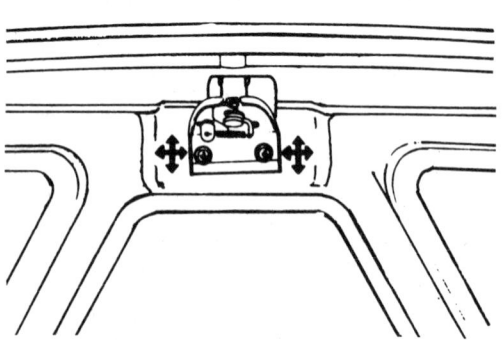

Fig. 12.39 Latch adjustment

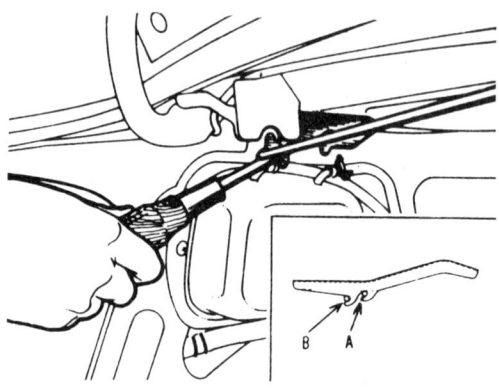

Fig. 12.40 Alternative positions of torsion bar

7   Adjust the height of the rubber bumper by turning the bolt, so that the body panel is flush with the tailgate panel.

21 Tailgate latch and lock – removal, refitting and adjustment

1   Remove the trim from the tailgate.
2   Slide back the clip and disconnect the rod from the lock cylinder.
3   Disconnect the operating rod from each of the latches, then remove the fixing screws and take off the lock assembly.
4   Remove the fixing screws from each of the latches and remove them.
5   Before refitting the lock assembly and the latches, lubricate all the moving parts with grease.
6   Adjust the lock assembly to give the standard clearance (Fig. 12.29) between the tailgate handle and the link assembly.
7   Adjust the two latches so that both sides operate in unison. Fit shims to give the latch to striker clearance shown in Fig. 12.27.

22 Door rattles – tracing and rectification

1   The most common cause of door rattle is a misaligned, loose, or worn striker plate. Other possible causes are:

   (a) Loose door handles, window winder handles or door hinges
   (b) Loose, worn or misaligned door lock components
   (c) Loose or worn remote control mechanism

2   If the striker catch is worn, renew it and adjust it as described in the relevant Section.
3   If the hinges are sufficiently worn to show excessive play in them, new hinges should be fitted.

23 Seatbelts – removal and refitting

Front
1   Remove the bolt securing the inertia reel and the bolt securing the shoulder anchor. Remove the combined lap and shoulder belt.
2   Remove the bolt securing the buckle stalk to the floor and disconnect the wiring harness of the driver's belt.
3   When refitting, the inertia reel must be vertical and must not foul the seat reclining adjuster for any position of the seat. Tighten the bolts to the specified torque.
4   Make sure that the belt is not twisted and that the shoulder anchor is free to rotate on its mounting bolt, which should be tightened to the specified torque.
5   After fitting the buckle stalk and tightening its fixing bolt to the required torque, re-connect the cable harness of the driver's belt.

Rear
6   Remove the rear seat belt by removing the single bolt which secures the end of each strap.
7   When refitting the belts, ensure that the anchor plate of the buckle side of the strap is at right angles to the axis of the car. The anchor plate of the tongue side should be upwards at an angle of 45° to the horizontal.

24 Bonnet – removal and refitting

1   Release the bonnet lock and lift the bonnet, then disconnect the windscreen washer pipe from the nozzle.
2   Mark the position of the hinges, so that the bonnet can be refitted in exactly the same position.
3   With an assistant supporting the bonnet, remove the four fixing bolts and lift the bonnet clear.

25 Bonnet lock – adjustment

1   Adjust the alignment between the lock and the hook by using the slotted holes on each of the two parts of the lock.
2   The engagement of the lock can be altered by adjusting the length of the bonnet lock bolt.

3   Set the bolt to the standard length of 2.2 in (56 mm) for models except the estate car and 2.1 in (53 mm) on the estate car version.
4   Check to see if locking is satisfactory. If locking is difficult, lengthen the bolt and if the front of the bonnet is high, shorten the bolt until the lock engages firmly.

26 Front wings – removal and refitting

1   Remove the front bumper and the grille.
2   Disconnect the wiring of the side marker light.
3   Remove the front clips of the skirt moulding.
4   Remove the attachment bolts and take off the wing assembly by moving it forwards.
5   When refitting the wing, ensure that the packing fits snugly between the wing and the car body. Fit the wing seals using adhesive. Ensure that if any bare metal is exposed, it is painted or otherwise protected from corrosion.

27 Boot lid – removal, refitting and adjustment

1   Mark the position of the hinges, so that the lid can be replaced in exactly the same position.
2   With an assistant supporting the lid, remove the four bolts attaching the hinges to the lid.
3   To remove the torsion bar, first remove the clamp from its midpoint and then prise each end of the car out of its end fitting (photo).
4   The lid may be adjusted both laterally and longitudinally by loosening the bolts attaching the hinges to the lid and pushing the lid into the required position.
5   The latch has a longitudinal adjustment by means of slotted holes for the fixing screws. The striker can be adjusted horizontally and vertically by loosening its fixing screws (photos).

28 Heater unit – removal and refitting

Except estate car
1   Disconnect the battery and drain the cooling system, with the water valve lever in the Off position.
2   Remove the parcel tray, the defroster nozzle and the console.
3   Disconnect all the controls from the heater unit, then remove the water hoses and the air duct connections.
4   Remove the screws and nuts from the four heater fixing points and lift out the heater assembly.

Estate car
5   Disconnect the battery and drain the cooling system.
6   Remove the parcel tray, glove box, floor console and defroster duct.
7   Disconnect all the controls from the heater and then remove the control unit as an assembly.
8   Disconnect the water hoses and remove the centre ventilator duct.
9   Remove the top mounting bolt and the centre mounting nut, then remove the heater as an assembly.
10 Refitting is the reversal of removal, but it is necessary to take care that all hoses are pushed on fully and clamped securely.
11 With the water valve fully open, refill the cooling system and run the engine for a short time to expel air. Stop the engine and top-up the cooling system.

29 Heater unit – adjustment

1   Turn the air control lever to Inside, close the heater unit outside air inlet port and ensure that the air outlet ports, to the car interior, are fully open. Clamp the control wire with the valve and control in these positions. Make sure that the wire is inserted in the clip and is secured by the clip.
2   Turn the water valve lever to Off and ensure that the water valve is closed, then tighten the wire. After tightening, run the engine and check for leaks.
3   With the control lever in the Def position and with the heater unit butterfly on the Def side, tighten the wire.

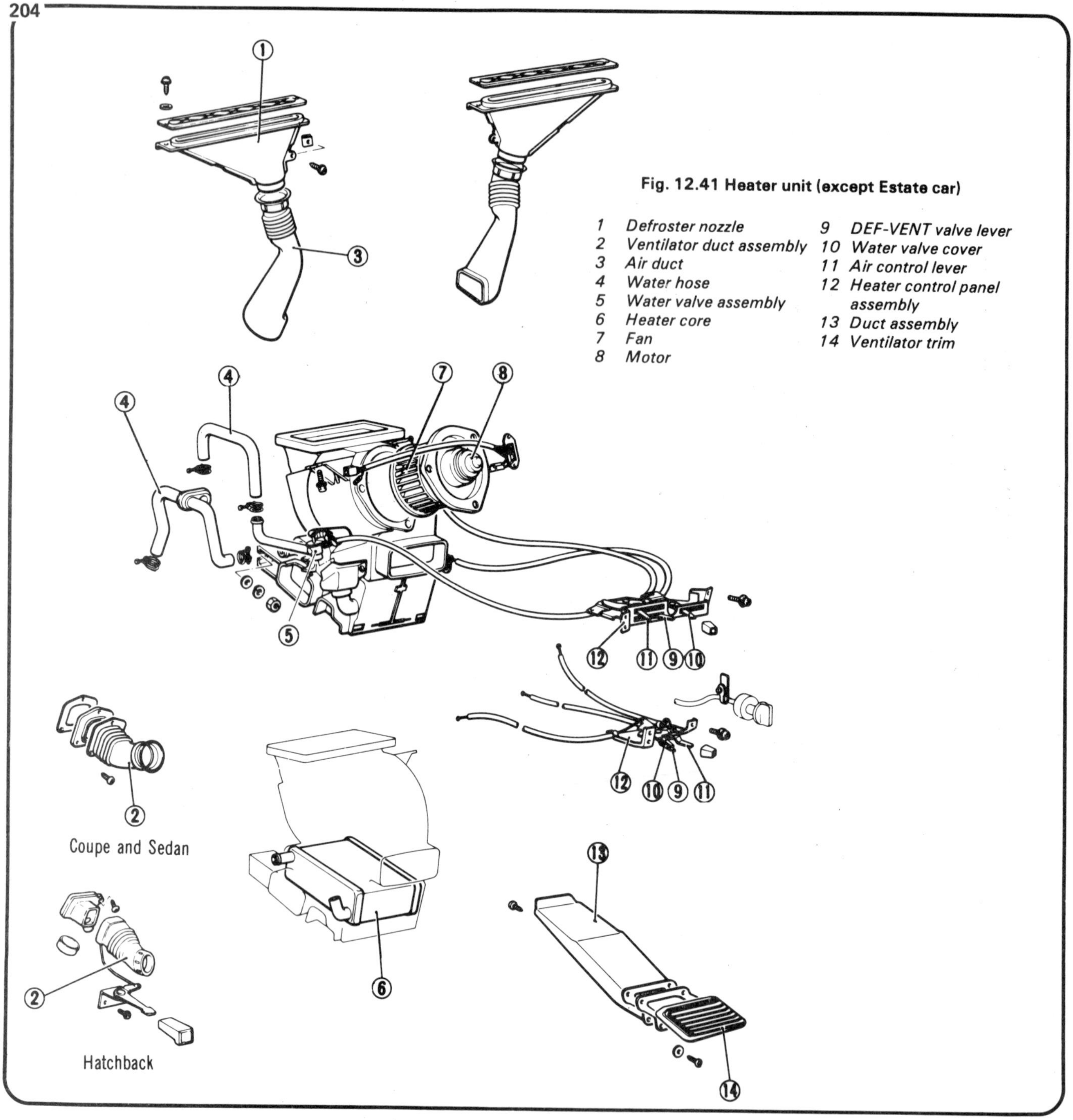

Fig. 12.41 Heater unit (except Estate car)

1 Defroster nozzle
2 Ventilator duct assembly
3 Air duct
4 Water hose
5 Water valve assembly
6 Heater core
7 Fan
8 Motor

9   DEF-VENT valve lever
10 Water valve cover
11 Air control lever
12 Heater control panel
     assembly
13 Duct assembly
14 Ventilator trim

Coupe and Sedan

Hatchback

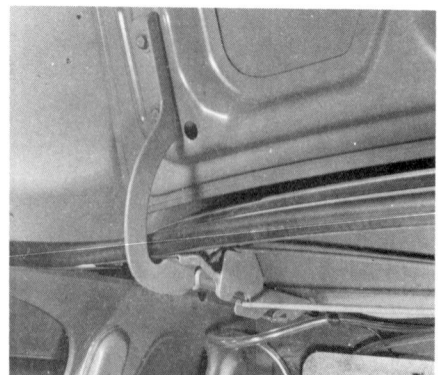

27.3 Boot lid torsion bar

27.5a Boot latch

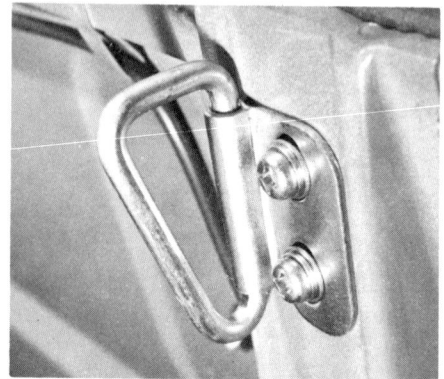

27.5b ... and striker

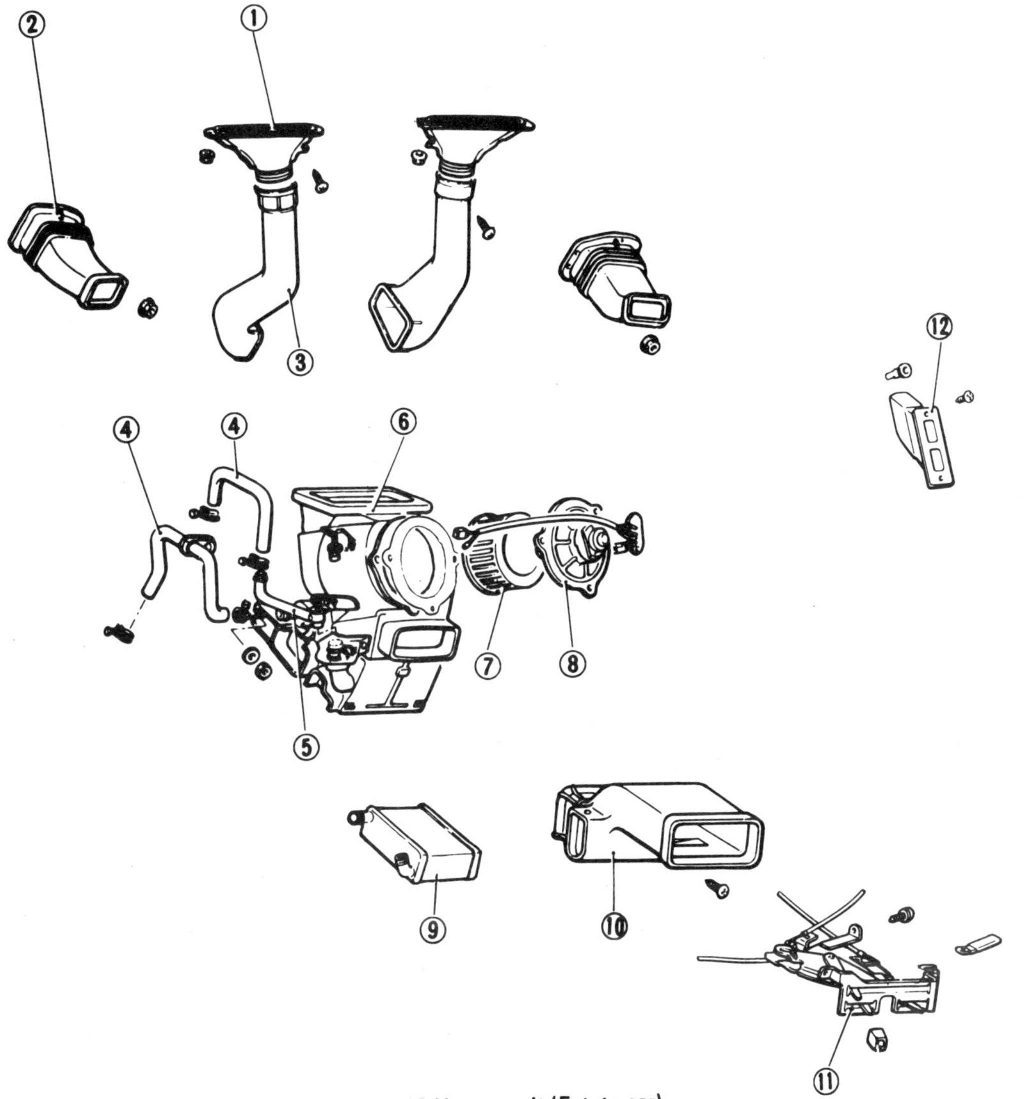

Fig. 12.42 Heater unit (Estate car)

1 Defroster nozzle	5 Water valve assembly	8 Motor	11 Heater control panel
2 Side ventilator duct	6 Heater assembly	9 Motor core	assembly
3 Air duct	7 Fan	10 Centre ventilator duct	12 Rear ventilator
4 Water hose			

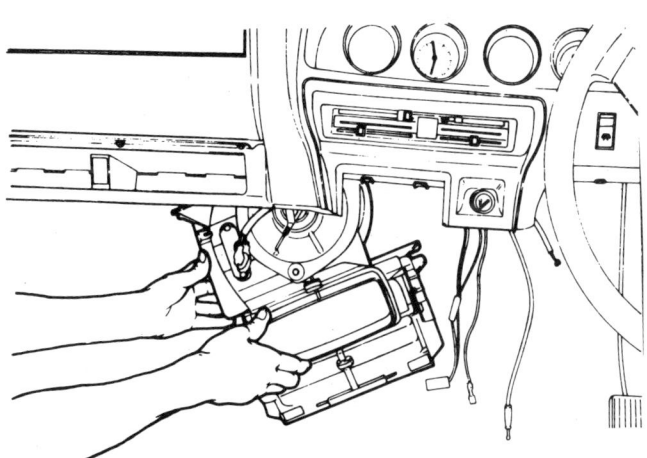

Fig. 12.43 Removing the heater (except Estate car)

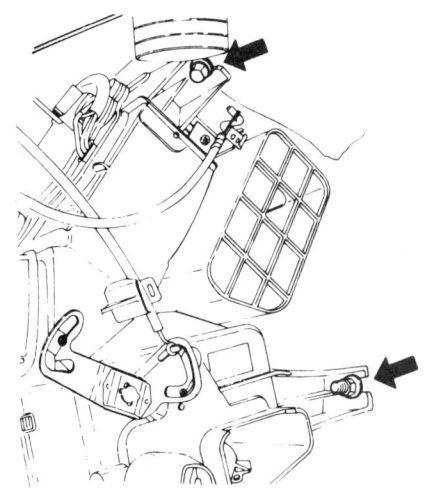

Fig. 12.44 Removing the heater (Estate car)

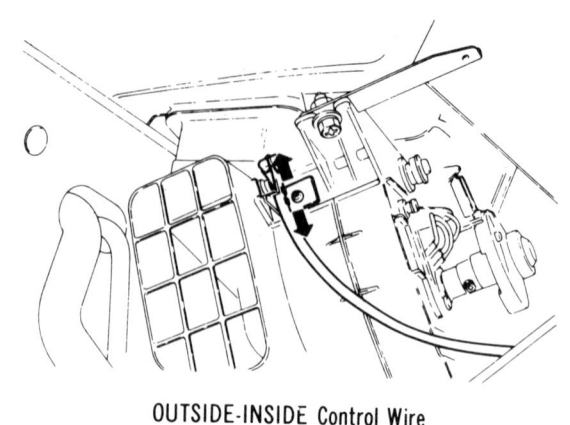

OUTSIDE-INSIDE Control Wire

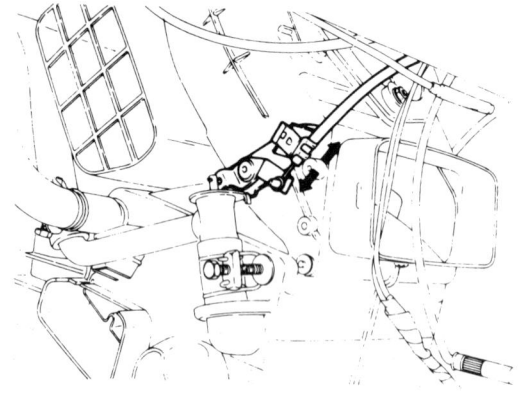

Water Valve Control Wire

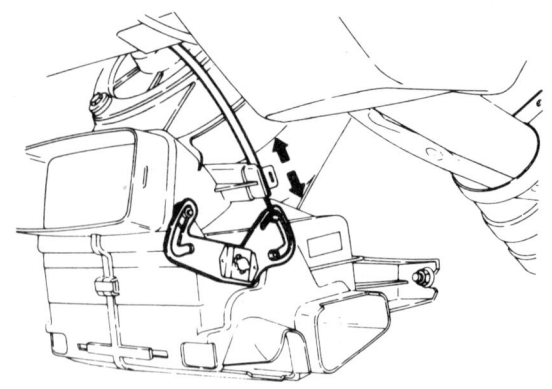

DEF-HEAT-VENT Control Wire

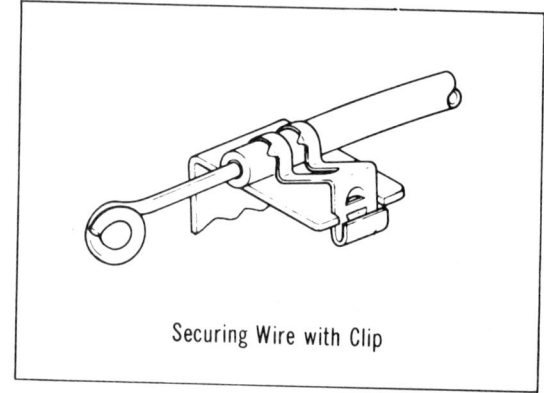

Securing Wire with Clip

Fig. 12.45 Heater control adjustments

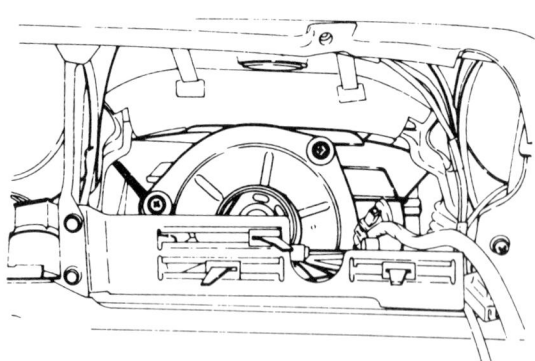

Fig. 12.46 Removing the motor assembly (Coupe and Saloon)

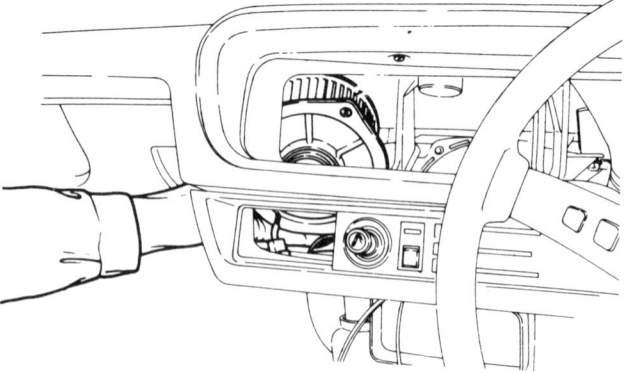

Fig. 12.47 Removing the motor assembly (Hatchback)

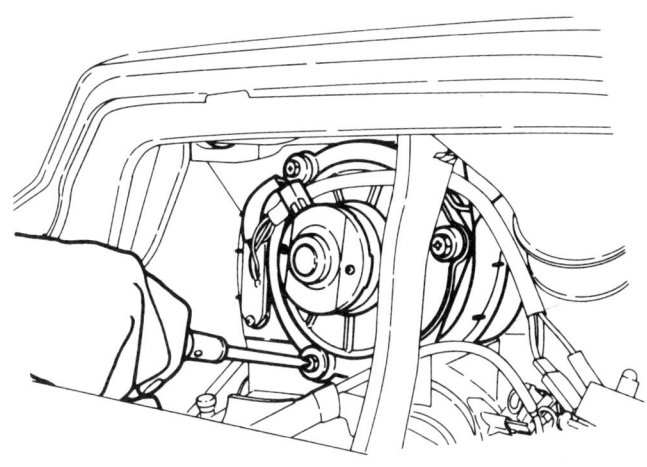

Fig. 12.48 Removing the motor assembly (Estate car)

30 Heater unit – motor removal

Except estate car

1 Remove the instrument cluster and on the hatchback also remove the glove box.

2 Remove the bolts securing the heater control bracket and remove the bracket.

3 Remove the three motor assembly fixing screws and pull the motor leads from their connectors.

4 On the coupe and sedan, pull the motor horizontally whilst pressing down on the control bracket.

5 On the hatchback, withdraw the motor through the glove box opening.

Estate car

6 Remove the meter cover and combination meter.

7 Pull the motor leads from their connectors.

8 Remove the three motor assembly fixing screws and lift out the motor.

31 Air conditioning

Air conditioning is available on some models, but when fitted should only be removed, serviced and refitted by a competent air conditioning specialist. When it is necessary to depressurise the system, for example, if the engine is to be removed, this must also be entrusted to a specialist.

Safety First!

Professional motor mechanics are trained in safe working procedures. However enthusiastic you may be about getting on with the job in hand, do take the time to ensure that your safety is not put at risk. A moment's lack of attention can result in an accident, as can failure to observe certain elementary precautions.

There will always be new ways of having accidents, and the following points do not pretend to be a comprehensive list of all dangers; they are intended rather to make you aware of the risks and to encourage a safety-conscious approach to all work you carry out on your vehicle.

Essential DOs and DON'Ts

DON'T start the engine without first ascertaining that the transmission is in neutral.

DON'T suddenly remove the filler cap from a hot cooling system – cover it with a cloth and release the pressure gradually first, or you may get scalded by escaping coolant.

DON'T attempt to drain oil until you are sure it has cooled sufficiently to avoid scalding you.

DON'T grasp any part of the engine, exhaust or silencer without first ascertaining that it is sufficiently cool to avoid burning you.

DON'T allow brake fluid or antifreeze to contact the machine's paintwork or plastic components.

DON'T syphon toxic liquids such as fuel, brake fluid or antifreeze by mouth, or allow them to remain on your skin.

DON'T inhale dust – it may be injurious to health (see Asbestos heading).

DON'T allow any spilt oil or grease to remain on the floor – wipe it up straight away, before someone slips on it.

DON'T use ill-fitting spanners or other tools which may slip and cause injury.

DON'T attempt to lift a heavy component which may be beyond your capability – get assistance.

DON'T rush to finish a job, or take unverified short cuts.

DON'T allow children or animals in or around an unattended vehicle.

DON'T inflate a tyre to a pressure above the recommended maximum. Apart from overstressing the carcase and wheel rim, in extreme cases the tyre may blow off forcibly.

DO ensure that the machine is supported securely at all times. This is especially important when the machine is blocked up to aid wheel or fork removal.

DO take care when attempting to slacken a stubborn nut or bolt. It is generally better to pull on a spanner, rather than push, so that if slippage occurs you fall away from the machine rather than on to it.

DO wear eye protection when using power tools such as drill, sander, bench grinder etc.

DO use a barrier cream on your hands prior to undertaking dirty jobs – it will protect your skin from infection as well as making the dirt easier to remove afterwards; but make sure your hands aren't left slippery.

DO keep loose clothing (cuffs, tie etc) and long hair well out of the way of moving mechanical parts.

DO remove rings, wristwatch etc, before working on the vehicle – especially the electrical system.

DO keep your work area tidy – it is only too easy to fall over articles left lying around.

DO exercise caution when compressing springs for removal or installation. Ensure that the tension is applied and released in a controlled manner, using suitable tools which preclude the possibility of the spring escaping violently.

DO ensure that any lifting tackle used has a safe working load rating adequate for the job.

DO get someone to check periodically that all is well, when working alone on the vehicle.

DO carry out work in a logical sequence and check that everything is correctly assembled and tightened afterwards.

DO remember that your vehicle's safety affects that of yourself and others. If in doubt on any point, get specialist advice.

IF, in spite of following these precautions, you are unfortunate enough to injure yourself, seek medical attention as soon as possible.

Asbestos

Certain friction, insulating, sealing, and other products – such as brake linings, clutch linings, gaskets, etc – contain asbestos. Extreme care must be taken to avoid inhalation of dust from such products since it is hazardous to health. If in doubt, assume that they do contain asbestos.

Fire

Remember at all times that petrol (gasoline) is highly flammable. Never smoke, or have any kind of naked flame around, when working on the vehicle. But the risk does not end there – a spark caused by an electrical short-circuit, by two metal surfaces contacting each other, or even by static electricity built up in your body under certain conditions, can ignite petrol vapour, which in a confined space is highly explosive.

Always disconnect the battery earth (ground) terminal before working on any part of the fuel or electrical system, and never risk spilling fuel on to a hot engine or exhaust.

It is recommended that a fire extinguisher of a type suitable for fuel and electrical fires is kept handy in the garage or workplace at all times. Never try to extinguish a fuel or electrical fire with water.

Fumes

Certain fumes are highly toxic and can quickly cause unconsciousness and even death if inhaled to any extent. Petrol (gasoline) vapour comes into this category, as do the vapours from certain solvents such as trichloroethylene. Any draining or pouring of such volatile fluids should be done in a well ventilated area.

When using cleaning fluids and solvents, read the instructions carefully. Never use materials from unmarked containers – they may give off poisonous vapours.

Never run the engine of a motor vehicle in an enclosed space such as a garage. Exhaust fumes contain carbon monoxide which is extremely poisonous; if you need to run the engine, always do so in the open air or at least have the rear of the vehicle outside the workplace.

The battery

Never cause a spark, or allow a naked light, near the vehicle's battery. It will normally be giving off a certain amount of hydrogen gas, which is highly explosive.

Always disconnect the battery earth (ground) terminal before working on the fuel or electrical systems.

If possible, loosen the filler plugs or cover when charging the battery from an external source. Do not charge at an excessive rate or the battery may burst.

Take care when topping up and when carrying the battery. The acid electrolyte, even when diluted, is very corrosive and should not be allowed to contact the eyes or skin.

If you ever need to prepare electrolyte yourself, always add the acid slowly to the water, and never the other way round. Protect against splashes by wearing rubber gloves and goggles.

Mains electricity

When using an electric power tool, inspection light etc which works from the mains, always ensure that the appliance is correctly connected to its plug and that, where necessary, it is properly earthed (grounded). Do not use such appliances in damp conditions and, again, beware of creating a spark or applying excessive heat in the vicinity of fuel or fuel vapour.

Ignition HT voltage

A severe electric shock can result from touching certain parts of the ignition system, such as the HT leads, when the engine is running or being cranked, particularly if components are damp or the insulation is defective. Where an electronic ignition system is fitted, the HT voltage is much higher and could prove fatal.

Conversion factors

Length (distance)

Inches (in)	X	25.4	= Millimetres (mm)	X	0.0394	= Inches (in)
Feet (ft)	X	0.305	= Metres (m)	X	3.281	= Feet (ft)
Miles	X	1.609	= Kilometres (km)	X	0.621	= Miles

Inches (in) X 25.4 = Millimetres (mm) X 0.0394 = Inches (in)
Feet (ft) X 0.305 = Metres (m) X 3.281 = Feet (ft)
Miles X 1.609 = Kilometres (km) X 0.621 = Miles

Volume (capacity)
Cubic inches (cu in; in^3) X 16.387 = Cubic centimetres (cc; cm^3) X 0.061 = Cubic inches (cu in; in^3)
Imperial pints (Imp pt) X 0.568 = Litres (l) X 1.76 = Imperial pints (Imp pt)
Imperial quarts (Imp qt) X 1.137 = Litres (l) X 0.88 = Imperial quarts (Imp qt)
Imperial quarts (Imp qt) X 1.201 = US quarts (US qt) X 0.833 = Imperial quarts (Imp qt)
US quarts (US qt) X 0.946 = Litres (l) X 1.057 = US quarts (US qt)
Imperial gallons (Imp gal) X 4.546 = Litres (l) X 0.22 = Imperial gallons (Imp gal)
Imperial gallons (Imp gal) X 1.201 = US gallons (US gal) X 0.833 = Imperial gallons (Imp gal)
US gallons (US gal) X 3.785 = Litres (l) X 0.264 = US gallons (US gal)

Mass (weight)
Ounces (oz) X 28.35 = Grams (g) X 0.035 = Ounces (oz)
Pounds (lb) X 0.454 = Kilograms (kg) X 2.205 = Pounds (lb)

Force
Ounces-force (ozf; oz) X 0.278 = Newtons (N) X 3.6 = Ounces-force (ozf; oz)
Pounds-force (lbf; lb) X 4.448 = Newtons (N) X 0.225 = Pounds-force (lbf; lb)
Newtons (N) X 0.1 = Kilograms-force (kgf; kg) X 9.81 = Newtons (N)

Pressure
Pounds-force per square inch (psi; lbf/in^2; lb/in^2) X 0.070 = Kilograms-force per square centimetre (kgf/cm^2; kg/cm^2) X 14.223 = Pounds-force per square inch (psi; lbf/in^2; lb/in^2)
Pounds-force per square inch (psi; lbf/in^2; lb/in^2) X 0.068 = Atmospheres (atm) X 14.696 = Pounds-force per square inch (psi; lbf/in^2; lb/in^2)
Pounds-force per square inch (psi; lbf/in^2; lb/in^2) X 0.069 = Bars X 14.5 = Pounds-force per square inch (psi; lbf/in^2; lb/in^2)
Pounds-force per square inch (psi; lbf/in^2; lb/in^2) X 6.895 = Kilopascals (kPa) X 0.145 = Pounds-force per square inch (psi; lbf/in^2; lb/in^2)
Kilopascals (kPa) X 0.01 = Kilograms-force per square centimetre (kgf/cm^2; kg/cm^2) X 98.1 = Kilopascals (kPa)

Torque (moment of force)
Pounds-force inches (lbf in; lb in) X 1.152 = Kilograms-force centimetre (kgf cm; kg cm) X 0.868 = Pounds-force inches (lbf in; lb in)
Pounds-force inches (lbf in; lb in) X 0.113 = Newton metres (Nm) X 8.85 = Pounds-force inches (lbf in; lb in)
Pounds-force inches (lbf in; lb in) X 0.083 = Pounds-force feet (lbf ft; lb ft) X 12 = Pounds-force inches (lbf in; lb in)
Pounds-force feet (lbf ft; lb ft) X 0.138 = Kilograms-force metres (kgf m; kg m) X 7.233 = Pounds-force feet (lbf ft; lb ft)
Pounds-force feet (lbf ft; lb ft) X 1.356 = Newton metres (Nm) X 0.738 = Pounds-force feet (lbf ft; lb ft)
Newton metres (Nm) X 0.102 = Kilograms-force metres (kgf m; kg m) X 9.804 = Newton metres (Nm)

Power
Horsepower (hp) X 745.7 = Watts (W) X 0.0013 = Horsepower (hp)

Velocity (speed)
Miles per hour (miles/hr; mph) X 1.609 = Kilometres per hour (km/hr; kph) X 0.621 = Miles per hour (miles/hr; mph)

Fuel consumption*
Miles per gallon, Imperial (mpg) X 0.354 = Kilometres per litre (km/l) X 2.825 = Miles per gallon, Imperial (mpg)
Miles per gallon, US (mpg) X 0.425 = Kilometres per litre (km/l) X 2.352 = Miles per gallon, US (mpg)

Temperature
Degrees Fahrenheit = (°C x 1.8) + 32   Degrees Celsius (Degrees Centigrade; °C) = (°F - 32) x 0.56

*It is common practice to convert from miles per gallon (mpg) to litres/100 kilometres (l/100km), where mpg (Imperial) x l/100 km = 282 and mpg (US) x l/100 km = 235

Index

Printed by
J H Haynes & Co Ltd
Sparkford Nr Yeovil
Somerset BA22 7JJ England